COMPUTER
KNOWLEDGE

For SBI/ IBPS Clerk/ PO/ RRB/ RBI/ SSC/ Railway/ Insurance Exams

- **Head Office :** B-32, Shivalik Main Road, Malviya Nagar, New Delhi-110017
- **Sales Office :** B-48, Shivalik Main Road, Malviya Nagar, New Delhi-110017
  Tel. : 011-26691021 / 26691713

Typeset by Disha DTP Team

Compiled & Edited by Vinit Garg

DISHA PUBLICATION

ALL RIGHTS RESERVED

For further information about the books from DISHA,

Log on to **www.dishapublication.com** or email to **info@dishapublication.com**

CONTENTS

Fundamentals of Computer

C - Common; O - Operating; M - Machine; P - Particularly; U - Used for; T - Trade; E - Education; R - Research.

In this age of computers there is no such activity that cannot be achieved without computers. Computer has become an indispensable and multipurpose tool. We are breathing in the computer age and gradually computer has become such a desire necessity of life that it is difficult to imagine life without it. This book will help you to gain an understanding of the basic as well as advanced concepts of computers. It will cover a foundational study of the computer hardware, software, operating systems, Internet Technology, DBMS (Database Management system) & computer Network & Its security, or more.

CONCEPT OF COMPUTER SYSTEM

A computer is an advanced electronic device that takes raw data as input from the user and processes this data under the control of set of instructions (called program) and gives the result (output) and saves output for the future reference and usage.

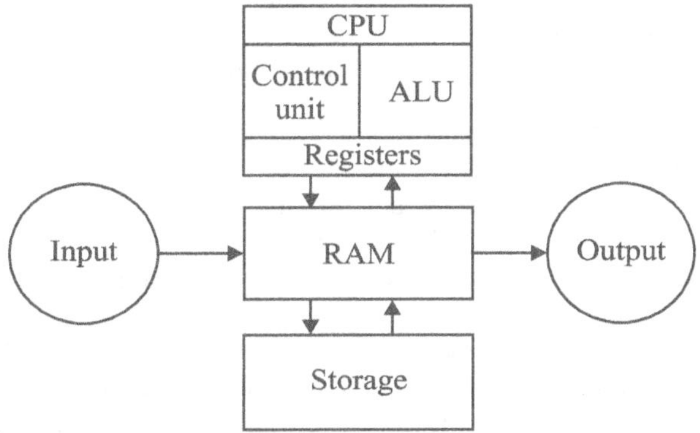

A basic computer system

To know about the working of a computer, first need to understand various terms such as Data, Processing and Information. First of all, lets start with three basic terms:-

1. **Data : Data** is a collection of basic facts and figure without any sequence. This data is also called as raw data. When the data is collected as facts and figures, there is no meaning to it, at that time, for example, name of people, names of employees etc.

    In other words computer data is information processed or stored by a computer. This information may be in the form of text documented images, audio clip, software programme or other type of data.

2. **Processing : Processing** is the set of instructions given by the user to the related data that was collected earlier to output meaningful information. The computer does the required processing by making the necessary calculations, comparisons and decisions.

3. **Information : Information** is the end point or the final output of any processed work. This meaningful output data is called information.

CHARACTERSTICS OF COMPUTER

The major characteristics of computers are the following:

- **Speed :** A powerful computer is capable of executing about 3 million calculations per second.
- **Accuracy :** A computer's accuracy is consistently high; if there are errors, they are due to errors in instructions given by the programmer.
- **Reliability :** The output generated by the computer is very reliable as long as the data is reliable.
- **Memory/Storage Capacity :** The computer can store large volumes of data and makes the retrieval of data an easy task.
- **Versatility:** The computer can accomplish many different things. It can accept information through various input-output devices, perform arithmetic and logic operations, generate a variety of outputs in a variety of forms, etc.
- **Automation:** Once the instructions are fed into computer it works automatically without any human intervention.
- **Diligence :** A computer will never fail to perform its task due to distraction or laziness.
- **Convenience :** Computers are usually easy to access, and allow people to find information easily that without a would be very difficult.
- **Flexibility :** Computers can be used for entertainment, for business, by people who hold different ideals or who have varied goals. Almost anyone can use a computer, and computers can be used to assist with almost any goal.

GOALS OF COMPUTERS

1. Problem-solving techniques using the computer.
2. Analysis of complex problems and the synthesis of solutions .
3. Comprehension of modern software engineering principles.
4. A vast breadth and depth of knowledge in the discipline of computer science.

COMPUTER CAPABILITIES

Like all machines, a computer needs to be directed and controlled in order to perform a task successfully. Until such time as a program is prepared and stored in the computer's memory, the computer 'knows' absolutely nothing, not even how to accept or reject data. Even the most sophisticated computer, no matter how capable it is, must be told what to do. Until the capabilities and the limitations of a computer are recognized, its usefulness cannot be thoroughly understood.

In the first place, it should be recognized that computers are capable of doing repetitive operations. A computer can perform similar operations thousands of times, without becoming bored, tired, or even careless.

Secondly, computers can process information at extremely rapid rates. For example, modern computers can solve certain classes of arithmetic problems millions of times faster than a skilled mathematician. Speeds for performing decision-making operations are comparable to those for arithmetic operations but input-output operations, however, involve mechanical motion and hence require more time. On a typical computer system, cards are read at an average speed of 1000 cards per minute and as many as 1000 lines can be printed at the same rate.

Thirdly, computers may be programmed to calculate answers to whatever level of accuracy is specified by the programmer. In spite of newspaper headlines such as 'Computer Fails', these machines are very accurate and reliable especially when the number of operations they can perform every second is considered. Because they are man-made machines, they sometimes malfunction or break down and have to be repaired. However, in most instances when the computer fails, it is due to human error and is not the fault of the computer at all.

In the fourth place, general-purpose computers can be programmed to solve various types of problems because of their flexibility. One of the most important reasons why computers are so widely use today is that almost every big problem can be solved by solving a number of little problems-one after another.

Finally, a computer, unlike a human being, has no intuition. A person may suddenly find the answer to a problem without working out too many of the details, but a computer can only proceed as it has been programmed to.

HISTORY OF THE DEVELOPMENT OF COMPUTERS

In beginning, there were no computers. To add or subtract , man used his fingers and toes. Abacus is known to be the first mechanical calculating device. The main purpose of abacus was that additions and subtraction coud be performed quickly. Abacus was developed by the Egyptians in the 10th centuary B.C, but the final structure was given in the 12th centuary A.D. by the Chinese educationists. Abacus is made up of a frame in which rods are fitted across with rounds beads sliding on the rod.

Napier

Napier's Bones in an Abacus invented by John Napier.Napier's used the bone rods for counting purpose where numbers were printed on them. With the help of these rods ,one could do addition, subtraction, multiplication and division speediy.

Pascal's calculator called 'Pascaline'

In the year 1642, Blaise Pascal a French scientist invented an adding machine called Pascal's calculator, which represents the position of digit with the help of gears in it. Though these machines were early forerunners to computer engineering, the calculator failed to be a great commercial success.

Leibniz Calculator

Leibniz was successfully introduced as a calculator onto the market in the year 1646. It was designed further in 1673 but it took until 1694 to complete. The calculator could perform the basic mathematical operations such as add, subtract, multiply, and divide. Wheels were placed at right angles which could be displaced by a special stepping mechanism.

Analytical Engine "The first Computer"

This analytical engine, the first fully-automatic calculating machine, was constructed by British computing pioneer Charles Babbage (1791-1871), who first conceived the idea of an advanced calculating machine to calculate and print mathematical tables in 1812. This Analytical Engine incorporated an arithmetic logic unit, control flow in the form of conditional branching and loops, and integrated memory, making it the first design for a general-purpose computer that could be described in modern terms as Turing-complete.

GENERATIONS OF COMPUTERS

There are five Generation of Computer, these are :

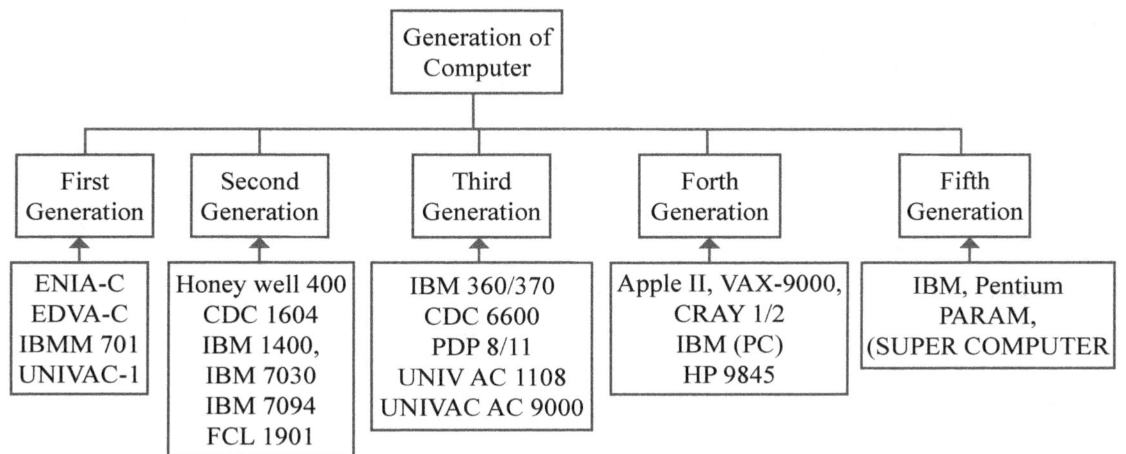

COMPUTER GENERATIONS

Generation	Device	Hardware feature	Characteristics	System names
First (1942-1959)		▶ Vacuum Tubes ▶ Punch Cards	▶ Support machine laguage only ▶ Very costly ▶ Generate lot of heat ▶ Hhuge size ▶ Consumed lot of electricity	▶ ENIAC ▶ EDVAC ▶ **IBM 701** ▶ UNIVAC-1
Second (1959-1965)		▶ Transistors ▶ Magnetic Tapes	▶ Batch operating system ▶ Faster, smaller and reliabe than previous generation ▶ Costly	▶ **Honeywell 400** ▶ **CDC 1604** ▶ **IBM 7030, IBM1400** ▶ **IBM 7094** ▶ **ICL 1901**
Third (1965-1975)		▶ ICs ▶ Large capacity disk and Magnetic Tapes ▶ **Size 1/4 of Sq. INCH**	▶ Time Sharing OS ▶ Faster, smaller and reliabe cheaper ▶ Easier to update	▶ IBM 360/370 ▶ CDC 6600 ▶ PDP 8/11 ▶ **UNIVAC 1108** ▶ **UNIVAC AC 9000**
Fourth (1975-1988)		▶ **Ics with LSI & VLSI Technology** ▶ **Semiconductor Memory** ▶ **Magnetic tapes and floppy as portable**	▶ Multiprocessing & GUI OS ▶ Object oriented programs ▶ Small, affordable, easy to Use ▶ Easier to update	▶ **Apple II** ▶ **VAX 9000** ▶ **CRAY 1/2** ▶ **IBM PERSONAL COMPUTER (PC)** ▶ **HP 9845**
Fifth (1988-Present)		▶ ICs with ULSI Technology ▶ Large capacity hard disk with RAID Support ▶ Optical disks as portable read-only storage media ▶ powerful servers, internet, Cluster computing	▶ Powerful, cheaper, reliable, easy to use, portable ▶ Rapid software development possible	▶ IBM ▶ Pentium ▶ PARAM ▶ **SUPER COMPUTER**

A. First Generation of Computers (1942-1959)

The beginning of commercial computer age is from UNIVAC (Universal Automatic Computer). The first generation computers were used during 1942-1959. They were based on vacuum tubes. Examples of first generation computers are **ENIVAC** and **UNIVAC-1.**

Advantages :

*   Vacuum tubes were the only electronic component available during those days.
*   Vacuum tube technology made possible to make electronic digital computers.
*   These computers could calculate data in millisecond.

Disadvantages :

*   The computers were very large in size.
*   They consumed a large amount of energy.
*   Non-portable.
*   Limited commercial use.
*   Very slow speed.
*   Used machine language only.
*   Used magnetic drums which provide very less data storage.

B. Second Generation Computers (1959-1965)

The **second generation computers** used transistors. The size of the computers was decreased by replacing vacuum tubes with transistors. The examples of second generation computers are **IBM 7094 series, IBM 1400 series and CDC 1604** etc.

Advantages :

- Smaller in size as compared to the first generation computers.
- Used less energy and were not heated.
- Better speed and could calculate data in microseconds
- Used faster peripherals like tape drives, magnetic disks, printer etc.
- Used Assembly language instead of Machine language.

Disadvantages :

- Cooling system was required
- Constant maintenance was required
- Only used for specific purposes
- Costly and not versatile

C. Third Generation Computers (1965-1975)

The **Third generation computers** used the integrated circuits (IC). The first IC was invented and used in 1961. The size of an IC is about ¼ square inch. A single IC chip may contain thousands of transistors. The computer became smaller in size, faster, more reliable and less expensive. The examples of third generation computers are **IBM 370, IBM System/360, UNIVAC 1108** and **UNIVAC AC 9000** etc.

An integrated circuit (IC), sometimes called a chip or microchip, is a semiconductor wafer on which thousands or millions of tiny resistors, capacitors, and transistors are fabricated.

Advantages :

- Smaller in size as compared to previous generations.
- More reliable.
- Used less energy.
- Better speed and could calculate data in nanoseconds.

Disadvantages :

- Air conditioning was required.
- Highly sophisticated technology required for the manufacturing of IC chips.

D. Fourth Generation Computers (1975-1988)

The **fourth generation computers** started with the invention of Microprocessor. The Microprocessor contains thousands of ICs. The LSI (Large Scale Integration) circuit and VLSI (Very Large Scale Integration) circuit was designed. It greatly reduced the size of computer. The size of modern Microprocessors is usually one square inch. It can contain millions of electronic circuits. The examples of fourth generation computers are **Apple Macintosh & IBM PC.**

Advantages :

- More powerful and reliable than previous generations.
- Small in size

- Fast processing power with less power consumption
- Fan for heat discharging and thus to keep cold.
- Cheapest among all generations
- All types of High level languages can be used in this type of computers

Disadvantages :

- The latest technology is required for manufacturing of Microprocessors.

E. Fifth Generation Computers (1988 to Present)

Scientists are working hard on the **5th generation computers** with quite a few breakthroughs. It is based on the technique of Artificial Intelligence (AI). Computers can understand spoken words & imitate human reasoning. IBM Watson computer is one example that outsmarts Harvard University Students.

CLASSFICATION OF COMPUTERS

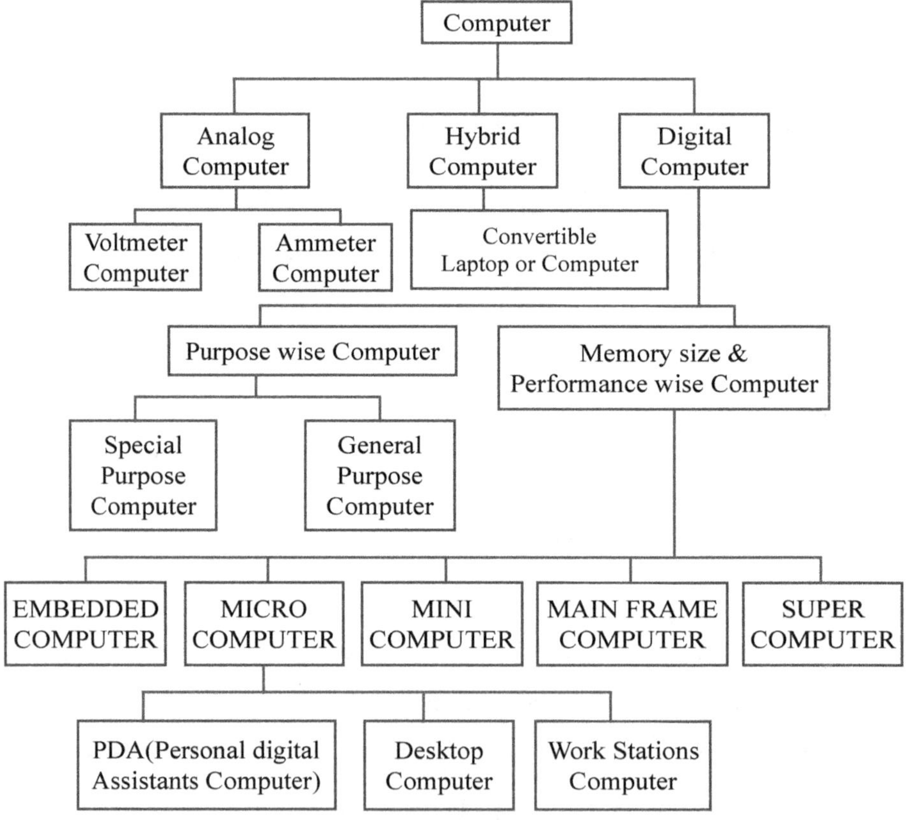

Computers can be classified according to the following types:

(a) Analog

The analog computers are computer systems that measure variations in quantities such as temperature, voltage, speed, etc. Analog computers are known to measure the data that varies continuously. Other examples of analog computers include Voltmeter and Ammeter.

(b) Digital

Digital computers are the computer systems that count things by manipulation of certain discontinuous numbers and letters through representation of binary digits (also called bits) in contrast to analog computers that measures the variations in quantities). In other words texts and graphics are treated numerically.

Today the digital computers have replaced the analog ones .Examples of digital computers are desktop , personal computers, workstations,tablet PC etc

(c) Hybrid

Hybrid computers as the name suggests are a good mix of analog as well as digital computers, using an analog computer front-end, which is then fed into a digital computer's repetitive process. Hybrid computers are used for scientific calculations, in defence and systems.

DIGITAL COMPUTER ARE DIVIDED INTO TWO PART

(1) Based on Purpose

(2) Based on Memory size and Performance

1. Based on Purpose

On the basis of purpose, computers are categorised as follows –

(i) General Purpose

These computers are designed to work on different types of applications. In these types of computers the programs are not stored permanently rather programs are input at the time of their execution. Personal computers, including desktops, notebooks, smart phones and tablets, are all examples of general-purpose computers. Various tasks can be accomplished by using general purpose computers : For example writing and editing (word processing), manipulating different facts and figures in various databases, tracking manufacturing inventory, making scientific calculations, controlling organization's security system, electricity consumption, building temperature etc.

(ii) Special Purpose

Special-Purpose computers are task specific computers and are designed to solve a particular problem. They are also known as dedicated computers, because these computers are dedicated to perform a single particular task repetitively. Examples of such computer systems include the traffic control system ,they are also used in video games ,navigational systems in an aircraft, weather forecasting, satellite launch tracking, oil exploration, and in automotive industries, keeping time in a digital watch, or Robot helicopter.

2. Based on Memory Size and Performance

Computers can be classified by memory size and performance as follows –

(i) Micro Computer

A microcomputer is a computer that uses a microprocessor as its central processing unit. Microcomputers are physically smaller in size as compared to mainframe and minicomputers. Many microcomputers when equipped with a keyboard and screen for input and output respectively can be used as personal computers (in the generic sense) .Microcomputers are easier to use and also inexpensive as the memory used by them i.e microprocessors and semi conductors have become cheaper in the last few years.

E.g. : The various micro computers widely available are IBM pcs , APPLE mac etc.the small types of pcs like the palmtop and handheld are now becoming available.

(ii) Minicomputer

It is a midsize computer. In the past few years the difference between large minicomputers and small mainframes has decreased significantly just like the distinction between small minicomputers and workstations. A minicomputer can support upto 200 users at the same time.

E.g. : The various machines widely available are vax series 8200 and 8300, honeywell(xps-100), icl's series 36 level 20,50,60 galaxy-21, hcl-4, nelco-5000 and others.

(iii) Mainframe

Mainframe computers known as the "Big Iron" are computers that are used primarily by corporate and governmental organizations . Modern mainframe design is generally defined by the following features:

- High reliability and security
- Extensive input-output facilities with the ability to offload to separate engines
- Strict backward compatibility with older version of software

(iv) Supercomputer

Supercomputer is a term used for one of the fastest computers that exist today. They are deployed for specialized applications that require processing of highly critical data and immense amounts of mathematical calculations. **E.g. :-** Weather forecasting requires a supercomputer.

- PARAM is a series of supercomputers designed and assembled by the Centre for Development of Advanced Computing (C-DAC) in Pune, India. The latest machine in the series is the PARAM Yuva II.
- China's vast Tianhe-2 is the fastest supercomputer in the world.

PERSONAL COMPUTERS

Personal Computers are computers that are designed for an individual user. These computers are small and a relatively cheaper. In price, personal computers can range anywhere from a few hundred pounds to over five thousand pounds. Personal Computers use the microprocessor technology as they enable manufacturers to put an entire CPU onto one chip. They serve myriad purposes and can be put to use by various businesses for word processing, accounting, desktop publishing, and for running spreadsheet and database management applications. People across the globe use internet for playing games,surfing net and other online applications at their homes and personal use.

Types of Personal Computers

Personal computers can be classified on the basis of its size .There are two basic types of the traditional designs i.e the desktop models and tower models. There are several variations on these two basic types also.

(i) Tower model

This model of personal computer refers to a computer in which the power supply, motherboard, and other mass storage devices are stacked on top of each other in a cabinet.

(ii) Desktop model

Desktop model means computer that are designed to fit comfortably on top of a desk, with the monitor sitting on top of the computer. Desktop model computers as compared to the tower model are broad and low, whereas tower model computers are narrow and tall.

(iii) Notebook computer

Also called ultra book. These are extremely popular because they are extremely lightweight and portable. Because of their small size ,typically less than 6 pounds or lesser than that,they have become so popular. These flat-panel technologies can produce a lightweight and non-bulky display screen. The quality of notebook display screens also differs considerably. Modern notebook computers are very similar to personal computers in terms of computing power.

(iv) Laptop computer

Laptop are now a days also called notebook computers .These are small and portable .You can make them sit on your lap and work on them.

(v) Subnotebook computer

Subnotebook computers are portable computers that are even lighter and smaller than a full-sized notebook computer. They are light weight because they use a small keyboard and screen as compared to a notebook computer.

(vi) Hand-held computer

These computers are portable enough to be carried in one's hand. They are extremely convenient for use but due to extremely small size of their keyboards and screens they have still not succeeded in to replacing notebook computers.

(vii)Palmtop

These computers as the name suggest fit in your palm. Due to extremely small size their use is limited to phone books and calendars .

(viii)   PDA

PDA's have electronic pens rather than keyboards for inputs unlike laptop. They also incorporate handwriting recognition features. and voice recognition technologies i.e can also react to voice input . PDAs are also called palmtops, hand-held computers and pocket computers.

(ix) Smart phones

Smart phones are cellular phones that function both as a phone and a small pc. They may use a pen or may have a small keyboard. They can be connected to the internet using wifi (wireless fidelity). Apple, Samsung, Sony are some manufacturers of smart phones.

USES OF COMPUTERS

Computers have their application or utility everywhere. Some of the prominent areas of computer applications are:

A. In the Field of Education

Computers have taken the education systems in the entire world to a different level altogether. Following are the uses of computers in education-

1.   **Making classrooms effective :** The traditional classes have become modern and high-tech with the advent of computers. Students now see multimedia presentations, clips, images, etc. with the help of computers. This gives them a better experience of education as compared to the monotonous blackboard teaching. This way, the power of students to remember or recollect the taught concepts increases as the classroom learning becomes interesting.

2. **Providing online education :** Computers not only strengthen the traditional education system but also provide a new mode of pursuing educational courses and degrees. This mode is called as online training mode of education. Online education system offers several benefits to the students which they can't avail in traditional education system.

3. **Helps in research work :** Computers help students of schools, colleges and universities in their research works. Gone are the days when students would go to libraries, and other Knowledge processing units to complete their research work. With the help of computers students now pursue their research work with ease and get ample amount of information for the same with easy clicks.

B. In the Field of Office

1. **Document Management system :** Document Management system consists of different applications like word processing, desktop publishing, spreadsheets etc.
   - **Word Processing :** is used to create documents electronically. It is used to produce high-quality letters, proposals, reports and brochures etc.
   - **Desktop Publishing :** is used to make these documents attractive with photos and graphics etc. it is used to publish the documents.
   - **Spreadsheet Application :** is used to maintain records and calculate expenses, profits and losses. It is also used to perform mathematical, statistical and logical processing.

2. **Office Support System :** It is used to coordinate and manage the activities of a workgroup. The members of a workgroup can share their work and coordinate with one another. Groupware and desktop organizers are examples of this system.

C. In the Field of Medicine

1. **Hospital Administration :** Hospital is an important organization. We can use computer for the administration of a hospital. We can computerize the accounting, payroll and stock system of the hospital. We can keep the record of different medicines, their distribution and use in different wards etc.

2. **Recording Medical History :** Computer can be used to store medical history of patients. We can store important facts about patients in computer we can keep record if his past treatment, suggested medicines and their results. Such systems can be very effective and helpful for doctors.

3. **Monitoring systems :** Some serious patients must be monitored continuously. Monitoring is needed especially in operation theatres and intensive care units. Many computerized device are used to monitor the blood pressure, heartbeat and brain of the patients.

4. **Life Support System :** life support systems are used to help the disabled persons. Many devices are used that help deaf person to hear, scientists are trying to create a device to help blind person to see.

5. **Diagnosis of Diseases :** Different software are available to store data about different diseases and their symptoms. Diagnosis of disease is possible by entering the symptoms of a patient. Different computerized devices are used in laboratories for different tests of blood.

D. In the Field of Defence

There are many uses computers in defence such as:

1. Computers are used to track incoming missiles and help slew weapons systems onto the incoming target to destroy them.

2. Computers are used in helping the military find out where all their assets are (Situational Awareness) and in Communications/Battle Management Systems.

3. Computers are used in the logistic and ordering functions of getting equipment to and around the battlefield.

4. Computers are used in tanks and planes and ships to target enemy forces, help run the platform and more recently to help diagnose any problems with the platforms.

5. Computers are used as gateways between different computer networks and to host security functions (crypto systems).

Past Exercise

1. Which of the following are computers that can be carried around easily ?   **[SBI Clerk, 2009]**
   (a) Minicomputers   (b) Supercomputers
   (c) PCs   (d) Laptops
   (e) None of these

2. The basic goal of computer process is to convert data into   **[SBI Clerk, 2009]**
   (a) files   (b) tables
   (c) information   (d) graphs
   (e) None of these

3. Which of the following refers to the fastest, biggest and most expensive computers ?
   (a) Personal Computers   **[SBI Clerk, 2009]**
   (b) Supercomputers
   (c) Laptops
   (d) Notebooks
   (e) None of these

4. A central computer that holds collections of data and programs for many PCs, workstations and other computers is a(n) —— **[SBI Clerk, 2009]**
   (a) supercomputer   (b) minicomputer
   (c) laptop   (d) server
   (e) None of these

5. A —— is an electronic device that process data, converting it into information.
   [SBI Clerk, 2009]
   (a) computer   (b) processor
   (c) case   (d) stylus
   (e) None of these

6. Processor's speed of a computer is measured in
   [SSC CGL, 2010]
   (a) BPS   (b) MIPS
   (c) Baud   (d) Hertz

7. The first computer made available for commercial use was: **[SSC CGL, 2011]**
   (a) MANIAC   (b) ENIAC
   (c) UNIVAC   (d) EDSAC

8. A central computer that holds collections programs for many PCs, workstations computers is a(n)   **[IBPS PO, 2011]**
   (a) supercomputer   (b) minicomputer
   (c) laptop   (d) server
   (e) None of these

9. Personal computers can be connected together to form a   **[IBPS PO, 2011]**
   (a) server   (b) supercomputer
   (c) network   (d) enterprise
   (e) None of these

10. Portable computer, also known as laptop computer, weighing between 4 and 10 pounds is called   **[SBI PO, 2011]**
    (a) general-purpose application
    (b) Internet
    (c) scanner
    (d) printer
    (e) notebook computer

11. Which of the following is the fastest type of computer?   **[IBPS Clerk, 2011]**
    (a) Laptop   (b) Notebook
    (c) Personal computer   (d) Workstation
    (e) Supercomputer

12. A computer system   **[SBI Clerk, 2011]**
    (a) hardware   (b) software
    (c) peripheral devices   (d) All of these
    (e) None of these

13. A ________ is a large and expensive computer capable of simultaneously processing data for hundreds or thousands of users.
    [SBI Clerk, 2011]
    (a) handheld computer
    (b) mainframe computer
    (c) personal computer
    (d) tablet computer
    (e) None of these

14. A personal computer is designed to meet the computing needs of a(n)   **[SBI Clerk, 2011]**
    (a) individual   (b) department
    (c) company   (d) city
    (e) None of these

15. Ctrl, shift and alt are called ________ keys.
    [SBI Clerk, 2011]
    (a) adjustment   (b) function
    (c) modifier   (d) alphanumeric
    (e) None of these

16. A Group Ware is a   **[SSC CGL, 2011]**
    (a) Hardware   (b) Network
    (c) Software   (d) Firmware

17. Super computer developed by Indian scientists
    [IBPS Clerk, 2012]
    (a) Param   (b) Super30l
    (c) Compaq Presario   (d) Cray YMP
    (e) Blue Gene
18. A computer used at supermarkets, departmental stores and restaurant etc is called _______ terminal   **[IBPS Clerk, 2012]**
    (a) P-O-S (Point of scale)
    (b) Dumb
    (c) Intelligent
    (d) Smart
    (e) calculating
19. Supercomputers________   **[SBI Clerk, 2012]**
    (a) are smaller in size and processing capability than mainframe computers
    (b) are common in majority of households
    (c) contain thousands of microprocessors
    (d) are rarely used by researchers due to their lack of computing capacity
    (e) are of the same size as laptops
20. What type of information system would be recognised by digital circuits ?
    (a) Hexadecimal system   **[SSC CGL, 2013]**
    (b) Binary system
    (c) Both hexadecimal and binary system
    (d) Only Roman system
21. The first computer mouse was built by
    [SSC CGL, 2013]
    (a) Douglas Engelbart   (d) William English
    (c) Oaniel Coogher   (d) Robert Zawacki
22. Which of the following is contained on chips connected to the system board and is a holding area for data instructions and information? (processed data waiting to be output to secondary storage)   **[IBPS Clerk, 2014]**
    (a) program   (b) mouse
    (c) Internet   (d) memory
    (e) modem
23. Codes consisting of lines of varying widths or lengths that are computer-readable are known as _______   **[IBPS Clerk, 2014]**
    (a) an ASCII code   (b) a magnetic tape
    (c) an OCR scanner   (d) a bar code
    (e) None of these
24. Help Menu is available at which button?
    [IBPS Clerk, 2014]
    (a) End   (b) Start
    (c) Turnoff   (d) Restart
    (e) Reboot

25. What is the process of copying software programs from secondary storage media to the hard disk called?   **[SBI Clerk, 2014]**
    (a) configuration   (b) download
    (c) storage   (d) upload
    (e) installation
26. Which of the following is true ?
    [SBI Clerk, 2014]
    (a) Byte is a single digit in a binary number.
    (b) Bit represents a grouping of digital numbers
    (c) An eight-digit binary number is called a byte.
    (d) An eight-digit binary number is called a bit.
    (e) None of these
27. Information on a computer is stored as
    [SBI Clerk, 2014]
    (a) analog data   (b) digital data
    (c) modern data   (d) watts data
    (e) None of these
28. When a ________is deleted, the original application, folder, or file is not deleted.
    [SBI Clerk, 2014]
    (a) Option   (b) Task
    (c) Shortcut   (d) Suite
    (e) None of these
29. Who among the following introduced the world's first laptop computer in the market?
    (a) Hewlett-Packard   **[SSC CGL, 2014]**
    (b) Epson
    (c) Laplink travelling software Inc
    (d) Microsoft
30. Who is father of modern computers?
    (a) Abraham Lincoln   **[IBPS Clerk, 2015]**
    (b) James Gosling
    (c) Charles Babbage
    (d) Gordon E. Moore
    (e) None of these
31. How many generations of computers we have?
    [IBPS Clerk, 2015]
    (a) 6   (b) 7
    (c) 5   (d) 4
    (e) None of these

32. _________ controls the way in which the computer system functions and provides a means by which users can interact with the computer. **[IBPS Clerk, 2015]**
    (a) The operating system
    (b) The motherboard
    (c) The platform
    (d) Application software
    (e) None of these

33. Which of the following is NOT a component of the Central Processing Unit of the computer? **[IBPS Clerk, 2015]**
    (a) Universal Serial Bus
    (b) Uninterrupted Power Supply
    (c) CU
    (d) Both A & B
    (e) None of these

34. __________ Is a mechanism by which all the content in a specified storage areas are written as output. **[IBPS Clerk, 2015]**
    (a) Scheduling　　　(b) Logging
    (c) Chumping　　　(d) Dumping
    (e) None of these

35. VLSI technology is used in __________ generation computers. **[IBPS Clerk, 2015]**
    (a) First　　　(b) Second
    (c) Third　　　(d) Fourth
    (e) None of these

36. Different types of modern digital computers come under which generation. **[IBPS Clerk, 2015]**
    (a) Forth　　　(b) Third
    (c) Second　　　(d) Fifth
    (e) None of these

37. What computers are used for fastest type of computer that can perform complex operations at very high speed? **[IBPS Clerk, 2015]**
    (a) Micro　　　(b) Mini
    (c) Mainframe　　　(d) Super
    (e) None of these

38. The operating system does all of the following EXCEPT: **[IBPS Clerk, 2015]**
    (a) provide a way for the user to interact with the computer.
    (b) enable users to perform a specific task such as document editing.
    (c) manage memory and storage
    (d) manage the central processing unit (CPU)
    (e) None of these

39. Which of the following is machine independent program? **[SBI Clerk, 2015]**
    (a) High level language
    (b) Low level language
    (c) Assembly level language
    (d) Machine language
    (e) None of these

40. Transformation of input into output is performed by ____? **[SBI Clerk, 2015]**
    (a) Peripherals　　　(b) Memory
    (c) Storage　　　(d) CPU
    (e) None of these

41. The operating system determines the manner in which all of the following occurs except **[IBPS PO, 2015]**
    (a) user creation of a document
    (b) user interaction with the processor
    (c) printer output
    (d) data displayed on the monitor
    (e) None of these

42. CPU Scheduler is also known as ______ .
    (a) Job Scheduler　　　**[SSC CGL, 2016]**
    (b) Resource Scheduler
    (c) Short-term Scheduler
    (d) Process Scheduler

43. China now has more of the world's fastest supercomputers than other countries. Which among the following is a Chinese super computer? **[IBPS PO Mains, 2016]**
    (a) BlueGene/Q system
    (b) Cray XC30
    (c) Shaheen II
    (d) Fujitsu's K

44. Which among the given options is IBM's Supercomputer? **[IBPS PO Mains, 2016]**
    (a) Tihane-2
    (b) SunwayTaihu Light
    (c) Watson
    (d) Shasra-T
    (e) Brain

45. Which of the following character set supports Japanese and Chinese font? **[IBPS Clerk Mains, 2016]**
    (a) EBCDIC　　　(b) ASCII
    (c) BCD　　　(d) EDCBI
    (e) None of these

46. Faster Supercomputer in the world as of June 2016, **[IBPS Clerk Mains, 2016]**
    (a) Sunway Taihulight (b) IBM HS20
    (c) Cray xc40 (d) SAGA
    (e) PARAM

47. Weibo is a micro-blogging site popular in **[IBPS Clerk Mains, 2016]**
    (a) India (b) USA
    (c) South Korea (d) China
    (e) New Zealand

48. Why do you log off from your computer when going out from your office? **[IBPS Clerk Mains, 2016]**
    (a) Someone might steal your files, passwords etc.
    (b) In order to save electricity
    (c) Logging off is essential to increase performance
    (d) Logging off is mandatory you before go out
    (e) Logging off is a good exercise to perform regularly

49. Which of the following is not responsible for the performance of the computer? **[IBPS Clerk Mains, 2016]**
    (a) no of keys in the keyboard
    (b) Name of the video/graphics card
    (c) Memory in the video/graphics card
    (d) The clock speed of the processor
    (e) No of cores available in the processor

50. Integrated Chips or IC's were started to be in use from which generation of Computers? **[IBPS Clerk Mains, 2016]**
    (a) 1st Generation (b) 2nd Generation
    (c) 3rd Generation (d) 4th Generation
    (e) 5th Generation

51. Which among the following is the smallest unit in an image in a computer screen? **[IBPS Clerk Mains, 2016]**
    (a) Unit (b) Pixel
    (c) Array (d) Resolution
    (e) Clip

52. Which of the following is the combination of numbers, alphabets along with username used to get access to a user account? **[IBPS Clerk Mains, 2016]**
    (a) password (b) Username
    (c) Title name (d) host-id
    (e) Screen name

53. Which among the following cycle consists of an Input, processing, output and storage as its constituents? **[IBPS Clerk Mains, 2016]**
    (a) Processing (b) Output
    (c) Input (d) Storage
    (e) Data

54. Which of the following system is a function of dedicated PCs? **[IBPS Clerk Mains, 2016]**
    (a) Meant for a single user
    (b) meant for the single task
    (c) Deal with single software
    (d) Deal with only editing
    (e) Deal for music purpose

55. BCC in the Email refer to **[IBPS RRB, 2016]**
    (a) Blind Carbon Copy
    (b) Black Carbon Copy
    (c) Blank Carbon Copy
    (d) Blue Carbon Copy
    (e) None of these

56. In which generation of computer, Integrated Circuit was introduced? **[IBPS RRB, 2016]**
    (a) First Generation
    (b) Second Generation
    (c) Third Generation
    (d) Fourth generation
    (e) Fifth Generation

57. What is called, a concentric circle on a disk? **[IBPS RRB, 2016]**
    (a) Sector (b) Track
    (c) Section (d) Arc
    (e) Directory

58. Which function key is used to refresh the current window? **[IBPS RRB, 2016]**
    (a) F1 (b) F5
    (c) F3 (d) F6
    (e) F4

59. JPEG stands for – **[IBPS RRB, 2016]**
    (a) Joint Photographic Expert group
    (b) Joint Photographic Expert graphics
    (c) Join Photographic Expert group
    (d) Join Photographic Expert graphics
    (e) None of these

60. 1000000 bytes =? **[IBPS RRB, 2016]**
    (a) TB (b) KB
    (c) MB (d) GB
    (e) None of these

61. ICMP stands for _______ **[IBPS RRB, 2016]**
    - (a) Internet Communication Message Protocol
    - (b) Internal Communication Message Protocol
    - (c) Internal Control Message Protocol
    - (d) Internet Control Message Protocol
    - (e) Intranet Control Message Protocol

62. Which of the following is a large and expensive, computer capable of simultaneously processing data for hundreds or thousands of users?
    - (a) Handheld Computer   **[IBPS RRB, 2016]**
    - (b) Tablet
    - (c) Personal Computer
    - (d) Mainframe Computer
    - (e) None of these

63. Which of the following type of computer could be found in a digital watch? **[IBPS RRB, 2016]**
    - (a) Handheld Computer
    - (b) Tablet
    - (c) Personal Computer
    - (d) Mainframe Computer
    - (e) Embedded Computer

64. To access a mainframe or super computer, users need _______ **[IBPS RRB, 2016]**
    - (a) Node
    - (b) Laptop
    - (c) Tablet
    - (d) CPU
    - (e) Terminal

65. Which of the following shortcut is used to repeat the last action performed?
    [IBPS RRB, 2016]
    - (a) F3
    - (b) F4
    - (c) F5
    - (d) F6
    - (e) F2

ANSWER KEY

1.	(d)	12.	(d)	23.	(b)	34.	(d)	45.	(e)	56.	(c)
2.	(c)	13.	(b)	24.	(b)	35.	(d)	46.	(a)	57.	(b)
3.	(b)	14.	(a)	25.	(c)	36.	(d)	47.	(d)	58.	(b)
4.	(d)	15.	(c)	26.	(c)	37.	(d)	48.	(a)	59.	(a)
5.	(b)	16.	(c)	27.	(b)	38.	(b)	49.	(a)	60.	(c)
6.	(b)	17.	(a)	28.	(c)	39.	(a)	50.	(c)	61.	(d)
7.	(c)	18	(a)	29.	(b)	40.	(d)	51.	(b)	62.	(d)
8.	(d)	19.	(c)	30.	(c)	41.	(b)	52.	(a)	63.	(e)
9.	(c)	20.	(b)	31.	(c)	42.	(c)	53.	(a)	64.	(e)
10.	(e)	21.	(a)	32.	(a)	43.	(c)	54.	(b)	65.	(b)
11.	(e)	22.	(d)	33.	(d)	44.	(c)	55.	(a)		

Practice Exercise

1. Which of the following is NOT associated with Computers?
   - (a) Bit
   - (b) Binary
   - (c) Pencil
   - (d) Mouse
   - (e) Screen

2. The first computer which provides storage is
   - (a) EDSAC
   - (b) EDBAC
   - (c) MARK-I
   - (d) ACE
   - (e) None of these

3. Microcomputer hardware consists of three basic categories of physical equipment __________.
   - (a) keyboard, monitor, hard drive
   - (b) system unit, input/output, memory
   - (c) system unit, input/output, secondary storage
   - (d) system unit, primary storage, secondary storage
   - (e) None of these

4. A desktop computer is also known as a –
   - (a) Palm Pilot
   - (b) PC
   - (c) laptop
   - (d) mainframe
   - (e) None of these

5. The benefit of using computers is that __________.
   - (a) Computers are very fast and can store huge amounts of data
   - (b) Computers provide accurate output even when input is incorrect
   - (c) Computers are designed to be inflexible
   - (d) All of these
   - (e) None of these

6. In latest generation computers, the instructions are executed
   - (a) Parallel only
   - (b) Sequentially only
   - (c) Both sequentially and parallel
   - (d) All of above
   - (e) None of these

7. Which of the following are computers that can be carried around easily?
   - (a) Laptops
   - (b) Supercomputers
   - (c) PCs
   - (d) Minicomputers
   - (e) None of these

8. The basic goal of computer process is to convert data into __________.
   - (a) information
   - (b) tables
   - (c) files
   - (d) graphs
   - (e) None of these

9. Computers gather data, which means they allow users to __________ data.
   - (a) present
   - (b) store
   - (c) output
   - (d) input
   - (e) None of these

10. Which of the following is not the major function of a computer?
    - (a) Processing data into information
    - (b) Storing data or information
    - (c) Gathering data
    - (d) Analysing data or information
    - (e) None of these

11. When your computer stops working suddenly, it is referred to as a __________.
    - (a) crash
    - (b) die
    - (c) death
    - (d) penalty
    - (e) None of these

12. First supercomputer developed in India is
    - (a) PARAM
    - (b) ARYA BHATT
    - (c) BUDDHA
    - (d) SHIVA
    - (e) None of these

13. Consider the following :
    - I.   C
    - II. C++
    - III. COBOL
    Which among the above is/are high-level languages (HLL)
    - (a) Only I
    - (b) I & II
    - (c) II & III
    - (d) I, II & III

14. What do we call an input/output device on a computer, reserved for communication between the computer operator or maintenance engineer and the computer?
    - (a) EDP Device
    - (b) Console
    - (c) Jokey
    - (d) Link Device

15. Dynamic Ad-hoc Wireless Networks (DAWN) usually comes under___?
    - (a) 2G
    - (b) 3G
    - (c) 4G
    - (d) 5G

16. A __________ is a small hand-held computer that helps you surf the Web and perform simple tasks.
    - (a) desktop computer
    - (b) mobile phone
    - (c) notebook computer
    - (d) minicomputer
    - (e) PDA

17. A portable, personal computer, small enough to fit on your lap, is called a __________.
    (a) notebook computer
    (b) handheld computer
    (c) mainframe computer
    (d) desktop computer
    (e) super computer
18. Computers manipulate data in many ways, and this manipulation is called
    (a) upgrading   (b) processing
    (c) batching   (d) utilising
    (e) downloading
19. Microprocessor was introduced in which generation of computer?
    (a) Second Generation
    (b) Fourth Generation
    (c) Both (a) and (b)
    (d) Fourth Generation
    (e) None of these
20. A__________ computer is a large and expensive computer capable of simultaneously processing data for hundreds or thousands of users
    (a) server   (b) mainframe
    (c) desktop   (d) tablet
    (e) None of these
21. Compatibility in regard to computers refers to
    (a) the software doing the right job for the user
    (b) it being versatile enough to handle the job
    (c) the software being able to run on the computer
    (d) software running with other previously installed software
    (e) None of the above
22. The first computers were programmed using
    (a) assembly language
    (b) machine language
    (c) spaghetti code
    (d) source code
    (e) None of the above
23. __________ are specially designed computer chips that reside inside other devices, such as your car or your electronic thermostat.
    (a) Server
    (b) Embedded computers
    (c) Robotic computers
    (d) Main frames
    (e) None of these
24. Every computer has a(n) __________; many also have __________.
    (a) operating system; a client system
    (b) operating system; instruction sets

    (c) application programs; an operating system
    (d) application programs; a client system
    (e) operating system; application programs
25. Computers that are portable and convenient for users who travel are known as
    (a) supercomputers   (b) planners
    (c) minicomputers   (d) file servers
    (e) laptops
26. The computer's capability of distinguishing spoken words is called
    (a) voice analysis
    (b) speech acknowledgment
    (c) voice recognition
    (d) speech interpretation
    (e) vocalisation
27. What is an embedded system?
    (a) A program that comes wrapped in a box.
    (b) A program that is permanent part of a computer
    (c) A computer that is part of a larger computer
    (d) A computer and software system that controls a machine or appliance
    (e) None of these
28. All computers must have
    (a) a word processing software
    (b) an operating system
    (c) an attached printer
    (d) a virus checking program
    (e) None of these
29. Computers excel at
    (a) performing the same action(s) over and over the same way.
    (b) keeping track of large numbers of small details.
    (c) providing creative solutions to problems.
    (d) working in fractions of seconds.
    (e) All of these
30. Which of the following refers to the fastest, biggest and most, expensive computers?
    (a) Notebooks
    (b) Personal Computers
    (c) Laptops
    (d) Supercomputers
    (e) PDAs
31. Which is not a basic function of a computer?
    (a) Accept and process data
    (b) Accept input
    (c) Process data
    (d) Store data
    (e) Scan text

32. Choose the odd one out.
    (a) Microcomputer
    (b) Minicomputer
    (c) Supercomputer
    (d) Notebook computer
    (e) Digital computer
33. A computer system that is old and perhaps not satisfactory is referred to as a(n)
    (a) Ancient system   (b) Historical system
    (c) Age old system   (d) Legacy system
    (e) Legal system
34. The basic goal of a computer process is to convert data into
    (a) graphs   (b) tables
    (c) files   (d) information
    (e) diagram
35. Analog computer works on the supply of
    (a) continuous electrical pulses
    (b) Electrical pulses but not continuous
    (c) Magnetic strength
    (d) Physical strength
    (e) Natural strength
36. Laptops are
    (a) Computers used in chemical laboratories
    (b) Portable, light weight and fit into briefcases
    (c) Hearing voice recognition system
    (d) Desktop
    (e) All of the above
37. _________ is not a microcomputer
    (a) Desktop computer
    (b) Tablet PC
    (c) Handled computer
    (d) Mainframe computer
    (e) Laptop
38. General purpose computer are used for
    (a) Accounting
    (b) Creating a small database
    (c) Performs calculation
    (d) All of the above
    (e) None of these
39. Which is not the example of special purpose computer ?
    (a) Automatic Aircraft Landing
    (b) Word Processor
    (c) Multimedia computer
    (d) All of the above
    (e) None of these
40. Palmtop computer is also known as
    (a) Personal computer
    (b) Notebook computer
    (c) Tablet PC
    (d) Handled computer
    (e) None of these

ANSWER KEY

1.	(c)	8.	(a)	15.	(d)	22.	(b)	29.	(e)	36.	(b)
2.	(a)	9.	(d)	16.	(c)	23.	(b)	30.	(d)	37.	(d)
3.	(b)	10.	(d)	17.	(a)	24.	(e)	31.	(e)	38.	(d)
4.	(b)	11.	(a)	18.	(b)	25.	(e)	32.	(d)	39.	(b)
5.	(a)	12.	(a)	19.	(d)	26.	(c)	33.	(d)	40.	(d)
6.	(c)	13.	(d)	20.	(b)	27.	(d)	34.	(d)		
7.	(a)	14.	(b)	21.	(d)	28.	(b)	35.	(a)		

Components of Computer System

Chapter 2

Any computer system consists of the four basic units; namely input unit, storage unit, central processing unit and output unit. Central Processing unit consists of Arithmetic logic unit and Control unit.

A computer performs five major functions no matter what size they are of as follows:

*   Data or Instructions are accepted as input,
*   Data and Instruction are stored
*   Processing of data as per the instructions,
*   Control of all operations inside the computer
*   Result in the form of output.

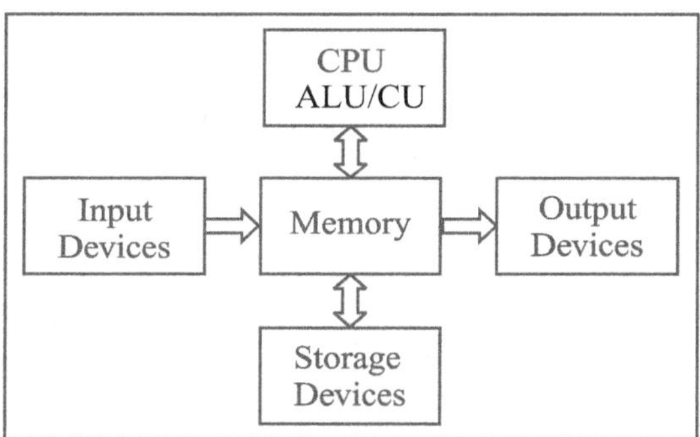

Functional Unit of a computer

BASIC COMPONENTS OF COMPUTER SYSTEMS

Following are the various components of a computer system–

Input Unit

Data and instructions must enter the computer system before any computation can be performed on the supplied data. The input unit that links the external environment with the computer system performs this task. An input unit performs the following functions :

*   It accepts (or reads) the list of instructions and data from the outside world.
*   It converts these instructions and data in computer acceptable format.
*   It supplies the converted instructions and data to the computer system for further processing.

Output Unit

The job of an output unit is just the reverse of that of an input unit. It supplied information and results of computation to the outside world. Thus it links the computer with the external environment. As computers work with binary code, the results produced are also in the binary form. Hence, before supplying the results to the outside world, it must be converted to human acceptable (readable) form. This task is accomplished by units called output interfaces.

Following functions are performed by an output unit.

- It accepts the results produced by the computer which are in coded form and hence cannot be easily understood by us.
- It converts these coded results to human acceptable (readable) form.
- It supplied the converted results to the outside world.

Storage Unit

The data and instructions that are entered into the computer system through input units have to be stored inside the computer before the actual processing starts. Similarly, the results produced by the computer after processing must also be kept somewhere inside the computer system before being passed on to the output units. The Storage Unit or the primary / main storage of a computer system is designed to do all these things. It provides space for storing data and instructions, space for intermediate results and also space for the final results.

The specific functions of the storage unit are to store:

- All the data to be processed and the instruction required for processing (received from input devices).
- Final results of processing before these results are released to an output device.
- Intermediate result of processing.

CENTRAL PROCESSING UNIT (CPU)

Central Processing Unit

The main unit inside the computer is the CPU. This unit is responsible for all events inside the computer. It controls all internal and external devices, performs "Arithmetic and Logical operations". The operations a Microprocessor performs are called "instruction set" of this processor. The instruction set is "hard wired" in the CPU and determines the machine language for the CPU. The more complicated the instruction set is, the slower the CPU works. Processors differed from one another by the instruction set. If the same program can run on two different computer brands they are said to be compatible. Programs written for IBM compatible computers will not run on Apple computers because these two architectures are not compatible.

The control Unit and the Arithmetic and Logic unit of a computer system are jointly known as the Central Processing Unit (CPU). The CPU is the brain of any computer system. In a human body, all major decisions are taken by the brain and the other parts of the body function as directed by the brain. Similarly, in a computer system, all major calculations and comparisons are made inside the CPU and the CPU is also responsible for activating and controlling the operations of other units of a computer system.

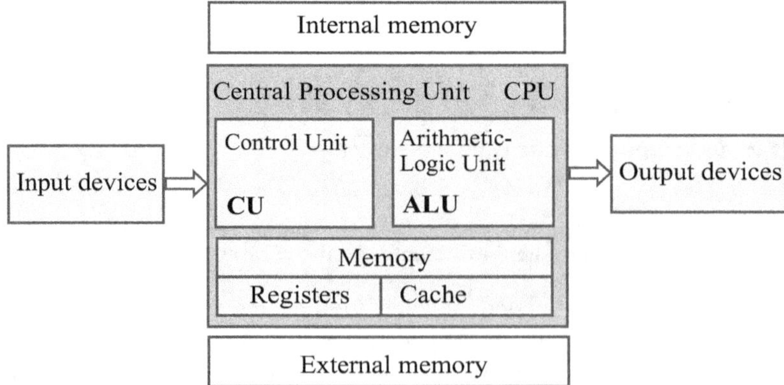

Arithmetic and Logic Unit (ALU)

The arithmetic and logic unit (ALU) of a computer system is the place where the actual execution of the instructions take place during the processing operations. All calculations are performed and all comparisons (decisions) are made in the ALU. The data and instructions, stored in the primary storage prior to processing are transferred as and when needed to the ALU where processing takes place. No processing is done in the primary storage unit. Intermediate results generated in the ALU are temporarily transferred back to the primary storage until needed at a later time. Data may thus move from primary storage to ALU and back again as storage many times before the processing is over. After the completion of processing, the final results which are stored in the storage unit are released to an output device.

The arithmetic and logic unit (ALU) is the part where actual computations take place. It consists of circuits that perform arithmetic operations (e.g. addition, subtraction, multiplication, division over data received from memory and capable to compare numbers (less than, equal to, or greater than).

Control Unit

The control unit directs and controls the activities of the internal and external devices. It interprets the instructions fetched into the computer, determines what data, if any, are needed, where it is stored, where to store the results of the operation, and sends the control signals to the devices involved in the execution of the instructions.

by the help of control unit, ALU known what should be done with the data, once it is received data then, how is it that only the final results are sent to the output devices and the control unit is also able to maintain order and directs the operation of the entire system.

> **Register :** In a computer, a register is one of a small set of data holding places that are part of a computer processor. A register may hold a computer instruction, a storage address, or any kind of data (such as a bit sequence or individual characters).

COMPUTER DEVICES

Computer devices are divide into two parts : (i) Input Device (ii) Output Device

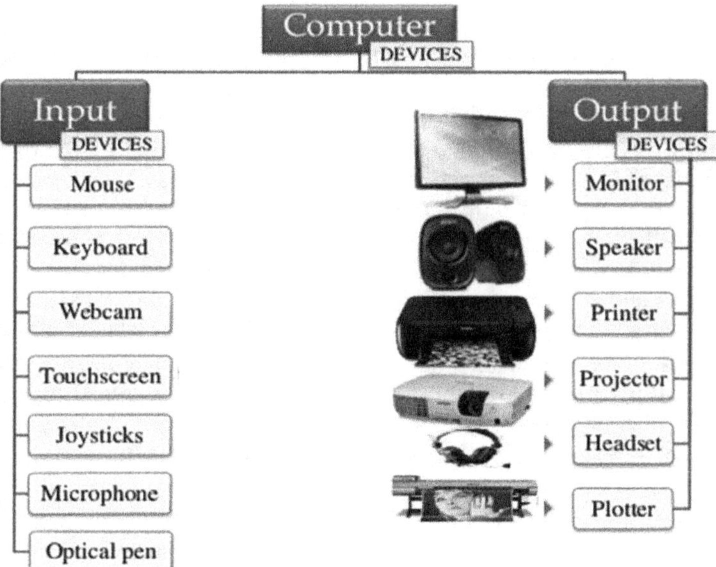

Functional of Computer Devices Components

Input Devices

Input devices include those devices with the help of which we enter data into computer as they make a link between user and computer. These devices translate the human readable information into the form understandable by computer. The various devices are as follows –

1.   **Keyboard :** Keyboard is used to input the data to the computer. In traditional times the typewriter was used. The keyboard has the layout similar to that of a typewriter but some additional keys are present that have additional functions.

The keys are following :

Sr. No.	Keys	Description
1	Typing Keys	These keys include the letter keys (A-Z) and digits keys (0-9) .
2	Numeric Keypad	It is used to enter numeric data or cursor movement. It has a set of 17 keys that are in the same layout as that of calculators.
3	Function Keys	There are twelve functions keys present on the keyboard. These are arranged in a row along the top of the keyboard. Each function key has unique meaning and is used for some specific purpose.
4	Control keys	These keysare used to provide cursor and screen control. It includes four directional arrow key. Control keys also include Home, End, Insert, Delete, Page Up, Page Down, Control(Ctrl), Alternate(Alt), Escape(Esc).
5	Special Purpose Keys	Keyboard also contains some special purpose keys such as Enter, Shift, Caps Lock, Num Lock, Space bar, Tab, and Print Screen.

2. **Mouse :** Mouse is a cursor-control device . It is a pointing and drop device. It's size is good enough to fit the palm. It has a palm size box with a round ball at its base .It senses the movement of mouse and sends corresponding signals to CPU on pressing of the buttons. There are two buttons that provide the left click and the right click. A scroll bar is present in the mid .Mouse is only used to control the position of cursor on screen.

3. **Joystick :** Just like the mouse , Joystick is also a pointing device, which is used to move cursor position on a monitor screen. It has a stick that has a spherical ball at its both lower and upper ends. The lower spherical ball moves in a socket. The joystick can be moved in four directions. It is mainly used in Computer Aided Designing (CAD) and playing computer games.

4. **Light Pen :** Light pen is also a pointing device. Its structure is similar to that of a pen. It is based on an optical system placed in a small tube. It is used to select a displayed menu item or draw pictures on the monitor screen. When light pen's tip is moved over the monitor screen and pen button is pressed, its photocell sensing element, detects the screen location and sends the corresponding signal to the CPU.

5. **Track Ball :** Track ball are used mostly in notebook or laptop computer. This is a ball, which is half inserted and by moving fingers on ball, pointer can be moved. A track ball requires less space than a mouse as the whole device is not moved. A track ball can come in various shapes like a ball, a button and a square.

6. **Scanner :** Scanner is an input device, which works on a similar principle of a photocopy machine. It is used when some information is available on a paper and it is to be transferred to the hard disc of the computer for further manipulation.

    Scanner captures images from the source which are then converted into the digital form that can be stored on the disc. These images can be edited before they are printed.

7. **Touch Screen :** A touchscreen is an electronic visual display that the user can control through simple or multi-touch gestures by touching the screen with a special stylus/pen and-or one or more fingers. Some touch screens use an ordinary or specially coated gloves to work while others use a special stylus/pen only. The user can use the touchscreen to react to what is displayed and to control how it is displayed (for example by zooming the text size).

8. **Digitizer :** Digitizer is an input device which converts analog signal from the television camera into a strings of binary digits that can be stored in a computer. It converts the analog information into a digital form. Digitizer is also known as Tablet or Graphics tablet. They can be used by the computer to create a picture of whatever the camera had been pointed at.

9. **Magnetic Ink Card Reader (MICR) :** We see in banks, libraries etc using MICR as an input device . As large number of cheques are processed everyday MICR serves a very useful purpose. A special type of ink that contains particles of magnetic material that is machine readable, is used to read the code number and

cheque number that are printed on the cheques in banks. This reading process is called Magnetic Ink Character Recognition (MICR). The main advantage of MICR is that it is highly accurate and fast in reading.

10. **Optical Character Reader (OCR) :** OCR is an input device that is used to read a printed text. The role of OCR is to scan the text optically character by character by converting them into a machine readable code and store the text on the system. The OCR is used for the preparation of electricity bills, insurance premium, telephone bills.

11. **OMR (Optical Mark Recognition):** Optical mark recognition (also called optical mark reading and OMR) is the process of capturing human-marked data from document forms such as surveys and test.

12. **SCR (Smart Card Readers):** A small electronic device about the size of a credit card that contains electronic memory, and possibly an embedded integrated circuit (IC). Smart cards containing an IC are sometimes called Integrated Circuit Cards (*ICCs*).

    Smart cards are used for a variety of purposes, including:
    – Storing a patient's medical records
    – Storing digital cash
    – Generating network IDs (similar to a token)
    To use a smart card, either to pull information from it or add data to it, you need a smart card reader, a small device into which you insert the smart card.

13. **Bar Code Readers :** Bar Code Reader is a device used for reading bar coded data (data in form of light and dark lines). Bar coded data is generally used in labelling goods, numbering the books, etc .Bar Code Reader scans a bar code image by converting it into an alphanumeric values . This value is then fed to the computer to which bar code reader is connected.

14. **Microphone :** A microphone,is an acoustic-to-electric transducer or sensor that converts sound in air into an electrical signal. Microphones are used in many applications such as telephones, hearing aids, public address systemsfor concert halls and public events, motion picture production, live and recorded audio engineering, two-way radios, megaphones, radio and television broadcasting, and in computers for recording voice, speech recognition, VoIP, and for non-acoustic purposes such as ultrasonic checking or knock sensors.

15. **Webcam :** A webcam is a video camera that feeds or streams its image in real time to or through a computer to computer network. When "captured" by the computer, the video stream may be saved, viewed or sent on to other networks via systems such as the internet, and email as an attachment. When sent to a remote location, the video stream may be saved, viewed or on sent there. Unlike an IP camera (which connects using Ethernet or Wi-Fi), a webcam is generally connected by a USB cable, or similar cable, or built into computer hardware, such as laptops.

Output Devices

An output device is that component of computer hardware that communicates the results of data that is processed by the computer and converts the digital   information into a form easily read and understood by humans. Various Output devices are used in Computers.

1. **Monitors :** Monitor or the Visual Display Unit (VDU) is the main output device of a computer. It forms images in the form of tiny dots, known as pixels. The sharpness of the image can be determined by the number of the pixels.

    Two kinds of viewing screens are used for monitors:
    • Cathode-Ray Tube (CRT)
    • Flat-Panel Display

    (a) **Cathode-Ray Tube (CRT) Monitor :** In the CRT, display consists of small picture elements known as pixels and determine the resolution of the image. Smaller are the pixels the better is the image clarity or resolution. Finite number of characters can be displayed on a screen at once. The screen can be divided into a series of character boxes that serve as a fixed location on the screen where a standard character can be placed.

Most screens are capable of displaying 80 characters of data horizontally and 25 lines vertically. CRT has some disadvantages as

(i).   It is large in Size

(ii).   Has a high power consumption.

(b)   **Flat-Panel Display Monitor :** The flat panel displays overcome the disadvantages of CRT as they have reduced volume, weight and power requirement compared to the CRT. They come in different shapes and size. You can hang them on walls or wear them on your wrists. They are used in all modern day calculators, video games, monitors, laptop computer, graphics display etc as displays.

The flat-panel display are of two main types :

(i)   **Emissive Displays :** The emissive displays convert electrical energy into light. Example are plasma panel and LED (Light-Emitting Diodes).

(ii)   **Non-Emissive Displays :** The Non-emissive displays use optical effects to convert sunlight or light from some other source into graphics patterns. Example is LCD (Liquid-Crystal Device).

(c)   **3-D Monitors:** It is a television that conveys depth perception to the viewer. 3-D describes an image that provides the perception of length. When 3-D images are made interactive then user feel involved with the scene and this experience is called virtual reality.

2.   **Printers :** Printer is among the most common output device, which is used to print information on paper.

There are two types of printers:

- Impact Printers
- Non-Impact Printers

(a)   **Impact Printers :** The printers that print the characters by striking against a ribbon and then onto the paper, are called impact printers.

Impact Printers are low of cost but they happen to be very noisy. Due to their low cost they are useful for bulk printing. There is physical contact with the paper to produce an image.

Impact printers can be further divided into two types:

(i)   **Character printers :** These printers print one character at a time. These further divided into two such as the Dot Matrix Printer and the daisy wheel printer.

Dot matrix printer (DMP) : They are the most popular printers because of their ease of printing features. They come at a low cost.

Each character is printed in the form of pattern of Dot's and head .These dots and heads consist of a matrix of pins of size (5*7, 7*9, 9*7 or 9*9) that result in forming a character. Hence they are called as Dot Matrix Printer.

Disadvantage of Dot Matrix Printer are

(i). Slow Speed   (ii). Poor Quality.

Daisy Wheel : These are known as daisy wheel printers as the head lies on the wheel and Pins correspond to characters like petals of Daisy flower. These printers are used for word-processing in offices and offer very nice quality representation. Disadvantage of Daisy wheel Printer (i) it is Slower then DMP, Noisy. (ii) More expensive then DMP.

(ii)   **Line Printers :** Line printers are printers, which print one line at a time. Speed of line printers is limited by the speed of cartridge used.

These can be divided into two types: The drum printer and the Chain printer

Drum Printer : This printer looks like a drum in shape that's why it is called a drum printer. The Drum surface has a number of tracks. Total tracks are equal to size of paper, i.e., for a paper width of 132 characters, Drum will have 132 tracks. A character set is embossed on track. The different character sets available in market are 48 character set, 64 and 96 characters set. One rotation of drum leads to printing of one line. These printers print between 300 to 2000 lines per minute. Hence they have a very high speed.

Disadvantage of this Printer are: (i) It is very expensive. (ii) Character fonts can't changed.

Chain Printer : In this printer because chain of character sets are used hence they are called as Chain Printers. A standard character set may have 48, 64, 96 characters.

Advantage of chain Printer is character fonts can easily be changed & different language can be used with same printer, less noisy then drum printer.

(b) **Non-impact Printers :** These printers print the characters without the physical contact with the paper i.e without striking against the ribbon and onto the paper. These printers print one complete page at a time, and are also called as Page Printers. It is support many fonts & different character size, high quality printing, not noisy, faster then impact printer.

These printers are of two types: Laser Printers and the Ink-jet Printers.

   (i) **Laser Printers :** These are non-impact page printers. They use laser lights to produce the dots needed to form the characters to be printed on a page.

   (ii) **Inkjet Printers :** Ink-jet printers are new technology non-impact character printers. They print characters via spraying small drops of ink onto paper. Ink-jet printers produce very high quality output with presentable features.

   They are noiseless printers and have many styles of printing modes available. These are also called as the coloured printers. Models of Ink-jet printers can produce multiple copies of printing also.

3. **Headphones :** Headphones are referred to as earphones, headphones are a hardware device that either plugs into your computer (line out) or your speakers and allow you to privately listen to audio without disturbing anyone else. The picture is an example of a USB headset from Logitech with a microphone and a popular solution for computer gaming.

4. **Speaker :** A hardware device connected to a computer's sound card that outputs sounds generated by the computer. It needs a sound card connected to a CPU, that generates sound via a card. These are used for listening music, for being audible in seminars etc.

5. **Projector :** A projector is an output device that can take images generated by a computer and reproduce them on a large, flat (usually lightly colored) surface. For example, projectors are used in meetings to help ensure that all participants can view the information being presented.

Some important points –
- External devices such as printers key boards and modems are known as peripherals.
- The higher the resolution of a monitor the closer together the pixels.
- The rate at which scanning is repeated in a CRT is called refresh rate best position for
- Tail towards the user is the best position for operating the mouse.

MAINTAINING COMPUTER SYSTEMS

We must ensure that the computer is well looked after. It can only run smoothly if it is protected valuable from malicious viruses which can wreak havoc on your PC or Mac.

Computers that become overloaded or vulnerable to viruses can freeze or crash. This can lead to loss of information .Hackers who hack professionally can be a threat to the computers. There are some extremely sophisticated and technologically advanced group or individuals who are hackers and can destabilise operating systems and bring computer networks crashing down.

This can lead to a slow computer. Each time a web page is opened or an attachment is downloaded certain data on the computer gets collected, much of it is not needed to be used again .This data gets clogged up on your hard drive and can affect your computer's performance if you don't do a spring clean once .Your computer must be given a general assessment every couple of months. A general assessment should be done more frequently (around once a month) if your computer is used a lot.

Backing Up

It is a very important thing to get into the habit of backing up your files on a regular basis. This means having a recent copy of important data held onto your computer. The important documents on your system include the invoices, legal documents or personal files such as photo albums.

You can copy your files to a USB memory stick. USB memory stick do not have enough data to store. They can be quite expensive to buy. They have been popular because of their portability as they're easy to use.

Disk imaging is one of the most effective methods of backing up .This is a more expensive method as it is the most fail-safe method of restoring everything on your computer if you lose everything on your hard drive. With the advent of various online backup you can enlist to help with the storage of your computer's data, which are incredibly convenient as the backup is done automatically and your files are kept in a safe online environment that you can access at any time.

Deleting files

Storing huge data and big files on your computer can bring performance speeds immediately down. In order to make sure your computer is running efficiently it's important to delete unnecessary files from time to time. Windows operating systems has a disk cleanup function that is extremely quick and easy to use. Disk cleanup doesn't take too long to run .This utility on your computer cleans up all the unwanted files that are stored in your computer's cache.

Scanning your hard drive

It is really important to Scan your hard drive as an another routine task which you should get into the habit of doing regularly. This utility examines the hard drive for some errors that could have a direct affecte on your computer's efficiency. This needs to be done around once a week to use your computer every day or once in a month incase if you use it less frequently.

Defragmenting your hard drive

The computer's hard drive can become clogged up with numerous files that are broken up across various locations around the drive. The drive becomes really chaotic. Due to the drive getting chaotic your computer gradually slow's down in its speed as it tries to access information from files scattered all over the drive. Hence it's really important to carry out a process that rationalises the various files from time to time.

Defragmentation collects all the different parts of one file back together in one place in the hard drive. Then it in turns reorganizes information and places the files that are used most frequently. Defragmention process leads to a much faster running computer.

Clearing your cache (cookies and Internet files)

This folder cache is of temporary Internet files folder that is a record of files which have been viewed or downloaded from the web, including web pages, images, music and cookies (small files that websites can create on your computer to help them deliver personalised content when you next visit.

Automatic updating

Computer hackers are determined to destabilise computer software through their malicious programs. A number of big companies like Microsoft , 'patch' their products in order to ensure their safety. If you run on windows then make sure your computer is set to update automatically. These updates can be automated by clicking on the start then programs. Windows updates ensure that you're set to install updates automatically.

Checking for viruses

Installing some form of anti-virus software is a must. The computer is vulnerable to a range of viruses. These viruses are transmitted to your computer via infected email attachments. These viruses are called as worms and can spread over the Internet. The viruses are used by criminals in order to gather personal information.

These worms can have serious consequences. Viruses have the capability of gathering financial information and secret data such as passwords and user names.

Hence making adequate arrangements of prevention is always better than cure. Installing enough anti virus protection programs for virus protection on your computers is the best way to protect your computer.

Anti-virus software can be bought as stand-alone or as a comprehensive security suite. Example of various software manufacturers include Mc Afee and AVG.

Installing anti malware, spyware and adware

Malware, spyware and adware all pose a significant threat to your online privacy and the smooth-running of your computer .It is extremely essential to install alongwith anti-virus software , the anti spyware software also. The spyware can spy on your online activities, as it installs unwanted program on your computer. Adware is used by commercial companies to find out more about consumers and track the effectiveness of their advertising, but it can have more dire consequences. Malicious adware or spyware is very hard to remove from your computer. It can cause to block access to certain websites, stop you running anti virus software, scan your hard disk and locate sensitive personal information, such as credit card numbers and other personal information which can then be used for criminal activities.

In order to ensure that you don't fall victim you can install an anti-spyware software. They work in the same way as anti-virus software. These free Downloadable products include AdAware and Microsoft Defender. As with anti-virus software, the free versions may not be quite as comprehensive as their paid for counterparts but they should provide a decent level of protection.

Set up a Firewall

Firewalls are a significant way of protecting your computer from some of the threats that have crept up in the cyberspace world. Firewalls are an effective way to safeguard you from hackers, viruses and worms . These viruses can endanger the personal information that is kept on your computer. Firewalls are a barrier between your computer and the world outside . But firewalls are not enough to be relied on only. They alone cannot protect your computer from online threats. Your firewall should be used in conjunction with other forms of computer security, such as your anti-virus software.

Windows packages contain a 'desktop firewall', for which you don't need to pay for and provide a basic level of security. The broadband internet router that is used for an internet connection also a firewall built into it, which can be controlled via your computer and which is password protected.

Cleaning your computer

Ensuring that your computer is clean of dust and dirt can make sure that your computer is kept under hygienic conditions. Make sure your computer is turned off and unplugged before you clean it. You can buy specialist computer cleaning products or use a damp, lint-free soft cloth to gently dislodge dirt from the keyboard or the exterior of the computer. A computer mouse is particularly susceptible to dirt, making it difficult to control. To clean your mouse turn the retaining ring on the bottom of the mouse anti-clockwise to remove the mouse ball. You can then use a clean soft cloth to remove any dust or dirt from inside the mouse.

It's important to deal with any spillages on your keyboard quickly. Turn off your computer and then turn the keyboard on its side to drain off the excess. Use a soft cloth to mop up any remaining liquid and then let your keyboard dry off before using it again.

Past Exercise

1. A printer is this kind of device

   [SBI Clerk, 2009]
   - (a) input
   - (b) word processing
   - (c) processing
   - (d) output
   - (e) None of these

2. The name of the computer's brain is

   [SBI Clerk, 2009]
   - (a) monitor
   - (b) hardware
   - (c) CPU
   - (d) byte
   - (e) None of these

3. The output devices make it possible to

   [SBI Clerk, 2009]
   - (a) view or print data
   - (b) store data
   - (c) scan data
   - (d) input data
   - (e) None of these

4. The most common method of entering text and numerical data into a computer system is through the use of a   **[SBI Clerk, 2009]**
   - (a) keyboard
   - (b) scanner
   - (c) printer
   - (d) plotter
   - (e) None of these

5. Which of the following groups consist of only input devices?   **[SBI Clerk, 2009]**
   - (a) Mouse, Keyboard, Monitor
   - (b) Mouse, Keyboard, Printer
   - (c) Mouse, Keyboard, Plotter
   - (d) Mouse, Keyboard, Scanner
   - (e) None of these

6. Which of the following groups consist of only output devices?   **[SBI Clerk, 2009]**
   - (a) Scanner, Printer, Monitor
   - (b) Keyboard, Printer, Monitor
   - (c) Mouse, Printer, Monitor
   - (d) Plotter, Printer, Monitor
   - (e) None of these

7. A keyboard is this kind of device

   [SBI Clerk, 2009]
   - (a) black
   - (b) input
   - (c) output
   - (d) word processing
   - (e) None of these

8. Arithmetic operations   **[SBI Clerk, 2009]**
   - (a) involve matching one data item to another to determine if the first item is greater than, equal to, or less than the other item
   - (b) sort data items according to standard, predefined criteria in ascending order or descending order
   - (c) use conditions with operators such as AND, OR and NOT
   - (d) include addition, subtraction, multiplication, and division
   - (e) None of these

9. A series of instructions that tells a computer what to do and how to do it is called a

   [SBI Clerk, 2009]
   - (a) program
   - (b) command
   - (c) user response
   - (d) processor
   - (e) None of these

10. Which part of the computer displays the work done ?   **[SBI Clerk, 2009]**
    - (a) RAM
    - (b) Printer
    - (c) Monitor
    - (d) ROM
    - (e) None of these

11. Any data or instruction entered into the memory of a computer is considered as   **[SBI Clerk, 2009]**
    - (a) storage
    - (b) output
    - (c) input
    - (d) information
    - (e) None of these

12. For seeing the output, you use————

    [SBI Clerk, 2009]
    - (a) Monitor
    - (b) Keyboard
    - (c) Mouse
    - (d) Scanner
    - (e) None of these

13. A scanner scans————   **[SBI Clerk, 2009]**
    - (a) Pictures
    - (b) Text
    - (c) Both Pictures and Text
    - (d) Neither Pictures nor Text
    - (e) None of the above

14. Which of the following is not an input device?

    [SBI Clerk, 2009]
    - (a) Keyboard
    - (b) Monitor
    - (c) Joystick
    - (d) Microphone
    - (e) None of these

15. Back up of the data files will help to prevent
———— **[SBI Clerk, 2009]**
    (a) loss of confidentiality
    (b) duplication of data
    (c) virus infection
    (d) loss of data
    (e) None of the above
16. Which is the part of the computer system that one can physically touch ? **[SBI Clerk, 2009]**
    (a) data   (b) operating system
    (c) hardware   (d) software
    (e) None of these
17. ———— is processed by the computer into information. **[SBI Clerk, 2009]**
    (a) Data   (b) Numbers
    (c) Alphabets   (d) Pictures
    (e) None of these
18. To access properties of an object, the mouse technique to use is—. **[SBI Clerk, 2009]**
    (a) right-clicking   (b) shift-clicking
    (c) dragging   (d) dropping
    (e) None of these
19. A —— can make it easier to play games.
[SBI Clerk, 2009]
    (a) mouse   (b) joystick
    (c) keyboard   (d) pen
    (e) None of these
20. Codes consisting of lines of varying widths or lengths that are computer-readable are known as **[IBPS PO, 2011]**
    (a) an ASCII code   (b) a magnetic tape
    (c) a bar code   (d) an OCR scanner
    (e) None of these
21. Which one is the world's first electric compter? **[IBPS PO, 2011]**
    (a) EDVAC   (b) UNIVAC
    (c) ENIAC   (d) All of the above
    (e) None of these
22. Video processors consist of_____and_____ which store and process images.
[IBPS PO, 2011]
    (a) CPU and VGA
    (b) CPU and memory
    (c) VGA and memory
    (d) VGI and DVI
    (e) None of these
23. The system unit   **[SBI PO, 2011]**
    (a) coordinates input and output devices
    (b) is the container that houses electronic components
    (c) is a combination of hardware and software
    (d) controls and manipulates data
    (e) does the arithmetic operations
24. The main circuit-board of the system unit is the **[SBI PO, 2011]**
    (a) computer program (b) control unit
    (c) motherboard   (d) RAM
    (e) None of these
25. Which keys enable the input of numbers quickly? **[IBPS Clerk, 2011]**
    (a) ctrl, shift and alt (b) function keys
    (c) the numeric keypad (d) arrow keys
    (e) None of these
26. Form which language the word "Compter" is derived? **[IBPS Clerk, 2011]**
    (a) Spanish   (b) English
    (c) Latin   (d) Greek
    (e) None of these
27. Which of the following can input graphical images and pictures for a computer?
[IBPS Clerk, 2011]
    (a) Plotter   (b) Scanner
    (c) Mouse   (d) Printer
    (e) Keyboard
28. Why is the Caps Lock key referred to as a toggle key? **[IBPS Clerk, 2011]**
    (a) Because its function goes back and forth every time it is pressed
    (b) Because it cannot be used for entering numbers
    (c) Because it cannot be used to delete
    (d) Because it cannot be used to insert
    (e) None of these
29. Using output devices one can
[IBPS Clerk, 2011]
    (a) input data   (b) store data
    (c) scan data   (d) view or print data
    (e) None of these
30. Which of the following categories would include a keyboard? **[IBPS Clerk, 2011]**
    (a) Printing Device (b) Output Device
    (c) Pointing Device (d) Storage Device
    (e) Input Device
31. What type of keys are 'ctrl' and 'shift'?
[IBPS Clerk, 2011]
    (a) adjustment   (b) function
    (c) modifier   (d) alphanumeric
    (e) None of these

32. The term __________ refers to data storage systems that make it possible for a computer or electronic device to store and retrieve data. **[SBI Clerk, 2011]**
    (a) retrieval technology
    (b) input technology
    (c) output technology
    (d) storage technology
    (e) None of these

33. The term __________ refers to any computer component that is required to perform work. **[SBI Clerk, 2011]**
    (a) bootstrap   (b) kernel
    (c) resource   (d) source code
    (e) None of these

34. The __________ is responsible for performing calculations and contains decision-making mechanisms. **[SBI Clerk, 2011]**
    (a) Central Processing Unit
    (b) Memory Unit
    (c) Arithmetic and Logic Unit
    (d) Output Unit
    (e) None of these

35. You use a (n) __________, such as a keyboard or mouse, to input information. **[SBI Clerk, 2011]**
    (a) storage device   (b) processing device
    (c) input device   (d) output device
    (e) None of these

36. What is output? **[SBI Clerk, 2011]**
    (a) What the processor takes from the user
    (b) What the user gives to the processor
    (c) What the processor gets from the user
    (d) What the processor gives to the user
    (e) None of these

37. Computer__________ is whatever is typed, submitted, or transmitted to a computer system. **[SBI Clerk, 2011]**
    (a) input   (b) output
    (c) data   (d) circuitry
    (e) None of these

38. Which process checks to ensure the components of the computer are operating and connected properly? **[SBI Clerk, 2011]**
    (a) Booting   (b) Processing
    (c) Saving   (d) Editing
    (e) None of these

39. Which one of the following is true for RAM? **[SBI Clerk, 2011]**
    (a) It is volatile memory
    (b) It is temporary memory

(c) It is primary memory
(d) All of the above
(e) None of these

40. Ctrl, shift and alt are called __________ keys. **[SBI Clerk, 2011]**
    (a) adjustment   (b) function
    (c) modifier   (d) alphanumeric
    (e) None of these

41. What is the function of the Central Processing Unit of a Computer ? **[SBI Clerk, 2012]**
    (a) Creates invoices
    (b) Performs calculations and processing
    (c) Deletes Data
    (d) Corrupts the data
    (e) None of these

42. All the characters that a device can use is called its ? **[SBI Clerk, 2012]**
    (a) Skill Set
    (b) Character Alphabet
    (c) Character Codes
    (d) Keyboard Characters
    (e) Character Set

43. Which unit controls the movement of signals between CPU and I/O ? **[SBI Clerk, 2012]**
    (a) ALU
    (b) Control Unit
    (c) Memory Unit
    (d) Secondary Storage
    (e) None of these

44. The three main parts of the processor are __________ **[SBI Clerk, 2012]**
    (a) ALU, Control Unit and Registers
    (b) ALU, Control Unit and RAM
    (c) Cache, Control Unit and Registers
    (d) Control Unit, Registers and RAM
    (e) RAM, ROM and CD-ROM

45. Which of the following does not relate to Input Unit ? **[SBI Clerk, 2012]**
    (a) If accepts data from the outside world.
    (b) It converts data into binary code that is understandable by the computer
    (c) It converts binary data into the human readable form that is understandable to the users.
    (d) It sends data in binary form to the computer for further processing
    (e) None of these

46. Which printer cannot print more than one character at a time ? **[SSC, CHSL, 2012]**
    (a) Line   (b) Daisy-wheel
    (c) Laser   (d) Dot-matrix
    (e) None of these

47. _________key is the example of Toggle key
[IBPS Clerk, 2012]
(a) Alt
(b) Shift
(c) Control
(d) Escape
(e) Caps Lock

48. Video controller **[IBPS Clerk, 2012]**
(a) Controls the resolution of images on screen
(b) Controls the signals to be sent and received from processor for display
(c) Handles the entire electronic work behind the formation of images on the screen
(d) Is responsible for allocating pixels for formation of images
(e) Is responsible for the refresh rate of the screen / monitor

49. Which of these is a point-and-draw device ?
[IBPS PO, 2012]
(a) mouse
(b) scanner
(c) printer
(d) CD-ROM
(e) Keyboard

50. When a key is pressed on the keyboard, which standard is used for converting the keystroke into the corresponding bits? **[IBPS PO, 2013]**
(a) ANSI
(b) ASCII
(c) EBCDIC
(d) ISO
(e) None of the above

51. _______ devices convert human-understandable data and programs into a form that the computer can process. **[SBI PO, 2013]**
(a) Printing
(b) Output
(c) Solid State
(d) Monitor
(e) Input

52. The CPU comprises of Control, Memory, and _________ units. **[SBI PO, 2013]**
(a) Microprocessor
(b) Arithmetic/Logic
(c) Output
(d) ROM
(e) Input

53. A joystick is primarily used to/for ___________.
[SBI PO, 2013]
(a) Control sound on the screen
(b) Computer gaming
(c) Enter text
(d) Draw pictures
(e) Print text

54. ________ plug into slots on the motherboard and provide additional functionality for your computer. **[SBI Clerk, 2014]**
(a) Network Interface Card
(b) USB
(c) Expansion Card
(d) UPS
(e) None of these

55. The most widely used computer device is ________. **[IBPS Clerk, 2015]**
(a) Solid state disks
(b) External hard disk
(c) Internal hard disk
(d) Mouse
(e) None of these

56. Which among the following is an important circuitry in a computer system that directs the operation of the processor?
[IBPS PO Mains, 2016]
(a) Memory
(b) Address Bus
(c) Accumulator
(d) ALU
(e) Control Unit

57. The combination of ALU and Control Unit jointly known as **[IBPS RRB 2016]**
(a) Hard disk
(b) Monitor
(c) CPU
(d) UPS
(e) Software

58. Which key launched the start button?
[IBPS RRB 2016]
(a) Windows
(b) Esc
(c) Shift
(d) Function key
(e) Num lock

59. Which of the following houses the most important parts of a computer system?
[IBPS RRB 2016]
(a) Input Device
(b) Client
(c) Server
(d) Hardware
(e) None of these

ANSWER KEY

1.	(d)	11.	(c)	21.	(d)	31.	(c)	41.	(b)	51.	(e)
2.	(c)	12.	(a)	22.	(d)	32.	(d)	42.	(d)	52.	(b)
3.	(a)	13.	(c)	23.	(c)	33.	(c)	43.	(b)	53.	(b)
4.	(a)	14.	(b)	24.	(c)	34.	(c)	44.	(a)	54.	(c)
5.	(d)	15.	(d)	25.	(c)	35.	(c)	45.	(c)	55.	(c)
6.	(d)	16.	(c)	26.	(c)	36.	(d)	46.	(b)	56.	(e)
7.	(b)	17.	(a)	27.	(b)	37.	(a)	47.	(e)	57.	(c)
8.	(d)	18.	(a)	28.	(a)	38.	(a)	48.	(c)	58.	(a)
9.	(a)	19.	(b)	29.	(d)	39.	(d)	49.	(a)	59.	(d)
10.	(c)	20.	(c)	30.	(e)	40.	(c)	50.	(a)		

Practice Exercise

1. Most of the commonly used personal computers/ laptops do not have a command key known as __________.
   (a) Turnover   (b) Shift
   (c) Alter   (d) Delete
   (e) Insert

2. Most of the commonly available personal computers/laptops have a keyboard popularly known as __________.
   (a) QWERTY   (b) QOLTY
   (c) ALTER   (d) UCLIF
   (e) None of these

3. Whenever we have to give space between the two words while typing on PC we have to press a key known as __________.
   (a) Backspace   (b) Shift
   (c) Control   (d) Escape
   (e) Space Bar

4. Every component of your computer is either
   (a) software or CPU/RAM
   (b) hardware or software
   (c) application software or system software
   (d) input devices or output devices
   (e) None of these

5. What is equipment used to capture information and commands?
   (a) Output device
   (b) Input device
   (c) Storage device
   (d) Telecommunication device
   (e) None of these

6. This type of hardware consists of devices that translate data into a form the computer can process
   (a) application   (b) input
   (c) system   (d) All of these
   (e) None of these

7. Which of the following will translate images of text, drawings, and photos into digital form?
   (a) digitizer   (b) modem
   (c) scanner   (d) keyboard
   (e) None of these

8. The computer is made of which of the following hardware equipments?
   (a) Monitor, CPU (Central Processing Unit), Keyboard, Mouse, Software and Network
   (b) Monitor, CPU (Central Processing Unit), Keyboard, Mouse, Programme and Network
   (c) Monitor, CPU (Central Processing Unit), Keyboard, Mouse, Printer and Modem
   (d) Monitor, CPU (Central Processing Unit), Keyboard, Mouse, Applications and Network
   (e) None of these

9. For selecting or highlighting, which of the following is generally used?
   (a) Icon   (b) Keyboard
   (c) Mouse   (d) Floppy Disk
   (e) None of these

10. Scanner scans
    (a) Picture
    (b) Text
    (c) Both Picture and Text
    (d) Neither Picture Nor Text
    (e) None of these

11. Which of the following is not a function of the control unit?
    (a) Read instructions
    (b) Execute instructions
    (c) Interpret instructions
    (d) Direct operations
    (e) None of these

12. The most common input devices include –
    (a) Monitor and mouse
    (b) Monitor and keyboard
    (c) Printer and mouse
    (d) None of these
    (e) All of the above

13. Holding the mouse button down while moving an object of text is known as –
    (a) moving   (b) dragging
    (c) dropping   (d) highlighting
    (e) None of these

14. ___________ helps in capturing row data and entering into computer system.
    (a) CPU   (b) Integrated circuit
    (c) Input device   (d) Motherboard
    (e) None of these

15. The most widely used input device is the ___________.
    (a) mouse   (b) keyboard
    (c) modem   (d) monitor
    (e) None of these

16. A CPU contains ___________
    (a) a card reader and a printing device
    (b) an analytical engine and a control unit
    (c) a control unit and an arithmetic logic unit
    (d) an arithmetic logic unit and a card reader
    (e) None of these

17. Computations and logical operations are performed by the ___________.
    (a) RAM   (b) ALU
    (c) Register   (d) Control unit
    (e) None of these

18. The term used to define all input and output devices in a computer system is ___________.
    (a) Monitor   (b) Software
    (c) Shared resources   (d) Hardware
    (e) None of these

19. What type of resource is most likely to be a shared common resource in a computer network?
    (a) Printers   (b) Speakers
    (c) Floppy disk drives (d) Keyboards
    (e) None of these

20. Which of the following is part of the System Unit?
    (a) Monitor   (b) CPU
    (c) CD-ROM   (d) Floppy Disk
    (e) None of these

21. What is output?
    (a) Processor takes from user
    (b) User gives to processor
    (c) Processor gets from user
    (d) None of these

22. Dumb terminals have terminals and ___________.
    (a) Mouse   (b) Speaker
    (c) Harddish   (d) Mouse or Speaker
    (e) None of these

23. Which of the following is not an output device?
    (a) Plotter   (b) Printer
    (c) Scanner   (d) Monitor
    (e) None of these

24. Devices that let the computer communicate with you.
    (a) input   (b) output
    (c) type   (d) print
    (e) None of these

25. Devices that allow you to put information into the
    (a) input   (b) output
    (c) type   (d) print
    (e) None of these

26. The primary device that a computer uses to store information.
    (a) TV   (b) storehouse
    (c) desk   (d) hard drive
    (e) None of these

27. Pick the odd one –
    (a) Mouse   (b) Scanner
    (c) Printer   (d) Keyboard
    (e) None of these

28. An output device that lets you see what the computer is doing –
    (a) a disk drive   (b) monitor-screen
    (c) shift key   (d) printer
    (e) None of these

29. A ___________ is an example of an most popular input device.
    (a) keyboard
    (b) monitor
    (c) Mouse
    (d) central processing unit
    (e) None of these

30. The function of CPU is –
    (a) to provide external storage of text
    (b) to communicate with the operator
    (c) to read, interpret and process the information and instruction
    (d) to provide a hard copy
    (e) None of these

31. Printed information, called ___________, exists physically and is a more permanent form of output than that presented on a display device.
    (a) soft copy   (b) carbon copy
    (c) hard copy   (d) desk copy
    (e) None of these

32. Which of the following is considered an input device?
    - (a) Keyboard
    - (b) Monitor
    - (c) Floppy disk
    - (d) Printer
    - (e) CD

33. Decreasing the amount of space required to store data and programs is accomplished by __________.
    - (a) pressing
    - (b) disk caching
    - (c) RAID
    - (d) crashing
    - (e) file compression

34. A device that copies or reproduces text and images is also called a(n) __________.
    - (a) optical scanner
    - (b) bar code reader
    - (c) character device
    - (d) digital camera
    - (e) printer

35. Which of the following is the equipment which holds the screen of a computer?
    - (a) Video
    - (b) Desktop
    - (c) Modem
    - (d) Monitor
    - (e) Scanner

36. What is usually used for displaying information at public places?
    - (a) Monitor
    - (b) Overhead Projections
    - (c) Monitors and Overhead Projections
    - (d) Touch Screen Kiosks
    - (e) None of these

37. Which of the following is not an output device?
    - (a) Plotter
    - (b) Printer
    - (c) Monitor
    - (d) Touch Screen
    - (e) None of these

38. The operation of computer is controlled by
    - (a) Memory system
    - (b) Controlling system
    - (c) Operating system
    - (d) Processing system
    - (e) None of these

39. The computer monitor is which type of device?
    - (a) Input
    - (b) Output
    - (c) Processing
    - (d) Software
    - (e) None of the above

40. The primary output device for computers is a
    - (a) video monitor
    - (b) printer
    - (c) keyboard
    - (d) mouse
    - (e) None of the above

41. The output which is made up of pictures, sounds, and video is called
    - (a) COM
    - (b) hard copy
    - (c) graphics
    - (d) multimedia
    - (e) None of the above

42. __________ provides the means to move the pointer on the screen and give information to the computer by clicking its buttons.
    - (a) Scanner
    - (b) Mouse
    - (c) Keyboard
    - (d) Program
    - (e) None of the above

43. Which of the following could be digital input devices for computers?
    - (a) Digital camcorder
    - (b) Microphone
    - (c) Scanner
    - (d) All of the above
    - (e) None of these

44. When speaking of computer input and output, input refers to
    - (a) any data processing that occurs from new data input into computer.
    - (b) retrieval of data or information that has been entered into the computer.
    - (c) data or information that has been entered into the computer.
    - (d) the transmission of data that has been entered into the computer.
    - (e) Both (c) and (d)

45. A means of capturing an image (drawing or photo) so that it can be stored on a computer is
    - (a) Modem
    - (b) Software
    - (c) Scanner
    - (d) Keyboard
    - (e) Mouse

46. Access control based on a person's fingerprints is an example of
    - (a) biometric identification
    - (b) characteristic identification
    - (c) fingerprint security
    - (d) logistics
    - (e) None of these

47. The patterns of printed lines on most products are called
    - (a) prices
    - (b) striping
    - (c) scanners
    - (d) OCR
    - (e) barcodes

48. Which of the following is needed for sound recording?
   (a) Speaker   (b) Microphone
   (c) Talker   (d) Mouse
   (e) Telephone
49. Which of the following is not associated with hardware?
   (a) CPU   (b) Monitor
   (c) Key board   (d) COBOL
   (e) None of these
50. In a computer most processing takes place in __________.
   (a) Memory   (b) RAM
   (c) Motherboard   (d) CPU
   (e) None of these
51. Keyboards, scanners, and microphones are examples of __________.
   (a) software programs (b) input devices
   (c) output devices   (d) utilities
   (e) None of these
52. Which of the following is part of the System Unit?
   (a) Monitor   (b) CPU
   (c) CD-ROM   (d) Floppy Disk
   (e) Printer
53. A __________ is an example of an input device.
   (a) printer
   (b) monitor
   (c) scanner
   (d) central processing unit
   (e) None of these
54. A hard copy of a document is __________.
   (a) printed on the printer
   (b) stored on a floppy
   (c) stored on a CD
   (d) stored in the hard disk
   (e) scanned
55. The ALU performs __________ operations.
   (a) logic   (b) ASCII
   (c) algorithm-based (d) logarithm-based
   (e) final
56. __________ is the part of the computer that does arithmetical calculations.
   (a) OS   (b) ALU
   (c) CPU   (d) Memory
   (e) printer

57. ALU works on the instructions and data held in the
   (a) Notebook   (b) Registers
   (c) Copy Pad   (d) I/O devices
   (e) None of these
58. What is a device that can change images into codes for the computer?
   (a) Mouse   (b) Printer
   (c) Joystick   (d) Keyboard
   (e) Scanner
59. Which of the following functions is not performed by the CPU?
   (a) Graphical display of data
   (b) Arithmetic calculations
   (c) Managing memory
   (d) Managing input and output
   (e) None of these
60. Which part of the computer can display the user's work?
   (a) Mouse   (b) Keyboard
   (c) Disk Drive   (d) Monitor
   (e) None of these
61. Which of the following is a secondary device?
   (a) Keyboard   (b) CD
   (c) ALU   (d) Mouse
   (d) Printer
62. When the mouse is moved, it causes a picture to move on the screen which is referred to as in a
   (a) menu   (b) icon
   (c) pointer   (d) tab
   (e) None of these
63. The mouse __________ usually appears in the shape of an arrow.
   (a) indicator   (b) marker
   (c) meter   (d) pointer
   (e) None of these
64. Which of the following is part of the system unit?
   (a) Keyboard   (b) Floppy disks
   (c) Monitor   (d) Memory
   (e) CD
65. In a computer, most of the processing takes place in
   (a) Memory   (b) RAM
   (c) CPU   (d) Motherboard
   (e) ALU

66. The central processing unit contains which of the following as a component?
    (a) Memory Regulation Unit
    (b) Flow Control Unit
    (c) Arithmetic Logic Unit
    (d) Instruction Manipulation Unit
    (e) None of these
67. The part of the CPU that accesses and decodes program instructions, and coordinates the flow of data among various system components is the
    (a) ALU   (b) control unit
    (c) megahertz   (d) motherboard
    (e) None of these
68. The main job of a CPU is to __________.
    (a) carry out program instructions
    (b) store data/information for future use
    (c) process data and information
    (d) Both (a) and (c)
    (e) None of these
69. All of the logic and mathematical calculations done by the computer happen in/on the
    (a) system board
    (b) central control unit
    (c) central processing unit
    (d) mother board
    (e) memory
70. The physical components of a computer system.
    (a) Software   (b) Hardware
    (c) ALU   (d) Control Unit
    (e) None of the above

ANSWER KEY

1.	(a)	13.	(b)	25.	(a)	37.	(e)	49.	(d)	61.	(e)
2.	(a)	14.	(c)	26.	(d)	38.	(d)	50.	(d)	62.	(c)
3.	(e)	15.	(b)	27.	(c)	39.	(b)	51.	(b)	63.	(d)
4.	(b)	16.	(c)	28.	(b)	40.	(a)	52.	(b)	64.	(d)
5.	(b)	17.	(b)	29.	(a)	41.	(d)	53.	(c)	65.	(c)
6.	(b)	18.	(d)	30.	(c)	42.	(b)	54.	(a)	66.	(c)
7.	(c)	19.	(a)	31.	(c)	43.	(d)	55.	(a)	67.	(b)
8.	(a)	20.	(b)	32.	(a)	44.	(c)	56.	(b)	68.	(d)
9.	(c)	21.	(d)	33.	(e)	45.	(c)	57.	(b)	69.	(c)
10.	(c)	22.	(c)	34.	(a)	46.	(a)	58.	(e)	70.	(b)
11.	(d)	23.	(c)	35.	(d)	47.	(e)	59.	(e)		
12.	(c)	24.	(b)	36.	(c)	48.	(b)	60.	(d)		

3 — Memory Organisation

Computer organisation is the way in which the components are built in computers whereas Computer architecture is the science of integrating those components to achieve a level of functionality and performance this chapter we shall study a high level view of computer architecture that may be concerned with how the central processing unit (CPU) acts and how it uses computer memory.

Computer Architecture is the field of study of selecting and interconnecting hardware components to create computers that satisfy functional performance and cost goals. It refers to those attributes of the computer system that are visible to a programmer and have a direct effect on the execution of a program.

Computer Architecture concerns with machine Organization, interfaces, application, technology, measurement & simulation that Includes:

* Instruction set
* Data formats
* Principle of Operation
* Features (organization of programmable storage, registers used, interrupts mechanism, etc.)

In short, it is the combination of Instruction Set Architecture, Machine Organization and the related hardware.

INTERCONNECTION OF UNITS

CPU sends data, instructions and information to the components inside the computer as well as to the peripherals and devices attached to it. Bus is a set of electronic signal pathways that allows information and signals to travel between components inside or outside of a computer.

The features and functionality of a bus are as follows

* A bus is a set of wires used for interconnection, where each wire can carry one bit of data.
* A computer bus can be divided into two types; **internal bus** and **external bus**.
* The internal bus connects components inside the motherboard like, CPU and system memory. It is also called the **system bus**.
* The external bus connects the different external devices; peripherals, expansion slots, I/O ports and drive connections to the rest of computer. It is also referred to as the **expansion bus**.
* The command to access the memory or the I/O device is carried by the **control bus**.
* The address of I/O device or memory is carried by the address bus. The data to be transferred is carried by the **data bus**.

INSTRUCTION CYCLE

The instruction cycle represents the sequence of events that takes place as an instruction is read from memory and executed.

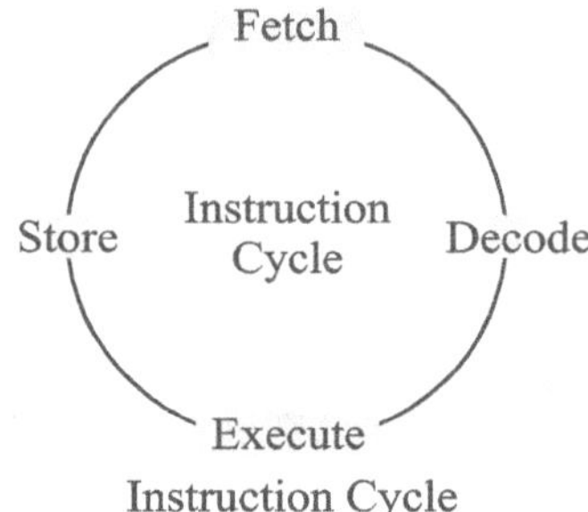

Instruction Cycle

A simple instruction cycle consists of the following steps

- *Fetching* the instruction from the memory.
- *Decoding* the instruction for operation.
- *Executing* the instruction.
- *Storing* in memory.

INSTRUCTIONS FORMAT

Computer understand instructions only in terms of 0s and 1s, which is called the machine language. A computer program is a set of instruction that describe the steps to be performed for carrying out a computational task. The processor must have two inputs; *instructions* and *data.*

The instruction tell the processor what actions are needed to be performed on the data. An instruction is divided into two parts; *operation* (*op-code*) and *operand.*

The op-code represents action that the processor must execute and the operand defines the parameters of the action and depends on the operation.

MEMORY HIERARCHY

The hierarchical arrangement of storage in current computer architectures is called the memory hierarchy. It is designed to take advantage of memory locality in computer programs. Each level of the hierarchy is of higher speed and lower latency, and is of smaller size, than lower levels.

Following diagram shows memory hierarchy in a modern computer system

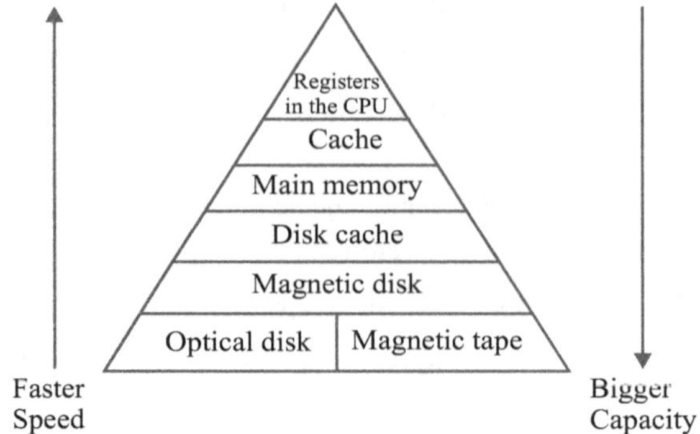

MEMORY ORGANISATION

Computer memory is the storage space in computer where data is to be processed and instructions required for processing are stored. The memory is divided into large number of small parts. Each part is called **cell**. Each location or cell has a unique address, which varies from zero to memory size minus one.

SOME IMPORTANT DEFINITIONS –

ACCUMULATOR AND GENERAL AND SPECIAL PURPOSE REGISTERS:

A CPU contains a number of register to store data temporarily during the execution of a program. The number differ from processor to processor. Registers are classified as follows :

GENERAL PURPOSE REGISTERS : These registers store data and intermediate results during the execution of a program.

ACCUMULATORS : It is most efficient in data movement, arithmetic and logical operation. It has some special features that the other general purpose registers do not have. After the execution of arithmetic and logical instructions, the result is placed in the accumulator. All data transfer between the CPU and device/port are performed through the accumulator.

Special Purpose Registers : A CPU contains a number of special purpose registers for different purpose. These are

(i) PROGRAM COUNTER (PC) : The program counter keeps track of the address of the instruction which is to be executed next. So it holds the address of the memory location, which contains the next instruction to be fetched from the memory. Its contents is automatically incremented after an instruction has been fetched.

(ii) STACK POINTER (SP) : The stack is a sequence of memory location defined by the user. It is used to save the contents of a register if it is required during the execution of a program. the stack pointer holds the address of the last occupied memory location of the stack.

(iii) INSTRUCTION REGISTER : It holds an instruction until it is decoded. Some computers have two types of instruction registers, and so they can fetch and save the next instruction while the execution of the previous instruction is going on.

(iv) MEMORY ADDRESS REGISTER : The memory address register holds the address of the next memory location where the next instruction is to be executed. While the first instruction is being executed, the address of the next memory location is held by it. The computer's CPU uses the address bus to communicate which memory address it wants to access, and the memory controller reads the address and then puts the data stored in that memory address back onto the address bus for the CPU to use.

Memory- Memory is made up of large number of cells.

(v) MEMORY DATA ADDRESS : The memory data register (MDR) is the register of a computer's control unit that contains the data to be stored in the computer storage (e.g. RAM), or the data after a fetch from the computer storage. It acts like a buffer and holds anything that is copied from the memory ready for the processor to use it.

Classification of Computer Memory :

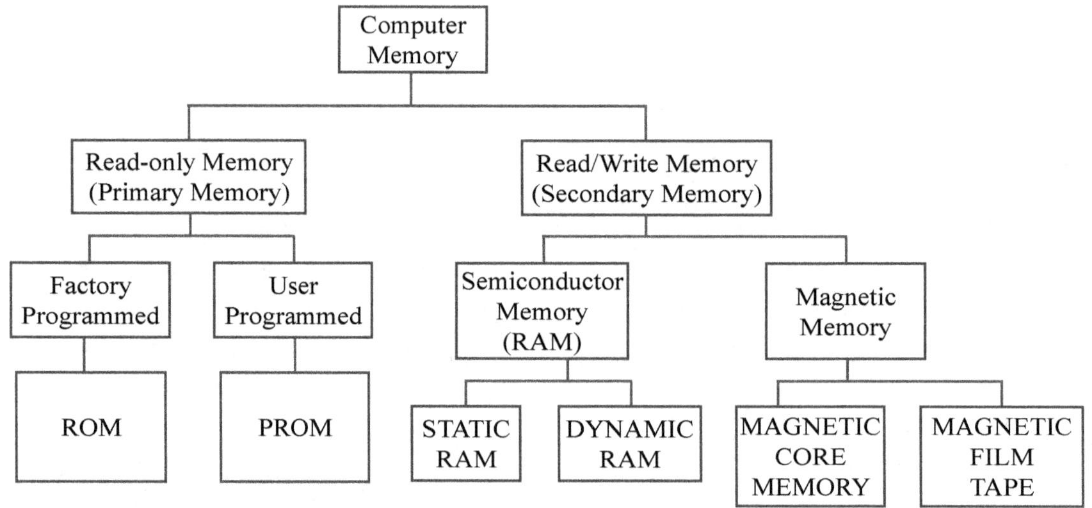

Memory is primarily of two types:

1. Primary Memory / Main Memory/Volatile Memory
2. Secondary Memory / Non Volatile Memory

Buffer : It is a temporary physical storage used to hold data during execution of process from one place to another.

1. Primary Memory (Main Memory)

Primary memory holds only those data and instructions on which computer is currently working. It has limited capacity and data gets lost when power is switched off.

It is generally made up of semiconductor device. These memories are not as fast as registers. The data and instructions required to be processed earlier reside in main memory.

It is divided into two subcategories: **RAM** and **ROM.**

Characteristic of Primary Main Memory

*   These are semiconductor memories.
*   It is known as main memory.
*   Usually volatile memory.
*   Data is lost in case power is switched off.
*   It is working memory of the computer.
*   Faster than secondary memories.
*   A computer cannot run without primary memory.

COMPARISON BETWEEN RAM & ROM

Description	RAM	ROM
Definition	Random Access Memory or RAM is a form of data storage that can be accessed randomly at any time, in any order and from any physical location, allowing quick access and manipulation.	Read-only memory or ROM is also a form of data storage that can not be easily altered or reprogrammed. Stores instructions that are not necessary for rebooting up to make the computer operate when it is switched off. They are hard wired.

Stands for	Random Access Memory	Read-only memory.
Use	RAM allows the computer to read data quickly to run applications. It allows reading and writing.	ROM stores the program required to initially boot the computer. It only allows reading.
Volatility	RAM is volatile i.e. its contents are lost when the device is powered off.	It is non-volatile i.e. its contents are retained even when the device is powered off.
Types	The two main types of RAM are static RAM and dynamic RAM.	The types of ROM include PROM, EPROM and EEPROM.

(i) RAM (RANDOM ACCESS MEMORY)

There are two types of Random Access Memory or RAM, each has its own advantages and disadvantages compared to the other.

A. SRAM (Static RAM)

B. DRAM (Dynamic RAM)

COMPARISON BETWEEN SRAM (STATIC RANDOM ACCESS MEMORY) AND DRAM (DYNAMIC RANDOM ACCESS MEMORY):

	SRAM	DRAM
Definition	It is a type of RAM. SRAM essentially uses latches to store charge.	It is also a type of RAM. DRAM makes use of capacitors to store bits in the form of charge.
Speed	Faster	Slower
Size	Bigger	Smaller
Cost	More expensive per bit	Less expensive per bit
Capacity (same technology)	Less	5 to 10 times more than SRAM
Applications	Generally in smaller applications like CPU cache memory and hard drive buffers	Commonly used as the main memory in personal computers
Types	Asynchronous SRAM Synchronous SRAM Pipeline Burst SRAM	Fast Page Mode DRAM Extended Data Out DRAM Burst EDO DRSSM Synchronous DRAM
Power Consumption	Less	More

(ii) ROM (READ ONLY MEMORY)

ROM has further classified into three types.

Each type has unique characteristics, but all types of ROM memory have two things in common they are:-

*   Data stored in these chips is non-volatile i.e it is not lost when power is removed.
*   Data stored in these chips is either unchangeable or requires a special operation to change.

A. Programmable Read-Only Memory (PROM) : This form of ROM is initially blank. The user or manufacturer can write data/program on it by using special devices. However, once the program or data is written in PROM chip, it cannot be changed. If there is an error in writing instructions or data in PROM, the error cannot be erased. PROM chip becomes unusable.

B. **Erasable Programmable Read-Only Memory (EPROM) :** This type of ROM can have its contents erased by ultraviolet light and then reprogrammed by user/manufacturer. This procedure can be carried out many times; however, the constant erasing and rewriting will eventually render the chip useless.

C. **Electrically Erasable Programmable Read-Only Memory (EEPROM) :** This type of ROM works in a similar way to Flash memory in that it can its contents can be 'flashed' for erasure ad then written to without having to remove the chip from its environment. EEPROMs are used to store a computer system's BIOS, and can be updated without returning the unit to the factory. In many cases, BIOS updates can be carried out by computer users wishing a BIOS update.

CACHE MEMORY

CPU is much faster than memory. The problem comes when the CPU issues a memory request, it will not get the data it need for many CPU cycles. The slower the memory the more cycles the CPU will have to wait. This problem can be overcome by introducing a small and very fast memory near the CPU. The small, fast memory is called. Cache memory is a very high speed semiconductor memory, which can speed up CPU. It acts as a buffer between the CPU and main memory.

It is used to hold those parts of data and program which are most frequently used by CPU. The parts of data and programs are transferred from disk to cache memory by operating system, from where CPU can access them.

Advantage

- Cache memory is faster than main memory.
- It consumes less access time as compared to main memory.
- It stores the program that can be executed within a short period of time.
- It stores data for temporary use.

Disadvantage

- Cache memory has limited capacity.
- It is very expensive

FLASH MEMORY

Flash memory is an example of quite a recent type of storage technology known as solid state devices. This type of portable storage has become very popular because of its low price and high storage capacity compared to its rivals, e.g. floppy disk.

Solid state devices are regarded as being robust and reliable because they have no moving parts with the data stored in semiconductor chips. This technology already exists in the form of flash memory used to store the Basic Input/Output System (BIOS) of a motherboard.

Unlike ROM, flash memory can be read form and written to and unlike RAM does not require power to retain its data. Although these devices typically cannot hold as much data as hard disks, CD-ROMs and DVDs, the storage capacity is continually increasing.

VIRTUAL MEMORY

Virtual memory is a technique that allows the execution of processes which are not completely available in memory. The main visible advantage of this scheme is that programs can be larger than physical memory. Virtual memory is the separation of user logical memory from physical memory.

This separation allows an extremely large virtual memory to be provided for programmers when only a smaller physical memory is available. Following are the situations, when entire program is not required to be loaded fully in main memory. User written error handling routines are used only when an error occured in the data or computation. Certain options and features of a program may be used rarely. Many tables are assigned a fixed amount of address space even though only a small amount of the table is actually used.

2. Secondary Memory (Auxillary Memory)

The size of the **main memory** is very small if large data need to be stored in it. Further, the main memory is volatile in nature i.e. the contents are lost when power supply is stopped. To overcome these another memory is used in a computer system called secondary memory or the auxiliary memory. This is large as well as non-volatile in nature. This type of memory is also known as external memory or non-volatile. It is slower than main memory. These are used for storing Data/Information permanently.

CPU directly does not access these memories, instead they are accessed via input-output routines. Contents of secondary memories are first transferred to main memory and then CPU can access it. For example, disk, CD-ROM, DVD, etc.

Characteristics of Secondary Memory
*   These are magnetic and optical memories.
*   It is known as backup memory.
*   It is non-volatile memory.
*   Data is permanently stored even if power is switched off.
*   It is used for storage of the data in the computer.
*   Computer may run without secondary memory.
*   Slower than primary memories.

Storage Devices

Storage devices are also called storage media. It is a hardware device that can hold information. Two main storage devices are used in computers. The primary storage device also known as RAM and the secondary storage device such as a computer hard drive. Secondary storage can be either internal or external storage. Storage device is required by the computer to save any settings or additional information.

Following are the different types of computer Storage Devices/Secondary memories –

Secondary Memory devices includes:

A. **Magnetic Disks :** Magnetic disks play two roles in computer systems:
    *   Long-term, nonvolatile storage for files, even when no programs are running
    *   A level of the memory hierarchy below main memory used as a backing store for virtual memory during program execution

    A magnetic disk consists of a collection of platters (generally 1 to 12), rotating on a spindle at 3,600 to 15,000 revolutions per minute (RPM). These platters are metal or glass disks covered with magnetic recording material on both sides, so 10 platters have 20 recording surfaces. The disk surface is divided into concentric circles, called tracks. Each track in turn is divided into sectors. A sector is the smallest unit that can be read or written.

B. **Optical Disks :** Optical disks are another type of secondary memory. Many types of optical disks are available in the market like CD(Compact disks), DVD (Digital versatile disks) etc. CD-R are write once CDs i.e. data can be written to them only once. CD-RW on the other hand are rewritable CDs i.e. data can be written and erased many times. Similar variations DVD-R and DVD-RW are also available in the market.

C. **Magnetic Tape :** Magnetic tape is a long and narrow strip of plastic that thin magnetic material is coated on. Nearly all recording tape is of this type, whether used for recording audio or video or computer data storage.

    Magnetic tape recording uses magnetic tape which moves on a recording head. Electrical signals are fed to the recording head, inducing a pattern of magnetization similar to the signal. A playback head can then pick up the changes in magnetic field from the tape and convert it into an electrical signal.

D. **Floppy diskette :** A Floppy Disk Drive is a computer disk drive that helps a user to save data to removable diskettes. 8 inch disk drives were first made available in 1971, which were later replaced with 3 ½ inch floppy disk drives. Due to the limited capacity and reliability of floppy diskettes in many computers they are no longer used with floppy disk drives . They are being replaced with CD-R, other writable discs, and flash drives.

E.   **CD-ROM disc :** Compact Disc-Read Only Memory, CD-ROM drives or optical drives are CD players inside computers that can have speeds in the range from 1x and beyond, and have the capability of playing audio CDs and computer data CDs.

F.   **CD-R and CD-RW disc :** It is also called as a CD writer, CD-WO (Write once), WORM (Write Once Read Many) drive. CD-R is used for CD-Recordable and is a writable disc and drive that is capable of having information written to the disc once and then having that disc read many times after that. If the data is not written to the disc properly, has errors, or has the incorrect information that disc or portions of that disc cannot be erased and is often jokingly referred to as a coaster.

G.   **Recordable DVD (Digital video Disk) drives :** These DVD drives are alternatively referred to as a **DVD writer, recordable DVD drives**. The recordable DVD drives are capable of creating DVD discs. They are different from recordable CD drives as they have many different competing standards for creating DVD discs. For example, DVD-R, DVD-RW, DVD + R, DVD + RW, DVD + R DL (DVD + R9), and DVD-RAM are all different competing standards.

     (i)   **DVD-R** DVD-R is called as Digital Versatile Disc-Recordable. DVD-R has features similar to CD-R, where the drive is capable or recording once to a disc and then read many times after it has been created. DVD-R is an approved standard by DVD Forum and the drives are capable of recording to DVD-R discs. These discs are also known as DVD-5 and DVD -10. DVD-R discs are compatible with most stand alone DVD players and computer DVD-ROM drives.

     (ii)   **DVD-RW (DVD-R/W)** These are called as Digital Versatile Disc-Read/Write. DVD-RW is an approved standard by DVD Forum.It is based on a technology that enables a user to read and write to a DVD-RW or DVD-R disc several times. DVD-RW discs are compatible with most stand-alone DVD players and computer DVD-ROM drives.

H.   **Jump drive and USB flash drive :** USB flash drive is a portable drive that is as small as the size of your thumb. Other such portable drives include data stick, pen drive, keychain drive ,thumb drive .It connects to the computer USB port. Flash drives are available in different sizes such as 256MB, 512MB, 1GB, 5GB, and 16GB . They can easily store and transfer information.

A flash drive is used by inserting it onto the front or back of USB port or hub. After inserting the flash drive , open the My Computer , you can see as "Removeable Disk", "Flash drive", or as the manufacturer's name. When the drive has been identified , data can be copied onto the flash drive by a simple copy paste or just dragging and dropping onto the flash drive icon.

I.   **Hard Drive :** It is called as the hard disk drive. It is represented sometimes by its short name as HD or HDD. It is the computer's main storage area that permanently stores the data on to the computer. It consists of one or more hard drive platters inside of air sealed casing. The hard drives are contained in an internal drive bay at the front of the computer . They connect to the mother board using ATA, SCSI or a SATA cable .

J.   **Memory card :** These are referred to as a flash memory card or a memory card . The memory card type of storage media is used in digital cameras, digital camcorders, handheld computers,printers , MP3 players and cell phones. They can store a huge number of pictures, videos, music, and other data. MicroSD flash memory card is one such example of a memory card . There are a number of different types of memory cards in the market that vary in size, compatibility, and storage capacity.

K.   **Memory stick :** Sony Memory Stick was first invented by Sony in October 1998 . It is a flash memory card used with Sony digital cameras . This flash memory card is used with other Sony products also. The capacity of the Memory Sticks range from sizes of 4MB to 256GB . They can have maximum capacity of 2TB, although till now the sticks of this capacity have not been produced .

Tape cassette

A tape cassette is magnetically thin coated piece that is wrapped with plastic around wheels. These are capable of storing data. Tape is far cheaper than other storage mediums but is much slower than the jump drives , memory sticks etc . Tapes are not much in use these days for faster and more reliable solutions like disc drives, hard drives, and flash drives.

L. **Zip Diskette :** Zip Diskette are made out of a much harder plastic and are much bigger than the standard floppy diskette. Zip drive is a medium capacity removable floppy disk storage system. Zip drives are not much in use because of need of mass portable storage .

M. **Blue ray disk :** Blu-ray (not Blue-ray) also known as Blu-ray Disc (BD), is the name of a new optical disc format jointly developed by the Blu-ray Disc Association (BDA), a group of the world's leading consumer electronics, personal computer and media manufacturers (including Apple, Dell, Hitachi, HP, JVC, LG, Mitsubishi, Panasonic, Pioneer, Philips, Samsung, Sharp, Sony, TDK and Thomson). The format was developed to enable recording, rewriting and playback of high-definition video (HD), as well as storing large amounts of data. The format offers more than five times the storage capacity of traditional DVDs and can hold up to 25GB on a single-layer disc and 50GB on a dual-layer disc. This extra capacity combined with the use of advanced video and audio codecs will offer consumers an unprecedented HD experience.

Secondary Memory Device and their storage Method and capacity.

Secondary memory Device	Storage Method	Capacity
Floppy disk (5.25 inch)	Magnetic	1.2 MB
Hard Disk	Magnetic	upto 1 T B
CD-ROM	optical	640 MB to 680 MB
DVD-ROM	optical	4.7 GB to 17 GB
Pen-Drive	solid state	1 GB to 512 GB
Magnetic Tape	Magnetic	upto 1 TB

MEMORY MANAGEMENT TABLE
Approximate/Actual Values

Unit	Abbreviation	Approximate	Actual
Bit	b (common 'b')		0 or 1
Byte	B (Capital 'B')		8 bites
Kilobytes	KB	1000 bytes	1024 bytes
Megabte	MB	1 million bytes	1024 KB
Gigabyte	GB	1 billion bytes	1024 MB
Terabyte	TB	1 trillion bytes	1024 GB
Petabyte	PB	10^{15} Bytes	1024 TB
Exa Byte	EB	10^{18} Bytes	1024 PB
Zetta Byte	ZB	10^{21} Bytes	1024 EB
Yotta Byte	YB	–	1024 ZB
Bronta Byte	BB	–	1024 YB

(KB, MB, GB, TB — All upper cases)

IMPORTANT MEASUREMENT :

1 Bit = Binary digit

The term 'Bit' is short for Binary digit.

1 Nibble = 4 Bits

8 bits = 1 Byte = 2 Nibble

Past Exercise

1. A collection of related information sorted and deal with as a unit is a   **[SBI Clerk, 2009]**
   - (a) disk
   - (b) data
   - (c) file
   - (d) floppy
   - (e) None of these

2. CDs are of which shape?   **[SBI Clerk, 2009]**
   - (a) Square
   - (b) Rectangular
   - (c) Round
   - (d) Hexagonal
   - (e) None of these

3. A disk's content that is recorded at the time of manufacture and that cannot be changed or erased by the user is——
     [SBI Clerk, 2009; IBPS PO, 2011]
   - (a) memory-only
   - (b) write-only
   - (c) read-only
   - (d) run-only
   - (e) None of these

4. Reusable optical storage will typically have the acronym——
     [SBI Clerk, 2009; IBPS PO, 2011]
   - (a) CD
   - (b) DVD
   - (c) ROM
   - (d) RW
   - (e) None of these

5. The most common type of storage devices are———   **[SBI Clerk, 2009]**
   - (a) persistent
   - (b) optical
   - (c) magnetic
   - (d) flash
   - (e) None of these

6. During the — portion of the Information Processing Cycle, the computer acquires data from some source.   **[SBI Clerk, 2009]**
   - (a) storage and output
   - (b) storage
   - (c) input
   - (d) output
   - (e) None of these

7. The most common type of storage devices are   **[IBPS PO, 2011]**
   - (a) persistent
   - (b) optical
   - (c) magnetic
   - (d) flash
   - (e) steel

8. Computers use the _________ number system to store data and perform calculations.   **[IBPS PO, 2011]**
   - (a) binary
   - (b) octal
   - (c) decimal
   - (d) hexadecimal
   - (e) None of these

9. What is the permanent memory built into your computer called?   **[IBPS PO, 2011]**
   - (a) RAM
   - (b) Floppy
   - (c) CD-ROM
   - (d) ROM
   - (e) None of these

10. When you save to this, your data will remain when the computer is turned off.
    - (a) RAM   **[IBPS PO, 2011]**
    - (b) motherboard
    - (c) secondary storage device
    - (d) primary storage
    - (e) None of these

11. The contents of _____ are lost when the computer turns off.   **[IBPS PO, 2011]**
    - (a) storage
    - (b) input
    - (c) output
    - (d) memory
    - (e) None of these

12. A DVD is an example of a(n) **[IBPS PO, 2011]**
    - (a) hard disk
    - (b) optical disc
    - (c) output device
    - (d) solid-state storage device
    - (e) None of these

13. The computer abbreviation KB usually means
      [IBPS PO, 2011]
    - (a) Key Block
    - (b) Kernel Boot
    - (c) Key Byte
    - (d) Kit Bit
    - (e) Kilo Byte

14. Which of the following are advantages of CD-ROM as a storage media?   **[IBPS PO, 2011]**
    - (a) CD-ROM is an inexpensive way to store large amount of data and information.
    - (b) CD-ROM disks retrieve data and information more quickly than magnetic disks do.
    - (c) CD-ROMs make less errors than magnetic media.
    - (d) All the above
    - (e) None of these

15. Which of the following is a storage device that uses rigid, permanently installed magnetic disks to store data/information?   **[IBPS PO, 2011]**
    (a) floppy diskette   (b) hard disk
    (c) permanent disk   (d) optical disk
    (e) None of these

16. Which of the following is billion of a second?
                                    [SBI PO, 2011]
    (a) Gigabyte   (b) Terabyte
    (c) Nanosecond   (d) Microsecond
    (e) Terasecond

17. How many megabytes make a gigabyte?
                                    [IBPS Clerk, 2011]
    (a) 1024   (b) 128
    (c) 256   (d) 512
    (e) 64

18. The time for the actual data transfer after receiving the request for data from secondary storage is referred to as the disk's
                                    [IBPS Clerk, 2011]
    (a) transfer time   (b) movement time
    (c) access time   (d) data input time
    (e) None of these

19. What happens when we try to delete the files on the floppy?   **[IBPS Clerk, 2011]**
    (a) The files get moved to the Recycle Bin
    (b) Files on a floppy cannot be deleted
    (c) The files get deleted and can be restored again from Recycle Bin .
    (d) The files get deleted and cannot be restored again
    (e) The file gets copied on the Hard disk

20. The following computer's memory is characterised by low cost per bit stored
                                    [IBPS Clerk, 2011]
    (a) Primary   (b) Secondary
    (c) Hard Disk   (d) All of these
    (e) None of these

21. On a CD-RW you can   **[IBPS Clerk, 2011]**
    (a) read and write information
    (b) only read information
    (c) only write information
    (d) read, write and rewrite information
    (e) None of these

22. Which contents are lost when the computer turn off ?   **[IBPS Clerk, 2011]**
    (a) storage   (b) input
    (c) output   (d) memory
    (e) None of these

23. Which of the following is not an example of hardware?   **[IBPS Clerk, 2011]**
    (a) Scanner   (b) Printer
    (c) Monitor   (d) Mouse
    (e) Interpreter

24. _________ is the maximum amount of data that can be stored on a storage medium.
                                    [SBI Clerk, 2011]
    (a) Magnetic storage   (b) Optical storage
    (c) Solid-state storage (d) Storage capacity
    (e) None of these

25. Secondary storage   **[SBI Clerk, 2011]**
    (a) does not require constant power
    (b) does not use magnetic media
    (c) consists of four main types of devices
    (d) does not store information for later retrieval
    (e) None of these

26. _______ acts as temporary high-speed holding area between the memory and the CPU thereby improving processing capabilities
                                    [IBPS Clerk, 2012]
    (a) ROM
    (b) RAM
    (c) Temporary memory
    (d) Cache memory
    (e) Flash memory

27. What type of device is a 3½ inch floppy drive ?
                                    [SBI Clerk, 2012]
    (a) Input   (b) Output
    (c) Software   (d) Storage
    (e) None of these

28. Which of the following memory chip is faster ?
                                    [SBI Clerk, 2012]
    (a) There is no certainty
    (b) DRAM
    (c) SRAM
    (d) DRAM is faster for larger chips
    (e) None of these

29. Which of the following is the second largest measurement of RAM ?   **[SBI Clerk, 2012]**
    (a) Terabyte   (b) Megabyte
    (c) Byte   (d) Gigabyte
    (e) Mega Hertz

30. Of the following, which is the fastest?
    [SSC, CGL, 2012]
    (a) CD-ROM   (b) RAM
    (c) CPU Registers   (d) Cache
31. A nibble is equal to ______________ bits.
    [SSC, CHSL, 2012]
    (a) 16   (b) 32
    (c) 4   (d) 8
32. ____________ a document means the file is transferred from another computer to your computer.   **[IBPS PO, 2012]**
    (a) Uploading
    (b) Really Simple Syndication (RSS)
    (c) Accessing
    (d) Downloading
    (e) Upgrading
33. Which computer memory is used for storing programs and data currently being processed by the CPU ?   **[IBPS PO, 2012]**
    (a) Mass memory
    (b) Internal memory
    (c) Non-volatile memory
    (d) PROM
    (e) None of these
34. Which part of the computer is used for calculating and comparing ?   **[IBPS PO, 2012]**
    (a) ALU   (b) Control unit
    (c) Disk unit   (d) Modem
    (e) None of these
35. Of the following, which is the fastest?
    [SSC CGL, 2012]
    (a) CD-ROM   (b) RAM
    (c) Registers   (d) Cache
36. Which computer was the first to use the magnetic drum for memory ?   **[SSC, CGL, 2013]**
    (a) IBM - 650   (b) IBM - 7090
    (c) IBM - 701   (d) IBM - 360
37. EPROM can be used for   **[IBPS PO, 2013]**
    (a) erasing the contents of ROM
    (b) reconstructing the contents of ROM
    (c) erasing and reconstructing the contents of ROM
    (d) duplicating the ROM
    (e) None of the above
38. Which is not a storage device?**[SBI PO, 2013]**
    (a) A CD   (b) A DVD
    (c) A floppy disk   (d) A printer
    (e) A Hard disk

39. An organization's profitability depends on
    [SSC CGL, 2013]
    (a) Quality of data processed
    (b) Quantity of data processed
    (c) Speed of processing the data
    (d) Both (a) and (c)
40. Which computer was the first to use the magnetic drum for memory?
    [SSC CGL, 2013]
    (a) IBM - 650   (b) IBM - 7090
    (c) IBM - 701   (d) IBM - 360
41. ______ is the process of dividing the disk into tracks and sectors.   **[IBPS Clerk, 2014]**
    (a) Tracking   (b) Formatting
    (c) Crashing   (d) Allotting
    (e) None of these
42. What is the permanent memory built into your computer called?   **[IBPS Clerk, 2014]**
    (a) RAM   (b) Floppy
    (c) CPU   (d) CD-ROM
    (e) ROM
43. What characteristic of read-only memory (ROM) makes it useful ?   **[SBI Clerk, 2014]**
    (a) ROM information can be easily updated.
    (b) ROM provides very large amounts of inexpensive data storage.
    (c) Data in ROM is nonvolatile, that is , it remains there even without electrical power.
    (d) ROM chips are easily swapped between different brands of computer.
    (e) None of these
44. Where are programs and data kept while the processor is usingthem?   **[SBI Clerk, 2014]**
    (a) Main memory   (b) Secondary memory
    (c) Disk memory   (d) Program memory
    (e) None of these
45. SAN, Google Docs, and Network drive are all examples of __________ Storage
    [SBI Clerk, 2014]
    (a) Primary   (b) RAM
    (c) Remote   (d) Volatile
    (e) None of these
46. What is the main folder on a storage device called?   **[SBI Clerk, 2014]**
    (a) Home page   (b) Platform
    (c) Interface   (d) Root Directory
    (e) None of these

47. Which computer memory is used for storing programs and data currently being processed by the CPU?   **[IBPS Clerk, 2015]**
    (a) Internal memory
    (b) Mass memory
    (c) Non-volatile memory
    (d) PROM
    (e) None of these

48. All of the following statements concerning files are true EXCEPT: **[IBPS Clerk, 2015]**
    (a) Files should be organized in folders
    (b) Files are stored in RAM.
    (c) Files can be generated from an application.
    (d) A file is a collection of related pieces of information stored together for easy reference.
    (e) None of these

49. Rearranging and allocating space in memory to provide for multiple computing tasks is called
                              [SSC CGL, 2015]
    (a) Multiprogramming
    (b) Multitasking
    (c) Memory Management
    (d) Networking

50. Which of the following is in the ascending order of Data hierarchy ?
                              [SSC CGL, 2015]
    (a) Bit – Byte – Record – Field – Database – File
    (b) Byte – Bit – File – Record – Database – Field
    (c) Bit – Byte – Field – Record – File – Database
    (d) Field – Byte – Bit – Record – File– Database

51. Which among the following is a term representing unit of data storage in computer memory?   **[IBPS PO Mains, 2016]**
    (a) Pixel   (b) Decimal
    (c) Octet   (d) Point
    (e) Fragment

52. Which of the following error occurs when software tries to access protected memory?
                              [IBPS PO Mains, 2016]
    (a) Segmentation Fault
    (b) Display time Error
    (c) IO Error
    (d) Runtime Error
    (e) Zero Division Error

53. Which of the following is false about the clock of the system?   **[IBPS Clerk Mains, 2016]**
    (a) It is the property of the toolbar
    (b) The system can periodically refresh the time by synchronizing with a time source
    (c) System time is the current date and time of day.
    (d) The system keeps time so that your applications have ready access to accurate time.
    (e) The system bases system time on coordinated universal time (UTC).

54. Which of the following is used to access a file from the computer store?
                              [IBPS Clerk Mains, 2016]
    (a) Insert   (b) Retrieve
    (c) File   (d) Print
    (e) find

55. During the execution of instructions, a copy of instruction is placed in the
                              [IBPS Clerk Mains, 2016]
    (a) Register   (b) RAM
    (c) System heap   (d) Cache
    (e) ROM

56. Which of the following is the correct use of Buffer or Block cashes?   **[IBPS RRB, 2016]**
    (a) Improve disk performance
    (b) Handle interrupts
    (c) Increase the capacity of main memory
    (d) Speed up main memory read operations
    (e) None of these

57. What is the full form of 'RAID'?
                              [IBPS RRB, 2016]
    (a) Random Access of Inexpensive disks
    (b) Redundant Array of Inexpensive data
    (c) Random Array of Inexpensive data
    (d) Random Array of Internet data
    (e) Redundant Array of Inexpensive disks

58. Which is designed to reorganize noncontiguous files into contiguous files and optimize their placement on the hard drive?
                              [IBPS RRB, 2016]
    (a) Backup
    (b) Restore
    (c) Disk Cleanup
    (d) Disk Defragmenter
    (e) None of these

ANSWER KEY

1.	(b)	13.	(e)	25.	(a)	37.	(c)	49.	(c)
2.	(c)	14.	(a)	26.	(d)	38.	(d)	50.	(c)
3.	(c)	15.	(b)	27.	(d)	39.	(d)	51.	(c)
4.	(d)	16.	(c)	28.	(c)	40.	(a)	52.	(a)
5.	(b)	17.	(a)	29.	(d)	41.	(b)	53.	(a)
6.	(c)	18.	(c)	30.	(c)	42.	(e)	54.	(e)
7.	(c)	19.	(d)	31.	(c)	43.	(e)	55.	(d)
8.	(a)	20.	(b)	32.	(d)	44.	(a)	56.	(d)
9.	(e)	21.	(d)	33.	(e)	45.	(c)	57.	(e)
10.	(c)	22.	(d)	34.	(a)	46.	(d)	58.	(d)
11.	(d)	23.	(e)	35.	(c)	47.	(a)		
12.	(b)	24.	(d)	36.	(a)	48.	(b)		

Practice Exercise

1. A CD-RW disk __________.
   (a) has a faster access than an internal disk
   (b) is a form of optical disk, so it can only be written once
   (c) holds less data than a floppy disk
   (d) can be erased and rewritten
   (e) None of these

2. Information on a computer is stored as ________.
   (a) analog data   (b) digital data
   (c) modem data   (d) watts data
   (e) None of these

3. A directory within a directory is called.
   (a) Mini Directory   (b) Junior Directory
   (c) Part Directory   (d) Sub Directory
   (e) None of these

4. DVDs are of which shape?
   (a) Square   (b) Rectangular
   (c) Round   (d) Hexagonal
   (e) None of these

5. Which part is the "brain" of the Computer?
   (a) CPU   (b) Monitor
   (c) RAM   (d) ROM
   (e) None of these

6. __________ Store data or information temporarily and pass it on as directed by the control unit
   (a) Address   (b) Register
   (c) Number   (d) Memory

7. Where are programs and data kept while the processor is using them?
   (a) Main memory
   (b) Secondary memory
   (c) Disk memory
   (d) Program memory
   (e) None of these

8. What does storage unit provide?
   (a) Place for typing data
   (b) Storage for information and instruction
   (c) Place for printing information
   (d) All of the above
   (e) None of these

9. Which type of memory is closely related to processor?
   (a) Main Memory
   (b) Secondary Memory
   (c) Disk Memory
   (d) Tape Memory
   (e) None of these

10. Which of the following is not true about RAM?
    (a) RAM is a temporary storage area
    (b) RAM is the same as hard disk storage
    (c) RAM is volatile
    (d) Information stored in RAM is gone when you turn the computer off
    (e) None of these

11. By CD you can
    (a) Read
    (b) Write
    (c) Read and Write
    (d) Either Read or Write
    (e) None of these

12. Which of the following storage media provides sequential access only?
    (a) Floppy disk   (b) Magnetic disk
    (c) Magnetic tape   (d) Optical disk
    (e) None of these

13. The main directory of a disk is called the __________ Directory.
    (a) root   (b) sub
    (c) folder   (d) network
    (e) None of these

14. What is the difference between a CD-ROM and a CD-RW?
    (a) They are the same – just two different terms used by different manufacturers
    (b) A CD-ROM can be written to and a CD-RW cannot
    (c) A CD-RW can be read & written to, but a CD-ROM can only be read from CD.
    (d) A CD-ROM holds more information than a CD-RW
    (e) None of these

15. A group of 8 bits is known as a –
    (a) byte   (b) kilobyte
    (c) binary digit   (d) megabit
    (e) None of these

16. If a user needs information instantly available to the CPU, it should be stored –
    (a) on a CD
    (b) in secondary storage
    (c) in the CPU
    (d) in RAM
    (e) None of these

17. To what temporary area can you store text and other data, and later paste them to another location?
    (a) The clipboard　　(b) ROM
    (c) CD-ROM　　(d) The hard disk
    (e) None of these

18. All of the following are included in removable media Except –
    (a) CD-ROMs　　(b) Diskette
    (c) DVDs　　(d) Hard Disk Drive
    (e) None of these

19. When you make graph and picture in document, then your computer holds the data in ____________.
    (a) Restore file　　(b) Backup drive
    (c) Clipboard　　(d) Memory
    (e) None of these

20. The storage element for a Static RAM is the ______.
    (a) diode　　(b) resistor
    (c) capacitor　　(d) flip-flop
    (e) None of these

21. With a CD you can __________.
    (a) Read
    (b) Write
    (c) Neither Read nor Write
    (d) Both Read and Write
    (e) None of these

22. Which of the following is the largest unit of storage?
    (a) GB　　(b) KB
    (c) MB　　(d) TB
    (e) None of these

23. __________ is the process of dividing the disk into tracks and sectors.
    (a) Tracking　　(b) Formatting
    (c) Crashing　　(d) Allotting
    (e) None of these

24. The portion of the CPU that coordinates the activities of all the other computer components is the __________.
    (a) motherboard
    (b) coordination board
    (c) control unit
    (d) arithmetic logic unit

25. Memory, also called random access memory, or RAM, __________.
    (a) contains the electronic circuits that cause processing to occur.
    (b) makes the information resulting from processing available for use

    (c) allots data, programs, commands, and user responses to be entered into a computer
    (d) consists of electronic components that store data
    (e) None of these

26. A device that reads the information contained on a disk and transfers it to the computer's memory.
    (a) monitor　　(b) screen
    (c) keyboard　　(d) disk drive
    (e) None of these

27. A disk on which you store information.
    (a) plate　　(b) data disk
    (c) paper disk　　(d) TV disk
    (e) None of these

28. The smallest unit of useful information a computer can handle.
    (a) bite　　(b) byte
    (c) bit　　(d) bait
    (e) None of these

29. The unit which acts as an intermediate agent between memory and backing store to reduce process time is ______.
    (a) TLB's　　(b) Registers
    (c) Page tables　　(d) Cache

30. A place in the computer system where data and programs are temporarily stored.
    (a) paste　　(b) open
    (c) memory　　(d) pocket
    (e) None of these

31. A removable magnetic disc that holds information.
    (a) floppy disk　　(b) hard drive
    (c) monitor　　(d) portable
    (e) None of these

32. Which type of memory holds only the program and data that the CPU is presently processing?
    (a) CMOS　　(b) ROM
    (c) RAM　　(d) ASCII
    (e) None of these

33. Bit in short for –
    (a) binary system　　(b) digital byte
    (c) binary digit　　(d) binary unit
    (e) None of these

34. Processors of all computers, whether micro, mini or mainframe must have:
    (a) ALU　　(b) Primary Storage
    (c) Control Unit　　(d) All of the above
    (e) None of the above

35. What characteristic of read-only memory (ROM) makes is useful?
    (a) ROM information can be easily updated
    (b) Data in ROM is nonvolatile, that is, it remains there even without electrical power
    (c) ROM provides very large amounts of inexpensive data storage
    (d) ROM chips are easily swapped between different brands of computers
    (e) None of these
36. To put information in a file on a magnetic disk, or in a computer's memory, so it can be used later __________.
    (a) store   (b) ship
    (c) shift   (d) centre
    (e) None of these
37. Which is not a factor when categorizing a computer?
    (a) Speed of the output device
    (b) Amount of main memory the CPU can use
    (c) Cost of the system
    (d) Capacity of the Hard Disk
    (e) Where it was purchased
38. Which of the following is not true about RAM?
    (a) RAM is a temporary storage area
    (b) RAM is the same as hard disk storage
    (c) RAM is volatile
    (d) Information stored in RAM is gone when you turn the computer off
    (e) None of these
39. What is the control unit's function in the CPU?
    (a) To transfer data to primary storage
    (b) To store program instruction
    (c) To perform logic operations
    (d) To decode program instructions
    (e) None of the above
40. Which of the following require large computer memory?
    (a) Imaging   (b) Graphics
    (c) Voice   (d) All of the above
    (e) None of the above
41. Which of the following require large computer memory?
    (a) Minicomputer
    (b) Laptop Computer
    (c) Notebook Computer
    (d) All of the above
    (e) None of the above
42. The amount of time required by a storage device to retrieve data and programs is its __________.

    (a) retrieval speed   (b) capacity
    (c) memory   (d) storage
    (e) access speed
43. A 32-bit-word computer can access __________ byte at a time.
    (a) 4   (b) 8
    (c) 16   (d) 32
    (e) 30
44. A megabyte is actually equal to __________ kilobytes.
    (a) 100   (b) 1000
    (c) 1024   (d) 1024×1024
    (e) None of these
45. The main memory of a computer must be large enough to contain the active parts of __________.
    (a) the operating system
    (b) the applications
    (c) input/output storage & working storage
    (d) All of these
    (e) None of these
46. Which of the following types of memory improves processing by acting as a temporary high-speed holding area between the memory and the CPU?
    (a) RAM   (b) ROM
    (c) Cache memory   (d) Flash memory
    (e) EPROM
47. The BOOT sector files of the system are stored in ______.
    (a) Hard disk
    (b) ROM
    (c) RAM
    (d) Fast solid state chips in the motherboard
48. The computer's processor consists of which of the following parts?
    (a) CPU and Main Memory
    (b) Hard Disk and Floppy Drive
    (c) Main Memory and Storage
    (d) Operating system and Applications
    (e) Control Unit and ALU
49. The most common storage device for the personal computer is
    (a) Floppy disk   (b) USB thumb drive
    (c) Zip disk   (d) Hard disk
    (e) Pen drive
50. Thick, rigid metal platters that are capable of storing and retrieving information at a high rate of speed are known as
    (a) hard disks   (b) soft disks
    (c) flash memory   (d) SAN
    (e) None of these

51. A DVD is an example of a(n) __________ .
    (a) hard disk
    (b) optical disk
    (c) output device
    (d) solid-state storage device
    (e) None of these

52. How many bits are there in a byte?
    (a) 20   (b) 4
    (c) 6   (d) 24
    (e) 8

53. Which of the following is another name for a chip?
    (a) Silicon chip   (b) Integrated circuit
    (c) Semiconductor   (d) All of these
    (e) None of these

54. Decreasing the amount of space required to store data and programs is accomplished by __________ .
    (a) pressing   (b) disk caching
    (c) RAID   (d) crashing
    (e) file compression

55. Data on a floppy disk is recorded in rings called __________ .
    (a) sectors   (b) ringers
    (c) rounders   (d) tracks
    (e) segments

56. Which type of memory holds only that program and data the CPU is presently processing?
    (a) CMOS   (b) ROM
    (c) RAM   (d) ASCII
    (e) CD

57. Storage that retains its data after the power is turned off is referred to as __________ .
    (a) volatile storage
    (b) sequential storage
    (c) direct storage
    (d) non-volatile storage
    (e) mobile storage

58. Which of the following is a secondary storage device?
    (a) Optical disks   (b) RAM
    (b) Microprocessor   (d) All of these
    (e) None of these

59. Which of the following is equal to 1,048,576 byte (approx one million byte)?
    (a) Byte   (b) Gigabyte
    (c) Memory   (d) Megabyte
    (e) Kilobyte

60. A hard disk drive is considered as a __________ storage.
    (a) flash   (b) non volatile
    (c) temporary   (d) non-permanent
    (e) None of these

61. A permanent memory is called
    (a) RAM   (b) ROM
    (c) CPU   (d) LCD
    (e) ALU

62. Name of round shining portable disk which can store large amount of information and softwares.
    (a) CD-ROM   (b) Floppy disk
    (c) Scanner   (d) Monitor
    (e) Laptop

63. A tape drive offers __________ access to data.
    (a) timely   (b) sporadic
    (c) random   (d) sequential
    (e) disastrous

64. How many values can be represented by a single byte?
    (a) 4   (b) 16
    (c) 64   (d) 256
    (e) 512

65. All the components of a computer are either __________ or __________ .
    (a) software, CPU/RAM
    (b) application software, system software
    (c) input device, output device
    (d) hardware, software
    (e) input, output

66. The result of computer processing of your input is called
    (a) output   (b) data
    (c) multi tasking   (d) tracking
    (e) intake

67. A disk's content that is recorded at the time of manufacture and that cannot be changed or erased by the user is
    (a) read-only   (b) memory-only
    (c) run-only   (d) write-only
    (e) None of these

68. When you save to __________ , your data will remain intact even when the computer is turned off.
    (a) RAM
    (b) motherboard
    (c) secondary storage device
    (d) primary storage device
    (e) None of these

69. Approximately how many bytes make one Megabyte?
    (a) One Thousand   (b) Ten Thousand
    (c) One Hundred   (d) One Million
    (e) None of these

70. A directory within a directory is called a __________.
    - (a) Mini Directory
    - (b) Junior Directory
    - (c) Part Directory
    - (d) Sub Directory
    - (e) None of these
71. What is the major disadvantage of RAM ?
    - (a) Its access speed is too slow.
    - (b) Its matrix size is too big.
    - (c) It is volatile.
    - (d) High power consumption
    - (e) None of these
72. What disk is used to cold-boot a PC?
    - (a) Setup disk
    - (b) System disk
    - (c) Diagnostic disk
    - (d) Program disk
    - (e) None of these
73. Data (information) is stored in computer as
    - (a) files
    - (b) directories
    - (c) floppies
    - (d) matter
    - (e) None of these
74. Memory unit is one part of __________.
    - (a) Control unit
    - (b) Central Processing Unit
    - (c) Input device
    - (d) Output device
    - (e) None of these
75. A character of information is represented by a(n) __________.
    - (a) byte
    - (b) bit
    - (c) field
    - (d) attribute
    - (e) None of these
76. Which of the following devices has a limitation that we can only read it but cannot erase or modify it?
    - (a) Tape Drive
    - (b) Hard Disk
    - (c) Compact Disk
    - (d) Floppy Disk
    - (e) None of these
77. Which of the following is the storage area within the computer itself which holds data only temporarily as the computer processes instructions?
    - (a) the hard disk
    - (b) main memory
    - (c) the control unit
    - (d) read-only memory
    - (e) None of these
78. If a memory chip is volatile, it will __________.
    - (a) explode if exposed to high temperatures
    - (b) lose its contents if current is turned off
    - (c) be used for data storage only
    - (d) to used to both read and write data
    - (e) None of these
79. A CD-ROM disk
    - (a) cannot be erased and rewritten
    - (b) has more storage capacity than a CD-R
    - (c) holds less data than a floppy disk
    - (d) can be written to only once
    - (e) None of the above
80. Storage device found inside the computer.
    - (a) CD-ROM
    - (b) Zip Disk
    - (c) Super Disk
    - (d) Hard Disk
    - (e) None of the above
81. Micro instructions are stored in the:
    - (a) Internal storage
    - (b) External storage
    - (c) Cache
    - (d) Control memory
82. RAM is __________ and __________.
    - (a) volatile, temporary
    - (b) nonvolatile, permanent
    - (c) nonvolatile, temporary
    - (d) volatile, permanent
    - (e) None of the above
83. The __________ indicates how much data a particular storage medium can hold.
    - (a) access
    - (b) capacity
    - (c) memory
    - (d) storage
    - (e) None of the above
84. How is it possible that both programs and data can be stored on the same floppy disk?
    - (a) A floppy disk has two sides, one for data and one for programs.
    - (b) Programs and data are both software, and both can be stored on any memory device.
    - (c) A floppy disk has to be formatted for one for the other.
    - (d) Floppy disk can only store data, not programs.
    - (e) None of the above
85. Secondary storage
    - (a) does not require constant power
    - (b) does not use magnetic media
    - (c) consists of four main types of devices
    - (d) does not store information for later retrieval
    - (e) None of the above
86. The process of preparing a floppy diskette for use is called __________.
    - (a) assembling
    - (b) translating
    - (c) parsing
    - (d) formatting
    - (e) None of the above
87. The access time of memory is __________ the time required for performing any single CPU operation.
    - (a) Longer than
    - (b) Shorter than
    - (c) Negligible than
    - (d) Same as

88. Which of the following are advantages of CD-ROM as a storage media?
    (a) CD-ROM is an inexpensive way to store large amount of data and information.
    (b) CD-ROM disks retrieve data and information more quickly than magnetic disks do.
    (c) CD-ROMs make less errors than magnetic media.
    (d) All of these
    (e) None of these
89. Even if a disk drive fails, the computer application running and using it can continue processing. This application is said to have been designed with this feature called
    (a) 100 percent up-time (b) Fault tolerance
    (c) High reliability   (d) All of these
    (e) None of these
90. Which media has the ability to have data/information stored (written) on them by users more than once?
    (a) CD-R disks
    (b) CD-RW disks
    (c) Zip disks
    (d) Opti-Disks
    (e) Both CD-RW disks and Zip disks
91. Storage media such as a CD read and write information using __________.
    (a) a laser beam of red light
    (b) magnetic dots
    (c) magnetic strips
    (d) All of these
    (e) None of these
92. Cache and main memory will lose their contents when the power is off. They are __________.
    (a) dynamic   (b) static
    (c) volatile   (d) non-volatile
    (e) faulty
93. Main memory works in conjunction with __________.
    (a) special function cards
    (b) RAM
    (c) CPU
    (d) Intel
    (e) All of these
94. Which of the following is a storage device that uses rigid, permanently installed magnetic disks to store data/information?
    (a) floppy diskette   (b) hard disk
    (c) permanent disk   (d) optical disk
    (e) None of these
95. Which of the following is an example of storage devices?
    (a) Magnetic disk   (b) Tapes
    (c) DVDs   (d) All of these
    (e) None of these
96. Which of the following is an example of an optical disk?
    (a) Digital versatile disks
    (b) Magnetic disks
    (c) Memory disks
    (d) Data bus disks
    (e) None of these
97. The main memory of a computer can also be called
    (a) Primary storage   (b) Internal memory
    (c) Primary memory   (d) All of these
    (e) None of these
98. The life span of a CD-ROM is
    (a) approximately one year
    (b) approximately two years
    (c) approximately five years
    (d) approximately twenty-five years
    (e) almost unlimited
99. Magnetic tape is not practical for applications where data must be quickly recalled because tape is
    (a) a random access medium
    (b) expensive
    (c) a read-only medium
    (d) fragile and easily damaged
    (e) a sequential access medium
100. How is it possible that both programs and data can be stored in the same floppy disk?
    (a) A floppy disk has two sides, one for data and one for programs.
    (b) A floppy disk has to be formatted for one or for the other
    (c) Programs and data are both software and both can be stored in any memory device.
    (d) Floppy disks can only store data, not programs.
    (e) Floppy disks are better than CDs.
101. The signal which shows that a computer is waiting for a command from the user is
    (a) prompt   (b) event
    (c) time slice   (d) interrupt
    (e) None of these
102. ROM tells the computer to
    (a) disconnect the computer
    (b) start up the operating system
    (c) connect to the hardware
    (d) turn on
    (e) pass on data to the RAM

103. Which of the following has the most capacity?
    (a) CD-R   (b) CD-RW
    (c) DVD   (d) VCD
    (e) Floppy Disk
104. __________ increase the accuracy of a search by fine-tuning the keywords in the search.
    (a) Indexes   (b) Italics
    (c) Compounds   (d) Links
    (e) Operators
105. The fastest component for accessing stored data/information is/are
    (a) cache   (b) DVDs
    (c) hard disks   (d) main memory
    (e) tape
106. A standard CD player accesses data/information using which method?
    (a) Sequential access
    (b) Random access
    (c) Multivariate access
    (d) All of these
    (e) None of these
107. In a computer most processing takes place in __________.
    (a) Memory   (b) RAM
    (c) Motherboard   (d) CPU
    (e) None of these
108. Which of the following is not a storage medium?
    (a) Hard disk   (b) Flash drive
    (c) DVD   (d) CD
    (e) keyboard/Monitor
109. __________ consists of volatile chips that temporarily store data or instructions.
    (a) CPU   (b) ROM
    (c) RMA   (d) RAM
    (e) None of these
110. A computer's ROM is __________.
    (a) ALU
    (b) computer software
    (c) operating system
    (d) computer hardware
    (e) CPU
111. Memory address refers to the successive memory words and the machine is called as __________.
    (a) Word addressable
    (b) byte addressable
    (c) bit addressable
    (d) Terra byte addressable

112. In a sequence of events that take place in an instruction cycle, the first cycle is called
    (a) store cycle   (b) execute cycle
    (c) fetch cycle   (d) decode cycle
    (e) code cycle
113. ROM is an example of which of the following?
    (a) Volatile memory
    (b) Cache memory
    (c) Nonvolatile memory
    (d) Virtual memory
    (e) None of these
114. A register that keeps track of the next instruction to be executed is called a/an
    (a) Data Register
    (b) Instruction Register
    (c) Action Register
    (d) Program Counter
    (e) Accumulator
115. The microprocessor of a computer
    (a) does not understand machine language.
    (b) understands machine language and high-level languages.
    (c) understands only machine language.
    (d) understands only high-level languages.
    (e) Program Read-Only Memory
116. What is the full form of PROM?
    (a) Programmable Read Only Memory
    (b) Progressive Read Only Memory
    (c) Periodic Read Only Memory
    (d) Perfect Read Only Memory
    (e) Program Read-Only Memory
117. Which of the following does not store data permanently?
    (a) ROM   (b) RAM
    (c) Floppy Disk   (d) Hard Disk
    (e) None of these
118. Which of the following is the smallest storage?
    (a) Megabyte   (b) Gigabyte
    (c) Kilobyte   (d) Terabyte
    (e) Nanobyte
119. Which of the following helps to protect floppy disks from data getting accidently erased?
    (a) Access notch
    (b) Write-protect notch
    (c) Entry notch
    (d) Input notch
    (e) None of these
120. CD and DVD drives are the examples of
    (a) coding media   (b) solid stage storage
    (c) Zip drives   (d) printers
    (e) storage devices

ANSWER KEY

1.	(d)	21.	(a)	41.	(a)	61.	(b)	81.	(d)	101.	(d)
2.	(b)	22.	(d)	42.	(a)	62.	(a)	82.	(a)	102.	(b)
3.	(d)	23.	(b)	43.	(d)	63.	(d)	83.	(b)	103.	(c)
4.	(c)	24.	(c)	44.	(c)	64.	(e)	84.	(b)	104.	(a)
5.	(a)	25.	(d)	45.	(b)	65.	(d)	85.	(a)	105.	(d)
6.	(b)	26.	(d)	46.	(c)	66.	(a)	86.	(d)	106.	(d)
7.	(a)	27.	(b)	47.	(b)	67.	(a)	87.	(a)	107.	(d)
8.	(b)	28.	(c)	48.	(e)	68.	(c)	88.	(b)	108.	(e)
9.	(a)	29.	(d)	49.	(d)	69.	(d)	89.	(b)	109.	(d)
10.	(b)	30.	(c)	50.	(a)	70.	(d)	90.	(b)	110.	(d)
11.	(a)	31.	(a)	51.	(b)	71.	(c)	91.	(a)	111.	(a)
12.	(b)	32.	(c)	52.	(e)	72.	(b)	92.	(c)	112.	(c)
13.	(a)	33.	(c)	53.	(b)	73.	(a)	93.	(c)	113.	(c)
14.	(c)	34.	(d)	54.	(e)	74.	(b)	94.	(b)	114.	(b)
15.	(a)	35.	(b)	55.	(d)	75.	(b)	95.	(d)	115.	(c)
16.	(b)	36.	(a)	56.	(c)	76.	(c)	96.	(a)	116.	(a)
17.	(a)	37.	(e)	57.	(d)	77.	(b)	97.	(c)	117.	(b)
18.	(d)	38.	(b)	58.	(a)	78.	(b)	98.	(d)	118.	(e)
19.	(d)	39.	(d)	59.	(d)	79.	(a)	99.	(e)	119.	(b)
20.	(d)	40.	(d)	60.	(b)	80.	(d)	100.	(c)	120.	(e)

Computer Software

Computer Programs are called as Computer software, or just software. A computer Software is set of programs that guides the hardware through its job. The computer program is the non-tangible component of a computer system. A Computer software is different from computer hardware, that is the physical component of a computer system. Computer hardware and software work hand in hand cannot function without the other.

TYPES OF SOFTWARE

Computer softwares are mainly divided into two parts:

(a) System Software   (b) Application Software

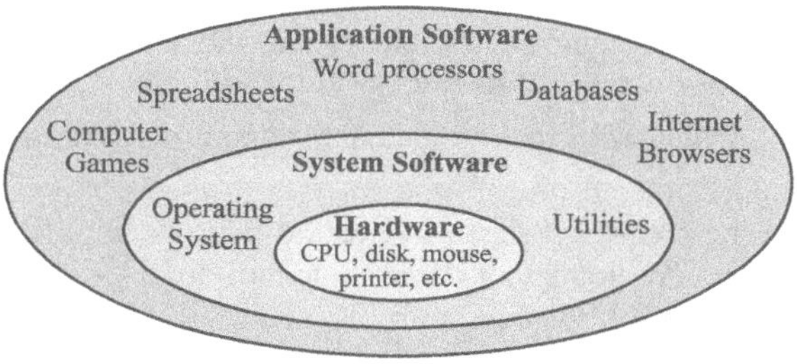

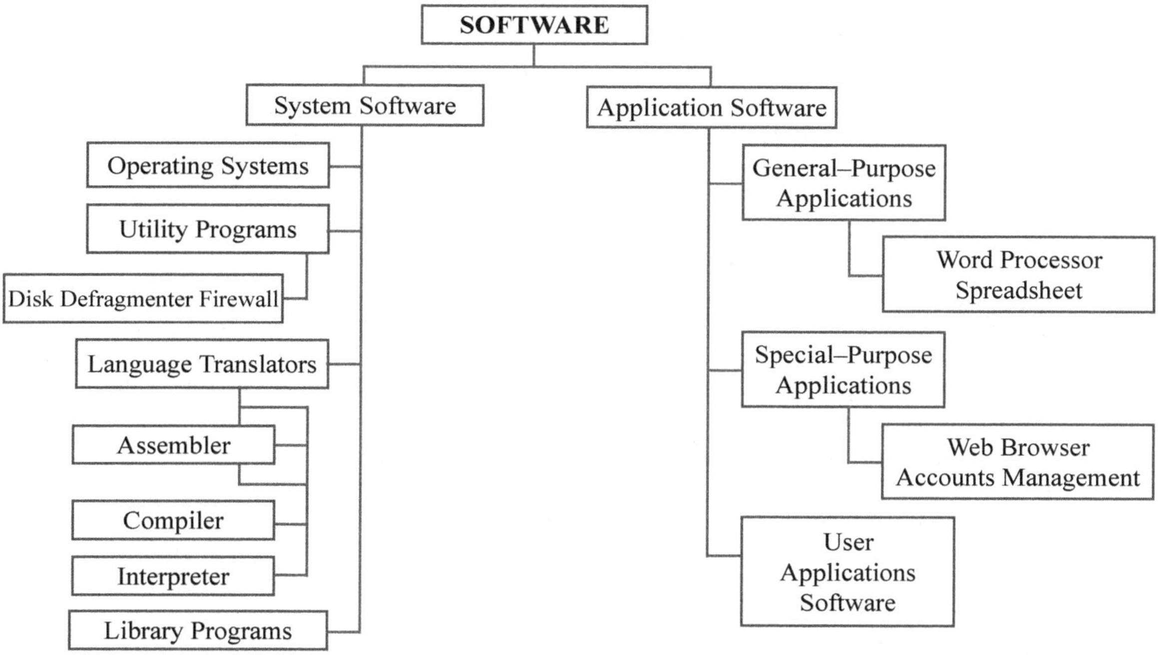

(A) System Software

System software is the software which manages and controls the hardware components and allows interaction between the hardware and the other different types of software. The computer's operating system is a type of system software. Device drivers are also a part of this category.

System software can be separated into two different categories: **Operating systems and Utility software.**

OPERATING SYSTEM :

A program that acts as an intermediary between a user of a computer and the computer hardware is called an operating system. The operating system is an essential component of the system software in a computer system. Application programs usually require an operating system to function.

Operating systems can be found on almost any device that contains a computer—from cellular phones and video game consoles to supercomputers and web servers. For example: UNIX, MS-DOS,WINDOWS, 98/2000/xp/7.

Functions of an operating system –

The basic functions of an operating system are:

I.   Booting the computer

II.   Performs basic computer tasks eg managing the various peripheral devices eg mouse, keyboard

III.   Provides a user interface, e.g. command line, graphical user interface (GUI)

IV.   Handles system resources such as computer's memory and sharing of the central processing unit (CPU) time by various applications or peripheral devices

V.   Provides file management which refers to the way that the operating system manipulates, stores, retrieves and saves data.

I.   Booting the computer : The process of starting or restarting the computer is known as **booting**. A cold boot is when you turn on a computer that has been turned off completely. A warm boot is the process of using the operating system to restart the computer.

II.   Performs basic computer tasks : The operating system performs basic computer tasks, such as managing the various peripheral devices such as the mouse, keyboard and printers. For example, most operating systems now are plug and play which means a device such as a printer will automatically be detected and configured without any user intervention.

III.   Provides a user interface : A user interacts with software through the user interface. The two main types of user interfaces are: command line and a graphical user interface (GUI). With a command line interface, the user interacts with the operating system by typing commands to perform specific tasks. An example of a command line interface is DOS (disk operating system). With a graphical user interface, the user interacts with the operating system by using a mouse to access windows, icons, and menus. An example of a graphical user interface is Windows Vista or Windows 7.

IV.   Handles system resources : The operating system also handles system resources such as the computer's memory and sharing of the central processing unit (CPU) time by various applications or peripheral devices. Programs and input methods are constantly competing for the attention of the CPU and demand memory, storage and input/output bandwidth. The operating system ensures that each application gets the necessary resources it needs in order to maximise the functionality of the overall system.

V.   Provides file management : The operating system also handles the organisation and tracking of files and directories (folders) saved or retrieved from a computer disk. The file management system allows the user to perform such tasks as creating files and directories, renaming files, coping and moving files, and deleting files. The operating system keeps track of where files are located on the hard drive through the type of file system. The type two main types of file system are File Allocation table (FAT) or New Technology File system (NTFS).

File Allocation table (FAT) : It uses the file allocation table which records, which clusters are used and unused and where files are located within the clusters.

NTFS : It is a file system introduced by Microsoft and it has a number of advantages over the previous file system, named FAT32 (File Allocation Table).NTFS also allows permissions (such as read, write, and execute) to be set for individual directories and files.

The three most common **operating systems** for personal computers are **Microsoft Windows, Mac OS X, and Linux.**

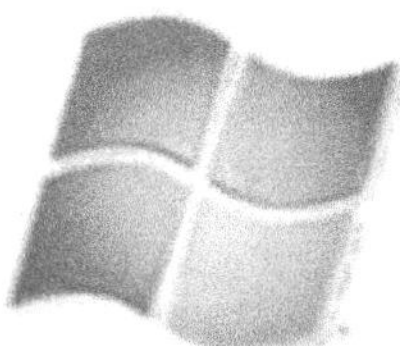

TYPES OF OPERATING SYSTEM

There are different types of operating system to support the computer system. Each type of operating system offers distinct facilities that are appropriate to the computer system in which it is used.

The operating systems are of mainly following types:

- **Single-user, single task Operating System** - This operating system is designed to manage the computer so that one user can effectively do one thing at a time. The Palm OS for Palm handheld computers is a good example of a modern single-user, single-task operating system.

- **Single-user, multi-tasking Operating System-** This operating system mostly used by people which are using desktop and laptop computers today. Microsoft's Windows and Apple's MacOS platforms are both examples of operating systems that will let a single user have several programs in operation at the same time. For example, it's entirely possible for a Windows user to be writing a note in a word processor while downloading a file from the Internet while printing the text of an e-mail message.

- **Multi-userOperating System :** A multi-user operating system allows many different users to take advantage of the computer's resources simultaneously. The operating system must make sure that the requirements of the various users are balanced, and that each of the programs they are using has sufficient and separate resources so that a problem with one user doesn't affect the entire community of users. Unix, VMS and mainframe operating systems, such as MVS, are examples of multi-user operating systems.

- **Real Time operating System :** Real time operating system controls the environment as they have a data processing system in which the time interval required to process and respond to inputs is very small. The time taken by the system to respond to an input and display the result of the required inputted information is termed as response time. A key characteristic of an RTOS is the level of its consistency concerning the amount of time it takes to accept and complete an application's task; the variability is jitter.A hard real-time operating system has less jitter than a soft real-time operating system. The chief design goal is not high throughput, but rather a guarantee of a soft or hard performance category. An RTOS that can usually or generally meet a deadline is a soft real-time OS, but if it can meet a deadline deterministically it is a hard real-time OS.

- **Time-sharing operating system :** Time sharing is a type of operating system that enables many people, located at various terminals, to use a particular computer system at the same time. Because of the above feature timesharing operating system is called multitasking operating system. In other words it is a logical extension of multiprogramming. Processor's time which is shared among multiple users simultaneously is termed as time-sharing.The main purpose of Multiprogrammed batch systems, is to maximize processor use, whereas in Time-Sharing Systems the primary objective is to minimize response time.

- **Distributed operating System :** Distributed systems use a number of central processors to serve multiple real time application and different users. Data processing jobs are distributed among the processors accordingly to which one can perform each job most efficiently.

- **Network operating System :** This operating system runs on a server.This server is responsible for managing data, users, groups, security, applications, and other networking functions. The network operating system allows shared file and printer access among multiple computers in a network. This can also be referred as a local area network (LAN), or a private network. Examples of network operating systems include Microsoft Windows Server 2003, Microsoft Windows Server 2008, UNIX, Linux, Mac OS X, Novell NetWare, and BSD.

SOME OTHER IMPORTANT OPERATING SYSTEM

Stand-Alone Operating System :

A stand-alone operating system is a complete operating system that works on a desktop computer, notebook computer, or mobile computing device. Some stand-alone operating systems are called client operating systems because they also work in conjunction with a server operating system. Client operating systems can operate with or without a network. Examples of currently used stand-alone operating systems are Microsoft Windows, Mac OS, and Linux.

(i) **Microsoft Windows :** Microsoft developed Windows operating system that has a graphical user interface. Some of the popular Windows Operating System are Windows 3.1, Windows 95, Windows 98, Windows 2000, Windows NT, Windows ME, Windows XP, Windows Vista and Windows 7.

Windows 8 is the latest Windows operating systems from Microsoft. It is a graphical user interface (GUI) operating system which is very easy to learn and operate. Windows 7 provides many ways to manage the files stored on your computer. You can open, rename, print, delete, move and search for files.

(ii) **Mac OS :** It is a series of graphical user interface-based operating systems developed by Apple Inc. for their Macintosh line of computer systems. The Macintosh user experience is credited with popularizing the graphical user interface.

(iii) **Linux :** It is a UNIX-based operating system that is available for free on the World Wide Web. Many companies, such as Red Hat, Corel and Mandrake, create easy-to-use versions of Linux that you can purchase. Red Hat Linux is a popular version that comes with the GNOME desktop environment. GNOME displays pictures on the screen to help you perform tasks.

Linux is an open source code operating system. It can be copied, modified and redistributed with few restrictions. This flexibility is one of the reasons why Linux is so popular among users.

Embedded Operating System :

An embedded system is a computer that is part of a different kind of machine. Examples include computers in cars, traffic lights, digital televisions, ATMs, airplane controls, point of sale (POS) terminals, digital cameras, GPS navigation systems, elevators, digital media receivers and smart meters, among many other possibilities.

In contrast to an operating system for a general-purpose computer, an embedded operating system is typically quite limited in terms of function – depending on the device in question, the system may only run a single application. However, that single application is crucial to the device's operation, so an embedded OS must be reliable and able to run with constraints on memory, size and processing power.

Thousands of connected embedded devices have been built on Windows Embedded platforms, from portable ultrasound machines to GPS devices and from ATMs to devices that power large construction machinery. With comprehensive features, easy-to-use and familiar Microsoft development tools, free evaluation kits and access to a large network of community support, working with Windows Embedded Products helps yield faster time to market for your devices and decreased development costs.

Mobile Operating System :

A mobile operating system, also called a mobile OS, is an operating system that is specifically designed to run on mobile devices such as mobile phones, smartphones, PDAs, tablet computers and other handheld devices. The mobile operating system is the software platform on top of which other programs, called application programs, can run on mobile device.

Examples of mobile operating systems include **Apple iOS**, **Windows Phone**, and **Google Android**.

Operating systems for mobile devices generally aren't as fully featured as those made for desktop or laptop computers, and they aren't able to run all of the same software. However, you can still do a lot of things with them, like watch movies, browse the Web, manage your calendar, and play games.

- The **BIOS** (basic input/output system) gets the computer system started after you turn it on and manages the data flow between the operating system and attached devices such as the hard disk, video adapter, keyboard, mouse, and printer.

- An **assembler** takes basic computer instructions and converts them into a pattern of bits that the computer's processor can use to perform its basic operations.

- A **device driver** controls a particular type of device that is attached to your computer, such as a keyboard or a mouse. The driver program converts the more general input/output instructions of the operating system to messages that the device type can understand.

- **Buffering is** the pre-loading of data into a reserved area of memory (the buffer). In streaming audio or video from the Internet, buffering refers to downloading a certain amount of data before starting to play the music or movie. Having an advance supply of audio samples or video frames in memory at all times prevents disruption if there are momentary delays in transmission while the material is being played. Even a live broadcast would have a few seconds of delay built in.

- **Spooling** is the overlapping of low-speed operations with normal processing. Spooling originated with mainframes in order to optimise slow operations such as reading cards and printing. Card input was read onto disk and printer output was stored on disk. In that way, the business data processing was performed at high speed, receiving input from disk and sending output to disk. Subsequently, spooling is used to buffer data for the printer as well as remote batch terminals.

GUI (Graphical User Interface) Based Operating System :

GUI is a program interface that takes advantage of the computer's graphics capabilities to make the program easier to use.

Basic Components of a GUI

Graphical user interfaces, such as Microsoft Windows and the one used by the Apple Macintosh, feature the following basic components:

- **Pointer :** A symbol that appears on the display screen and that you move to select objects and commands. Usually, the pointer appears as a small angled arrow. Text -processing applications, however, use an I-beam pointer that is shaped like a capital I.

- **Pointing device :** A device, such as a mouse or trackball, that enables you to select objects on the display screen.

- **Iicons :** Small pictures that represent commands, files, or windows. By moving the pointer to the icon and pressing a mouse button, you can execute a command or convert the icon into a window. You can also move the icons around the display screen as if they were real objects on your desk.

- **Desktop :** The area on the display screen where icons are grouped is often referred to as the desktop because the icons are intended to represent real objects on a real desktop.

- **Windows :** You can divide the screen into different areas. In each window, you can run a different program or display a different file. You can move windows around the display screen, and change their shape and size at will.

- **Menus :** Most graphical user interfaces let you execute commands by selecting a choice from a menu.

MS DOS (Microsoft Disk Operating System):

Short for Microsoft Disk operating system, MS-DOS is a non-graphical command line operating system derived from 86-DOS that was created for IBM compatible computers. MS-DOS originally written by Tim Paterson and introduced by Microsoft in August 1981 and was last updated in 1994 when MS-DOS 6.22 was released. MS-DOS allows the user to navigate, open, and otherwise manipulate files on their computer from a command line instead of a GUI like Window.

MS DOS based on character user interface. In this communication between a computer and the user can be done by using characters. In Dos, one has to key in the commands on the prompt. Prompt is a place where commands are issued. It may look like C:\> or C:\windows\>.

MS DOS Commands

Command	Description	Type
ansi.sys	Defines functions that change display graphics, control cursor movement, and reassign keys.	File
append	Causes MS-DOS to look in other directories when editing a file or running a command.	External
assign	Assign a drive letter to an alternate letter.	External
assoc	View the file associations.	Internal
attrib	Display and change file attributes.	External
call	Calls a batch file from another batch file.	Internal
cd	Changes directories.	Internal
chcp	Supplement the International keyboard and character set information.	External
chdir	Changes directories.	Internal
cls	Clears the screen.	Internal
cmd	Opens the command interpreter.	Internal
color	Change the foreground and background color of the MS-DOS window.	Internal
comp	Compares files.	External
convert	Convert FAT to NTFS.	External
date	View or change the systems date.	Internal
debug	Debug utility to create assembly programs to modify hardware settings.	External
delete	Recovery console command that deletes a file.	Internal

Command	Description	Type
dir	List the contents of one or more directory.	Internal
disable	Recovery console command that disables Windows system services or drivers.	Recovery
diskcomp	Compare a disk with another disk.	External
diskcopy	Copy the contents of one disk and place them on another disk.	External
echo	Displays messages and enables and disables echo.	Internal
edit	View and edit files.	External
erase	Erase files from computer.	Internal
exit	Exit from the command interpreter.	Internal
expand	Expand a Microsoft Windows file back to it's original format.	External
extract	Extract files from the Microsoft Windows cabinets.	External
find	Search for text within a file.	External
format	Command to erase and prepare a disk drive.	External
ftp	Command to connect and operate on an FTP server.	External
fType	Displays or modifies file types used in file extension associations.	Recovery
goto	Moves a batch file to a specific label or location.	Internal
help	Display a listing of commands and brief explanation.	External
if	Allows for batch files to perform conditional processing.	Internal
ipconfig	Network command to view network adapter settings and assigned values.	External
keyb	Change layout of keyboard.	External
label	Change the label of a disk drive.	External
lock	Lock the hard drive.	Internal
logoff	Logoff the currently profile using the computer.	External
logon	Recovery console command to list installations and enable administrator login.	Recovery
map	Displays the device name of a drive.	Recovery
mem	Display memory on system.	External
mkdir	Command to create a new directory.	Internal
move	Move one or more files from one directory to another directory.	Internal
ping	Test and send information to another network computer or network device.	External
power	Conserve power with computer portables.	External
print	Prints data to a printer port.	External
rd	Removes an empty directory.	Internal
rename	Renames a file or directory.	Internal
rmdir	Removes an empty directory.	Internal
share	Installs support for file sharing and locking capabilities.	External
shift	Changes the position of replaceable parameters in a batch program.	Internal
shutdown	Shutdown the computer from the MS-DOS prompt.	External

Command	Description	Type
set	Change one variable or string to another.	Internal
start	Start a separate window in Windows from the MS-DOS prompt.	Internal
sys	Transfer system files to disk drive.	External
telnet	Telnet to another computer or device from the prompt.	External
time	View or modify the system time.	Internal
Type	Display the contents of a file.	Internal
undelete	Undelete a file that has been deleted.	External
unformat	Unformat a hard drive.	External
unlock	Unlock a disk drive.	Internal
ver	Display the version information.	Internal
xcopy	Copy multiple files, directories, or drives from one location to another.	External

Utility Software

Utility software is software that helps to maintain and protect the computer system. It does not directly interface with the hardware. Examples include anti-virus software, firewalls, disk defragmenters and so on .

System utilities are the core software functions that allow you to manage your computer in ways that you would find it inconceivable to be without.

Functions of System Utility:

I. Disk Cleanup

Disk Cleanup is a function that comes with all versions of Windows Operating Systems. Disk Cleanup allows for you to scan your entire hard drive to search for extra room by deleting any unneccessary files such as temporary files from the Internet and cookies that are downloaded when you visit webpages. You can find Disk Cleanup in Windows XP by going to the Start menu → All Programs → Accessories → System Tools → Disk Cleanup.

II. Disk Defragmentation

Defragmentation is the process of locating the noncontiguous fragments of data into which a computer file may be divided as it is stored on a hard disk, and rearranging the fragments and restoring them into fewer fragments or into the whole file.

III. System Restore

System Restore is a Windows utility that allows a user to restore their computer data to a specific former state (known as a restore point), undoing changes made since that time. System Restore can be found by going to Start → All Programs → Accessories → System Tools → System Restore

IV. Disk Compression

Disk compression is a type of function that allows for a program to search your hard drive and compress files, particularly old or unused files. It also serves to free up space, which is the main function of disk compression software.

V. Antivirus

It is used to scan computer for viruses and prevent the computer system files from being corrupt.

(B)   APPLICATION SOFTWARE

(Also known as 'apps') are designed to achieve a complete task or a set of tasks. Application software consists of the programs for performing varied tasks particular to the machine's utilization. There are various examples of application software that include MS Word, MS Excel, a console game, database systems, desktop publishing systems, program development software, a library management system etc.

Table shows difference between System software and Application software :

System Software		Application Software
Enable the computer to function	Usage	Enable user to work effiently with documentation
Compulsory	Need	Optical depends on usage and needs
Each computer need one system system software	Number Software	Each computer cna have more than one application
Independent–can use without application software	Dependency	Depende – application software cannot work without Applicaiton software
Provide environment in which the applicaiton run	Function	Provides the environment to enable user to accomplish specific task

Following is a brief definition of different examples of softwares available in the market and the differences between them.

- *Retail software:* This type is sold off the shelves of retail stores. It involves expensive packaging that are designed to appeal customers .These are high on cost .

- *OEM software:* OEM stands for "Original Equipment Manufacturer" and refers to that sold in bulk to resellers, designed to be bundled with hardware.

- *Shareware :* It is a software that can be downloaded from the Internet. There is a license period in which the user is allowed to try the program for free .After the stipulated period (in the license usually thirty days), it must be purchased or uninstalled.

- *Adware:* This software has advertisements built into the program itself.It is a free software.These softwares use a live Internet feed and constant bandwidth to upload new advertisements..

- *Spyware:* Spyware is normally free. These can be shareware. For example, a multimedia player might profile what music and video the user wants to play.In such a case the software files the program whenever it is called upon to play

- *Freeware:* Freeware is also downloadable off the Internet and is free of charge.Freeware is only free for personal use. A paid license is required for commercial use. Freeware does not contain spyware or adware. If it is found to contain either of these, it is reclassified as such.

There are various types of application software :

I.   **Word Processing :** The most important computer application is that they are most commonly used to create, edit, and print documents. Word processing software allows users to create and manipulate documents that contain text and graphics. With word processing software, you can insert clip art into a document; change margins; find and replace text; use a spelling checker to check spelling; place a header and footer at the top and the bottom of a page; and vary font (character design), font size (character scale), and font style (character appearance).

E.g. *Microsoft Word, Google Docs, AppleWorks, Openoffice.org etc.*

II. **Spreadsheet :** A spreadsheet is a type of document that stores the entire data in a grid form consisting of horizontal rows and vertical columns. This row/column structure allows the analysis of data using formulas and calculations. With spreadsheet software, data is organized in rows and columns, which collectively are called a worksheet. The intersection of a row and column, called a cell, can contain a label (name of cells), a value (number), or aformula or function that performs calculations on the data and displays the result.

E.g. Microsoft Excel, Correl Quattro Pro etc

III. Presentation Graphics : Presentation Graphics also called as the presentation software is a type of application program that helps you to create different timing and organized sequence of information and pictures that present a story or help in giving a public presentation of information through a slide show.

E.g.Microsoft PowerPoint, Apple Keynote, OpenOffice Impress, Corel Presentations, Adobe Persuasion etc.

IV. Multimedia authoring : Multimedia authoring software helps you to create a a presentation that has a variety of feature such as the audio and video sequences. Business presentation software usually enables you to include images and sometimes audio and video developed with other tools.

V. Database software : Database software allows you to create and manage a database. A database is a collection of data organized to allow access, retrieval, and use of that data. A query is used to retrieve data according to specifiedcriteria, which are restrictions the data must meet.

E.g.Microsoft Access, Corel Paradox, Lotus Approach etc.

VI. Desktop publishing(DTP) : Desktop publishing(DTP) software is used to design and produce sophisticated documents. DTP is developed specifically to support page layout, which is the process of arranging text and graphics in a document. Complete DTP involves combination of type setting, graphic design, page layout and printing the document.

E.g.Adobe InDesign,Adobe PageMaker,Corel Ventura,Coreldraw,Microsoft Office Publisher etc.

A *videoconference* is a meeting between two or more geographically separated people who use a network or the Internet to transmit audio and video data.

PROGRAMMING LANGUAGES

A programming language is a set of commands, instructions, and other syntax use to create a software program. Languages that programmers use to write code are called "high-level languages." This code can be compiled into a "low-level language," which is recognized directly by the computer hardware.

(a) Low Level Languages : Low level computer languages are machine codes or close to it. Computer cannot understand instructions given in high level languages or in English. It can only understand and execute instructions given in the form of machine language i.e. language of 0 and 1. There are two types of low level languages:

I. Machine Language : The set of instructions executed directly by a computer's central processing unit (CPU) is called Machine code .In machine language each and every instruction performs specific operation. The machine code is in the form a numerical code (i.e. not assembly code) and is the lowest-level representation of a compiled and/or assembled computer program .Machine language is also called as a primitive and hardware-dependent programming language. Writing programs directly in numerical machine code is tedious task.

II. Assembly Language : A personal computer has a microprocessor of its own that manages the computer's arithmetical, logical and control activities. All these operations are managed through a set of instructions by each family of processors. These operations are handled by getting input from keyboard and displaying information on screen and performing various other jobs. These set of instructions are called machine language instructions.

Machine language instructions are in the form of strings of 1's and 0's. Machine language is quite obscure and complex for using in software development. For this very reason low-level assembly language is designed for representation of all the instructions in a symbolic code yet in a more understandable form for a specific family of processors.

(b) High-Level Language : Earlier languages that were developed ,during the development of computers required knowledge of the internal workings of the computer,hence attempts were made to ease the programming where the knowledge on the the internal workings of the computer was not required . High-level programming languages allowed the specification of writing a program closer to those used by human beings. With the advent of high level languages ,programming became far easier, less error-prone and also removed the programmer from having to know the details of the internal structure of a particular computer. Fortran II was one of the first high level language introduced in about 1958.

- **Assembler :** It is used to convert the assembly language into machine language (i.e. 0 or 1). This language consists of mnemonic codes which are difficult to lean and is machine dependent.

- **Compiler -** Compiler is a special program which reads a program in source language and translates into an equivalent other language. Also it reports the errors in the source program to its user, if there are any.

Types of Error. Errors are either syntactic or semantic:

Syntax errors are errors in the program text.

Semantic errors are mistakes concerning the meaning of a program construct.

- **Interpreter :** A high-level programming language translator that translates and runs the program at the same time. It converts one program statement into machine language, executes it, and then proceeds to the next statement. This differs from regular executable programs that are presented to the computer as binary-coded instructions. Interpreted programs remain in the source language the programmer wrote in, which is human readable text.

- **Loader :** In loading, a routine of a program is not loaded until it is called by the program. All routines are kept on disk in a re-locatable load format. The main program is loaded into memory and is executed. Other routines methods or modules are loaded on request. Dynamic loading makes better memory space utilization and unused routines are never loaded.

- **Linker :** Linking as the name suggests is the process of combining various pieces of code and data together to form a single executable that can be loaded in memory. Linking can be done at compile time, load time (by loaders) and at run time (by application programs) too.

- **Debugging :** In computers, debugging is the process of locating and fixing or bypassing bugs (errors) in computer program code or the engineering of a hardware device.

Many high level languages were developed since Fortran II (and many have also disappeared!), among the most widely used have been:

Language	Application Area	Developer
FORTRAN (Formula Translation)	Engineering & Scientific Applications	IBM in 1957
LISP (List Processing)	Artificial Intelligence	John Mc Zarthy in 1958
COBOL (Common Business Oriented Language)	Business applications	Grace Hopper in 1959
PASCAL	General use and as a teaching tool	Niklaus Irth in 1972
C & C++	General Purpose - currently most popular	Bjarne Stroustrup in 1983. Dennis Ritchie in 1972
JAVA	General Purpose - Internet Oriented Programming	James Gosling in 1995

Generation of Language:-

1GL or first-generation language was (and still is) the machine language generation.It refers to the level of instructions and data that is fed to the processor of a computer. (which in conventional computers is a string of 0s and 1s).

- 2GL or second-generation language is the assembly language generation. An assembler converts the assembler language statements into machine language.
- 3GL or third-generation language is a "high-level" programming language, such as C /C ++or Java.
- A 4GL or fourth generation (programming) language is a grouping of programming languages that attempt to get closer than 3GLs to human language, form of thinking and conceptualisation. 4th generation language, is known as the domain specific language, or a high productivity language.

4GLs are the programmer-friendly generation of programming. They are easier to write and hence improve the programming efficiency by using words and phrases close to the English language, with appropriate, use of icons, graphical interfaces and symbolical representations. 4GLs have also increased the number of professionals to be able to develop skills set in software development.

4GL and 5GL represent the leaps or the "generations" in the evolution of programming languages.

- 5GL or fifth-generation language is a programming language that has a visual or graphical development interface to develop the source code but compiled with a 3GL or 4GL language compiler. There are several business corporations that make these languages such as the Microsoft, Borland, IBM, etc.

NUMBER SYSTEM

In general, in any number system there is an ordered set of symbols known as digits with rules defined for performing arithmetic operations like addition, subtraction, multiplication and division. A collection of these digits makes a number which in general has two parts-integer and fractional.

The digits in a number are placed side by side and each position in the number is assigned a weight or index. Table below gives the details of commonly used number systems.

Table

Number System	Base or radix (b)	Symbol used or digits (di or d_{-f})	Weight assigned to position	example
Binary	2	(0,1)	2^{-i} 2^{-f}	1011.11
Octal	8	(0,1,2,3,4,5,6,7)	8^{-i} 8^{-f}	3567.25
Decimal	10	(0,1,2,3,4,5,6,7,8,9)	10^{-i} 10^{-f}	3974.57
Hexadecimal	16	(0,1,2,3,4,5,6,7,8,9 A,B,C,D,E,F)	16^{-i} 16^{-f}	3FA9.56

1. **Binary Number System**

    The number system with base (or radix) two is known as the binary number system. Only two symbols are used to represent numbers in this system and these are 0 and 1, these are known as bits. It is also known as base 2 system. It is a positional system, that is every position is assigned a specific weight left - most bit is known as **Most Significant Bit (MSB)** and the right - most bit is known as the **Least Significant Bit (LSB).** Any number of 0s can be added to the left of the number without changing the value of the number. A group of four bits is known as nibble and a group of eight bits is known as a byte. Table shows binary numbers and their equivalent decimal numbers.

Table : 4-bit binary numbers and their corresponding decimal numbers.

Binary Number				Hexa decimal	Decimal Number	
B_3	B_2	B_1	B_0	H	D_1	D_0
0	0	0	0	0	0	0
0	0	0	1	1	0	1
0	0	1	0	2	0	2
0	0	1	1	3	0	3
0	1	0	0	4	0	4
0	1	0	1	5	0	5
0	1	1	0	6	0	6
0	1	1	1	7	0	7
1	0	0	0	8	0	8
1	0	0	1	9	0	9
1	0	1	0	A	1	0
1	0	1	1	B	1	1
1	1	0	0	C	1	2
1	1	0	1	D	1	3
1	1	1	0	E	1	4
1	1	1	1	F	1	5

2. **Decimal Number System**

   It consists of ten digits from 0 to 9. These digits can be used to represent any numeric value. It is also known as Base 10 System.

3. **Octal Number System**

   It is one of the popular number system. It consists of 8 digits from 0 to 7. It is also known as Base 8 system.

4. **Hexadecimal Number System**

   Hexadecimal means 16. These are 16 combinations of 4-bit binary numbers and sets of 4-bit binary number can be entered in the microprocessor in the form of hexadecimal digits.

   Since 16 digits are used, the heights are in powers of 16. The decimal equivalent of a hexadecimal string equals sum of all hexadecimal digits multiplied by their weights.

   e.g., $(F\ 8\ E \cdot 2\ B)16 = F \times 16^2 + 8 \times 161 + E \times 160 + 2 \times 16^{-1} + B \times 16^{-2}$

   $$= 15 \times 16^2 + 8 \times 161 + 14 \times 16 + 2 \times 16^{-1} + 11 \times 16^{-2}$$

   $$= 3840 + 128 + 14 + \frac{2}{16} + \frac{11}{256} = (3982.16796875)_{10}.$$

NUMBER CONVERSIONS

Binary-Decimal Conversion

Any binary number can be converted into its equivalent decimal number using the weights assigned to each bit position. Since only two digits are used, the weights are powers of 2. These weights are 20 (Units), 2^1 (twos), 2^2 (fours) 2^3 (eights) and 2^4 (sixteen). If longer binary number involved, the weights continue in ascending powers of 2.

The decimal equivalent of a binary number equals the sum of all binary number equal the sum of all binary digits multiplied by their weights.

Example : Find the decimal equivalent of binary number 11111.

Solution: The equivalent decimal number is,

$$= 1 \times 2^4 + 1 \times 2^3 + 1 \times 2^2 + 1 \times 2^1 + 1 \times 20$$
$$= 16 + 8 + 4 + 2 + 1 = (31)_{10}$$

Decimal-to Binary Conversion

Any decimal number can be converted into its equivalent binary number. For integers, the conversion is obtained by continuous division by 2 and keeping track of the remainders, while for fractional parts, the conversion is effected by continuous multiplications by 2 and keeping track of the integers generated.

Example : Express the 25.5 decimal number in the binary form.

Solution: Integer Part:

Thus, $(25)_{10} = (11001)_2$

```
2 | 25
2 | 12 — 1
2 | 6  — 0
2 | 3  — 0
2 | 1  — 1
2 | 0  — 1
```

Read down to up

Fraction part

```
  0 . 5
× 	2
─────────
  1 . 0
```

i.e., $0.5_{10} = 0.1_2$

Therefore $25.5_{10} = 11001.1_2$

Decimal-Octal Conversion

This can be achieved by dividing the given decimal number repeatedly by 8, until a quotient of 0 is obtained.

Example : Convert conversion (444.499)10.

Solution :

Division		Generated Remainder
444 / 8	→	
55/ 8	→	4
6/8	→	7
0/8	→	6

On reading the remainders from bottom to top, the decimal (444)10(674)8. Now, fractional conversion

Division	Generated Remainder
Multiplication	Generated Integer
0.499 × 8 = 3.992	3
0.992 × 8 = 7.936	7
0.936 × 8 = 7.488	7
0.488 × 8 = 3.904	3

The process gets terminated when significant digits are acquired. Thus, octal equivalent is $(444.499)_{10} = (674.3773)_8$

Octal-Binary Conversion

It can be explained through the following example: To convert $(377)_8$ into binary, replace each significant digit by its 3-bit binary equivalent.

$(377)_8 = \quad 3 \quad 7 \quad \quad 7$

$= 011111 \quad 111$

Thus, $(377)_8 = (011111111)_2$

Binary-Hexadecimal Conversion

e.g., $(10100110111110)^2 = (0010\ 1001\ 1011\ 1110)^2 = (2\ 9\ B\ E)_{16} \times 1$

Hexadecimal-Binary Conversion

It can be explained through an example. To convert $(1D5)_{16}$ into binary, replace each significant digit by its 4-bit binary equivalent.

$(1D5)_{16} = \quad 1 \quad D \quad \quad 5$

$\qquad \quad = 0001 \quad 1101 \quad 0101$

Thus, $\quad (1D5)_{16} = (000111010101)_2$

SOME IMPORTANT TERMS IN COMPUTER SOFTWARE –

Kernel: The nucleus of an operating system. It is the closest part to the machine level and may activate the hardware directly or interface to another software layer that drives the hardware. The kernel orchestrates the entire operation of the computer by slicing time for each system function and each application as well as managing all the computer's resources. It typically resides in memory at all times.

Shell: The outer layer of a program that provides the user interface, or way of commanding the computer. The term originally referred to the software that processed the commands typed into the Unix operating system . For example, the Bourne shell was the original command line processor, and C shell and Korn shell were developed later. In DOS, the default shell was COMMAND.COM

Fork: fork creates a new process by duplicating the calling process. The new process, referred to as the child, is an exact duplicate of the calling process, referred to as the parent, except for the following points.The child has its own unique process ID, and this PID does not match the ID of any existing process group .The child's parent process ID is the same as the parent's process ID.

Thread: thread of execution is the smallest sequence of programmed instructions that can be managed independently by a scheduler (typically as part of an operating system). The implementation of threads and processes differs from one operating system to another, but in most cases, a thread is a component of a process. Multiple threads can exist within the same process and share resources such as memory, while different processes do not share these resources.

Deadlock: A condition that occurs when two processes are each waiting for the other to complete before proceeding. The result is that both processes hang. Deadlocks occur most commonly in multitasking and client/server environments. Ideally, the programs that are deadlocked, or the operating system, should resolve the deadlock, but this doesn't always happen.

Multiprocessing: Multiprocessing is the use of two or more central processing units (CPUs) within a single computer system. The term also refers to the ability of a system to support more than one processor and/or the ability to allocate tasks between them.

Past Exercise

1. _______ is a set of keywords, symbols, and a system of rules for constructing statements by which humans can communicate the instructions to be executed by a computer. **[SBI Clerk, 2009]**
   - (a) A computer program
   - (b) A programming language
   - (c) An assemble
   - (d) Syntax
   - (e) None of these

2. This can be another word for program **[SBI Clerk, 2009]**
   - (a) software
   - (b) disk
   - (c) floppy
   - (d) hardware
   - (e) None of these

3. A(n) _______ is device that electronically processes data, converting it to information. **[SBI Clerk, 2009]**
   - (a) algorithm
   - (b) computer
   - (c) software
   - (d) program
   - (e) None of these

4. The secret code that restricts entry to some programs is **[SBI Clerk, 2009]**
   - (a) password
   - (b) passport
   - (c) entry-code
   - (d) access-code
   - (e) None of these

5. The person who writes and tests computer programs is called a **[SBI Clerk, 2009]**
   - (a) programmer
   - (b) computer scientist
   - (c) software engineer
   - (d) project developer
   - (e) None of these

6. Processing involves **[SBI Clerk, 2009]**
   - (a) inputting data into a computer system
   - (b) transforming input into output
   - (c) displaying relevant answers
   - (d) providing relevant answers
   - (e) None of these

7. Which of the following controls the manner of interaction between the user and the operating system? **[SBI Clerk, 2009]**
   - (a) user interface
   - (b) language translator
   - (c) platform
   - (d) screensaver
   - (e) None of these

8. Computer language used on the Internet is —— **[SBI Clerk, 2009]**
   - (a) BASIC
   - (b) COBOL
   - (c) Java
   - (d) Pascal
   - (e) None of these

9. A compiler translates a program written in a high-level language into — **[SBI Clerk, 2009]**
   - (a) Machine language
   - (b) an algorithm
   - (c) a debugged program
   - (d) Java
   - (e) None of the above

10. What is correcting error in a program called? **[SBI Clerk, 2009]**
    - (a) Compiling
    - (b) Debugging
    - (c) Grinding
    - (d) Interpreting
    - (e) None of these

11. The ————— of a system includes the programs or instructions. **[SBI Clerk, 2009]**
    - (a) hardware
    - (b) icon
    - (c) information
    - (d) software
    - (e) None of these

12. The primary purpose of software is to turn data into———— **[SBI Clerk, 2009]**
    - (a) Websites
    - (b) information
    - (c) programs
    - (d) objects
    - (e) None of these

13. A————— contains specific rules and words that express the logical steps of an algorithm. **[SBI Clerk, 2009]**
    - (a) programming language
    - (b) syntax
    - (c) programming structure
    - (d) logic chart
    - (e) None of the above

14. A (n) — is a program that makes the computer easier to use. **[SBI Clerk, 2009]**
    - (a) utility
    - (b) application
    - (c) operating system
    - (d) network
    - (e) None of these

15. The —— tells the computer how to use its components **[SBI Clerk, 2009]**
    - (a) utility
    - (b) network
    - (c) application program
    - (d) operating system
    - (e) None of these

16. An error is also known as **[SBI Clerk, 2009, 2011]**
    - (a) bug
    - (b) debug
    - (c) cursor
    - (d) icon
    - (e) None of these

17. _____ is the process of carrying out commands.
    [SBI Clerk, 2009, IBPS Clerk 2011]
    (a) Fetching   (b) Storing
    (c) Executing   (d) Decoding
    (e) None of these
18. Which of the following is a programming language for creating special programs like applets? **[SBI PO, 2011]**
    (a) Java   (b) cable
    (c) domain name   (d) Net
    (e) COBOL
19. System software **[SBI PO, 2011]**
    (a) allows the user to diagnose and troubleshoot the device
    (b) is a programming language
    (c) is part of a productivity suite
    (d) is an optional form of software
    (e) helps the computer manage internal resources
20. Linux is a type of _______ software.
    [IBPS Clerk, 2011]
    (a) Shareware   (b) Commercial
    (c) Proprietary   (d) Open Source
    (e) Hidden type
21. Which of the following not a software?
    [IBPS Clerk, 2011]
    (a) excel
    (b) operating system
    (c) printer driver
    (d) central processing unit(CPU)
    (e) power point
22. The operating system, that is self-contained in a device and resident in the ROM .is
    [IBPS Clerk, 2011]
    (a) Batch Operating System
    (b) Real-time Operating System
    (c) Embedded Operating System
    (d) Mutli-Processor Operating System
    (e) None of these
23. Information that comes from an external source and fed into computer software is called
    [IBPS Clerk, 2011]
    (a) Output   (b) Input
    (c) Throughput   (d) Reports
    (e) None of these
24. To be able to "boot", the computer must have a(n) **[IBPS Clerk, 2011]**
    (a) Compiler   (b) Loader
    (c) Operating System   (d) Assembler
    (e) None of these

25. The binary system is a number system to the base **[IBPS Clerk, 2011]**
    (a) 2   (b) 4
    (c) 8   (d) 10
    (e) 16
26. Assembly language is **[IBPS Clerk, 2011]**
    (a) Machine Language
    (b) High-level programming language
    (c) A low-level programming language
    (d) Language for assembling computers
    (e) None of these
27. The simultaneous processing of two or more programs by multiple processors is
    [IBPS PO, 2011]
    (a) multiprogramming (b) multitasking
    (c) time-sharing   (d) multiprocessing
    (e) None of these
28. _________ are words that a programming language has set aside for its own use.
    [IBPS PO, 2011]
    (a) Control words   (b) Control structures
    (c) Reserved words   (d) Reserved keys
    (e) None of these
29. What is the process of copying software programs from secondary storage media to the hard disk called? **[IBPS PO, 2011]**
    (a) configuration   (b) download
    (c) storage   (d) upload
    (e) installation
30. Which of the following can only have sequential access? **[SBI Clerk, 2011]**
    (a) Disk   (b) Tape
    (c) CD-ROM   (d) DVD-ROM
    (e) None of these
31. What of the following means the altering of computer system software to archive a task for which it was not originally designed?
    [SBI Clerk, 2011]
    (a) breaking   (b) hacking
    (c) trekking   (d) pegging
    (e) None of these
32. A set of rules for telling the computer what operations to perform is called a __________.
    [IBPS PO, 2012]
    (a) procedural language
    (b) structures
    (c) natural language
    (d) command language
    (e) programming language
33. A detailed written description of the programming cycle and the program, along with

the test results and a printout of the program is called ___________. **[IBPS PO, 2012]**
(a) documentation   (b) output
(c) reporting   (d) spec sheets
(e) Directory

34. A(n)_________is a set of programs designed to manage the resources of a computer, including starting the computer, managing programs, managing memory, and coordinating tasks between input and output devices. **[IBPS PO, 2012]**
(a) application suite   (b) compiler
(c) input/output system   (d) interface
(e) operating system (OS)

35. In the absence of parentheses, the order of operation is _________. **[IBPS PO, 2012]**
(a) Exponentiation, addition or subtraction, multiplication or division
(b) Addition or subtraction, multiplication or division, exponentiation
(c) Multiplication or division, exponentiation, addition or subtraction
(d) Exponentiation, multiplication or division, addition or subtraction
(e) Addition or subtraction, exponentiation, Multiplication or division

36. An _____ program is one that is ready to run and does not need to be altered in any way. **[IBPS PO, 2012]**
(a) interpreter   (b) high-level
(c) compiler   (d) COBOL
(e) executable

37. A(n) _________ language reflects the way people think mathematically. **[IBPS PO, 2012]**
(a) cross-platform programming
(b) 3GL business programming
(c) event-driven programming
(d) functional
(e) None of these

38. Which of the following software could assist someone who cannot use their hands for computer input ? **[IBPS PO, 2012]**
(a) Video conferencing
(b) Speech recognition   (c) Audio digitizer
(d) Synthesizer   (e) None of these

39. ___________ software creates a mirror image of the entire hard disk, including the operating system, applications, files, and data. **[IBPS PO, 2012]**
(a) Operating system   (b) Backup software
(c) Utility programs   (d) Driver imaging
(e) None of these

40. Which of the following information systems focuses on making manufacturing processes more efficient and of higher quality ? **[IBPS PO, 2012]**
(a) Computer-aided manufacturing
(b) Computer-integrated manufacturing
(c) Computer-aided software engineering
(d) Computer-aided system engineering
(e) None of these

41. A mistake in an algorithm that causes incorrect results is called a ___________. **[IBPS PO, 2012]**
(a) logical error   (b) syntax error
(c) procedural error   (d) compiler error
(e) machine error

42. _______ is a feature for scheduling and multiprogramming to provide an economical interactive system of two or more users **[IBPS Clerk, 2012]**
(a) Time sharing   (b) Multitasking
(c) Time tracing   (d) Multiprocessing
(e) None of these

43. A programming language having a ______ is slow in execution **[IBPS Clerk, 2012]**
(a) Interpreter   (b) Compiler
(c) Assembler   (d) Linker
(e) (a) & (b)

44. The word processor used by DOS to write the programs or instructions **[IBPS Clerk, 2012]**
(a) WordStar   (b) WordPad
(c) Notepad   (d) MS-Word
(e) EDIT

45. Decimal equivalent of $(1111)_2 =$ **[IBPS Clerk, 2012]**
(a) 11   (b) 10
(c) 1   (d) 15
(e) 13

46. System proposal is prepared in ______ phase of SDLC **[IBPS Clerk, 2012]**
(a) Conception   (b) Initiation
(c) Analysis   (d) Design
(e) construction

47. The errors that can be find out by a compiler are **[IBPS Clerk, 2012]**
(a) Logical errors   (b) Internal errors
(c) Semantic errors   (d) Syntax errors
(e) Execution errors

48. The process that deals with the technical and management issues of software development is _______ **[IBPS Clerk, 2012]**
(a) Delivery process   (b) Control process
(c) Software process   (d) Testing process
(e) Monitoring process

49. Android is ______ **[IBPS Clerk, 2012]**
    (a) Operating system (b) Application
    (c) Interface   (d) Software
    (e) A collection of all these
50. Devices that enter information and let you communicate with the computer are called ______. **[SBI Clerk, 2012]**
    (a) Software   (b) Output devices
    (c) Hardware   (d) Input devices
    (e) Input/Output devices
51. In electronic device, operating under the control of information, that can accept data, process the data, produce output and store the results for future use ______ **[SBI Clerk, 2012]**
    (a) Input   (b) Computer
    (c) Software   (d) Hardware
    (e) None of these
52. By firmware or Remote control we understand ______ **[SBI Clerk, 2012]**
    (a) physical equipment used in a computer system
    (b) a set of instructions that causes a computer to perform one or more tasks.
    (c) the people involved in the computing process.
    (d) a set of programs that is pre-installed into the read only memory of a computer during the time of manufacturing
    (e) None of these
53. The basic computer processing cycle consists of ______ **[SBI Clerk, 2012]**
    (a) input, processing and output
    (b) systems and application
    (c) data, information and applications
    (d) hardware, software and storage
    (e) None of these
54. One of the following statements is not true for BUFFERS command **[IBPS PO, 2013]**
    (a) increasing numbers of BUFFERS can speed program execution, but only to a certain extent
    (b) the more buffers that exist the more sectors can be stored In memory; hence fewer accesses of disk are necessary
    (c) The BUFFERS command is used to establish the number ol disk buffers set up by MS-DOS during booting
    (d) All of the above
    (e) None of the above
55. A pixel is **[IBPS PO, 2013]**
    (a) a computer program that draws picture
    (b) a picture stored in the secondary memory
    (c) the smallest resolvable part of a picture

(d) a virus
(e) None of the above
56. Which switch should be used in the DIR command to view files or sub directories in a directories ? **[IBPS PO, 2013]**
    (a) /P   (b) /W
    (c) /S   (d) /L
    (e) None of these
57. Which of the following uses a handheld operating system? **[SBI PO, 2013]**
    (a) A supercomputer
    (b) A personal computer
    (c) A laptop
    (d) A mainframe
    (e) APDA (A Personal Digital Assistant)
58. In programming, repeating some statements is usually called **[SSC CGL, 2013]**
    (a) Looping   (b) Control structure
    (c) Compiling   (d) Structure
    (e) None of these
59. Identify the FIFO (First In First Out) structure among the following : **[SSC CGL, 2013]**
    (a) Stack   (b) Queue
    (c) De-queue   (d) Array
60. Where you are likely to find an embedded operating system? **[IBPS Clerk, 2014]**
    (a) on a desktop operating system
    (b) on a networked PC
    (c) on a network server
    (d) on a PDA
    (e) on a mainframe
61. System software– **[IBPS Clerk, 2014]**
    (a) allows the user to diagnose and troubleshoot the device
    (b) is a programming language
    (c) is part of a productivity suite
    (d) is an optional form of software
    (e) helps the computer manage internal resources
62. The term "User Interface" refers to ______ **[SBI Clerk, 2014]**
    (a) the monitor that is available for the computer
    (b) how the Operating System responds to user commands.
    (c) Error! Not a valid embedded object. the means by which the user interacts with the peripheral devices on the computer.
    (d) What the user sees on the screen and how they can interact with it
    (e) None of these

63. Which of the following computer languages is used for Artificial Intelligence(AI)?
    [SBI Clerk, 2014]
    (a) FORTRAN   (b) C
    (c) COBOL   (d) PROLOG
    (e) None of these

64. If a new device is attached to a computer, such as a printer or scanner, its __________ must be installed before the device can be used.
    [SBI Clerk, 2014]
    (a) Error! Not a valid embedded object. Server
    (b) Driver
    (c) Buffer
    (d) All of the above
    (e) None of the above

65. The software that allows users to surf the Internet is called a/an __________
    [SBI Clerk, 2014]
    (a) Error! Not a valid embedded object. Browser
    (b) Internet Service Provider
    (c) Multimedia application
    (d) Search Engine
    (e) None of these

66. __________ are software which is used to do particular task. **[IBPS Clerk, 2015]**
    (a) Operating system   (b) Program
    (c) Data   (d) Software
    (e) None of these

67. Finite number of sequential instructions are called **[IBPS Clerk, 2015]**
    (a) Flow chart   (b) Control flow
    (c) Program flow   (d) Algorithm
    (e) None of these

68. A ______ contains specific rules and words t hat express the logical steps of an algorithm
    (a) Programming language **[IBPS PO, 2015]**
    (b) Syntax error
    (c) Programming structure
    (d) Logic chart
    (e) None of these

69. Specialized programs that assist users in locating information on the Web are called
    (a) Information engines   **[SBI PO, 2015]**
    (b) locator engines   (c) web browsers
    (d) resource locators   (e) search engines

70. Compiling creates a(n)   **[SBI PO, 2015]**
    (a) error-free program
    (b) program specification
    (c) subroutine
    (d) algorithm
    (e) executable program

71. A computer executes programs in the sequence of : **[SSC CGL, 2015]**
    (a) Decode, Fetch, Execute
    (b) Execute, Fetch, Decode
    (c) Fetch, Decode, Execute
    (d) Store, Fetch, Execute

72. Which of the following is not an operating system? **[SSC CGL, 2016]**
    (a) Android   (b) Vista
    (c) iOS   (d) Opera

73. Assembly is a ______ based low-level language replacing binary machine-code instructions, which are very hard to remember, it is the classic and uncontroversial example of a low level language. **[IBPS PO Mains, 2016]**
    (a) Memory   (b) High Level
    (c) Key   (d) Mnemonic
    (e) FORTRAN

74. In Computer programming there is set of subroutine definitions, protocols, and tools for building software and applications. Which among the following is a term for sets of requirements that govern how one application can talk to another? **[IBPS PO Mains, 2016]**
    (a) UPS   (b) API
    (c) CGI   (d) J2EE
    (e) OLE

75. After a credit card transaction has been authorized by the issuing bank by sending an authorization code to the merchant, the settlement stage of the process begins. Which of the following is a system type used to process such statements? **[IBPS PO Mains, 2016]**
    (a) Multitasking   (b) Memory Processing
    (c) Level Processing   (d) Batch Processing
    (e) Online Processing

76. Which among the following is not an Object Oriented Programming Language?
    [IBPS PO Mains, 2016]
    (a) Python   (b) PASCAL
    (c) Java   (d) C++
    (e) Ruby

77. In Computer programming API is set of subroutine definitions, protocols, and tools for building software and applications. Which among the following is an application programming interface for the programming language Java, which defines how a client may access a database? **[IBPS PO Mains, 2016]**
    (a) J2EE   (b) JDK
    (c) JAVA SE   (d) JDBC
    (e) JSX

78. Android is a mobile operating system designed primarily for touch screen mobile devices such as smartphones and tablets. Which among the following was the first Android Operating System? **[IBPS PO Mains, 2016]**
    (a) Cupcake (b) Alpha
    (c) Gingerbread (d) Doughnut
    (e) Eclair

79. On August 25, 2016 Linux celebrated its 25 years of its existence, Features of LINUX are: **[IBPS Clerk Mains, 2016]**
    (a) Portability
    (b) Open source
    (c) Multi-user & Multi Programming
    (d) All of the above
    (e) None of the above

80. Which command is used to display the OS system name? **[IBPS Clerk Mains, 2016]**
    (a) OS (b) Unix
    (c) Kernel (d) Uname
    (e) Shell

81. _______ is used for very large files or where a fast response time is not critical. The files to be transmitted are gathered over a period and then send together as a batch. **[IBPS Clerk Mains, 2016]**
    (a) Batch processing (b) Online processing
    (c) File processing (d) Data processing
    (e) Text processing

82. Which is not an object oriented Programming language-? **[IBPS Clerk Mains, 2016]**
    (a) JAVA (c) C++
    (b) Python (d) FORTRAN
    (e) Ruby

83. Which among the following is not a mobile Operating System? **[IBPS Clerk Mains, 2016]**
    (a) Bada (b) Safari
    (c) Symbian (d) MeeGo
    (e) WebOS

84. Are we building the right product? This statement refers to **[IBPS RRB, 2016]**
    (a) Verification
    (b) Validation
    (c) Testing
    (d) Software quality assurance
    (e) None of these

85. Grammar of the programming is checked at which phase of compiler? **[IBPS RRB, 2016]**
    (a) Semantic analysis (b) Syntax analysis
    (c) Code generation
    (d) Code optimization (e) None of these

86. What is called the sharing of a medium and its path by 2 or more devices? **[IBPS RRB, 2016]**
    (a) Multiplexing (b) Multiprocessing
    (c) Multi-operating (d) Multitasking
    (e) Multi-sharing

87. A computer professional who writes and tests software are called a **[IBPS RRB, 2016]**
    (a) software consultant
    (b) librarian
    (c) hardware consultant
    (d) computer operator
    (e) data entry operator

88. Which of the following software could assist someone who cannot use their hands for computer input? **[IBPS RRB, 2016]**
    (a) Synthesizer
    (b) Speech Recognition
    (c) Audio Digitizer
    (d) Video Conferencing
    (e) None of these

89. UNIX Operating System is typically used for _______ **[IBPS RRB, 2016]**
    (a) Laptop (b) Web servers
    (c) Tablet (d) PC
    (e) None of these

ANSWER KEY

No.	Ans	No.	Ans	No.	Ans	No.	Ans	No.	Ans	No.	Ans	No.	Ans	No.	Ans
1.	(a)	12.	(b)	23	(b)	34	(e)	45.	(d)	56	(c)	67.	(d)	78.	(b)
2.	(a)	13.	(a)	24.	(c)	35.	(d)	46.	(b)	57.	(e)	68.	(a)	79.	(d)
3.	(b)	14.	(a)	25	(a)	36.	(e)	47.	(d)	58.	(a)	69.	(e)	80.	(d)
4.	(d)	15.	(d)	26	(c)	37.	(d)	48.	(c)	59.	(a)	70.	(e)	81.	(a)
5.	(a)	16.	(a)	27.	(d)	38.	(b)	49	(a)	60.	(d)	71.	(c)	82.	(d)
6.	(b)	17	(c)	28.	(c)	39.	(b)	50	(e)	61.	(e)	72.	(d)	83.	(b)
7.	(a)	18.	(a)	29.	(e)	40.	(a)	51.	(d)	62.	(d)	73.	(d)	84.	(b)
8.	(c)	19.	(e)	30.	(b)	41.	(a)	52	(c)	63.	(d)	74.	(b)	85.	(b)
9	(a)	20	(d)	31.	(b)	42.	(a)	53	(a)	64.	(b)	75.	(d)	86.	(b)
10.	(b)	21.	(d)	32.	(e)	43.	(e)	54.	(d)	65.	(a)	76.	(b)	87.	(c)
11.	(d)	22	(c)	33.	(a)	44.	(a)	55.	(c)	66.	(b)	77.	(d)	88.	(b)
														89.	(b)

Practice Exercise

1. Modern Computers represent characters and numbers internally using one of the following number systems __________.
   - (a) Penta
   - (b) Octal
   - (c) Hexa
   - (d) Septa
   - (e) Binary

2. Which of the following is NOT a computer programing language?
   - (a) C
   - (b) C++
   - (c) Java
   - (d) COBOL
   - (e) Microsoft

3. To prepare a presentation/slide show which application is commonly used?
   - (a) Photoshop
   - (b) Power Point
   - (c) Outlook Express
   - (d) Internet Explorer
   - (e) All of these

4. Which of the following is NOT a famous operating system?
   - (a) Windows Vista
   - (b) Mac OS X
   - (c) Linux
   - (d) Sun OS
   - (e) Virtual Box

5. What kind of software would you most likely use to keep track of a billing account?
   - (a) Word processing
   - (b) Electronic publishing
   - (c) Spreadsheet
   - (d) Web authoring
   - (e) None of these

6. Special effect used to introduce slides in a presentation are called __________.
   - (a) Effects
   - (b) Custom animation
   - (c) Transition
   - (d) Animation
   - (e) Preset animation

7. A compiler translates higher-level programs into a machine language program, which is called-
   - (a) source code
   - (b) object code
   - (c) compiled code
   - (d) beta code
   - (e) None of these

8. The two major categories of software include
   - (a) operating system and utility
   - (b) Personal productivity and system
   - (c) system and application
   - (d) system and utility
   - (e) None of these

9. A program that works like a calculator for keeping track of money and making budgets __________.
   - (a) calculator
   - (b) scholastic
   - (c) keyboard
   - (d) spreadsheet
   - (e) None of these

10. To take information from one source and bring it to your computer is referred to as __________.
    - (a) upload
    - (b) download
    - (c) transfer
    - (d) de-link
    - (e) None of these

11. Which is the best definition of a software package?
    - (a) An add-on for your computer such as additional memory
    - (b) A set of computer programs used for a certain function such as word processing
    - (c) A protection you can buy for a computer
    - (d) The box, manual and license agreement that accompany commercial software
    - (e) None of these

12. __________ is the process of finding errors in software code.
    - (a) Debugging
    - (b) Compiling
    - (c) Interpreting
    - (d) Testing
    - (e) None of these

13. Which of the following is not a common feature of software applications?
    - (a) Menus
    - (b) Windows
    - (c) Help
    - (d) Search
    - (e) None of these

14. A____________ contains specific rules and words that express the logical steps of an algorithm.
    (a) programming language
    (b) programming structure
    (c) syntax
    (d) logic chart
    (e) None of these
15. For seeing the output, you use
    (a) Monitor (b) Keyboard
    (c) Mouse (d) Scanner
    (e) None of these
16. The software tools that enable a user to interact with a computer for specific purposes are known as -
    (a) Hardware
    (b) Networked Software
    (c) Shareware
    (d) Applications
    (e) None of these
17. A____________ shares hardware, software, and data among authorized users.
    (a) network (b) protocol
    (c) hyperlink (d) transmitter
    (e) None of these
18. Computer programs are written in a high-level programming language; however, the human-readable version of a program is called -
    (a) cache (b) instruction set
    (c) source code (d) word size
    (e) None of these
19. Software for organizing storage and retrieval of information is a(an) -
    (a) operating system (b) database
    (c) database program (d) data warehouse
    (e) None of these
20. While running DOS on a PC, which command would be used to duplicate the entire diskette?
    (a) COPY (b) DISKCOPY
    (c) CHKDSK (d) TYPE
    (e) None of these
21. Data representation is based on the____________ number system, which uses two numbers to represent all data.
    (a) binary (b) biometric
    (c) bicentennial (d) byte
    (e) None of these
22. ____________ processing is used when a large mail-order company accumulates orders and processes them together in one large set.
    (a) Batch (b) Online
    (c) Real-time (d) Group
    (e) None of these
23. The____________ primarily take(s) of the behind-the-scenes details and manage(s) the hardware.
    (a) operating system
    (b) application software
    (c) peripheral devices
    (d) hard disk
    (e) None of these
24. Documents converted to ____________ can be published to the Web.
    (a) a doc file (b) http
    (c) machine language (d) HTML
    (e) None of these
25. Only____________ program(s) become(s) active even though we can open many programs at a time.
    (a) four (b) three
    (c) two (d) one
    (e) None of these
26. All of the followings are included in typical computer programming language which are in use currently Except
    (a) C++
    (b) Java
    (c) Visual Basic NET
    (d) Machine language
    (e) None of these
27. The ability of an OS to run more than one application at a time is called_________.
    (a) multitasking
    (b) object-oriented programming
    (c) multi-user computing
    (d) time-sharing
    (e) None of these
28. ____________ is the process of carrying out commands.
    (a) Fetching (b) Storing
    (c) Decoding (d) Executing
    (e) None of these

29. ___________ is a set of computer program that runs or controls computer hardware and acts as an interface with application programs and users.
    (a) Object code
    (b) A compiler
    (c) An operating system
    (d) The CPU
    (e) None of these

30. Errors in a computer program are referred to as ___________.
    (a) bugs   (b) mistakes
    (c) item overlooked   (d) blunders
    (e) None of these

31. A compiler is used to translate a program written in ___________.
    (a) a low level language
    (b) a high level language
    (c) assembly language
    (d) machine language
    (e) None of these

32. Computer programs are also known as ___________.
    (a) operating systems (b) documents
    (c) peripherals   (d) applications
    (e) None of these

33. Information that comes from an external source and is fed into computer software is called ___________.
    (a) Input   (b) Output
    (c) Throughput (d) Reports
    (e) None of these

34. A repair for a known software bug, usually available at no charge on the internet, is called a(n) ___________.
    (a) version   (b) patch
    (c) tutorial (d) FAQ
    (e) None of these

35. The operating system is the most common type of ___________ software.
    (a) Communication (b) Application
    (c) System   (d) Word-processing
    (e) None of these

36. Correcting errors in a program is referred to as ___________.
    (a) debugging (b) bugging
    (c) rectifying (d) modifying
    (e) None of these

37. An assembler is used to translate a program written in ___________.
    (a) a low level language
    (b) machine language
    (c) a high level language
    (d) assembly language
    (e) None of these

38. The capability of the operating system to enable two or more than two programs to execute simultaneously in a single computer system by using a single processor is ___________.
    (a) Multiprocessing   (b) Multitasking
    (c) Multiprogramming   (d) Multiexecution
    (e) None of these

39. Instructions that tell the computer what to do. Another name for software.
    (a) programs (b) CPU
    (c) options   (d) folder
    (e) None of these

40. Several programs run at same time and storage is shared especially in
    (a) microcomputers
    (b) mainframe computers
    (c) enquiry computers
    (d) dump computers

41. Programs designed specifically to address general purpose applications special purpose applications are called –
    (a) operating system
    (b) system software
    (c) application software
    (d) management information systems
    (e) None of these

42. Types of software programs usually includes
    (a) application programs
    (b) replicate programs
    (c) mathematical operations
    (d) both a and b

43. Programs or a set of electronic instructions that tell a computer what to do ___________.
    (a) Menu   (b) Monitor
    (c) Hardware (d) Software
    (e) None of these

44. The ability of an OS to run more than one application at a time is called –
   (a) multitasking
   (b) object-oriented programming
   (c) multi user computing
   (d) time-sharing
   (e) None of these

45. Coded entries which are used to gain access to a computer system are called its –
   (a) Entry codes
   (b) Passwords
   (c) security commands
   (d) code words
   (e) None of these

46. What is the name for the process that is used to convert a series of instructions, or program, written in a high-level language into instructions (or a program) that can be run on a computer?
   (a) Assembling
   (b) Compiling
   (c) Translating
   (d) Uploading
   (e) None of these

47. Set of programs with full set of documentation is considered as
   (a) database packages
   (b) file package
   (c) software
   (d) software packages

48. The software tools that enable a user to interact with a computer for specific purposes are known as ___________.
   (a) Hardware
   (b) Networked Software
   (c) Shareware
   (d) Applications
   (e) None of these

49. Programs used to control system performance are classified as
   (a) experimental programs
   (b) system programs
   (c) specialized program
   (d) organized programs

50. Software for organizing storage and retrieval of information is a(n) ___________.
   (a) operating system
   (b) database
   (c) database program
   (d) data warehouse
   (e) None of these

51. A set of step-by-step procedures for accomplishing a task is known as a(n) ___________.
   (a) algorithm
   (b) hardware program
   (c) software bug
   (d) firmware program
   (e) None of these

52. Compilers and translators are one form of ___________.
   (a) ROM
   (b) RAM
   (c) hard disk
   (d) software
   (e) None of these

53. Data representation is based on the ________ number system, which uses two numbers to represent all data
   (a) binary
   (b) biometric
   (c) bicentennial
   (d) byte
   (e) None of these

54. The ___________ primary take(s) care of the behind-the-scenes details and manage(s) the hardware.
   (a) operating system
   (b) application software
   (c) peripheral devices
   (d) hard disk
   (e) None of these

55. When a file contains instructions that can be carried out by the computer, it is often called a(n) ___________ pile.
   (a) data
   (b) information
   (c) executable
   (d) application
   (e) None of these

56. A software which you can use to create a budget is called
   (a) Word processing software
   (b) Graphics software
   (c) Utility software
   (d) Spreadsheet software
   (e) None of these

57. Which device uses a hand-held operating system?
   (a) PDA
   (b) A personal computer
   (c) A laptop
   (d) A mainframe
   (e) None of these

58. What is Software?
   (a) A type of computer code
   (b) A computer language
   (c) A set of instructions for your computer
   (d) A cover for the computer
   (e) None of these

59. Computers process binary numbers, which are composed of __________.
    (a) 1s and 2s   (b) 2s and 4s
    (c) 1s and 10s   (d) 2s and 3s
    (e) 0s and 1s

60. System programs examples includes
    (a) operating system of computer
    (b) trace program
    (c) compiler
    (d) all of above

61. __________ is the process of finding errors in software code.
    (a) Hacking   (b) Compiling
    (c) Testing   (d) Running
    (e) Debugging

62. Most application softwares today come with an interface called a(n) __________.
    (a) graphical user interface
    (b) character user interface
    (c) icon user interface
    (d) button user interface
    (e) voice instruction system

63. __________ are bundles of related software packages that are sold together.
    (a) Personal productivity tools
    (b) Word and PowerPoint
    (c) Screen savers
    (d) Excel and WordPerfect
    (e) Software suites

64. The __________ manual tells you how to use a software program.
    (a) documentation   (b) programming
    (c) technical   (d) user
    (e) dictionary

65. The __________ is an information system that must be reliable and capable of handling the expected workload.
    (a) hardware   (b) software
    (c) data input   (d) people
    (e) mobiles

66. Specialised programs that allow particular input or output devices to communicate with the rest of the computer system are called __________.
    (a) operating systems
    (b) utilities
    (c) device drivers
    (d) language translators
    (e) connectors

67. The primary purpose of a software is to turn data into __________.
    (a) Web sites   (b) graphs
    (c) programs   (d) objects
    (e) information

68. You must instruct the __________ to start the application software.
    (a) utility program   (b) memory
    (c) operating system   (d) processor
    (e) user

69. Professional designers can create sophisticated documents that contain text, graphics, and many colours, using __________ software.
    (a) computer aided design (CAD)
    (b) illustration
    (c) image editing
    (d) desktop publishing (DTP)
    (e) PowerPoint

70. Oracle is an example of __________ application software.
    (a) database
    (b) word processing
    (c) project management
    (d) presentation graphics
    (e) desktop

71. A collection of programmes which determines and controls how your computer system works and process information is called
    (a) Interpretor   (b) Computer
    (c) Office   (d) Compiler
    (e) Operating system

72. An error in a computer program is called
    (a) Crash   (b) Power failure
    (c) Bug   (d) Virus
    (e) Bugger

73. The real business and competitive value of information technology lies in
    (a) The software applications that are used by many companies
    (b) The capabilities of the software and value of the information a business acquires and used
    (c) The infrastructure of hardware, networks, and other IT facilities that are commonly used by many companies
    (d) The capabilities of the hardware and the speed at which it processes information
    (e) None of these

74. Companies use which of the following vendors to provide access to software and services rather than purchasing the applications and maintaining the applications themselves?
    (a) Open source vendors
    (b) Alliances
    (c) Application service providers
    (d) All of the above
    (e) None of these

75. In the information systems concept, the output function involves
    (a) Capturing and assembling elements that enter the system to be processed
    (b) Transformation processes that convert input into output
    (c) Transferring elements that have been produced by a transformation process to their ultimate destination
    (d) Monitoring and evaluating feedback to determine whether a system is moving toward the achievement of its goal
    (e) None of these

76. Which of the following is a popular programming language for developing multimedia web pages, websites, and web-based applications?
    (a) COBOL   (b) Java
    (c) BASIC   (d) Assembler
    (e) None of these

77. Compiling creates a(n) ___________
    (a) program specification
    (b) algorithm
    (c) executable program
    (d) subroutine
    (e) None of these

78. The ___________ manual tells you how to use a software program.
    (a) documentation   (b) programming
    (c) technical   (d) user
    (e) None of these

79. The ___________ tells the computer how to use its components.
    (a) utility
    (b) network
    (c) operating system
    (d) application program
    (e) None of these

80. The process of writing out computer instructions is known as

(a) assembling   (b) compiling
(c) executing   (d) coding
(e) None of these

81. Multiprogramming systems:
    (a) are easier to develop than single programming systems.
    (b) execute each job faster.
    (c) execute more jobs in the same time period.
    (d) use only one large mainframe computer.
    (e) None of these

82. Set of software authorized to specific users is considered as
    (a) software library   (b) program library
    (c) directory library   (d) library package

83. ___________ is a set of keywords, symbols, and a system of rules for constructing statements by which humans can communicate the instructions to be executed by a computer.
    (a) A computer program
    (b) A programming language
    (c) An assembler
    (d) Syntax
    (e) None of these

84. A program that converts a high-level language source file into a machine-language file is called as
    (a) translator   (b) assembler
    (c) compiler   (d) linker
    (e) None of the above

85. Housing all hardware, software, storage, and processing in one site location is called ______.
    (a) time-sharing
    (b) a distributed system
    (c) centralized processing
    (d) a host computer
    (e) None of the above

86. If program can cope data errors, program is called
    (a) robust   (b) reliable
    (c) unreliable   (d) stable functioning

87. The operating system determines the manner in which all of the following occur except
    (a) user creating of a document
    (b) user interaction with the processor
    (c) printer output
    (d) data displayed on the monitor
    (e) None of these

88. What are the two examples of freeware?
    (a) WinZip and Linux
    (b) Shareware and file sharing
    (c) Microsoft Word and the Google toolbar
    (d) Instant messaging and the Google toolbar
    (e) Microsoft Power Point and Microsoft Excel

89. Vendor-created program modifications are called
    (a) patches   (b) antiviruses
    (c) holes   (d) fixes
    (e) overlaps

90. A sales clerk at a checkout counter scanning a tag on an item rather than keying it into the system, is using __________.
    (a) input automation
    (b) item data automation
    (c) scanning automation
    (d) source data automation
    (e) None of these

91. Which of the following is not a type of computer software which can be bought?
    (a) Off-the-shelf
    (b) Tailor-made
    (c) Custom-developed
    (d) Off-the-shelf with alterations
    (e) All of these can be purchased

92. Computer software can be defined as __________.
    (a) the computer and its associated equipment.
    (b) the instructions that tell the computer what to do.
    (c) computer components that act to accomplish a goal.
    (d) an interface between the computer and the network
    (e) the interaction between the computer and its database.

93. The operating system called UNIX is typically used for
    (a) Desktop computers (b) Laptop computers
    (c) Super computers (d) Web servers
    (e) All of these

94. Program which exactly perform operations that manual says is classified as
    (a) unreliable   (b) stable functioning
    (c) robust   (d) reliable

95. Executing more than one program concurrently by one user on one computer is known as
    (a) multi-programming (b) multi-processing
    (c) time sharing   (d) multi-tasking
    (e) multi-action

96. Which of the following controls the manner of interaction between the user and the operating system?
    (a) Language translator
    (b) Platform
    (c) User interface
    (d) Icon
    (e) None of these

97. Collecting personal information and effectively posing as another individual is known as
    (a) spooling   (b) spoofing
    (c) hacking   (d) identity theft
    (e) None of these

98. A(n) __________ contains text as well as information about the text.
    (a) annotated language (b) browser language
    (c) markup language (d) protocol language
    (e) machine language

99. An operating system that can do multitasking means that
    (a) the operating system can divide up work between several CPUs.
    (b) multiple people can use the computer concurrently.
    (c) several programs can be operated concurrently.
    (d) All of these
    (e) None of these

100. Compilers and translators are one form of –
    (a) ROM   (b) RAM
    (c) hard disk   (d) software
    (e) None of these

101. The capability of the operating system to enable two or more than two programs to execute simultaneously in a single computer system by using a single processor is __________.
 (a) Multiprocessing   (b) Multitasking
 (c) Multiprogramming (d) Multiexecution
 (e) None of these

102. The simultaneous execution of two or more instructions is called
 (a) sequential access
 (b) reduced instruction set computing
 (c) multiprocessing
 (d) disk mirroring
 (e) None of these

103. Which of the following is an example of a binary number?
 (a) 6AH1   (b) 100101
 (c) 005   (d) ABCD
 (e) 23456

104. Which of the following is not true about computer files?
 (a) They are collections of data saved to a storage medium.
 (b) Every file has a filename.
 (c) A file extension is established by the user to indicate the date it was created
 (d) Usually files contains data.
 (e) None of these

105. How many kilobytes make a megabyte?
 (a) 128   (b) 1024
 (c) 256   (d) 512
 (e) 64

106. In a computer, how many bits does a nibble signify?
 (a) 4   (b) 8
 (c) 16   (d) 32
 (e) 64

107. Which of the following is not true about a compiler?
 (a) Translate instruction of a high level language into machine language
 (b) Translates entire source program into machine language program
 (c) It is involved in program's execution
 (d) Is a translating program
 (e) Is useful to run program

108. When machine instructions are being executed by a computer, the instruction phase followed by the execution phase is referred to as __________.
 (a) program cycle
 (b) machine instruction
 (c) execution cycle
 (d) task cycle
 (e) machine cycle

109. Which language is directly understood by the computer without translation program?
 (a) BASIC language
 (b) Assembly language
 (c) High level language
 (d) C language
 (e) Machine language

110. The translator program used in assembly language is called __________.
 (a) Compiler   (b) Assembler
 (c) Intepreter   (d) Translator
 (e) Operating System

111. A set of instructions telling the computer what to do is called __________.
 (a) mentor   (b) instructor
 (c) compiler   (d) program
 (e) None of these

112. Which of the following is not true about computer files?
 (a) They are a collection of data saved in a storage medium.
 (b) Every file has a filename.
 (c) A file extension is established by the user to indicate the computer on which it was created.
 (d) All files contain data.
 (e) None of these

113. Which of the following is not a software?
 (a) Excel   (b) Printer-Driver
 (c) Operating System (d) Powerpoint
 (e) Mouse

114. ASCII is a coding system that provides
  (a) 256 different characters
  (b) 512 different characters
  (c) 1024 different characters
  (d) 128 different characters
  (e) 1000 different characters

115. Which part of the computer is directly invoked in executing the instructions of the computer program?
  (a) The scanner
  (b) The main storage
  (c) The secondary storage
  (d) The printer
  (e) The processor

116. Which of the following is not a binary number?
  (a) 001 (b) 101
  (c) 202 (d) 110
  (e) 011

117. Large transaction processing systems in automated organisations use
  (a) Online processing
  (b) Batch Processing
  (c) Once-a-day Processing
  (d) End-of-day processing
  (e) Once-a-week processing

118. Which of the following is true for the octal system?
  (a) It needs less digits to represent a number than in the binary system.
  (b) It needs more digits to represent a number than in the binary system.
  (c) It needs the same number of digits to represent a number as in the binary system
  (d) It needs the same number of digits to represent a number as in the decimal system.
  (e) None of these

119. The language used in a computer that is similar to the language of humans and is easy to understand is referred to as
  (a) Source Code
  (b) Machine Language
  (c) High Level Language
  (d) Object Code
  (e) Assembly language

ANSWER KEY

1.	(e)	16.	(d)	31.	(b)	46.	(b)	61.	(e)	76.	(b)	91.	(d)	106.	(a)
2.	(e)	17.	(a)	32.	(d)	47.	(d)	62.	(a)	77.	(c)	92.	(b)	107.	(c)
3.	(b)	18.	(c)	33.	(a)	48.	(d)	63.	(e)	78.	(d)	93.	(e)	108.	(e)
4.	(e)	19.	(d)	34.	(b)	49.	(b)	64.	(a)	79.	(c)	94.	(d)	109.	(e)
5.	(c)	20.	(b)	35.	(c)	50.	(c)	65.	(b)	80.	(d)	95.	(d)	110.	(b)
6.	(c)	21.	(a)	36.	(a)	51.	(a)	66.	(a)	81.	(c)	96.	(c)	111.	(d)
7.	(a)	22.	(a)	37.	(d)	52.	(d)	67.	(e)	82.	(b)	97.	(d)	112.	(c)
8.	(c)	23.	(a)	38.	(c)	53.	(a)	68.	(c)	83.	(a)	98.	(c)	113.	(e)
9.	(d)	24.	(d)	39.	(a)	54.	(a)	69.	(a)	84.	(c)	99.	(c)	114.	(d)
10.	(b)	25.	(b)	40.	(b)	55.	(c)	70.	(a)	85.	(c)	100.	(d)	115.	(e)
11.	(b)	26.	(d)	41.	(c)	56.	(d)	71.	(e)	86.	(a)	101.	(c)	116.	(c)
12.	(d)	27.	(a)	42.	(d)	57.	(a)	72.	(c)	87.	(b)	102.	(c)	117.	(b)
13.	(b)	28.	(d)	43.	(d)	58.	(e)	73.	(b)	88.	(d)	103.	(b)	118.	(b)
14.	(a)	29.	(c)	44.	(a)	59.	(e)	74.	(c)	89.	(a)	104.	(c)	119.	(c)
15.	(a)	30.	(a)	45.	(b)	60.	(d)	75.	(a)	90.	(c)	105.	(b)		

Computer Hardware

Computer hardware is the collection of physical parts of a computer system. This includes the computer case, monitor, keyboard, and mouse. It also includes all the parts inside the computer case, such as the hard disk drive, motherboard, video card, and many others. Computer hardware is what you can physically touch.

All computers have a common structure. These components can be very different in terms of expense, speed and quality, but every computer has them to one degree or another.

The main components are as follows :

- **Form Factor** - This is the physical configuration of the computer: desktop, laptop, tablet or netbook
- **The Processor** - This is the 'brain' of the computer
- **Data Storage** - This is where your data are stored, as well as all the programmes and other files that your computer needs to run.
- **The Operating System** - The OS is the software that runs the computer on the lowest level - Windows, Macintosh or Linux are the most popular.
- **Monitor** - This is the viewing screen that you use to operate the computer. It is a very important part of the digital photography computer.

HARDWARE COMPONENTS OF COMPUTER

1. **The Processor :** The Processor (CPU) is the "brain" of your computer, the thing that carries out the tasks you give it. The speed that the computer can run an operation is largely determined by how fast the processor can make calculations. The CPU (Central Processing Unit), a complete computation engine that is fabricated on a single chip, is the computer's brain. It is sometimes referred to as the central processor, microprocessor, or just processor.

   Two typical components of a CPU are:

   (1) The Arithmetic Logic Unit (ALU), which performs arithmetic and logical operations.

   (2) The Control Unit, which extracts instructions from memory and decodes and executes them, calling on the ALU when necessary.

   There are three parts to determining how fast a processor can do its work: clock speed, number of cores, and chip generation.

- **Clock Speed :** Every processor has a speed rating, currently measured in Gigahertz or GHz. The higher the number, the faster it runs. In theory, a processor that is 2GHz will be twice as fast as a 1 GHz .
- **Number of Cores :** A core refers to part of the processor that actually does the calculations. One way that computer chip makers have increased the speed is by adding additional cores. A dual core processor can run operations twice as fast as a single core processor of the same design and clock speed. Multiple cores can make some computing tasks go quickly, and for others, there is no speed increase at all. In many cases, both clock speed and number of cores is less important than the chip generation.

- **Chip Generation :** Every few years, the companies that make processor chips will redesign the entire chip architecture to make them faster. Sometimes the clock speed of the newer chips will be slower, even as the real-world speed of the chip increases.

  Intel's Core 2 Duo chips that run at 3 GHz, for instance, will run Photoshop slower than an i7 chip running at 2 GHz, because the i7 is a newer generation.

There are 2 main chip manufacturers, **Intel** and **AMD**.

As of 2013,the current lineup of Core processors includes the latest Intel Core i7, Intel Core i5, and Intel Core i3, and the older Intel Core 2 Solo, Intel Core 2 Duo, Intel Core 2 Quad, and Intel Core 2 Extreme lines.

2. **The Motherboard :** The motherboard connects all the other components to one another, and is the physical base upon which everything build. It contains a lot of machine's core features, like the number of USB ports, the number of expansion cards can put in (such as video, sound, and Wi-Fi), and also partially determines how big a computer will be. Which motherboard can be pick will depend on whether want to build a low, medium, or high performance machine and how advanced of a user you are.

3. **The Case :** The case holds all of your computer's parts together. For the most part, a case is less about features that affect how computer runs and more about features that affect you and your home—that is, how quiet it is, how large it is, and of course, how it looks in office/home.

4. **The RAM :** RAM, or Random Access Memory (or "Memory" for short), is like your computer's short-term memory. It stores data what a computer needs quick access to to help your programs run faster, and help to run more programs at one time.

In general, you want to have as much RAM in your computer as you can afford. If you are running a 32 bit operating system, then each program can make use 2GB to 3 GB of RAM. If you have a 64bit OS, then each program can use as much RAM as you have available.

5. **The Graphics Card :** The Graphics card, or GPU, is a processor specifically designed to handle graphics. It's what you hook your monitor up to, and it's what draws your desktop and your windows on the screen. Some motherboards come with a GPU already integrated, which is enough to manage your desktop, but not enough for watching high definition video or playing 3D games. For those, you'll need a dedicated graphics card, since it can do the legwork needed to draw those complex images.

6. **The Hard Drive(s) :** Hard drive store all of data, ranging from operating system to documents, music, and movies. If the RAM is considered as computer's short-term memory, then hard drive is the long-term memory. It stores all the things want to keep around for a while. The kind of hard drive choose will be determined mainly by how much data need to store.

7. **The Optical Drive :** An optical drive, more commonly known as a CD or DVD drive, is what required to read CDs, DVDs, and even Blu-Ray discs.

8. **The Power Supply :** The power supply directs electricity to the other components in machine. Generally, if you have a high performance computer with a fast processor, a graphics card, and a few hard drives, you'll need a higher wattage power supply than you would if you were building a low-end PC.

9. **Sound Card :** A sound card is an electronic circuit board that is mounted inside the computer to control sound output to speakers or headphones, to record sound input from a microphone connected to the computer, and to manipulate sound stored on a disk. Sound cards are essential for multimedia applications and have become common on modern personal computers.

10. **Ports :** A port is an interface on a computer to which you can connect a device. Personal computers have various types of ports. Internally, there are several ports for connecting disk drives, monitors, and keyboards. Externally, personal computers have ports for connecting modems, printers, mice, and other peripheral devices.

There are three common types of external ports that usually come with a computer:

(i) Parallel ports (for most printers) : A parallel part is an interface for connecting eight or more data wires. The data flows through the eight wires simultaneously. They can transmit eight bits of data in parallel. As a result, parallel ports provide high speed data transmission. Parallel port is used to connect printer to computer.

(ii) Serial ports (for most modems and some mouse) : A serial port transmits one bit of data through a single wire. Since, data is transmitted serially as single bits. Serial ports provide slow speed data transmission. Serial port is used to connect external modems, plotters, barcode, reader etc.

(iii) USB (Universal Serial Bus) ports (for about every peripheral made in a USB version) : The USB (Universal Serial Bus) provides a single, standardized, easy-to-use way to connect up to 127 devices to a computer. The USB connectors let you attach everything from mice to printers to your computer more quickly and easily than the other two. The operating system supports USB as well, so the installation of the device drives is quick and easy, too.

A *"bus"* is a set of conductors that carry signals between different parts of a computer.

Firewire – It is used to connect audio and video multimedia devices like video camera it has data transfer rate of upto 400 Mb/s.

11. Input Output Peripherals : A computer peripheral is any external device that provides input and output for the computer. For example, a keyboard and mouse are input peripherals, while a monitor and printer are output peripherals. Computer peripherals, or peripheral devices, are sometimes called "I/O devices" because they provide input and output for the computer. Some peripherals, such as external hard drives, provide both input and output for the computer.

12. Expansion card : An expansion card is an electronic card/board that is used to add extra functionality to a computer. It is inserted into an expansion slot on the motherboard of a computer. Expansion cards contain edge connectors that are used to create an electronic link between motherboard and card, thus enabling these two to communicate.

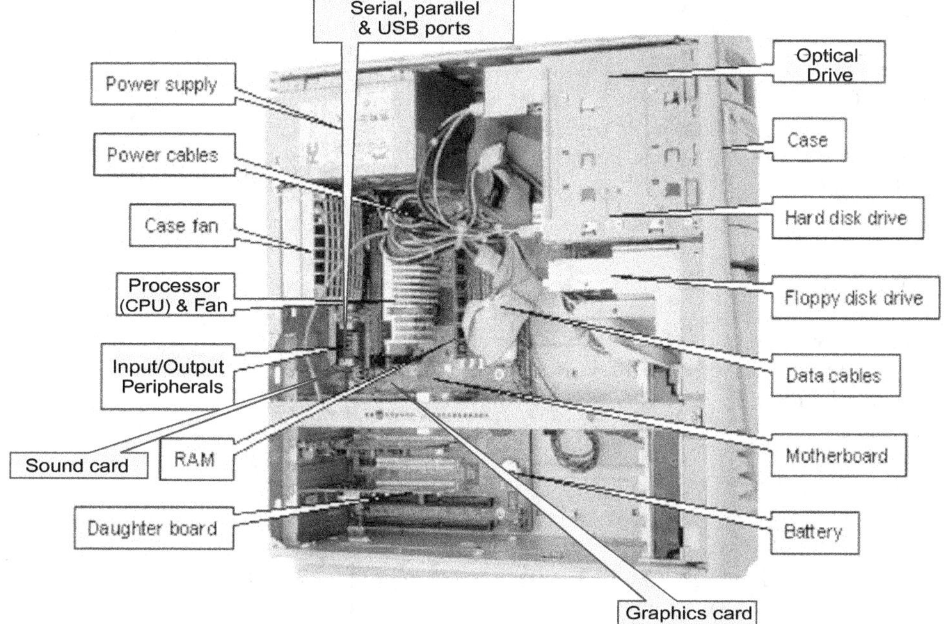

Hardware Component of Computer

Past Exercise

1. Restarting a computer that is already on is referred to as **[SBI Clerk, 2009]**
   (a) shut down   (b) cold booting
   (c) warm booting   (d) logging off
   (e) None of these

2. Hardware includes
   [SBI Clerk, 2009 ; IBPS PO, 2015]
   (a) all devices used to input data into a computer
   (b) sets of instructions that a computer runs or executes
   (c) the computer and all the devices connected to it that are used to input and output data
   (d) all devices involved processing information including the central processing unit, memory, and storage
   (e) None of these

3. Which part of the computer helps to store information ?   **[SBI Clerk, 2009]**
   (a) Disk drive   (b) keyboard
   (c) Monitor   (d) Printer
   (e) None of these

4. Which is the part of a computer that one can touch and feel?   **[SBI Clerk, 2009]**
   (a) Hardware   (b) Software
   (c) Programs   (d) Output
   (e) None of these

5. A complete electronic circuit with transistors and other electronic components on a small silicon chip is called a (n)–   **[SBI Clerk, 2009]**
   (a) workstation
   (b) CPU
   (c) magnetic disk
   (d) integrated circuit
   (e) None of these

6. ________ is the process of dividing the disk into tracks and sectors.   **[IBPS PO, 2011]**
   (a) Tracking   (b) Formatting
   (c) Crashing   (d) Allotting
   (e) None of these

7. Which ports connect special types of music instruments to sound cards?
   [IBPS PO, 2011; IBPS Clerk, 2014]
   (a) BUS   (b) CPU
   (c) USB   (d) MIDI
   (e) MINI

8. Which of the following is contained on chips connected to the system board and is a holding area for data instructions and information? (processed data waiting to be output to secondary storage)   **[SBI PO, 2011]**
   (a) program   (b) mouse
   (c) Internet   (d) memory
   (e) modem

9. Which of the following is hardware and not software ?   **[IBPS Clerk, 2011]**
   (a) Excel   (b) Printer driver
   (c) Operating System (d) Power Point
   (e) CPU

10. Where is the disk put in a computer?
    [SBI Clerk, 2011]
    (a) in the modem   (b) in the hard drive
    (c) into the CPU   (d) in the disk drive
    (e) None of these

11. Different components on the motherboard of a PC unit are linked together by sets of parallel electrical conducting lines. What are these lines called ?   **[IBPS PO, 2012]**
    (a) Conductors   (b) Buses
    (c) Connectors   (d) Consecutives
    (e) None of these

12. A USB communication device that supports data encryption for secure wireless communication for notebook users is called a ____________.
    [IBPS PO, 2012]
    (a) USB wireless network adapter
    (b) wireless switch
    (c) wireless hub
    (d) router
    (e) None of these

13. A device for changing the connection on a connector to a different configuration is-
    [IBPS PO, 2012]
    (a) a converter   (b) a component
    (c) an attachment   (d) an adapter
    (e) Voltmeter

14. The disks stores information in
    [IBPS Clerk, 2012]
    (a) Tables
    (b) Rows and columns
    (c) Blocks
    (d) Tracks and sectors
    (e) All of these

15. Tangible, physical computer equipment that can be seen and touched is called _________
    [SBI Clerk, 2012]
    (a) hardware   (b) software
    (c) storage   (d) input/output
    (e) None of these
16. What resides on the motherboard and connects the CPU to other components on the motherboard ?   **[SBI Clerk, 2012]**
    (a) Input Unit   (b) System Bus
    (c) ALU   (d) Primary Memory
    (e) None of these
17. The cost of a given amount of computing power has _________ dramatically with the progress of computer technology.   **[SBI Clerk, 2012]**
    (a) stayed the same
    (b) changed proportionally with the economy
    (c) increased
    (d) fluctuated
    (e) decreased
18. The indentations on CDs and DVDs are called:
    [SSC, CHSL, 2012]
    (a) pits   (b) clusters
    (c) tracks   (d) lands
19. Which of the following refers to too much electricity and may cause a voltage surge?
    [SBI PO, 2013]
    (a) Anomaly   (b) Shock
    (c) Spike   (d) Virus
    (e) Splash
20. Which of the following is an impact printe ?
    [SSC, CGL, 2013]
    (a) Daisy wheel printer
    (b) Ink jet printer
    (c) Bubble jet printer
    (d) Laser printer

21. A_________ is a non-impact printer that can produce very high-quality letter-perfect printing.   **[SBI Clerk, 2015]**
    (a) daisy wheel printer
    (b) laser printer
    (c) dot-matrix printer
    (d) thermal printer
    (e) drum printer
22. DVD is an example of   **[SBI Clerk, 2015]**
    (a) Hard disk
    (b) optical disk
    (c) Output device
    (d) Solid-state storage devices
    (e) None of these
23. BSoDs can be caused by poorly written device drivers or malfunctioning hardware, such as faulty memory, power supply issues, overheating of components, or hardware running beyond its specification limits. Which color screen is displayed when encountered a BSOD Error?
    [IBPS PO Mains, 2016]
    (a) Red   (b) Grey
    (c) Black   (d) Blue
    (e) Green
24. Hard drive is used to store:
    [IBPS Clerk Mains, 2016]
    (a) Volatile data   (b) Non volatile data
    (c) permanent data   (d) Temporary data
    (e) Intermediate data
25. Which of the following is properties of USB?
    [IBPS Clerk Mains, 2016]
    (a) Platform independent
    (b) Platform dependent
    (c) Source dependent
    (d) Software dependent
    (e) Software independent

ANSWER KEY

1.	(d)	8.	(d)	15.	(a)	22.	(b)
2.	(c)	9.	(e)	16.	(b)	23.	(d)
3.	(a)	10.	(d)	17.	(e)	24.	(c)
4.	(a)	11.	(b)	18.	(a)	25.	(a)
5.	(d)	12.	(a)	19.	(c)		
6.	(b)	13.	(d)	20.	(a)		
7.	(d)	14.	(d)	21.	(b)		

Practice Exercise

1. The __________ directory is mandatory for every disk.
   - (a) Root
   - (b) Base
   - (c) Sub
   - (d) Case
   - (e) None of these

2. Which of the following is NOT a hardware of a computer?
   - (a) Monitor
   - (b) Key Board
   - (c) Windows
   - (d) Central Processing Unit
   - (e) None of these

3. Permanent instructions that the computer uses when it is turned on and that cannot be changed by other instructions are contained in __________.
   - (a) ROM
   - (b) RAM
   - (c) ALU
   - (d) REM
   - (e) None of these

4. Which is not an item of hardware?
   - (a) An MP3 file
   - (b) A keyboard
   - (c) A disk drive
   - (d) A monitor
   - (e) None of these

5. Another word for the CPU is __________
   - (a) microprocessor
   - (b) execute
   - (c) microchip
   - (d) decode
   - (e) None of these

6. Hardware devices that are not part of the main computer system and are often added later to the system are
   - (a) clip art
   - (b) highlight
   - (c) execute
   - (d) peripheral
   - (e) None of these

7. Where is the disk put to enable the computer to read it?
   - (a) Disk drive
   - (b) Memory
   - (c) CPU
   - (d) ALU
   - (e) None of these

8. Which of the following is not an example of hardware?
   - (a) Mouse
   - (b) Printer
   - (c) Monitor
   - (d) EXCEL
   - (e) None of these

9. When you save the following the data would remain intact even after turning off computer?
   - (a) RAM
   - (b) Motherboard
   - (c) Secondary and Storage Device
   - (d) Primary Storage Device
   - (e) None of these

10. A computer's hard disk is __________.
    - (a) an arithmetic and logical unit
    - (b) computer software
    - (c) operating system
    - (d) computer hardware
    - (e) None of these

11. Devices that make up a computer system that you can see or touch –
    - (a) menu
    - (b) print
    - (c) software
    - (d) hardware
    - (e) None of these

12. The term used to define all input and output devices in a computer system is –
    - (a) Monitor
    - (b) Software
    - (c) Shared resources
    - (d) Hardware
    - (e) None of these

13. Which of the following peripheral devices displays information to a user?
    - (a) Monitor
    - (b) Keyboard
    - (c) Secondary storage devices
    - (d) Secondary storage media
    - (e) None of these

14. The hardware device commonly referred to as the "brain" of the computer is the __________.
    - (a) RAM chip
    - (b) data input
    - (c) CPU
    - (d) secondary storage
    - (e) None of these

15. What provide expansion capability for a computer system?
    - (a) Sockets
    - (b) Slots
    - (c) Bytes
    - (d) Bays
    - (e) None of these

16. The clock rate of a processor is measured in
    (a) milliseconds
    (b) microhertz
    (c) megabytes or gigabytes
    (d) nanoseconds
    (e) megahertz or gigahertz
17. Which of the following devices translate data and programs that humans can understand into a form that the computer can process?
    (a) Display   (b) Input
    (c) Output   (d) Hardware
    (e) None of these
18. ___________ ports connect special types of music instruments to sound cards.
    (a) BUS   (b) CPU
    (c) USB   (d) MIDI
    (e) MINI
19. If a processor has a word size of 32 bits, compared to a processor with a word size of 16 bits, it can process ___________ at a time.
    (a) thrice as much   (b) half as much
    (c) a fourth as much (d) the same amount
    (e) twice as much
20. Which of the following is an example of connectivity?
    (a) CD   (b) Floppy disk
    (c) Power cord   (d) Data
    (e) Internet
21. Any hardware component that allows you to enter data or instructions into a computer is called a(n) ___________.
    (a) printer   (b) storage device
    (c) output device   (d) system unit
    (e) input device
22. The new ___________ integrates the function of a processor, memory and video card on a single chip
    (a) micro processor
    (b) power processor
    (c) system on a chip
    (d) multimedia processor
    (e) chip processor
23. The main system board of a computer is called the
    (a) integrated circuit (b) motherboard
    (c) processor   (d) microchip
    (e) drive board

24. Peripheral devices such as printers and monitors are considered to be
    (a) hardware   (b) software
    (c) data   (d) information
    (e) source code
25. Which of the following is usually connected to a computer with the help of a cable?
    (a) Icon   (b) Virus
    (c) Database   (d) Pixel
    (e) Peripheral devices
26. Fax machines and imaging systems are examples of
    (a) bar-code readers
    (b) imaging systems
    (c) scanning devices
    (d) pen-based systems
    (e) None of these
27. A ___________ is a device that not only provides surge protection, but also furnishes your computer with battery backup power during a power outage.
    (a) surge strip   (b) USB
    (c) UPS   (d) battery strip
    (e) None of these
28. The motherboard is the
    (a) circuit board that houses peripheral devices
    (b) same as the CPU chip
    (c) the first chip that is accessed when the computer is turned on
    (d) circuit board that contains a CPU and other chips
    (e) None of these
29. A directory within a directory is called a ___________.
    (a) Mini Directory   (b) Junior Directory
    (c) Part Directory   (d) Sub Directory
    (e) None of these
30. When installing ___________, the user must copy and usually decompress program files from a CD-ROM or other medium to the hard disk.
    (a) programming software
    (b) system hardware
    (c) application hardware
    (d) applications software
    (e) None of these

31. If a new device is attached to a computer, such as a printer or scanner, its ___________ must be installed before the device can be used.
    - (a) buffer
    - (b) driver
    - (c) pager
    - (d) server
    - (e) None of these

32. The general term "peripheral equipment" is used for ___________.
    - (a) any device that is attached to a computer system
    - (b) large-scale computer systems
    - (c) a program collection
    - (d) other office equipment not associated with a desktop computer
    - (e) None of these

33. Which is not an item of hardware?
    - (a) An MP3 file
    - (b) A keyboard
    - (c) A monitor
    - (d) A mouse
    - (e) None of the above

34. The box that contains the central electronic components of the computer is the
    - (a) motherboard
    - (b) system unit
    - (c) peripheral
    - (d) input device
    - (e) None of the above

35. A device that provides emergency power to your computer, conditions the voltage, and protects against power surges is called a ___________.
    - (a) PSU = Power Supply Unit
    - (b) USP = Universal Surge Protector
    - (c) UPPS = Universal Power Protection and Supply
    - (d) UPS = Uninterruptible Power Supply
    - (e) None of the above

36. A device that is connected to the motherboard is ___________.
    - (a) called an external device
    - (b) called an adjunct device
    - (c) called a peripheral device
    - (d) must connect using ribbon cable
    - (e) None of these

37. The CPU, also called the ___________ when talking about PCs, does the vast majority of the processing for a computer
    - (a) macroprocessor
    - (b) RAM
    - (c) memory system
    - (d) microprocessor
    - (e) None of these

38. A computer's type, processor, and operating system define its
    - (a) brand
    - (b) size
    - (c) platform
    - (d) speed
    - (e) none of these

39. A microprocessor is the brain of the computer and is also called a(n)
    - (a) microchip
    - (b) macrochip
    - (c) macroprocessor
    - (d) calculator
    - (e) software

40. Storage and memory differ with respect to which of the following characteristics?
    - (a) Price
    - (b) Reliability
    - (c) Speed
    - (e) All of these
    - (e) None of these

41. What is the process of copying software programs from secondary storage media to the hard disk called?
    - (a) Configuration
    - (b) Download
    - (c) Storage
    - (d) Upload
    - (e) Installation

42. What is the most popular hardware for multimedia creations?
    - (a) PCs
    - (b) Minicomputers
    - (c) Mainframe Computers
    - (d) WANs
    - (e) Super Computers

43. Which of the following will you require to hear music on your computer?
    - (a) Video Card
    - (b) Tape Recorder
    - (c) Mouse
    - (d) Joy Stick
    - (e) Sound Card

44. For viewing video CDs, you would use
    - (a) CD Player
    - (b) Windows Media Player
    - (c) Windows Video Player
    - (d) Windows Movie Player
    - (e) None of these

45. A CPU-chip developed by Intel for wireless laptops is called the
   (a) Celeron   (b) Pentium-M
   (c) Xen   (d) Itanium
   (e) None of these

46. What is a backup?
   (a) Restoring the information backup
   (b) An exact copy of a system's information
   (c) The ability to get a system up and running in the event of a system crash or failure
   (d) All of these
   (e) None of these

47. Which of the following is hardware and not software?
   (a) Excel   (b) Printer driver
   (c) Operating System (d) Power Point
   (e) Control Unit

48. Peripheral devices such as printers and monitors are considered to be ____________.
   (a) data   (b) software
   (c) hardware   (d) information
   (e) None of these

49. Which of the following is not an example of a hardware?
   (a) Word   (b) Printer
   (c) Monitor   (d) Mouse
   (e) Scanner

50. Which of the following is a secondary memory device?
   (a) Keyboard   (b) Disk
   (c) ALU   (d) Mouse
   (e) Printer

51. The processor is a ____________ chip plugged onto the motherboard in a computer system.
   (a) LSI   (b) VLSI
   (c) ULSI   (d) XLSI
   (e) WLSI

52. The other name of a motherboard is
   (a) Mouse   (b) Computer Board
   (c) System Device   (d) Central Board
   (e) System Board

53. Which type of storage is a hard disc?
   (a) Non-permanent   (b) Volatile
   (c) Temporary   (d) Non-volatile
   (e) None of these

54. When a computer is switched on, the booting process performs
   (a) Integrity Test
   (b) Power-On-Self-Test
   (c) Correct Functioning Test
   (d) Reliability Test
   (e) Shut-down

ANSWER KEY

1.	(a)	10.	(d)	19.	(e)	28.	(d)	37.	(d)	46.	(d)
2.	(c)	11.	(d)	20.	(e)	29.	(d)	38.	(d)	47.	(e)
3.	(a)	12.	(d)	21.	(e)	30.	(d)	39.	(a)	48.	(c)
4.	(a)	13.	(a)	22.	(c)	31.	(b)	40.	(d)	49.	(a)
5.	(a)	14.	(c)	23.	(b)	32.	(a)	41.	(e)	50.	(b)
6.	(d)	15.	(a)	24.	(a)	33.	(a)	42.	(a)	51.	(b)
7.	(a)	16.	(e)	25.	(e)	34.	(b)	43.	(e)	52.	(e)
8.	(d)	17.	(e)	26.	(b)	35.	(d)	44.	(b)	53.	(d)
9.	(c)	18.	(d)	27.	(c)	36.	(c)	45.	(b)	54.	(b)

Database Management System

Chapter 6

Database Management Systems (DBMS) are specially designed software which is used to create and maintain a database. It acts as an interface between users and a database or multiple databases. DBMS is comprised of tables that made up of rows called records and columns called fields.

The important processes catered by existing DBMS are as below:

- Defining or constructing a data structure which is also called as data definition such as creating a table, deleting a table or modifying the existing one.
- Updating like inserting a record into a table, deleting or modifying a record.
- Retrieval or extracting information from the database by user queries for user applications, reporting or any other business purposes.
- Administration includes the activities like enforcing data security, maintaining data integrity,data backup and recovery, granting & revoking accesses, performance monitoring, disaster management etc. These activities are generally carried out by a DBA (database administrator).

SOME OF THE DATABASE MANAGEMENT SYSTEM ARE

(1) **Microsoft Access :** This is the database management system developed by Microsoft. It stores data in its own format based on the Access Jet Database Engine. It also has the facilities like importing or linking directly to data stored in other databases and applications.

(2) **MySQL :** MySQL is open source database management system, one of the most popular dbms on the web. It is reliable, fast and also flexible.

(3) **Oracle :** Developed by Oracle corporation. It is object relational database management system. The original version of Oracle software was developed by Software Development Laboratories (SDL). Oracle is regarded to be one of the safe DBMS.

(4) **Microsoft SQL Server :** Microsoft developed this relational database server. The primary function of this software is to store and retrieve the data as requested by other applications, whether those applications are on the same computer or running on other computers across the network (including internet).

COMPONENTS OF DATABASE SYSTEM

The database system can be divided into four components.

- **Users :** Users may be of various type such as DB administrator, System developer and End users.
- **Database application :** Database application may be Personal, Departmental,Enterprise and internal.
- **DBMS :** Software that allow users to define, create and manages databaseaccess. Ex : Mysql, Oracle etc.
- **Database :** Collection of logical data.

DATABASE TABULAR MODEL

Database in tabular form contain, Row and Column database.

Row database

In a database, a **row** also called a tuple represents a single row, implicitly structured data item in a table.

A database table can be thought of as consisting of *rows* and columns or fields. Each row in a table represents a set of related data, and every tuple in the table has the same structure.

Example : A table that represents companies, each row would represent a single company. Columns might represent things like company name, company street address, whether the company is publicly held, its TIN number, VET number, etc.

Column database

In a database, a **column** is a set of data values of a particular simple type, one for each row of the table. The columns provide the structure according to which the rows are composed.

In database terminology, column's equivalent is called attribute.

Example : A table that represents companies might have the following columns: ID (integer identifier, unique to each row), Name (text), Address line 1 (text), Address line 2 (text), Postal code (text), city (text), industry (text), etc.

	Column (Field) **1**	**Column** (Field) **2**
(Record) **Row 1**	Row 1, Column 1	Row 1, Column 2
(Record) **Row 2**	Row 2, Column 1	Row 2, Column 2
(Record) **Row 3**	Row 3, Column 1	Row 3, Column 2

DATABASE MODEL

A Database model defines the logical design of data. The model describes the relationships between different parts of the data. In history of database design, three models have been in use.

(i)   **Hierarchical Model :** In this model each entity has only one parent but can have several children . At the top of hierarchy there is only one entity which is called Root.

(ii) **Network Model :** In the network model, entities are organised in a graph,in which some entities can be accessed through several path.

(iii) **Relational Model :** In this model, data is organised in two-dimensional tables called relations. The tables or relation are related to each other.

DATABASE DESIGN

Database design is the process of producing a detailed data model of database. This data molel contains all the needed logical and physical design choices and physical storage parameters needed to generate a design in a data definations language, which can be used to create a database. A fully attributed data model contains detailed attributes of each entity.

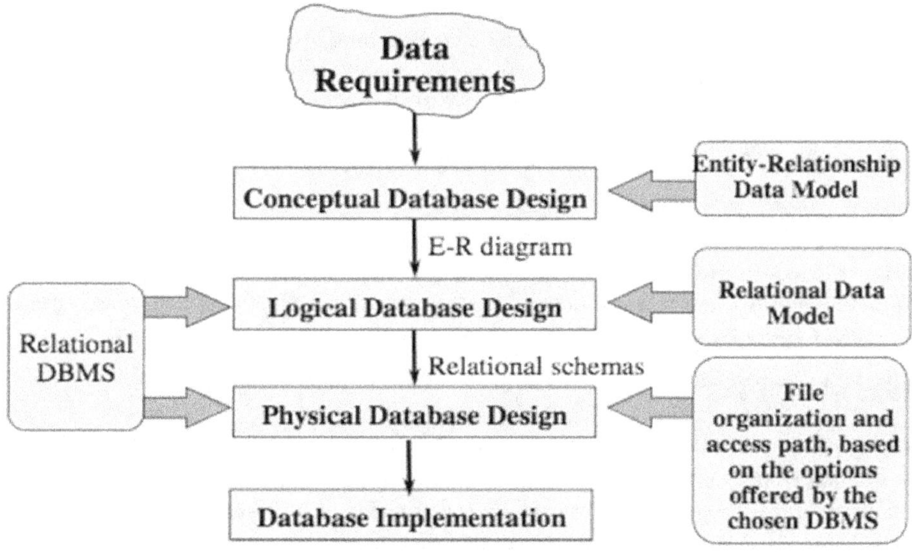

ENTITY RELATIONSHIP MODEL

E-R model is a very popular conceptual data model which is used to develop conceptual design of databases. This data model describes or perceives the real world data in form of entities.

The E-R Model: The enterprise is viewed as set of

- Entities
- Relationships among entities

Symbols used in E-R Diagram

- Entity – rectangle

- Attribute – oval

- Relationship – diamond

- Link - line

- Weak entity

- Weak entity Relationship

- Multivalued Attribute

- Composite Attribute

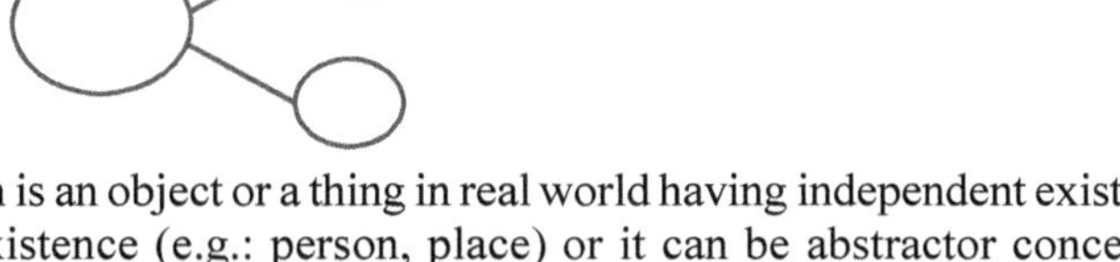

An **ENTITY** is a basic unit of E-R model which is an object or a thing in real world having independent existence. An entity may be concrete and a physical existence (e.g.: person, place) or it can be abstractor conceptual existence like loan, course. Entity is an object that is involved in the enterprise and that be distinguished from other objects.

- Can be person, place, event, object, concept in the real world
- Can be physical object or abstraction
- Ex: "John", "CSE305"

ENTITY SET : It is a collection of entities of a particular entity type at any point of time. For example: A firm is having many employees, these are defined as entities(e1, e2, e3, .en) and all these entities are having same attributes under entity type employee. The set of students(e1,e2,e3......) is entity set.

TYPES OF ENTITY SET

Weak : An entity set that does not have a primary key is referred to as a Weak entity set.

The existence of a weak entity set depends on the existence of a strong entity set; it must relate to the strong set via a one-to-many relationship set. The discriminator (or partial key) of a weak entity set is the set of attributes that distinguishes among all the entities of a weak entity set.

Example : We depict a weak entity set by double rectangles. We underline the discriminator of a weak entity set with a dashed line. *payment-number* – discriminator of the *payment* entity set
Primary key for *payment* – (*loan-number, payment-number*)

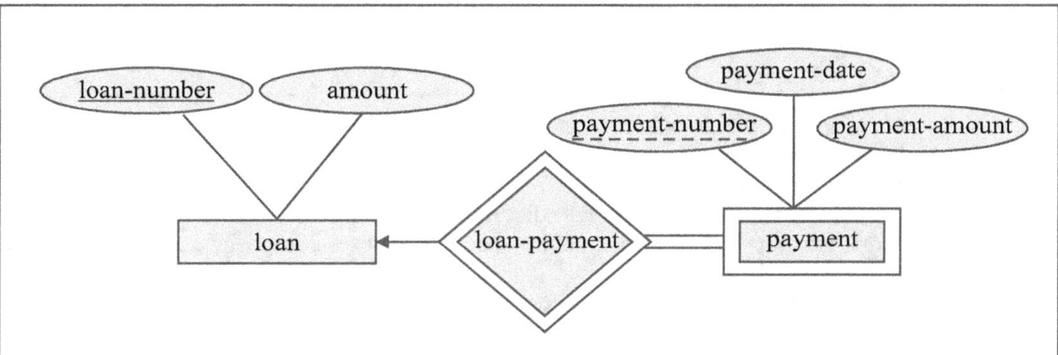

- **Strong :** An entity set that has a primary key is called as Strong entity set. Consider an entity set Payment which has three attributes: payment_number, payment_date and payment_amount. Although each payment entity is distinct but payment for different loans may share the same payment number. Thus, this entity set does not have a primary key and it is an entity set.

The table shows the difference between Strong Entity set and Weak Entity set

Strong Entity Set	Weak Entity Set
It has its own primary key.	I does not save sufficient attributes to form a primary key on its own.
It is represented by a rectangle.	It is represented by a double rectangle.
It contains a primary key represented by an underline.	It contains a Partial Key or discriminator represented by a dashed underline.
The member of strong entity set is called as dominant entity set.	The member of weak entity set is called as subordinate entity set.
The Primary key is one of its attributes which uniquely identifies its member.	The Primary Key of weak entity set is a combination of partial key and primary key of the strong entity set.
The relationship between two strong entity set is represent by a diamond symbol.	The relationship between one strong and a weak entity set is represented by a double diamond sign. It is known as identifying relationship.
The line connecting strong entity set with the relationship is single.	The line connecting weak entity set with the identifying relationship is double.
To participation in the relationship may or may not exist.	Total participation in the identifying relationship always exists.

VALUE SET OR DOMAIN VALUES

A set of possible values that can be assigned to a given attribute in individual entity. For example, the attribute employee name in employee entity type can have character data and integer value. Hence the values in this attribute will be a non-integer domain.

ENTITY TYPE

It is the set of similar objects or a category of entities; they are well defined
- A rectangle represents an entity set
- Ex: *students*, *courses*
- We often just say "entity" and mean "entity type"

ATTRIBUTE

It describes one aspect of an entity type; usually [and best when] single valued and indivisible (atomic)
- Represented by oval on E-R diagram
- Ex: *name, maximum enrollment*
- May be **multi-valued** – use double oval on E-R diagram
- May be **composite** – attribute has further structure; also use oval for composite attribute, with ovals for components connected to it by lines
- May be **derived** – a virtual attribute, one that is computable from existing data in the database, use dashed oval. This helps reduce redundancy

DOMAIN

It is the possible values of an attribute.
- Note that the value for an attribute can be a set or list of values, sometimes called "multi-valued" attributes
- This is in contrast to the pure relational model which requires atomic values
- E.g., (111111, John, 123 Main St, (stamps, coins))

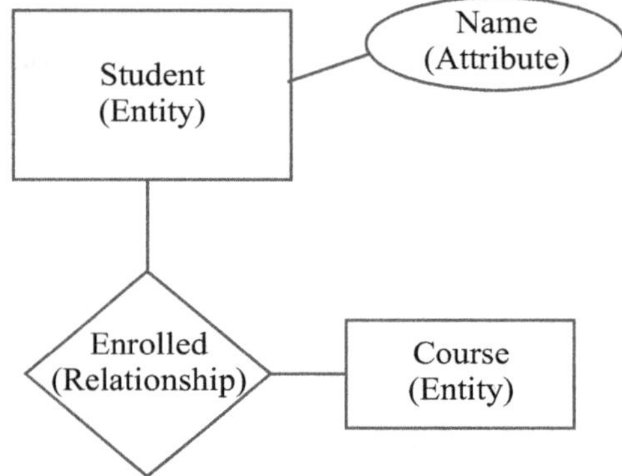

FUNCTIONS OF DBMS

- Provides data independence
- Concurrency Control
- Provides Recovery services
- Provides Utility services
- Provides a clear and logical view of the process that manipulates data.

ADVANTAGES OF DBMS

- Segregation of application program.
- Minimal data duplicacy.
- Easy retrieval of data
- Reduced development time and maintenance need.

DISADVANTAGES OF DBMS

- Complexity
- Costly
- Large in size

RDBMS (RELATIONAL DATABASE MANAGEMENT SYSTEM)

RDBMSs have become a predominant choice for the storage of information in new databases used for financial records, manufacturing and logistical information, personnel data, and much more since the 1980s. Relational databases have often replaced legacy hierarchical databases and network databases because they are easier to understand and use. However, relational databases have been challenged by object databases, which were introduced in an attempt to address the object-relational impedance mismatch in relational database, and XML databases.

Relational data model describes the world as "a collection of inter-related relations (or tables).

Relational databases are powerful because they require few assumptions about how data is related or how it will be extracted from the database. As a result, the same database can be viewed in many different ways. An important feature of relational systems is that a single database can be spread across several tables. This differs from flat-file databases, in which each database is self-contained in a single table.

Almost all full-scale database systems are RDBMS's. Small database systems, however, use other designs that provide less flexibility in posing queries.

KEYS

An important constraint on the entities is the key. The key is an attribute or a group of attributes whose values can be used to uniquely identify an individual entity in an entity set. Types of keys are described below:

1. Candidate Key

- a simple or composite key that is unique and minimal
- unique – no two rows in a table may have the same value at any time
- minimal – every column must be necessary for uniqueness
- For example, for the entity

Employee (EID, First Name, Last Name, SIN, Address, Phone, BirthDate, Salary, DepartmentID) Possible candidate keys are EID, SIN

FirstName and Last Name – assuming there is no one else in the company with the same name, Last Name and DepartmentID – assuming two people with the same last name don't work in the same department. EID, SIN are also candidate keys

2. Composite Key

- Composed of more than one attribute.
- For example, as discussed earlier. First Name and Last Name – assuming there is no one else in the company with the same name, Last Name and Department ID – assuming two people with the same last name don't work in the same department.
- A composite key can have two or more attributes, but it must be minimal.

3. Primary Key

- A candidate key is selected by the designer to uniquely identify tuples in a table. It must not be null.
- A key is chosen by the database designer to be used as an identifying mechanism for the whole entity set. This is referred to as the primary key. This key is indicated by underlining the attribute in the ER model.
- For example **Employee**(EID, First Name, Last Name, SIN, Address, Phone, BirthDate, Salary, DepartmentID) – EID is the Primary key.

4. Secondary Key

- An attribute used strictly for retrieval purposes (can be composite), for example: Phone number, Last Name and Phone number, etc.
- All other candidate keys not chosen as the primary key
- An attribute in one table that references the primary key of another table OR it can be null.
- Both foreign and primary keys must be of the same data type
  For example: **Employee**(EID, First Name, Last Name, SIN, Address, Phone, BirthDate, Salary, DepartmentID) – DepartmentID is the Foreign key.

5. Foreign Key

- An attribute in one table that references the primary key of another table OR it can be null.
- Both foreign and primary keys must be of the same data type
- For example: **Employee**(EID, First Name, Last Name, SIN, Address, Phone, BirthDate, Salary, DepartmentID) – DepartmentID is the Foreign key.

6. Unique Key
It is used to uniquely define the attribute of each row.

NULLS

This is a special symbol, independent of data type, which means either unknown or inapplicable. (it does not mean zero or blank)
* No data entry
* Not permitted in primary key
* Should be avoided in other attributes
* Can represent
    * An unknown attribute value
    * A known, but missing, attribute value
    * A "not applicable" condition
    * Can create problems when functions such as COUNT, AVERAGE, and SUM are used
    * Can create logical problems when relational tables are linked

NOTE : The result of a comparison operation is null when either argument is null. The result of an arithmetic operation is null when either argument is null (except functions which ignore nulls)

SOME IMPORTANT TERMS IN DBMS

SCHEMA of a database system is its structure described in a formal language supported by the database management system (DBMS) .

DATA MINING sometimes called data or knowledge discovery) is the process of analyzing data from different perspectives .

TABLES: Refers to data arranged in rows and columns. A *spreadsheet*, for example, is a table. In relational database management systems, all information is stored in the form of tables.

FIELDS : The smallest unit of information about a record in a datbas is called field.

RECORD: A complete set of information. Records are composed of fields, each of which contains one item of information. A set of records constitutes a file.

QUERIES: In database management systems, query by example (QBE) refers to a method of forming queries in which the database program displays a blank record with a space for each field. You can then enter conditions for each field that you want to be included in the query.

FORM : A program that generally has more user friendly interface than a DBMS is called a form

REPORTS : A formatted and organized presentation of data. Most database management systems include a report writer that enables you to design and generate reports.

CARDINALITY: In database design, the cardinality or fundamental principle of one data table with respect to another is a critical aspect. The relationship of one to the other must be precise and exact between each other in order to explain how each table links together.

In the relational model, tables can be related as any of "one-to-many" or "many-to-many." This is said to be the cardinality of a given table in relation to another.

DATA REDUNDANCY: Data redundancy occurs in database systems which have a field that is repeated in two or more table

DATA INTEGRITY: Data integrity refers to maintaining and assuring the accuracy and consistency of data over its entire life-cycle, and is a critical aspect to the design

DATA RELIABILITY: the accuracy and completeness of computer-processed data, given the uses they are intended for

DATA CONSISTENCY: Consistency, in the context of databases, states that data cannot be written that would violate the database's own rules for valid data. If a certain transaction occurs that attempts to introduce inconsistent data, the entire transaction is rolled back and an error returned to the user.

TUPLE : Tuple is the collection of information about the attributes of table for single instance. In simple this also can be called as a 'row' in a Table

ROLLBACK: The process of restoring a database or program to a previously defined state, typically to recover from an error.

IMPORTANT COMMANDS IN DATABASE:

Data Definition Language (DDL) statements are used to define the database structure or schema. Some examples:

- CREATE - to create objects in the database
- ALTER - alters the structure of the database
- DROP - delete objects from the database
- TRUNCATE - remove all records from a table, including all spaces allocated for the records are removed
- COMMENT - add comments to the data dictionary
- RENAME - rename an object

Data Manipulation Language (DML) statements are used for managing data within schema objects. Some examples:

- SELECT - retrieve data from the a database
- INSERT - insert data into a table
- UPDATE - updates existing data within a table
- DELETE - deletes all records from a table, the space for the records remain
- MERGE - UPSERT operation (insert or update)
- CALL - call a PL/SQL or Java subprogram
- EXPLAIN PLAN - explain access path to data
- LOCK TABLE - control concurrency

Data Control Language (DCL) statements. Some examples:

- GRANT - gives user's access privileges to database
- REVOKE - withdraw access privileges given with the GRANT command

Transaction Control (TCL) statements are used to manage the changes made by DML statements. It allows statements to be grouped together into logical transactions.

- COMMIT - save work done
- SAVEPOINT - identify a point in a transaction to which you can later roll back
- ROLLBACK - restore database to original since the last COMMIT
- SET TRANSACTION - Change transaction options like isolation level and what rollback segment to use

Past Exercise

1. Part number, part description, and number of parts ordered are examples of **[IBPS PO, 2011]**
   (a) control   (b) output
   (c) processing   (d) feedback
   (e) input

2. Grouping and processing all of a firm's transactions at one time is called
   [IBPS PO, 2011]
   (a) a database management system
   (b) batch processing
   (c) a real-time system
   (d) an on-line system
   (e) None of these

3. Forms that are used to organize business data into rows and columns are called __________.
   [IBPS PO, 2012]
   (a) transaction sheets   (b) registers
   (c) business forms   (d) sheet-spreads
   (e) spreadsheets

4. What refers to a set of characters of a particular design ? **[IBPS PO, 2012]**
   (a) keyface   (b) formation
   (c) calligraph   (d) stencil
   (e) typeface

5. __________ is used by public and private enterprises to publish and share financial information with each other and industry analysts across all computer platforms and the Internet. **[IBPS PO, 2012]**
   (a) Extensible Markup Language (EML)
   (b) Extensible Business Reporting Language (XBRL)
   (c) Enterprise Application Integration (EAI)
   (d) Sales Force Automation (SFA) software
   (e) None of these

6. ROLLBACK in a database is __________ statement **[IBPS Clerk, 2012]**
   (a) TCL   (b) DCL
   (c) DML   (d) DDL
   (e) SDL

7. __________ provides total solutions to reduce data redundancy, inconsistency, dependence and unauthorized access of data
   (a) DBMS   **[IBPS Clerk, 2012]**
   (b) Tables
   (c) Database
   (d) Protection passwords
   (e) Centralization of data

8. __________ is one reason for problems of data integrity **[IBPS Clerk, 2012]**
   (a) Data availability constraints
   (b) Data inconsistency
   (c) Security constraints
   (d) Unauthorized access of data
   (e) Data redundancy

9. Dr. E.F. Codd represented __________ rules that a database must obey if it has to be considered truly relational **[IBPS Clerk, 2012]**
   (a) 10   (b) 8
   (c) 12   (d) 6
   (e) 5

10. A data warehouse **[IBPS Clerk, 2012]**
    (a) Contains numerous naming conventions and formats
    (b) Is organized around important subject areas
    (c) Contains only current data
    (d) Can be updated by end users
    (e) Explains some observed event or condition

11. Which of these is considered intelligent CASE tool **[IBPS Clerk, 2012]**
    (a) Toolkit
    (b) Methodology companion
    (c) Workbench
    (d) Upper CASE
    (e) Lower CASE

12. A collection of conceptual tools for describing data, relationships, semantics and constraints is referred to as **[IBPS Clerk, 2012]**
    (a) ER model   (b) Data base
    (c) Data Model   (d) DBMS
    (e) None of these

13. __________ search method is conducted for a specific title, domain, URL, or host
    [IBPS Clerk, 2012]
    (a) Keyword   (b) Field
    (c) Boolean   (d) Miscellaneous
    (e) Logical

14. Attributes can be defined for **[IBPS PO, 2013]**
    (a) entity   (b) switch board
    (c) macro   (d) pages
    (e) None of the above

15. Where will we find the referential integrity command ? **[IBPS PO, 2013]**
    (a) Tools   (b) View
    (b) Format   (d) Table
    (e) None of these

16. Unlike filters queries can be saved as in a database. **[IBPS PO, 2013]**
    (a) objects   (b) filters
    (c) database   (d) Any of the above
    (e) None of these

17. What is a database ?   **[IBPS PO, 2013]**
    (a) It is a collection of data arranged in rows
    (b) It is a collection of data arranged in columns
    (c) It is a collection of data arranged in rows and columns
    (d) All of the above
    (e) None of the above

18. External database is   **[IBPS PO, 2013]**
    (a) Database created in EXCEL
    (b) Database created using DBMS package
    (c) Database created in MS-Word
    (d) All of the above
    (e) None of the above

19. Which command we will give if we want to show the database objects with it's decription ?   **[IBPS PO, 2013]**
    (a) Details   (b) Show
    (c) List   (d) Any of the above
    (e) None of the above

20. The software that is used to create text-based documents are referred to as _____________ .
    (a) DBMS   **[SBI PO, 2013]**
    (b) suites
    (c) spreadsheets
    (d) presentation software
    (e) word processors

21. In database, a field is a   **[SBI Clerk, 2014]**
    (a) label
    (b) table of information
    (c) group of related records
    (d) category of information
    (e) None of these

22. The particular field of a record that uniquely identifies each record is called the   **[SBI Clerk, 2014]**
    (a) key field   (b) primary field
    (c) master field   (d) order field
    (e) None of these

23. Data in database at a particular point of time is called as?   **[SSC CGL, 2016]**
    (a) Intension   (b) Extension
    (c) Back up   (d) Application

24. A relational database consists of a collection of   **[IBPS Clerk Mains, 2016]**
    (a) Tables   (b) Entities
    (c) Records   (d) Keys
    (e) ROM

25. Database ________ which is the logical design of the database, and the database ________ which is snapshot of the data in the database at given instant in time.   **[IBPS Clerk Mains, 2016]**
    (a) Instance, Schema   (b) Relation, Schema
    (c) Relation, Domain   (d) Schema, Instance
    (e) Trees, Attributes

26. Which of the following is the organized collection of large amount of interrelated data stored in a meaningfully way used for manipulation and updating?   **[IBPS Clerk Mains, 2016]**
    (a) Database   (b) File
    (c) Folder   (d) Data-mining
    (e) Data source

			ANSWER KEY						
1.	(e)	7.	(a)	13.	(b)	19.	(a)	25.	(d)
2.	(b)	8.	(e)	14.	(a)	20.	(e)	26.	(a)
3.	(e)	9.	(c)	15	(e)	21.	(b)		
4.	(c)	10.	(b)	16	(a)	22.	(a)		
5	(b)	11.	(c)	17.	(c)	23.	(b)		
6.	(a)	12.	(c)	18.	(b)	24.	(a)		

Practice Exercise

1. A field that uniquely identifies which person, thing, or event the record describes is a ________.
   - (a) file
   - (b) data
   - (c) field
   - (d) key
   - (e) None of these

2. The ability to find an individual item in a file immediately -
   - (a) sequential access
   - (b) file allocation table
   - (c) direct access
   - (d) directory
   - (e) None of these

3. Which of the following places the common data elements in order from smallest to largest?
   - (a) Character, file record, field, database
   - (b) Character, record, field, file, database
   - (c) Character, field, record, file, database
   - (d) Bit, byte, character, record, field, file, database
   - (e) None of these

4. Files are organised by storing them in ________.
   - (a) tables
   - (b) databases
   - (c) folders
   - (d) graphs
   - (e) None of these

5. A collection of unprocessed items is ________.
   - (a) information
   - (b) data
   - (c) memory
   - (d) reports
   - (e) None of these

6. Example of non-numeric data is
   - (a) Employee address
   - (b) Examination score
   - (c) Bank balance
   - (d) All of these
   - (e) None of these

7. Periodically adding, changing and deleting file records is called file
   - (a) updating
   - (b) upgrading
   - (c) restructiring
   - (d) renewing
   - (e) None of these

8. Which of the following statements best describes the batch method of input?
   - (a) Data is processed as soon as it is input
   - (b) Data is input at the time it is collected
   - (c) Data is collected in the form of source documents, placed into groups, and then input to the computer
   - (d) Source documents are not used
   - (e) None of these

9. ________ represents raw facts, whereas ________ is data made meaningful.
   - (a) Information, reporting
   - (b) Data, information
   - (c) Information, bits
   - (d) Records, bytes
   - (e) None of these

10. An ad hoc query is a ________.
    - (a) pre-planned question
    - (b) pre-scheduled question
    - (c) spur-of-the-moment question
    - (d) question that will not return any results
    - (e) None of these

11. A telephone number, a birth date, and a customer name are all examples of
    - (a) a record
    - (b) data
    - (c) a file
    - (d) a database
    - (e) None of these

12. A collection of interrelated files in a computer is a ________.
    - (a) file manager
    - (b) field
    - (c) record
    - (d) database
    - (e) None of these

13. Collecting personal information and effectively posing as another individual is known as the crime of ________.
    - (a) spooling
    - (b) identity theft
    - (c) spoofing
    - (d) hacking
    - (e) None of these

14. The first step in the transaction processing cycle is ________.
    - (a) database operations
    - (b) audit
    - (c) data entry
    - (d) user inquiry
    - (e) None of these

15. A tuple is a
    - (a) column of a table
    - (b) two-dimensional table
    - (c) row of a table
    - (d) key of a table
    - (e) None of these

16. The method of file organization in which data records in a file are arranged in a specified order according to key filed is known as the
    - (a) Direct access method
    - (b) Queuing method
    - (c) Predetermined method
    - (d) Sequential access method
    - (e) None of these

17. Numbers in table columns are usually
   (a) right-aligned   (b) left-aligned
   (c) justified   (d) centered
   (e) None of these

18. The simultaneous execution of two or more instructions is called
   (a) sequential access
   (b) reduced instruction set computing
   (c) multiprocessing
   (d) disk mirroring
   (e) None of these

19. A collection of interrelated records is called a
   (a) management information system
   (b) spreadsheet
   (c) database
   (d) text file
   (e) None of these

20. How many options does a binary choice offer?
   (a) One
   (b) Two
   (c) Three
   (d) It depends on the amount of memory in the computer
   (e) None of the above

21. The name of the location of a particular piece of data is its _____________.
   (a) address   (b) memory name
   (c) storage site   (d) data location
   (e) None of the above

22. A Field is a related group of _____________.
   (a) Records   (b) Files
   (c) Characters   (d) Cables
   (e) None of the above

23. A prescribed set of well-defined instructions for solving mathematical problems is called _____________.
   (a) a compiler   (b) a code
   (c) a description   (d) an algorithm
   (e) None of the above

24. A record is related to a file as a statement is related to a _____________.
   (a) procedure   (b) file
   (c) program   (d) data
   (e) None of the above

25. Meaningful filename helps in easy file _______.
   (a) Storing   (b) Accessing
   (c) Identification   (d) Printing
   (e) None of the above

26. You organise files by storing them in
   (a) archives   (b) folders
   (c) indexes   (d) lists
   (e) None of these

27. Distributed processing involves
   (a) solving computer component problems from a different computer
   (b) solving computing problems by breaking them into smaller parts that are seperately processed by different computers
   (c) allowing users to share files on a network
   (d) allowing users to access network resources away from the office
   (e) None of these

28. When data changes in multiple lists and all lists are not updated, this causes
   (a) data redundancy
   (b) information overload
   (c) duplicate data
   (d) data inconsistency
   (e) data repetition

29. The issues that deals with the collection and use of data about individuals is
   (a) access   (b) publicity
   (c) accuracy   (d) property
   (e) privacy

30. Participants can see and hear each other in a/an
   (a) electronic mail system
   (b) message system
   (c) teleconference
   (d) bulletin board
   (e) None of these

31. How do businesses protect their databases?
   (a) Security guards are hired to watch the databases at all times.
   (b) Databases are protected by file swapping.
   (c) Databases are naturally protected.
   (d) Databases are kept physically and electronically secure.
   (e) The computer room is kept locked after office hours.

32. The path of creation of an executable is
   (a) coding, linking, compiling, parsing
   (b) coding, parsing, compiling, linking.
   (c) coding, compiling, parsing, linking
   (d) coding, compiling, linking, parsing.
   (e) coding, parsing, linking, compiling

33. _____________ increase the accuracy of a search by fine-tuning the keywords in the search.
   (a) Indexes   (b) Italics
   (c) Compounds   (d) Links
   (e) Operators

34. The main purpose(s) of a database management program is to
    (a) allow users to retrieve and analyze stored records.
    (b) provide a way to store information about specified entities.
    (c) make it possible for users to store information as interrelated records.
    (d) translate hard-to-read data into more legible formats.
    (e) a, b, and c above

35. Files are organised by storing them in
    (a) tables   (b) databases
    (c) folders   (d) graphs
    (e) diagrams

36. Which of the following contains permanent data and gets updated during the processing of transactions?
    (a) Operating System File
    (b) Transaction file
    (c) Software File
    (d) Master file
    (e) None of these

37. The DBMS acts as an interface between what two components of an enterprise-class database system?
    (a) Database application and the database
    (b) Data and the database
    (c) The user and the database application
    (d) Database application and SQL
    (e) None of these

38. The following are components of a database except __________ .
    (a) user data   (b) metadata
    (c) reports   (d) indexes
    (e) None of these

39. An application where only one user accesses the database at a given time is an example of a(n) __________ .
    (a) single-user database application
    (b) multiuser database application
    (c) e-commerce database application
    (d) data mining database application
    (e) None of these

40. A DBMS that combines a DBMS and an application generator is __________ .
    (a) Microsoft's SQL Server
    (b) Microsoft's Access
    (c) IBM's DB2
    (d) Oracle Corporation's Oracle
    (e) None of these

41. The DBMS that is most difficult to use is __________ .
    (a) Microsoft's SQL Server
    (b) Microsoft's Access
    (c) IBM's DB2
    (d) Oracle Corporation's Oracle
    (e) None of these

42. In order to understand DBMS, it is important to understand ?
    (a) the physical schema
    (b) all sub schema that are system support
    (c) one sub schema
    (d) Both (a) and (b)
    (e) on demand report

43. Databases overall structure is maintained in a file called
    (a) Redolog file   (b) Data file
    (c) Control file   (d) All of the above
    (e) None of these

44. E-R modeling technique is a
    (a) top-down approach
    (b) bottom-up approach
    (c) left-right approach
    (d) both top-down and bottom-up
    (e) None of these

45. Data independency in DBMS is known as
    (a) Data modeling   (b) Data hiding
    (c) Data capturing   (d) Data consistency
    (e) None of these

46. A data dictionary doesn't provide information about
    (a) where data is located
    (b) the size of the disk storage disk
    (c) who owns or is responsible for the data
    (d) how the data is used
    (e) None of these

47. The database administrator is, in effect, the coordinator between the ______ and the ______ .
    (a) DBMS; database
    (b) application program; database
    (c) database, users
    (d) application programs; users
    (e) None of these

48. What does the data dictionary identify?
    (a) Field names   (b) Field types
    (c) Field formates   (d) All of the above
    (e) None of these

49. Which is one function of a database management system (DBMS)?
    - (a) Ensuring usability
    - (b) Identifying what a user needs
    - (c) Deciding what to do with legacy systems
    - (d) Preventing errors arising, while enabling multiple, simultaneous users
    - (e) None of these
50. A relation (from the relational database model) consists of a set of tuples, which implies that
    - (a) relational model supports multi-valued attributes whose values can be represented in sets.
    - (b) for any two tuples, the values associated with all of their attributes may be the same.
    - (c) for any two tuples, the value associated with one or more of their attributes must differ.
    - (d) all tuples in particular relation may have different attributes.
    - (e) None of these

ANSWER KEY

1.	(d)	10.	(c)	19.	(c)	28.	(d)	37.	(a)	46.	(b)
2.	(c)	11.	(a)	20.	(b)	29.	(e)	38.	(c)	47.	(c)
3.	(c)	12.	(d)	21.	(a)	30.	(c)	39.	(a)	48	(d)
4.	(c)	13.	(b)	22.	(a)	31.	(d)	40.	(b)	49.	(d)
5.	(b)	14.	(c)	23.	(d)	32.	(d)	41.	(d)	50.	(c)
6.	(a)	15.	(c)	24.	(d)	33.	(a)	42.	(c)		
7.	(a)	16.	(d)	25.	(b)	34.	(e)	43.	(c)		
8.	(c)	17.	(a)	26.	(b)	35.	(c)	44.	(a)		
9.	(b)	18.	(c)	27.	(b)	36.	(d)	45.	(a)		

7 Computer Networks

Chapter

A computer Network is a group of computer systems and other computing hardware devices that are linked together through communication channels to facilitate communication and resource-sharing among a wide range of users.

Generally, networks are distinguished based on their geographical span. A network can be as small as distance between your mobile phone and its Bluetooth headphone and as large as the Internet itself, covering the whole geographical world, i.e. the Earth.

TYPES OF COMPUTER NETWORKS

WAN
(Wide Area Network)

MAN
(Metropolitan Area Network)

LAN
(Local Area Network)

PAN
(Personal Area
Network)

	PAN	LAN	MAN	WAN
Standards	Bluetooth, UWB	802,11 HiperLAN2	802, 16 MMDS, LMDS	GSM, GPRS, CDMA, 2.5-3G,802.16
Speed	< 1 Mbps	11 to 54 Mbps	11 to 100 + Mbps	100 to 384Mbps
Range	Short	Medium	Medium-Long	Long
Applications	Peer-to-Peer Device-to-Device	Enterprise networks	T1 replacement, last mile access	PDAs, Mobile Phones, cellular access

There are many types of Networks including :

1. **Personal Area Network (PAN) :** A Personal Area Network or simply PAN, is smallest network which is very personal to a user. This may include Bluetooth enabled devices or infra-red enabled devices. PAN has connectivity range up to 10 meters. PAN may include wireless computer keyboard and mouse, Bluetooth enabled headphones, wireless printers and TV remotes for examples.

2. **Local Area Network (LAN) :** A computer network spanned inside a building and operated under single administrative system is generally termed as Local Area Network. Usually, Local Area Network covers

an organization such as offices, schools, college/universities etc. Number of systems may vary from as least as two to as much as 16 million LAN provides a useful way of sharing resources between end users. Resources like Printers, File Servers, Scanners and internet is easy sharable among computers. Local Area Networks are composed of inexpensive networking and routing equipment. It may contains local servers serving file storage and other locally shared applications. It mostly operates on private IP addresses and generally do not involve heavy routing. LAN uses either Ethernet or Token-ring technology. Ethernet is most widely employed LAN technology and uses Star topology while Token-ring is rarely seen.

Data transfer rate in LAN is of the order 10 to 100 mega bits per second(Mbps).

3. **Metropolitan Area Network (MAN) :** MAN, generally expands throughout a city such as cable TV network. It can be in form of Ethernet, Token-ring, ATM or FDDI. Metro Ethernet is a service which is provided by ISPs. This service enables its users to expand their Local Area Networks. For example, MAN can help an organization to connect all of its offices in a City. Backbone of MAN is high-capacity and high-speed fiber optics. MAN is works in between Local Area Network and Wide Area Network. MAN provides uplink for LANs to WANs or Internet.

4. **Wide Area Network (WAN) :** As name suggests, this network covers a wide area which may span across provinces and even a whole country. Generally, telecommunication networks are Wide Area Network. These networks provides connectivity to MANs and LANs. Equipped with very high speed backbone, WAN uses very expensive network equipment. WAN may use advanced technologies like Asynchronous Transfer Mode (ATM), Frame Relay and SONET. WAN may be managed under by more than one administration.

5. **Virtual Private Network (VPN) :** VPN is a network that is constructed by using public wires usually the Internet to connect to a private network, such as a company›s internal network. There are a number of systems that enable you to create networks using the Internet as the medium for transporting data. These systems use encryption and other security mechanisms to ensure that only authorized users can access the network and that the data cannot be intercepted.

6. **Internetwork :** A network of networks is called internetwork, or simply Internet. It is the largest network in existence on this planet. Internet hugely connects all WANs and it can have connection to LANs and Home networks. Internet uses TCP/IP protocol suite and uses IP as its addressing protocol. Present day, Internet is widely implemented using IPv4. Because of shortage of address spaces, it is gradually migrating from IPv4 to IPv6. Internet enables its users to share and access enormous amount of information worldwide. It uses www, ftp, email services, audio and video streaming etc. At huge level, internet works on Client-Server model. Internet uses very high speed backbone of fiber optics. To inter-connect various continents, fibers are laid under sea known to us as submarine communication cable. Internet is widely deployed on World Wide Web services using HTML linked pages and is accessible by some client software known as Web Browsers. When a user requests a page using some web browser located on some Web Server anywhere in the world, the Web Server responds with the proper HTML page. The communication delay is very low.

Internet is serving many proposes and is involved in many aspects of life. Some of them are:

*   Web sites
*   E-mail
*   Instant Messaging
*   Blogging
*   Social Media
*   Marketing
*   Networking
*   Resource Sharing
*   Audio and Video Streaming

COMPARISON OF OSI REFERENCE MODEL AND TCP/IP REFERENCE MODEL

Following are some major difference between OSI Reference Model and TCP/IP Reference Model, with diagrammatic comparison below :

OSI (Open System Interconnection)	TCP/IP (Transmission Control Protocol/Internet Protocol)
1. OSI provides layer functioning and also defines functions of all the layers.	1. TCP/IP model is more based on protocols and protocols are not flexible with other layers.
2. In OSI model the transport layer guarantees the delivery of packets.	2. In TCP/IP model the transport layer does not guarantees delivery of packets.
3. Follows horizontal approach.	3. Follows vertical approach.
4.OSI model has a separate presentation layer.	4. TCP/IP does not have a separate presentation layer.
5. OSI is a general model.	5. TCP/IP model cannot be used in any other application.
6. Network layer of OSI model provide both connection oriented and connectioniess service.	6. The Network layer in TCP/IP model provides connectioniness service.
7. OSI model has problem of fitting the protocols in the	7. TCP/IP model does not fit any protocol.
8. Protocols are hidden OSI model and are easily replaced as the technology changes.	8. In TCP/IP replacing protocol is not easy.
9. OSI model defines services, interfaces and protocols very clearly and makes clear distinction between them.	9. In TCP/IP it is not clearly separated its services, interfaces and protocols.
10. It has 7 layers.	10. It has 4 layers.

ETHERNET

Ethernet is a Local Area Network implementation technology which is widely deployed.

Ethernet is network technology which shares media. Network which uses shared media has high probability of data collision. Ethernet uses CSMA/CD technology to detect collisions. CSMA/CD stands for Carrier Sense Multi Access/Collision Detection. When a collision happens in Ethernet, all its host rolls back and waits for some random amount of time and then re-transmit data. Ethernet connector, i.e. Network Interface cards are equipped with 48-bits MAC address. This help other Ethernet devices to identify and communicate with remote devices in Ethernet. Traditional Ethernet uses 10BASE-T specifications.

Where 10 is for 10mpbs speed, BASE stands for using baseband and T stands for Thick net or Thick Ethernet. 10BASE-T Ethernet provides transmission speed up to 10mbps and uses Coaxial cable or Cat-5 Twisted Pair cable with RJ-5 connector. Ethernet follows Star Topology with segment length up to 100 meters. All devices are connected to a Hub/Switch in a Star Fashion.

Fast-Ethernet

To encompass need of fast emerging software and hardware technologies, Ethernet extends itself as Fast-Ethernet. It can run on UTP, Optical Fiber and can be wireless too. It can provide speed up to 100 mbps. This standard is named as 100BASE-T in IEEE 803.2 using Cat-5 Twisted pair cable. It uses CSMA/CD technique for wired media sharing among Ethernet hosts and CSMA/CA (Collision Avoidance) technique for wireless Ethernet LAN. Fast Ethernet on fiber is defined under 100BASE-FX standard which provides speed up to 100mbps on fiber. Ethernet over Fiber can be extended up to 100 meters in half-duplex mode and can reach maximum of 2000 meters in full-duplex over multimode fibers.

Giga-Ethernet

After being introduced in 1995, Fast-Ethernet could enjoy its high speed status only for 3 years till Giga-Ethernet introduced. Giga-Ethernet provides speed up to 1000 mbits/seconds. IEEE802.3ab standardize Giga-Ethernet over UTP using Cat-5, Cat-5e and Cat-6 cables. IEEE802.3ah defines Giga-Ethernet over Fiber.

Virtual LAN

LAN uses Ethernet which in turn works on shared media. Shared media in Ethernet create one single Broadcast domain and one single Collision domain. Introduction of switches to Ethernet has removed single collision domain issue and each device connected to switch works in its separate collision domain. But even Switches cannot divide a network into separate Broadcast domain. Virtual LAN is a method to divide a single Broadcast domain into more than one Broadcast domains. Host in one VLAN cannot speak to a host in another. By default, all hosts are placed into same VLAN.

COMPUTER NETWORK TOPOLOGIES

Network Topology is the way computer systems or network equipment connected to each other. Topologies may define both physical and logical aspect of the network. Both logical and physical topologies could be same or different in a same network. Topology can be referred as the physical arrangement of a computer system. Each computer system in a topology is known as node. In a fully connected network with n nodes, there are n(n-1)/2 direct links.

1. **Point-to-point Technology :** These networks contains exactly two hosts (computer or switches or routers or servers) connected back to back using a single piece of cable. Often, the receiving end of one host is connected to sending end of the other end and vice-versa. If the hosts are connected point-to-point logically, then may have multiple intermediate devices. But the end hosts are unaware of underlying network and see each other as if they are connected directly.

2. **Bus Topology :** In contrast to point-to-point, in bus topology all device share single communication line or cable. All devices are connected to this shared line. Ethernet is commonly well protocol in networks connected in bus topology.

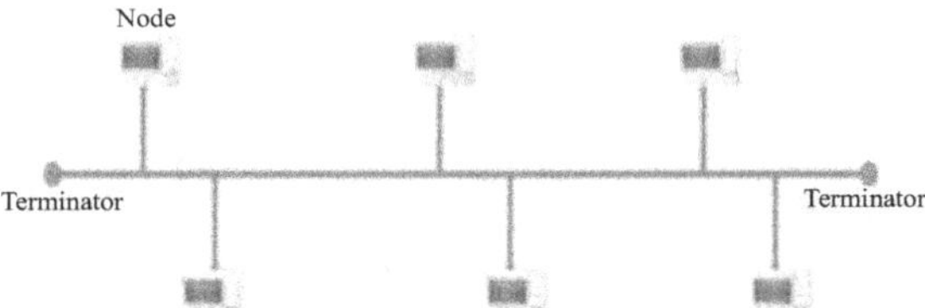

3. **Ring Topology :** In ring topology, each host machine connects to exactly two other machines, creating a circular network structure. This topology use the token ring protocol for controlling access. Each workstation is connected to two other components on either side, and it communicates with these two adjacent neighbours. Data travels around the network, in one direction. Sending and receiving of data takes place by the help of TOKEN.

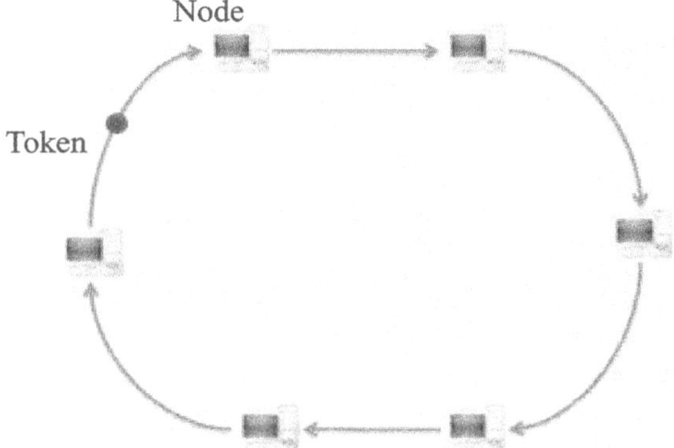

4. **Star Topology :** In Star topology, all the components of network are connected to the central device called "hub" which may be a hub, a router or a switch. All the data on the star topology passes through the central device before reaching the intended destination. Hub acts as a junction to connect different nodes present in Star Network, and at the same time it manages and controls whole of the network. Depending on which central device is used, "hub" can act as repeater or signal booster.

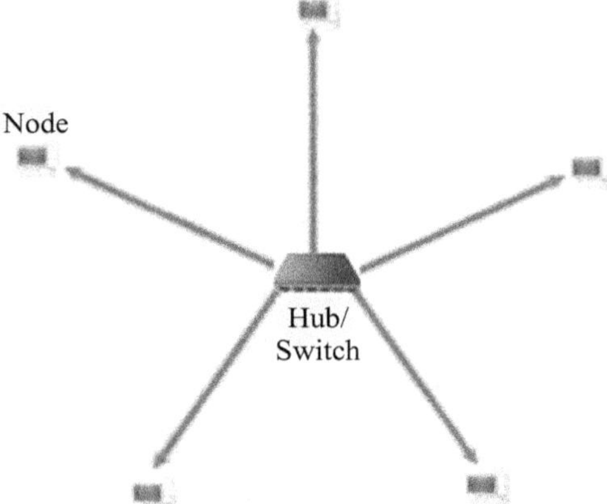

5. **Mesh Topology :** In this type of topology, a host is connected to one or two or more than two hosts. This topology may have hosts having point-to-point connection to every other hosts or may also have hosts which are having point to point connection to few hosts only.

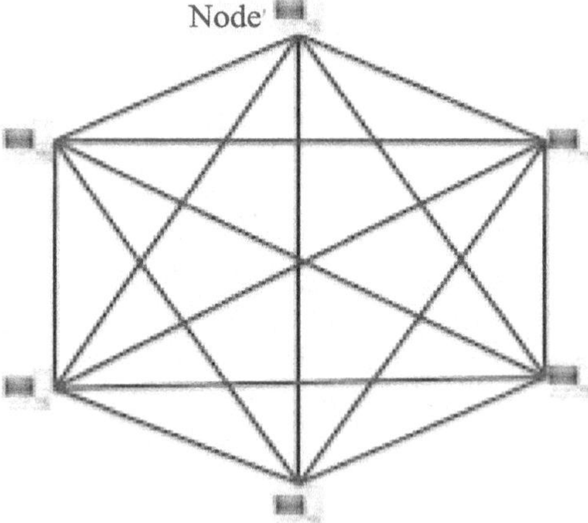

Hosts in Mesh topology also work as relay for other hosts which do not have direct point-to-point links. Mesh technology comes into two flavors:

Full Mesh: All hosts have a point-to-point connection to every other host in the network. Thus for every new host n(n-1)/2 cables (connection) are required. It provides the most reliable network structure among all network topologies.

Partially Mesh: Not all hosts have point-to-point connection to every other host. Hosts connect to each other in some arbitrarily fashion. This topology exists where we need to provide reliability to some host whereas others are not as such necessary.

6. **Tree Topology :** Also known as Hierarchical Topology is the most common form of network topology in use present day. This topology imitates as extended Star Topology and inherits properties of Bus topology.

This topology divides the network in to multiple levels/layers of network. Mainly in LANs, a network is bifurcated into three types of network devices. The lowest most is access-layer where user"s computer are attached. The middle layer is known as distribution layer, which works as mediator between upper layer and lower layer. The highest most layer is known as Core layer, and is central point of the network, i.e. root of the tree from which all nodes fork.

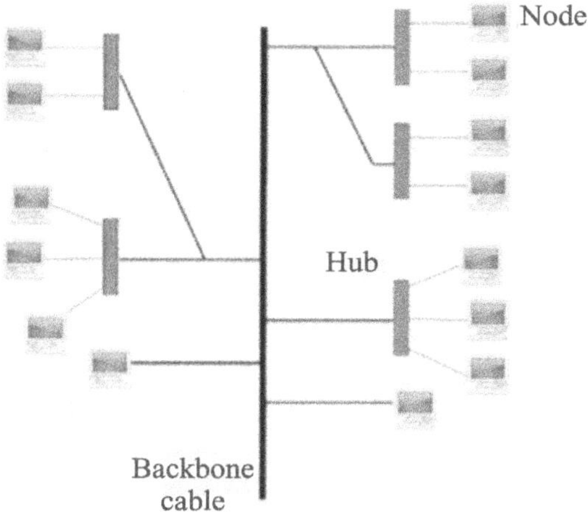

7. **Daisy Chain :** This topology connects all its hosts in a linear fashion. Similar to Ring topology, all hosts in this topology are connected to two hosts only, except the end hosts. That is if the end hosts in Daisy Chain are connected then it represents Ring topology. Each link in Daisy chain topology represents single point of failure. Every link failure splits the network into two segment. Every intermediate host works as relay for its immediate hosts.

8. **Hybrid Topology :** A network structure whose design contains more than one topology is said to be Hybrid Topology. Hybrid topology inherits merits and demerits of all the incorporating topologies. The above picture represents an arbitrarily Hybrid topology. The combining topologies may contain attributes of Star, Ring, Bus and Daisy-chain topologies. Most WANs are connected by means of dual Ring topology and networks connected to them are mostly Star topology networks. Internet is the best example of largest Hybrid topology.

NETWORK DEVICES

1. **Network Repeater :** Network repeaters regenerate incoming electrical, wireless or optical signals. With physical media like Ethernet or Wi-Fi, data transmissions can only span a limited distance before the quality of the signal degrades. Repeaters attempt to preserve signal integrity and extend the distance over which data can safely travel. Actual network devices that serve as repeaters usually have some other name. Active hubs, for example, are repeaters. Active hubs are sometimes also called Multiport Repeaters but more commonly they are just "hubs." Other types of passive hubs are not repeaters. In Wi-Fi, access points function as repeaters only when operating in so-called Repeater mode .

2. **Network Hub :** A hub is a small Network Device. A hub joins multiple computers (or other network devices) together to form a single network segment. On this network segment, all computers can communicate directly with each other. Ethernet hubs are by far the most common type, but hubs for other types of networks such as USB also exist.

A hub includes a series of ports that each accept a network cable, one port is reserved for "uplink" connections to another hub or similar device.

3. **Network Bridge :** It reads the outermost section of data on the data packet, to tell where the message is going only the outermost hardware address of the packet. It reduces the traffic on other network segments, since it does not send all packets. Bridges can be programmed to reject packets from particular networks Bridging occurs at the data link layer of the OSI model. Bridge cannot read IP addresses. Bridge can read the ethernet data which gives the hardware address of the destination address. Bridges forward all broadcast messages.

4. **Network Router :** It is a network device with interfaces in multiple networks whose task is to copy packets from one network to another. Router gives path to data packet to destination. Routers provide connectivity inside enterprises, between enterprises and the Internet, and within an Internet Service Provider (ISP). It operates at Layer 3 (Network Layer) of the OSI Model. Router works with Static Routing manually configure by Network Administrator. Router works with Dynamic Routing which routers calculate automatically by different methods. Router stores calculate path in his Routing Table. The network router will then use its routing table to make intelligent decisions about which packets to copy to which of its interfaces. The router will use this information to create a routing table. This process is known as routing.

5. **Network Switch :** Network Switch is a small hardware device that joins multiple computers together within one local area network (LAN).

    Network Switches operate at layer two (Data Link Layer) of the OSI model . Network switches appear nearly identical to network hubs, but a switch generally contains more intelligence (and a slightly higher price tag) than a hub. Unlike hubs, Switches are capable of inspecting data packets as they are received, determining the source and destination device of each packet, and forwarding them appropriately. By delivering messages only to the connected device intended. Switch conserves network bandwidth and offers generally better performance than a hub. Switch supports different bandwidth either 10/100 Mbps Fast Ethernet or Gigabit Ethernet (10/100/1000) standards.

6. **Gateway :** A gateway is an interconnecting device which joins two different network together they are also known as protocol converters. It accepts packet formed for one protocol and converts the formated packet into another protocol.

7. **CSU/DSU (Channel Service Unit/Data Service Unit) :** CSU/DSU is a hardware device about the size of an external modem that converts a digital data frame from the communications technology used on a local area network (LAN) into a frame appropriate to a wide-area network (WAN) and vice versa. The Channel Service Unit (CSU) receives and transmits signals from and to the WAN line and provides a barrier for electrical interference from either side of the unit. The CSU can also echo loopback signals from the phone company for testing purposes. The Data Service Unit (DSU) manages line control, and converts input and output between RS-232C, RS-449, or V.xx frames from the LAN and the time-division multiplexed (TDM) DSX frames on the T-1 line. The DSU manages timing errors and signal regeneration. The DSU provides a modem-like interface between the computer as Data Terminal Equipment (DTE) and the CSU.

8. **Modem :** Modem is a device that converts digital signal to analog signal (modulator) at the sender's end and converts back analog signal to digital signal (demodulator) at the receiver's end. A modem is always placed between a telephone line and a computer. A modem links home network to the Internet through **Internet Service Provider (ISP).** The high speed types of data outside your home aren't suitable for your direct use, so modems convert the data into digital Ethernet, which all the network equipment in your home can use.

The internet services that are outside your home (or business) which are supplied by your ISP are either DSL, cable, dial-up, or satellite. Modems are often combined with a router into a single unit, which then also gives you a firewall protecting of your network from attack. If your modem is not also a router, then you will probably want a router in addition to your modem.

9. **Ethernet Card :** An Ethernet card is one kind of network adapter. These adapters support the Ethernet standard for high-speed network connections via cables. Ethernet cards are sometimes known as network interface cards (NICs).

DATA SIGNALS

When data is sent over physical medium it needs to be first converted into electromagnetic signals. Data itself can be analog such as human voice, or digital such as file on the disk. Data (both analog and digital) can be represented in digital or analog signals.

Digital Signals

Digital signals are discrete in nature and represents sequence of voltage pulses. Digital signals are used within the circuitry of a computer system.

Analog Signals

Analog signals are in continuous wave form in nature and represented by continuous electromagnetic waves.

BASIC COMMUNICATION MODES OF OPERATION

There are three basic modes of operation that can exist for any network connection, communications channel, or interface.

1. **Simplex Operation :** In simplex operation, a network cable or communications channel can only send information in one direction; it's a "one-way street".

2. **Half-Duplex Operation :** Technologies that employ half-duplex operation are capable of sending information in both directions between two nodes, but only one direction or the other can be utilized at a time. This is a fairly common mode of operation when there is only a single network medium (cable, radio frequency and so forth) between devices.

3. **Full-Duplex Operation :** In full-duplex operation, a connection between two devices is capable of sending data in both directions simultaneously. Full-duplex channels can be constructed either as a pair of simplex links (as described above) or using one channel designed to permit bidirectional simultaneous transmissions. A full-duplex link can only connect two devices, so many such links are required if multiple devices are to be connected together.

COMMUNICATION MEDIUM

The Communication Medium plays an important role in Networks. If the medium works well and properly, then the speed of transferring data is good but if the medium is not working properly, then your data would be delayed or would not be sent or even can be lost during transmission. In Computer Networks, we call this speed of transmitting data, as **date rate**. The medium over which the information between two computer systems is sent, called Transmission Media.

Transmission media comes in two forms:

- **Guided Media** - All communication wires/cables comes into this type of media, such as UTP, Coaxial and Fiber Optics. In this media the sender and receiver are directly connected and the information is send (guided) through it.

- **Unguided Media** - Wireless or open air space is said to be unguided media, because there is no connectivity between the sender and receiver. Information is spread over the air, and anyone including the actual recipient may collect the information.

CHANNEL CAPACITY : The speed of transmission of information is said to be the channel capacity. We count it as data rate in digital world. It depends on numerous factors

BANDWIDTH: The physical limitation of underlying media.

ERROR-RATE: Incorrect reception of information because of noise.

ENCODING: Number of levels used for signaling.

MULTIPLEXING : Multiplexing is a technique to mix and send multiple data stream over a single media. This technique requires system hardware called Multiplexer for multiplexing streams and sending them on a media and De-Multiplexer which takes information from the media and distributes to different destinations.

SWITCHING : Switching is a mechanism by which data/information sent from source towards destination which are not directly connected. Networks have interconnecting devices, which receives data from directly connected sources, stores data, analyze it and then forwards to the next interconnecting device closest to the destination.

THROUGHPUT : Throughput is the amount of work that a computer can do in a given time period.

VARIOUS TYPES OF GUIDED OR WIRED TECHNOLOGIES

1. **Ethernet Cable or Twisted Pair Cable :** A twisted pair cable is made of two plastic insulated copper wires twisted together to form a single media, which are surrounded by an insulating material and outer layer called jacket.
   Out of these two wires only one carries actual signal and another is used for ground reference. The twists between wires is helpful in reducing noise (electromagnetic interference) and crosstalk. It is used as a short distance communication. E.g. Local Area networks used twisted pair cable.
   There are two types of twisted pair cables available:
   (a) Shielded Twisted Pair (STP) Cable -STP cables comes with twisted wire pair covered in metal foil. This makes it more indifferent to noise and crosstalk.
   (b) Unshielded Twisted Pair (UTP) Cable -UTP has seven categories, each suitable for specific use. In computer networks, Cat-5, Cat-5e and Cat-6 cables are mostly used. UTP cables are connected by RJ45 connectors.

2. **Coaxial Cable :** Coaxial cables has two wires of copper. The core wire lies in center and is made of solid conductor. Core is enclosed in an insulating sheath. Over the sheath the second wire is wrapped around and that too in turn encased by insulator sheath. This all is covered by plastic cover. Because of its structure coax cables are capable of carrying high frequency signals than that of twisted pair cables. The wrapped structure provides it a good shield against noise and cross talk. Coaxial cables provide high bandwidth rates of up to 450 mbps. There are three categories of Coax cables namely, RG-59 (Cable TV), RG-58 (Thin Ethernet) and RG-11 (Thick Ethernet. RG stands for Radio Government. Cables are connected using BNC connector and BNC-T. BNC terminator is used to terminate the wire at the far ends.

3. **Power Lines :** Power Line communication is Layer-1 (Physical Layer) technology which uses power cables to transmit data signals. Send in PLC modulates data and sent over the cables. The receiver on the other end de-modulates the data and interprets. Because power lines are widely deployed, PLC can make all powered devices controlled and monitored. PLC works in half-duplex. Two types of PLC exists:

Narrow band PLC - Narrow band PLC provides lower data rates up to 100s of kbps, as they work at lower frequencies (3-5000 kHz). But can be spread over several kilometers.

Broad band PLC - Broadband PLC provides higher data rates up to 100s of Mbps and works at higher frequencies (1.8 – 250 MHz). But cannot be much extended as Narrowband PLC.

4. **Fiber Optics :** Fiber Optic works on the properties of light. When light ray hits at critical angle it tends to refracts at 90 degree. This property has been used in fiber optic. The core of fiber optic cable is made of high quality glass or plastic. From one end of it light is emitted, it travels through it and at the other end light detector detects light stream and converts it to electric data form. Fiber Optic provides the highest mode of speed. It comes in two modes:

    (a) Single mode fiber - Single mode fiber can carries single ray of light.

    (b) Multimode fiber- Multimode is capable of carrying multiple beams of light.

    Fiber Optic also comes in unidirectional and bidirectional capabilities. To connect and access Fiber Optic special type of connectors are used.

    Optical fibers allow transmission over longer distance at higher bandwidth which is not affected by electromagnetic field. The speed of optical fiber is hundred of times faster than coaxial cable. E.g. Wavelength Division Multiplexing and SONET network.

VARIOUS TYPES OF UNGUIDED OR WIRELESS TECHNOLOGIES

1. **Wireless Transmission :** Wireless transmission is a form of unguided media. Wireless communication involves no physical link established between two or more devices, communicating wirelessly. Wireless signals are spread over in the air and are received and interpret by appropriate antennas. When an antenna is attached to electrical circuit of a computer or wireless device, it converts the digital data into wireless signals and spread all over within its frequency range. The receptor on the other end receives these signals and converts them back to digital data. A little part of electromagnetic spectrum can be used for wireless transmission.

2. **Radio Transmission :** Radio frequency is easier to generate and because of its large wavelength it can penetrate through walls and alike structures. Radio waves can have wavelength from 1 mm – 100,000 km and have frequency ranging from 3 Hz (Extremely Low Frequency) to 300 GHz (Extremely High Frequency). Radio frequencies are sub-divided into six bands. Radio waves at lower frequencies can travel through walls whereas higher RF travel in straight line and bounces back. The power of low frequency waves decreases sharply as it covers longer distance. High frequency radio waves have more power. Lower frequencies like (VLF, LF, MF bands) can travel on the ground up to 1000 kilometers, over the earth's surface.

3. **Microwave Transmission :** Electromagnetic waves above 100 MHz tend to travel in a straight line and signals over them can be sent by beaming those waves towards one particular station. Because Microwaves travels in straight lines, both sender and receiver must be aligned to be strictly in line-of-sight. Microwaves can have wavelength ranging from 1 mm – 1 meter and frequency ranging from 300 MHz to 300 GHz. Microwave antennas concentrate the waves making a beam of it. Microwaves are higher frequencies and do not penetrate wall like obstacles. Microwaves transmission depends highly upon the weather conditions and the frequency it is using.

4. **Infrared Transmission :** Infrared waves lies in between visible light spectrum and microwaves. It has wavelength of 700 nm to 1 mm and frequency ranges from 300 GHz to 430 THz. Infrared waves are used for very short range communication purposes such as television and it's remote. Infrared travels in a straight line so they are directional by nature. Because of high frequency range, Infrared do not cross wall like obstacles.

5. **Light Transmission :** Highest most electromagnetic spectrum which can be used for data transmission is light or optical signaling. This is achieved by means of LASER. Because of frequency light uses, it tends to travel strictly in straight line. So the sender and receiver must be in the line-of-sight. Because laser transmission is unidirectional, at both ends of communication laser and photo-detectors needs to be

installed. Laser beam is generally 1mm wide so it is a work of precision to align two far receptors each pointing to lasers source.

CLIENT-SERVER MODEL

In client-server model, any process can act as Server or Client. This not the machine or size of the machine or its computing power which makes it server but it is the feature of serving request that makes it server.

Client-server architecture (client/server) is a network architecture in which each computer or process on the network is either a *client* or a *server*. Servers are powerful computers or processes dedicated to managing disk drives (*file servers*), printers (*print servers*), or network traffic (*network servers*). Clients are PCs or workstations on which users run applications. Clients rely on servers for resources, such as files, devices, and even processing power.

PEER TO PEER MODEL

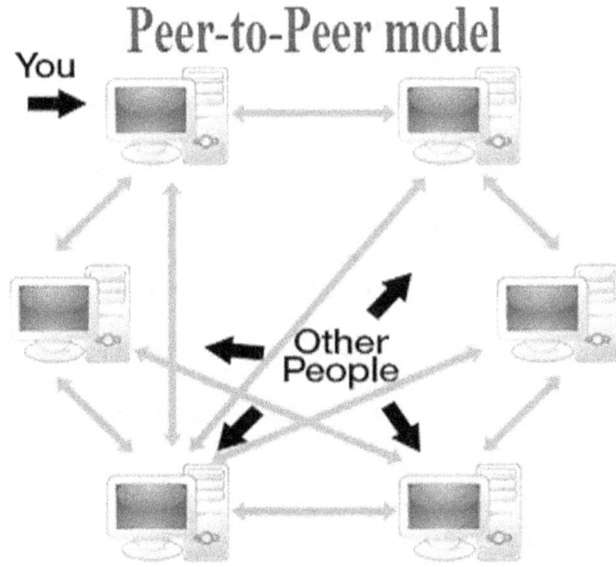

Another type of network architecture is known as a *peer-to-peer* architecture because each *node* has equivalent responsibilities. This computer network selies on computing power at the edges of a connection rather than in the network itself.

Peer to Peer computing or Networking is a distributed application architecture that partitions tasks or work loads between Peers, Peers are equaly privileged and equivalent participants in the Application Architecture so this Network is known as peer to peer architecture.

Past Exercise

1. Computer and communication technology, such as communication links to the Internet, that provide help and understanding to the end user is known as **[SBI PO, 2011]**
   (a) presentation file
   (b) information technology
   (c) program
   (d) worksheet file
   (e) FTP

2. A device that connects to a network without the use of cables is said to be **[IBPS PO, 2011]**
   (a) distributed   (b) free
   (c) centralized   (d) open source
   (e) wireless network

3. What is a modem connected to ? **[SBI Clerk, 2011]**
   (a) processor   (b) motherboard
   (c) printer   (d) phone line
   (e) None of these

4. Computers connected to a LAN can **[SBI Clerk, 2011]**
   (a) run faster
   (b) go on line
   (c) share information and/or share peripheral equipment
   (d) E-mail
   (e) None of these

5. A device that connects to a network without the use of cables is said to be **[SBI Clerk, 2011]**
   (a) distributed   (b) centralised
   (c) open source   (d) wireless
   (e) None of these

6. If you want to connect to your own computer through the Internet from another location, you can use **[IBPS PO, 2011]**
   (a) e-mail   (b) FTP
   (c) instant message   (d) Telnet
   (e) None of these

7. A communication network which is used by large organizations over regional, national or global area is called: **[SSC-CGL , 2011]**
   (a) LAN   (b) WAN
   (c) MAN   (d) VAN

8. Computers that control processes accept data in a continuous __________. **[IBPS PO, 2012]**
   (a) data traffic pattern   (b) data highway
   (c) infinite loop   (d) feedback loop
   (e) slot

9. The method of Internet access that requires a phone line, but offers faster access speeds than dial-up is the ______ connection. **[IBPS PO, 2012]**
   (a) cable access
   (b) satellite access
   (c) fiber-optic service
   (d) Digital Subscriber Line (DSL)
   (e) modem

10. __________ is a technique that is used to send more than one call over a single line. **[IBPS PO, 2012]**
    (a) Digital transmission
    (b) Infrared transmission
    (c) Digitizing
    (d) Streaming
    (e) Multiplexing

11. Codec refers to **[IBPS Clerk, 2012]**
    (a) Coder-decoder
    (b) Co-declaration
    (c) Command declaration
    (d) Command decoding
    (e) None of these

12. To connect networks of similar protocols ________ are used **[IBPS Clerk, 2012]**
    (a) Routers   (b) Bridges
    (c) Gateways   (d) Dial-up routers
    (e) None of these

13. Telnet is a ________ based computer protocol **[IBPS Clerk, 2012]**
    (a) Sound   (b) Text
    (c) Image   (d) Animation
    (e) Digits

14. P2P is a ________ application architecture **[IBPS Clerk, 2012]**
    (a) Client/ server   (b) Distributed
    (c) Centralized   (d) 1- tier
    (e) None of these

15. Which of the following terms is just the collection of networks that can be joined together ? **[SBI Clerk, 2012]**
    (a) virtual private network
    (b) LAN   (c) intranet
    (d) extranet   (e) internet

16. An alternate name for the completely interconnected network topology is **[SSC, CGL, 2012]**

(a) Mesh   (b) Star
(c) Tree   (d) Ring

17. The transfer of date from a CPU to peripheral devices of computer is achieved through **[SSC-CGL , 2012]**
(a) interfaces   (b) buffer memory
(c) modems   (d) computer ports

18. Which of the following items is not used in Local Area Networks (LANs)? **[SSC-CGL , 2012]**
(a) Interface Card   (b) Cable
(c) Computer   (d) Modem

19. An alternate name for the completely interconnected network topology is **[SSC-CGL , 2012]**
(a) Mesh   (b) Star
(c) Tree   (d) Ring

20. ___________ is the most important/powerful computer in a typical network. **[SBI PO, 2013]**
(a) Desktop   (b) Network client
(c) Network server   (d) Network station
(e) Network switch

21. In a client/server model, a client program **[SBI Clerk, 2014]**
(a) asks for information
(b) provides information and files
(c) Serves Software files to other computers
(d) Distributes Software files to other computers
(e) None of the above

22. 'Blue tooth' technology allows **[IBPS Clerk, 2015]**
(a) Satellite communication
(b) Signal transmission on mobile phones only
(c) Wireless communication between equipments
(d) Landline phone to mobile phone communication
(e) None of these

23. What is the commonly used unit for measuring the sped of data transmission? **[IBPS Clerk, 2015]**
(a) Mega Hertz
(b) Characters per second
(c) Nano seconds
(d) Bits per second
(e) None of these

24. What is the other name of LAN card? **[SBI Clerk, 2015]**
(a) Modem
(b) Network connector
(c) Internet card
(d) NIC
(e) None of these

25. Distributed processing involves **[IBPS PO, 2015]**
(a) solving computer component problems from a different computer
(b) solving computing problems by breaking them into smaller parts that are separately processed by different computers
(c) allowing users to share files on a network
(d) allowing users to access network resources away from the office
(e) None of these

26. Office LANs that are spread geographically apart on a large scale can be connected using a corporate **[IBPS PO, 2015]**
(a) CAN   (b) LAN
(c) DAN   (d) WAN
(e) None of these

27. AT&T designed its first commercial modem, specifically for converting digital computer data to analog signals for transmission across its long distance network. What is the name of the modem? **[IBPS PO, 2016]**
(a) Telex   (b) Memex
(c) CompuServe   (d) Bell 103 dataset
(e) Dataphone

28. There is a network that can connect networks ranging from small location or area to a bigger range including public packet network and large corporate networks. That network's enterprise allows users to share access to applications, services and other centrally located resources. Its ability for a huge geographical access has transformed networking. Which among the following is that network? **[IBPS PO, 2016]**
(a) SAN   (b) CAN
(c) LAN   (d) WAN
(e) MAN

29. Which cloud is a cloud computing environment that uses a mix of on-premises, private cloud and third-party, public cloud services with orchestration between the two platforms and it is particularly valuable for dynamic or highly changeable workloads? **[IBPS PO, 2016]**
(a) Dynamic Cloud   (b) Advance Cloud
(c) Hybrid Cloud   (d) Sharing Cloud
(e) Combined Cloud

30. A router is a networking device that forwards data packets and is connected to two or more data lines from different networks. Which among the following was the earliest device

which had almost the same functionality as that of a router? **[IBPS PO, 2016]**
- (a) Interface Delay Device
- (b) Interface Traffic Manager
- (c) Interface Routing Processor
- (d) Interface Message Processor
- (e) Interface Data Manager

31. When collection of various computers seems a single coherent system to its client, then it is called **[IBPS Clerk, 2016]**
- (a) Computer Network
- (b) Distributed System
- (c) Both (a) & (b)
- (d) None of the above
- (e) Server

32. In computer network nodes are:
[IBPS Clerk, 2016]
- (a) The computer that originates the data
- (b) The computer that routes the data
- (c) The computer that terminates the data
- (d) All of the mentioned
- (e) None of the above

33. Bluetooth is an example of
[IBPS Clerk, 2016]
- (a) Personal area network
- (b) Local area network
- (b) Virtual private network
- (d) None of the above
- (e) Wireless fidelity

34. Which of the following extends a private network across public networks?
[IBPS Clerk, 2016]
- (a) Local area network
- (b) Virtual private network
- (c) Enterprise private network
- (d) Storage area network
- (e) DSL-LINE

35. _______ allows wireless mobile device to access the internet and its services such as the web and email. **[IBPS RRB, 2016]**
- (a) TCP
- (b) Ethernet
- (c) WAP
- (d) Token ring
- (e) None of these

36. Which of the following protocol have file edit capability in remote logging?
[IBPS RRB, 2016]
- (a) FTP
- (b) TFTP
- (c) Telnet
- (d) SMTP
- (e) None of these

37. End to End connectivity is provided from which of the following layer? **[IBPS RRB, 2016]**
- (a) Network layer
- (b) Session layer
- (c) Transport layer
- (d) Data link layer
- (e) None of these

38. ICMP stands for _______
[IBPS RRB, 2016]
- (a) Internet Communication Message Protocol
- (b) Internal Communication Message Protocol
- (c) Internal Control Message Protocol
- (d) Internet Control Message Protocol
- (e) Intranet Control Message Protocol

39. ICMP used for _______
[IBPS RRB, 2016]
- (a) Forwarding
- (b) Addressing
- (c) Multicasting
- (d) Error Reporting
- (e) None of these

40. Which of the following is the process of extracting large amount of information from a website?
[IBPS RRB, 2016]
- (a) Trackback
- (b) Spoofing
- (c) SYN Flood
- (d) Scraping
- (e) None of these

41. Which is a small hardware device that joins multiple computers together within one LAN?
[IBPS RRB, 2016]
- (a) Network Interface Card
- (b) Switch
- (c) Bridge
- (d) Router
- (e) None of these

ANSWER KEY

1.	(b)	8.	(c)	15.	(c)	22.	(c)	29.	(c)	36.	(c)
2	(e)	9.	(e)	16.	(a)	23.	(d)	30.	(d)	37.	(c)
3.	(d)	10.	(e)	17.	(a)	24.	(d)	31.	(b)	38.	(d)
4.	(c)	11.	(a)	18.	(c)	25.	(b)	32.	(d)	39.	(d)
5.	(d)	12.	(b)	19.	(a)	26.	(d)	33.	(a)	40.	(d)
6.	(d)	13.	(b)	20.	(c)	27.	(e)	34.	(b)	41.	(b)
7.	(b)	14.	(a)	21.	(a)	28.	(d)	35.	(c)		

Practice Exercise

1. A MODEM is connected in between a telephone line and a ___________.
   (a) Network
   (b) Computer
   (c) Communication Adapter
   (d) Serial Port

2. A device that connects to a network without the use of cables is said to be ___________.
   (a) distributed
   (b) wireless network
   (c) centralized
   (d) open source
   (e) None of these

3. Computers send and receive data in the form of ___________ signals.
   (a) Analog
   (b) Digital
   (c) Modulated
   (d) Demodulated
   (e) All of these

4. Computers connected to a LAN (Local Area Network) can ___________.
   (a) run faster
   (b) go on line
   (c) share information and/or share peripheral equipment
   (d) E-mail
   (e) None of these

5. An example of a telecommunications device is a ___________.
   (a) keyboard
   (b) mouse
   (c) printer
   (d) modem
   (e) None of these

6. Which device is used to access your computer by other computer or for talk over phone?
   (a) RAM
   (b) CD ROM Drive
   (c) Modem
   (d) Hard Disk
   (e) None of these

7. The vast network of computers that connects millions of people all over the world is called ___________.
   (a) LAN
   (b) Web
   (c) Hypertext
   (d) Internet
   (e) None of these

8. An example of a telecommunications device is a
   (a) keyboard
   (b) mouse
   (c) printer
   (d) modem
   (e) None of these

9. Several computers linked to a server to share programs and storage space.
   (a) Network
   (b) grouping
   (c) library
   (d) integrated system
   (e) None of the above

10. A ___________ typically connects personal computers within a very limited geographical area, usually within a single building.
    (a) LAN
    (b) BAN
    (c) TAN
    (d) NAN
    (e) None of these

11. Networks are monitored by security personnel and supervised by ___________ who set(s) up accounts and passwords for authorized network users.
    (a) IT managers
    (b) the government
    (c) network administrators
    (d) password administrators

12. Protocols are?
    (a) Agreements on how communication components and DTE's are to communicate
    (b) Logical communication channels for transferring data
    (c) Physical communication channels sued for transferring data
    (d) None of above

13. A collection of computers and devices connected together via communication devices and transmission media is called a ___________.
    (a) workgroup
    (b) server
    (c) mainframe
    (d) network
    (e) computer lab

14. A device which can be connected to a network without using cable is called
    (a) Distributed device
    (b) Centralised device
    (c) Open-source device
    (d) Wireless device
    (e) Without code device

15. A modem
    (a) translates analog signals from a computer into digital signals that can travel along conventional telephone lines.
    (b) translates digital signals from a computer into analog signals that, can travel along conventional telephone lines.
    (c) demodulates digital signals from a computer.
    (d) modulates signals from an analog telephone lines.
    (e) None of these
16. The collection of links throughout the Internet creats an interconnected network called the

    ____________.
    (a) WWW   (b) Web
    (c) World Wide Web   (d) All of the above
    (e) None of the above
17. A(n) ____________ is composed of several computers connected together to share resources and data.
    (a) Internet   (b) network
    (c) backbone   (d) hyperlink
    (e) protocol
18. A popular way to learn about computers without ever going to a classroom is called

    ____________.
    (a) i-learning   (b) isolated learning
    (c) e-learning   (d) close learning
    (e) distance learning
19. A ____________ is a set of rules.
    (a) resource locator (b) domain
    (c) hypertext   (d) URL
    (e) protocol
20. The connection between your computer at home and your local ISP is called ____________.
    (a) the last mile
    (b) the home stretch
    (c) the home page
    (d) the backbone
    (e) the vital mile
21. If you wish to extend the length of the network without having the signal degrade, you would use a
    (a) resonance   (b) router
    (c) gateway   (d) switch
    (e) repeater

22. The Internet is
    (a) a large network of networks
    (b) an internal communication system for a business
    (c) a communication system for the indian government
    (d) a communication system for some states of India
    (e) a communication system for some cities of India
23. A term related to sending data to a satellite is
    (a) downlink   (b) modulate
    (c) demodulate   (d) uplink
    (e) inter-relate
24. What is a benefit of networking your computer with other computers?
    (a) Increase in the computer's speed
    (b) Sharing of cables to cut down on expenses and clutter
    (c) You have another computer if yours has a breakdown
    (d) Increase in the speed of the network
    (e) Sharing of resources to cut down on the amount of equipment needed
25. Officer LANs that are spread geographically apart on a large scale can be connected using a corporate
    (a) CAN   (b) LAN
    (c) DAN   (d) WAN
    (e) TAN
26. The common name for a modulator-demodulator is ____________.
    (a) modem   (b) joiner
    (c) networker   (d) connector
    (e) demod
27. A modem is connected to
    (a) a telephone line (b) a keyboard
    (d) a printer   (d) a monitor
    (e) a scanner
28. Bluetooth is an example of ____________.
    (a) Personal area network
    (b) Local area network
    (c) Virtual private network
    (d) Wide area network
    (e) None of these
29. Frames from one LAN can be transmitted to another LAN via the device
    (a) Router   (b) Bridge
    (c) Repeater   (d) Modem
    (e) None of these

30. Which of the following is not a disadvantage of wireless LAN?
    (a) Slower data transmission
    (b) higher error rate
    (c) interference of transmissions from different computers
    (d) All of the above
    (e) None of these

31. Which of the following device is used to connect two systems, especially if the systems use different protocols?
    (a) hub   (b) bridge
    (c) gateway   (d) repeater
    (e) None of these

32. The synchronous modems are more costly than the asynchronous modems because
    (a) they produce large volume of data
    (b) they contain clock recovery circuits
    (c) they transmit the data with stop and start bits.
    (d) they operate with a larger bandwidth
    (e) None of these

33. A distributed network configuration in which all data/information pass through a central computer is
    (a) bus network
    (b) star network
    (c) ring network
    (d) Point-to-point network
    (e) None of these

34. The slowest transmission speeds are those of
    (a) twisted-pair wire   (b) coaxial cable
    (c) fiber-optic cable   (d) microwaves

35. To connect a computer with a device in the same room, you might be likely to use
    (a) a coaxial cable   (b) a dedicated line
    (c) a ground station   (d) All of the above
    (e) None of these

36. Which of the following types of channels moves data relatively slowly?
    (a) wideband channel
    (b) voiceband channel
    (c) narrowband channel
    (d) broadband channel
    (e) None of these

37. Which of the following is required to communicate between two computers?
    (a) communications software
    (b) protocol
    (c) communications hardware
    (d) access to transmission medium
    (e) All of the above

38. What device separates a single network into two segments but lets the two segments appear as one to higher protocols?
    (a) Switch   (b) Bridge
    (c) Gateway   (d) Router
    (e) None of these

39. In a synchronous modem, the digital-to-analog converter transmits signal to the
    (a) equalizer   (b) modulator
    (c) demodulator   (d) terminal
    (e) None of these

40. Which of the following communications modes support two-way traffic but in only one direction of a time?
    (a) simplex
    (b) half-duplex
    (c) three-quarters duplex
    (d) All of the above
    (e) None of these

ANSWER KEY

1.	(b)	8.	(d)	15.	(c)	22.	(a)	29.	(b)	36.	(c)
2.	(b)	9.	(a)	16.	(d)	23.	(d)	30.	(d)	37.	(e)
3.	(b)	10.	(a)	17.	(b)	24.	(e)	31.	(c)	38.	(b)
4.	(c)	11.	(c)	18.	(c)	25.	(d)	32.	(b)	39.	(a)
5.	(d)	12.	(a)	19.	(e)	26.	(a)	33.	(b)	40.	(b)
6.	(c)	13.	(d)	20.	(c)	27.	(a)	34.	(a)		
7.	(d)	14.	(d)	21.	(e)	28.	(a)	35.	(a)		

Basics of Internet Technology

*The **Internet** is a global system of interconnected computer networks that use the standard Internet protocol suite(TCP/IP) to link various billion devices worldwide. It is an international network of networks that consists of millions of private, public, academic, business, and government packet switched networks, linked by a broad array of electronic, wireless, and optical networking technologies. The Internet carries a wide range of information resources and services, such as the inter-linked hypertext documents and applications of the World Wide Web (WWW), theinfrastructure to support email, and peer-to-peer networks for file sharing and telephony.*

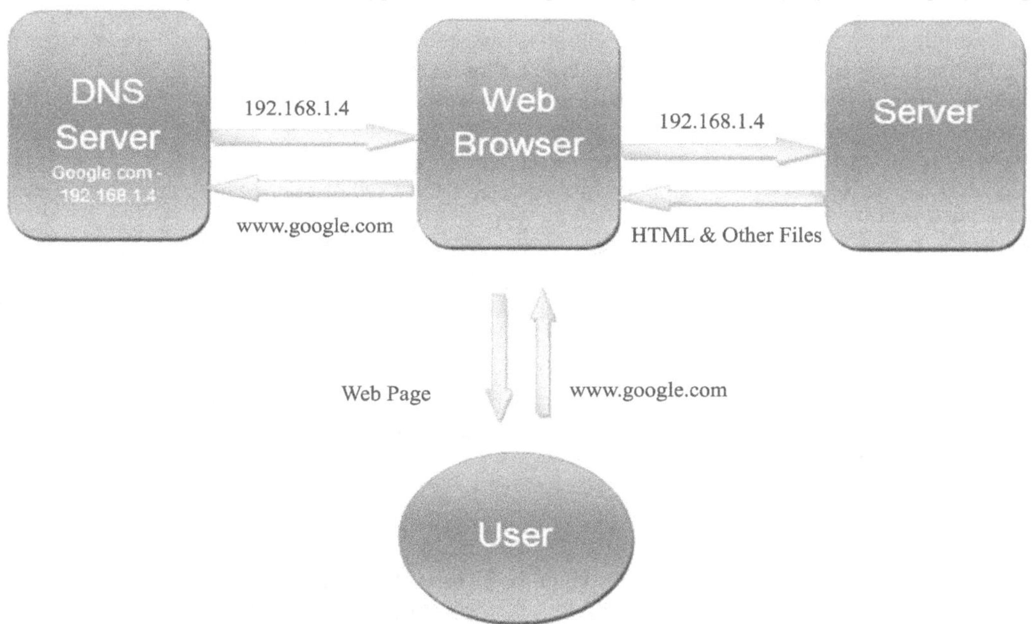

USES AND WORKING OF INTERNET

Internet is today one of the most important part of our daily life. There are large numbers of things that can be done using the internet and so it is very important. You can say that with the progress in the internet we are progressing in every sphere of life as it not only makes our tasks easier but also saves a lot of time.

1. **Communication :** Earlier the communication used to be a daunting task but all that chanced once internet came into the life of the common people. Now people can not only chat but can also do the video conferencing. It has become extremely easy to contact the loved ones who are in some other part of the world. Communication is the most important gift that the internet has given to the common man. Email, social networking sites are some of the prime example of it.

2. **Research :** In order to do research you need to go through hundreds of books as well as the references and that was one of the most difficult jobs to do earlier. Since the internet came into life, everything is available just a click away. You just have to search for the concerned topic and you will get hundreds of references that may be beneficial for your research. And since internet is here to make your research public, you can then benefit a large amount of people from the research work that you have done.

3. **Education :** There are a number of books, reference books, online help centres, expert's views and other study oriented material on the internet that can make the learning process very easier as well as a fun learning experience. There are lots and lots of websites which are related to different topic. You can visit them and can gain endless amount of knowledge that you wish to have. With the use of internet for education, you are non-longer dependent on some other person to come and teach you. There are various number of tutorials available over the internet using which you can learn so many thing very easily.

4. **Financial Transaction :** Now you don't need to stand in the queue at the branch of your particular bank rather you can just log in on to the bank website with the credential that has been provided to you by the bank and then can do any transaction related to finance at your will. With the ability to do the financial transaction easily over the internet you can purchase or sell items so easily.

5. **Real time Updates :** There are various websites on the internet which provides you with the real time updates in every field be it in business, sports, finance, politics, entertainment and others. Many a time the decisions are taken on the real time updates that are happening in various parts of the world and this is where internet is very essential and helpful.

INTERNET CONNECTIONS

While determining which type of Internet connection is right for you or your family, it's important to make sure the difference between each connection. In today's age, there are numerous ways to connect laptops, desktops, mobile phones, gaming consoles, e-readers and tablets to the Internet. Some of the most widely used Internet connections are described below.

1. **Dial-Up :** Dial-up connections require users to link their phone line to a computer in order to access the Internet. This particular type of connection also referred to as analog does not permit users to make or receive phone calls through their home phone service while using the Internet.

2. **Broadband :** This high-speed Internet connection is provided through either cable or telephone companies. One of the fastest options available, broadband Internet uses multiple data channels to send large quantities of information. The term broadband is shorthand for broad bandwidth. Broadband Internet connections such as DSL and cable are considered high-bandwidth connections. Although many DSL connections can be considered broadband, not all broadband connections are DSL.

   - **DSL :** DSL which stands for Digital Subscriber Line, uses existing 2-wire copper telephone line connected to one's home so service is delivered at the same time as landline telephone service. Customers can still place calls while surfing the Internet.

   - **Cable :** Cable Internet connection is a form of broadband access. Through use of a cable modem, users can access the Internet over cable TV lines. Cable modems can provide extremely fast access to the Internet.

3. **Wireless Connection :** Wireless Internet enables wireless connectivity to the Internet via radio waves rather than wires on a person's home computer, laptop, smart phone or similar mobile device.

   Some ways to connect the internet wirelessly are:

   - **Wireless (WiFi) :** wireless fidelity (wifi) allows high speed internet connections without use the use of cable or wires radio frequency bands are used in place of telephone or cable networks. One of the greatest advantages of wireless Internet connections is the "always-on" connection that can be accessed from any location that falls within network coverage. Wireless connections are made possible through the use of a modem, which picks up Internet signals and sends them to other devices.

   - **Mobile :** Many cell phone and smart phone providers offer voice plans with Internet access. Mobile Internet connections provide good speeds and allow you to access the Internet on the go.

   - **Hotspots :** Hot-spots are sites that offer Internet access over a wireless local area network (WLAN) by way of a router that then connects to an Internet service provider. Hot-spots utilize Wi-Fi technology, which allows electronic devices to connect to the Internet or exchange data wirelessly through radio waves. Hotspots can be phone-based or free-standing, commercial or free to the public.

   - **Satellite :** In certain areas where broadband connection is not yet offered, a satellite Internet option may be available. Similar to wireless access, satellite connection utilizes a modem.

- **ISDN :** ISDN (Integrated Services Digital Network) allows users to send data, voice and video content over digital telephone lines or standard telephone wires. The installation of an ISDN adapter is required at both ends of the transmission—on the part of the user as well as the Internet access provider.

  There are quite a few other Internet connection options available, including T-1 lines, T-3 lines, OC (Optical Carrier) and other DSL technologies.

INTERNET CONNECTING PROTOCOLS

A protocol is set of rules that define how computers will act when talking to each other. A protocol is the special set of rules that end points in a telecommunication connection use when they communicate. Protocols specify interactions between the communicating entities.

TCP (TRANSMISSION CONTROL PROTOCOL)

TCP (Transmission Control Protocol) is a standard that defines how to establish and maintain a network conversation via which application programs can exchange data. TCP works with the Internet Protocol (IP), which defines how computers send packets of data to each other. Together, TCP and IP are the basic rules defining the Internet.

TCP is a connection-oriented protocol, which means a connection is established and maintained until the application programs at each end have finished exchanging messages. It determines how to break application data into packets that networks can deliver, sends packets to and accepts packets from the network layer, manages flow control, and—because it is meant to provide error-free data transmission—handles retransmission of dropped or garbled packets as well as acknowledgement of all packets that arrive.

ISO/OSI NETWORK MODEL

The standard model for networking protocols and distributed applications is the International Standard Organization's Open System Interconnect (ISO/OSI) model. It defines seven network layers.

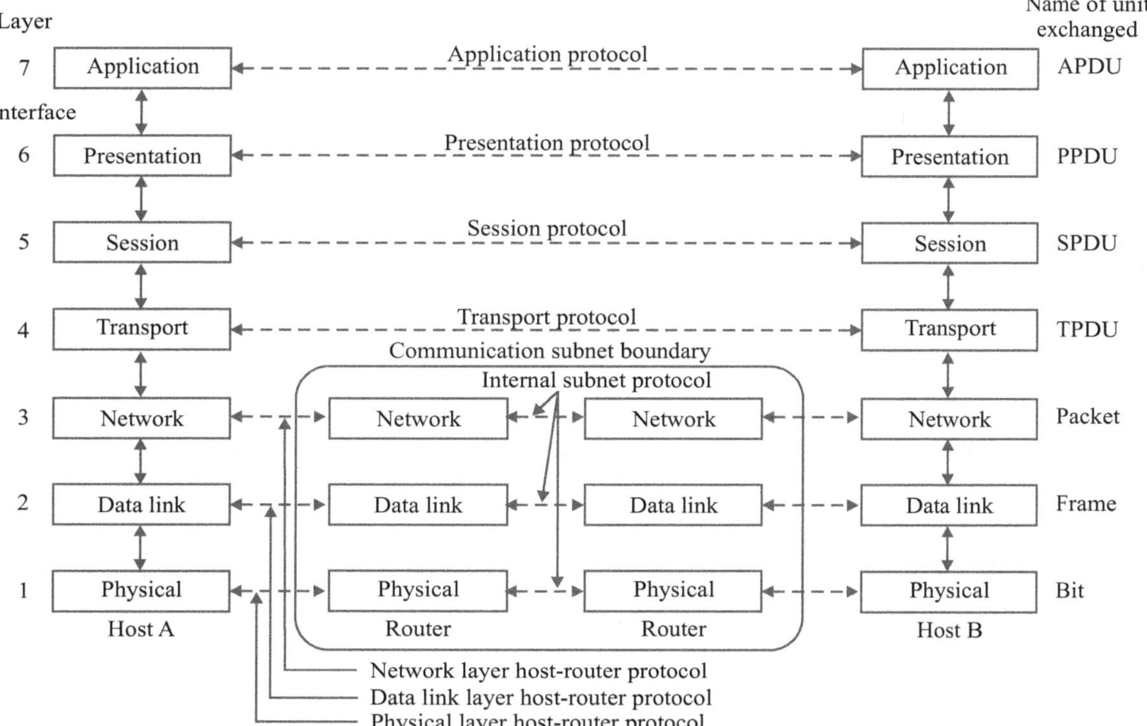

Layer 1 – Physical - Physical layer defines the cable or physical medium itself, e.g., thinnet, thicknet, unshielded twisted pairs (UTP). All media are functionally equivalent. The main difference is in convenience and cost of installation and maintenance. Converters from one media to another operate at this level.

Layer 2 – Data Link - Data Link layer defines the format of data on the network. A network data frame, aka packet, includes checksum, source and destination address, and data. The largest packet that can be sent through a data link layer defines the Maximum Transmission Unit (MTU). The data link layer handles the physical and logical connections to the packet's destination, using a network interface. A host connected to an Ethernet would have an Ethernet interface to handle connections to the outside world, and a loopback interface to send packets to itself. Ethernet addresses a host using a unique, 48-bit address called its Ethernet address or Media Access Control (MAC) address. MAC addresses are usually represented as six colon-separated pairs of hex digits, e.g., 8:0:20:11:ac:85. This number is unique and is associated with a particular Ethernet device. Hosts with multiple network interfaces should use the same MAC address on each. The data link layer's protocol-specific header specifies the MAC address of the packet's source and destination. When a packet is sent to all hosts (broadcast), a special MAC address (ff:ff:ff:ff:ff:ff) is used.

Layer 3 – Network - NFS uses Internetwork Protocol (IP) as its network layer interface. IP is responsible for routing, directing datagrams from one network to another. The network layer may have to break large datagrams, larger than MTU, into smaller packets and host receiving the packet will have to reassemble the fragmented datagram. The Internetwork Protocol identifies each host with a 32-bit IP address. IP addresses are written as four dot-separated decimal numbers between 0 and 255, e.g., 129.79.16.40. The leading 1-3 bytes of the IP identify the network and the remaining bytes identify the host on that network.

Even though IP packets are addressed using IP addresses, hardware addresses must be used to actually transport data from one host to another. The Address Resolution Protocol (ARP) is used to map the IP address to it hardware address.

Layer 4 - Transport - Transport layer subdivides user-buffer into network-buffer sized datagrams and enforces desired transmission control. Two transport protocols, Transmission Control Protocol (TCP) and User Datagram Protocol (UDP), sits at the transport layer. Reliability and speed are the primary difference between these two protocols. TCP establishes connections between two hosts on the network through 'sockets' which are determined by the IP address and port number. TCP keeps track of the packet delivery order and the packets that must be resent. Maintaining this information for each connection makes TCP a stateful protocol. UDP on the other hand provides a low overhead transmission service, but with less error checking. NFS is built on top of UDP because of its speed and statelessness. Statelessness simplifies the crash recovery.

Layer 5 - Session - The session protocol defines the format of the data sent over the connections. The NFS uses the Remote Procedure Call (RPC) for its session protocol. RPC may be built on either TCP or UDP. Login sessions uses TCP whereas NFS and broadcast use UDP.

Layer 6 - Presentation - External Data Representation (XDR) sits at the presentation level. It converts local representation of data to its canonical form and vice versa. The canonical uses a standard byte ordering and structure packing convention, independent of the host.

Layer 7 - Application - Provides network services to the end-users. Mail, ftp, telnet, DNS, NIS, NFS are examples of network applications.

TCP/IP NETWORK MODEL

TCP/IP is designed around a simple four-layer scheme. It does omit some features found under the OSI model. Also it combines the features of some adjacent OSI layers and splits other layers apart. The four network layers defined by TCP/IP model are as follows.

Layer 1 – Link - This layer defines the network hardware and device drivers.

Layer 2 – Network - This layer is used for basic communication, addressing and routing. TCP/IP uses IP and ICMP protocols at the network layer.

Layer 3 – Transport - Handles communication among programs on a network. TCP and UDP falls within this layer.

Layer 4 – Application - End-user applications reside at this layer. Commonly used applications include NFS, DNS, arp, rlogin, talk, ftp, ntp and traceroute.

INTERNET PROTOCOL

The Internet protocols are the world's most popular open-system (nonproprietary) protocol suite because they can be used to communicate across any set of interconnected networks and are equally well suited for LAN and WAN communications. The Internet protocols consist of a suite of communication protocols, of which the two best known are the Transmission Control Protocol (TCP) and the Internet Protocol (IP). The Internet protocol suite not only includes lower-layer protocols (such as TCP and IP), but it also specifies common applications such as electronic mail, terminal emulation, and file transfer.

IP Addresses (Internet Protocol)

The IP, which stands for Internet protocol, is an identifier which sends and receives information across the Internet. It is made of 4 octets consisting of 32 numbers between 0 and 255, separated by periods. Whenever you are browsing the web or sending an email, an IP address (assigned to your computer) is required.

Characteristics of IP address:

- Unique
- No two machines have same IP address

FILE TRANSFER PROTOCOL

The File Transfer Protocol (FTP) is a standard network protocol used to transfer computer files from one host to another host over a TCP-based network, such as the Internet.

FTP is built on a client-server architecture and uses separate control and data connections between the client and the server. FTP users may authenticate themselves using a clear-text sign-in protocol, normally in the form of a username and password, but can connect anonymously if the server is configured to allow it. For secure transmission that protects the user name and password, and encrypts the content, FTP is often secured with SSL/ TLS (FTPS). SSH File Transfer Protocol (SFTP) is sometimes also used instead, but is technologically different.

> **Hypertext :** Generally, any text that contains "links" to other documents - words or phrases in the document that can be chosen by a reader which cause another document to be retrieved and displayed.
>
> **Hyperlinks :** An element in an electronic document that links to another place in the same document or to an entirely different document.

Hypertext Transfer Protocol (HTTP)

Hypertext Transfer Protocol (HTTP) is the underlying protocol used by the World Wide Web. HTTP defines how messages are formatted and transmitted, and what actions Web servers and browsers should take in response to various commands. For example, when you enter a URL in your browser, this actually sends an HTTP command to the Web server directing it to fetch and transmit the requested Web page. The protocol for moving hypertext files across the Internet. Requires HTTP client program on one end, and HTTP server program on the other end. HTTP is most important protocol used in World Wide Web (WWW).

HyperText Markup Language (HTML)

HTML (Hypertext Markup Language) is the set of markup symbols or codes inserted in a file intended for display on a World Wide Web browser page. The <html> tag tells the browser that this is an HTML document. The <html> tag represents the root of an HTML document.

WEB BROWSER

A web browser is an interface that helps a computer user gain access to all the content that is on the Internet and the hard disk of the computer. It can view images, text documents, audio and video files, games, etc. More than one web browser can also be installed on a single computer. The user can navigate through files, folders and websites with the help of a browser. When the browser is used for browsing web pages, the pages may contain certain links which can be opened in a new browser. Multiple tabs and windows of the same browser can also be opened.

Some popular Web Browsers:

Internet Explorer : Internet Explorer (IE) is a product from software giant Microsoft. This is the most commonly used browser in the universe

Safari : Safari is a web browser developed by Apple Inc. and included in Mac OS X. It was first released as a public beta in January 2003. Safari has very good support for latest technologies like XHTML, CSS2 etc.

Firefox : Firefox is a browser derived from Mozilla. It was released in 2004 and has grown to be the second most popular browser on the Internet.

Opera : Opera is smaller and faster than most other browsers, yet it is full- featured. Fast, user-friendly, with keyboard interface, multiple windows, zoom functions, and more. Ideal for newcomers to the Internet, school children, handicap and as a front-end for CD-Rom and kiosks.

Google Chrome : This web browser was developed by Google. Its beta and commercial versions were released in September 2008 for Microsoft Windows. It has soon become the fourth-most widely used

DOMAIN NAME

It is the unique name that identifies an Internet site. Domain Names always have two or more parts, separated by dots. The part on the left is the most specific, the part on the right is the most general. A given machine can have more than one Domain name but a given Domain Name points to only one machine. For example: google.com etc

Domain abbreviation

Domain are organised by the type of organisations and by country. A three letter abbreviation indicating the organisation and usually two letter abbreviation indicating the country name. Most common abbreviations for organisation are –

.org	Organisation
.net	Network
.com	Commercial
.edu	Education
.gov	Government
.mil	Military

Some domain abbreviations for country are :

.in	India
.an	Australia
.fr	France
.nz	New Zealand
.uk	United kingdom

Domain Name System (DNS)

The DNS stores and associates many types of information with domain names, but most importantly, it translates domain names (computer host name) to IP address. It also lists mail exchange series accepting E-mail for each domain.

WWW (WORLD WIDE WEB)

The World Wide Web (abbreviated as WWW or W3 commonly known as the Web) is a system of interlinked hypertext documents that are accessed via the Internet. With a web browser, one can view web pages that may contain text, images, videos, and other multimedia and navigate between them via hyperlinks.

WEBSITE

A website is a collection of webpages that are under 1 domain (such as google.com). For example if there is a company that owns abccompany.com then this website will have several Webpages like Home, About Us, Contact Us, Testimonials, Products, Services, FAQ's, and others. All of these pages together make up a Website.

WEB PAGES

A webpage is an independent page of a Website. For example a webpage would be the testimonials page. A web page can be accessed by typically one URL in a browser and that page can be copied and or send to a friend for review whereas websites are collections of multiple page that must be navigated to view other content.

A web browser displays a web page on a monitor or mobile device. The web page is what displays, but the term also refers to a computer file, usually written in HTML or comparable markup language. Web browsers coordinate the various web resource elements for the written web page, such as style sheets, scripts and images, to present the web page.

A static web page is delivered exactly as stored, as web content in the web server's file system, while a dynamic web page is generated by a web application that is driven by server-side software or client-side scripting.

HOME PAGE

The home page is the first page that a visitor discovers when he wants to visit your site. There is usually just one.

WEB ADDRESS/URLS (UNIFORM RESOURCE LOCATOR)

A URL (Uniform Resource Locator; also known as a web address) is a distinct web address on the Internet for a web page, a PDF file or any other file format available. It is easy for humans to remember URLs but the computer cannot "understand" this format. For example, the URL of a web page may be www.xyz.com, and its IP address 123.456.789.011.

Syntax:

Every HTTP URL consists of the following, in the given order:

* the scheme name (commonly called protocol)
* a colon, two slashes
* a host, normally given as a domain name but sometimes as a literal IP address
* optionally a colon followed by a port number
* the full path of the resource

WEB SERVER

A web server is a computer system that processes requests via HTTP, the basic network protocol used to distribute information on the World Wide Web. The term can refer either to the entire system, or specifically to the software that accepts and supervises the HTTP requests. The most common use of web servers is to host websites, but there are other uses such as gaming, data storage, running enterprise applications, handling email, FTP, or other web uses.

Three of the most popular web servers on the web are:

* ### Apache HTTP Server

    Apache HTTP Server (also referred to as simply "Apache") has, at the time of writing, been the most popular web server on the web since 1996. Apache is developed and maintained by the Apache Software Foundation, which consists of a decentralized team of developers. The software is produced under the Apache licence, which makes it free and open source.

    Apache is available for a range of operating systems, including Unix, Linux, Novell Netware, Windows, Mac OS X, Solaris, and FreeBSD.

* ### Microsoft Internet Information Services (IIS)

    IIS is, at the time of writing, the second most popular web server on the web. It is however, gaining market share, and if the current trend continues, it won't be long before it overtakes Apache.

    IIS comes as an optional component of most Windows operating systems. You can install IIS by using Add/Remove Windows Components fromAdd or Remove Programs in the Control Panel.

- **Sun Java System Web Server**

  Based on the Sun One Web Server, the Sun Java System Web Server is designed for medium to large business applications. Sun Java System Web Server is available for most operating systems.

DIFFERENCE BETWEEN WEB SERVER AND APPLICATION SERVER

A Web server can be either a computer program or a computer running a program that is responsible for accepting HTTP requests from clients, serving back HTTP responses along with optional data contents, which usually are web pages such as HTML documents and linked objects on it.

An application server is the kind of software engine that will deliver various applications to another device. It is the kind of computer found in an office or university network that allows everyone in the network to run software off of the same machine.

SERVICES OF INTERNET

1. **E-MAIL (ELECTRONIC MAIL) :** E-MAIL is the electronic equivalent of sending a letter.
    Email consists of two parts, 1) the header, which contains information about where the message will be sent, and 2) the body, or message.
    First, the person goes to the head of the email message and types in:
    - the email addresses of the person(s) to receive it, i.e. the To:
    - the sender's email addresses, i.e. the From:
    - the sender may want the email reply sent elsewhere, i.e. Reply to:
    - the email addresses of the person(s) to receive the Cc: and Bcc: copies (normally this is used to create file and information copies),
    - the Subject: which tells the receiver of the email what the message is about. The user uses the Compose function of the particular email system included in the account and types in a text message, as one would use a word processor to create a document.

    Email Address : An email address is made up of two parts: the user ID, i.e. your account name, and the domain name, i.e. the Internet name of the computer where your mail is sent. The two parts are separated by a @. For example, the instructor's email address is: xyz@abc.com.

2. **WIRELESS APPLICATION PROTOCOL(WAP) :** Short for the Wireless Application Protocol, a secure specification that allows users to access information instantly via handheld wireless devices such as mobile phones, pagers, two-way radios, smartphones and communicators.
    WAP supports most wireless networks. These include CDPD, CDMA, GSM, PDC, PHS, TDMA, FLEX, ReFLEX, iDEN, TETRA, DECT, DataTAC, and Mobitex.

3. **VOIP :** A Voice over IP call, or VoIP call, utilizes packet-switched Voice over Internet Protocol (VoIP) or Internet telephony as opposed to the circuit-switched telephony used by the traditional Public Switched Telephone Network (PSTN). The advantage to VoIP phone calls is that unlike regular long-distance calls, calls made through a VoIP phone service are free – there are no fees beyond the cost of your Internet access.
    Also referred to as online phones or Internet phones, a VoIP phone can be a physical telephone with built-in IP technology and an RJ-45 Ethernet connector instead of the RJ-11 phone connector found in standard phones, or it can be a voice-capable computer that uses VoIP hardware such as MagicJack or VoIP software like Skype

4. **ONLINE BANKING :** Online banking is an electronic payment system that enables customers of a financial institution to conduct financial transactions on a website operated by the institution, such as a retail bank, virtual bank, credit union or building society. Online banking is also referred as Internet banking, e-banking, virtual banking and by other terms.

5. **E-COMMERCE :** E-commerce (electronic commerce or EC) is the buying and selling of goods and services, or the transmitting of funds or data, over an electronic network, primarily the Internet.

6. **M-COMMERCE :** M-commerce stands for Mobile Commerce wherein commercial transactions are done using cellular or mobile phones that have access to the Internet.

Difference between M- Commerce and E- Commerce

1. M-commerce and E-commerce are business transactions done online.
2. M-commerce stands for Mobile Commerce while E-commerce stands for Electronic Commerce.
3. M-commerce uses mobile devices for commercial transactions while E-commerce uses computers.
4. M-commerce is available anyplace you go, even if there is no Internet. For E-commerce, you still need to go to a place where there is Internet to access your online transactions.
5. M-commerce is very handy and easy to carry while E-commerce you cannot always bring with you your computer or laptop anywhere.
6. M-commerce is charged through the caller's rate, deduction of user's credit, and mobile banking. E-commerce is charged through the use of credit cards that are swiped in credit card machines.
7. In conclusion, M-commerce uses mobile devices for business transactions while E-commerce uses computers or laptops for business transactions.

7. **E.Shopping (Electronic shopping) :** It is the process of buying goods and services from merchants who seel an the Internet. some E-shopping websites are flipkart, amazon, jabong etc.
8. **E-Reservation (Electronic Reservation) :** Electronic Reservation means making a reservation for a services via Internet. Example of E-Reservation are - www.irctc.com, www.makingtrip.com etc.
9. **Social Networking :** Social Networking services is an online service, platform or site that focuses on facilitating the building of social networks or social relations among people. The most popular sites are facebook, Myspace etc.

VARIOUS INTERNET RELATED TERMS

INTERNET ADDRESS (NETWORK ADDRESS)

Internet site addresses come in two forms: as a set of numbers such as 202.54.1.18 and as alpha numerical such as giasbm01.vsnl.net.in (these can represent the same address, and either can be used, e.g., Telnet). (2) An individual's email address, e.g., at this site, Internet for You may look like i4u@giasbm02.vsnl.net.in.

ASCII

(American Standard Code for Information Interchange) – This is a de facto world-wide standard for the code numbers used by the computers to represent all the upper and lower-case Latin letters, numbers, punctuation, etc. There are 128 ASCII codes by a seven digit binary number 0000000 through 1111111.

EBCDIC

EBCDIC is an IBM code for representing characters as numbers. Although it is widely used on large IBM computers, most other computers, including PCs and Macintoshes, use ASCIIcodes.

BAUD

When transmitting data, the number of times the medium's state changes per second. For example a 14,400 baud modem changes the signal it sends on the phone line 14,400 times per second. Since each change in state can correspond to multiple bits of data, the actual bit rate of data transfer may exceed the baud rate.

BIT

(Binary Digit) A single digit number in base-2, in other words, either a 1 or zero. The smallest unit of computerized data. Bandwidth is usually measured in bits-per-second. See also: Bandwidth, Bps, Byte, Kilobyte, Megabyte.

BITS PER SECOND (BPS)

The speed at which bits are transmitted over a communication medium.

BYTE

A set of bits that represent a single character, usually there are 8 bits in a byte, sometimes more, depending on how the measurement is being made.

BANDWIDTH

How much "stuff " you can send through a connection. Usually measured in bit-per-second. A full page of English text is about 16,000 bits. A fast modem can move about 15,000 bits in one second. Full-motion full screen video will require roughly 10,000,000 bits-per-second, depending on compression.

CYBERSPACE

The term originated by author William Gibson in his novel "Neuromancer", the word cyberspace is currently used to describe the whole range of information resources available through computer networks.

COOKIE

A cookie, also known as an HTTP cookie, web cookie, Internet cookie, or browser cookie, is a small piece of data sent from a website and stored in a user's web browser while the user is browsing that website. Every time the user loads the website, the browser sends the cookie back to the server to notify the website of the user's previous activity.

CHAT

Real-time communication between two users via computer. Once a chat has been initiated, either user can enter text by typing on the keyboard and the entered text will appear on the other user's monitor. Most networks and online services offer a chat feature.

FREENET

A organization to provide free Internet access to people in a certain area, usually through public libraries.

Any computer on a network that is a repository for services available to other computers on the network. It is quite common to have one host machine provide several services, such as WWW and USENET.

IP NUMBER

Sometimes called a "dotted quad". A unique number consisting of four parts separated by dots, e.g. 202.54.1.1 is a IP number of one of the servers. Every machine that is on the Internet has an unique IP number - if a machine does not have an IP number, it is not really on the Internet. Most machines also have one or more Domain Names that are easier for people to remember.

ISDN

(Integrated Services Digital Network) – Basically a way to move more data over existing regular phone lines. ISDN is only slowly becoming available in Mumbai. It allows a very large bandwidth for transmission of data.

ISO

The International Organization for Standardization; An organization that has defined a different set of network protocols, called the ISO/OSI protocols. In theory, the ISO/OSI protocols will eventually replace the Internet protocols. When and if this will actually happen is a hotly debated topic.

INTERNET SERVICE PROVIDER (ISP)

An organization that provides connections to a part of Internet. If you want to connect you company's network, or even your personal computer, to the Internet, you have to talk to a "service provider". Also commonly known as ISP (Internet Service Provider).E.g. Airtel, MTNL etc.

KILOBYTE

A thousand bytes. Actually, usually, 1024 bytes.

LEASED LINE

A permanently-connected private telephone line between two locations. Leased lines are typically used to connect a moderate-sized local network to an Internet service provider.

MODEM

(Modulator, DEModulator) – a piece of equipment that connects a computer to a data transmission line (typically a telephone line of some sort). Presently the modems transfer data at speeds ranging from 1200 to 33,600 bits per second. There are also modems providing higher speeds and supporting other media. These are used for special purposes – for example, to connect a large local network to its network provider over a leased line.

NIC

(Network Information Center) – Generally, any office that handles information for a network a network. The most famous of these on the Internet is the InterNIC, which is where new domain names are registered.

NFS

(Network File System) – A set of protocols that allows you to use files on other network machines as if they were local. So rather than using FTP to transfer a file to your local computer, you can read it, write it or edit it on the remote computer – using the same commands that you'd use locally. NFS was originally developed by SUN Microsystem, Inc. and is currently in widespread use.

NETWORK

Anytime you connected two or more computers together so that they can share resources you have a computer network. Connect two or more network together you have internet.

OCTET

Internet standard-monger's lingo for a set of 8 bits, i.e., a byte.

PACKET

A bundle of data. On the Internet, data is broken up into small chunks, called "packet"; each packet traverses the network independently. Packet sizes can vary from roughly 40 to 32,000 bytes, depending on network hardware media, but the packets are normally less than 1500 bytes long.

PASSWORD

A code used to gain access to a locked system. Good passwords contain letters and non-letters and are not simple combinations such as "shanti8". A good password might be: Albert12@45$

PPP

(Point to Point Protocol) – most well known as a protocol that allows a computer to use a regular phone line and a modem to make a TCP/IP connection and thus be really and truly on the Internet. PPP is gradually replacing SLIP for this purpose.

SEARCH ENGINE

An automatized way to index and find documents on the internet. Search engines will "crawl," or explore, the internet and index every file they find. Examples of search engines are www.google.com and www.bing.com.

TELNET

The command and program used to login from one Internet site to another. The Telnet command/program gets you to the "login" prompt of another host.

UDP

(The User Datagram Protocol) – Another of the protocols on which the Internet is based. For the techies, UDP is a connectionless unreliable protocol. If you're not techie don't let the word "unreliable" worry you.

USENET

A world wide system of discussion groups, with comments passed among hundreds of thousands of machines. Not all Usenet machines are on the Internet, may be half. Usenet is completely decentralized, with over 15,000 discussion areas, called news groups.

Past Exercise

1. E-mail (electronic mail) is   **[SBI Clerk, 2009]**
   (a) an internet standard that allows users to upload and download files
   (b) a real-time typed conversation that takes place on a computer
   (c) an online area in which users conduct written discussions about a particular subject
   (d) the transmission of messages and files via a computer network
   (e) None of these

2. A chat is   **[SBI Clerk, 2009]**
   (a) an internet standard that allows users to upload and download files
   (b) a typed conversation that takes place on a computer or Mobile.
   (c) an online area in which users conduct written discussions about a particular subject
   (d) the transmission of messages and files via a computer network
   (e) None of these

3. Sending an e-mail is similar to
                          [SBI Clerk, 2009, 2011]
   (a) picturing an event   (b) narrating a story
   (c) writing a letter   (d) creating a drawing
   (e) None of these

4. The process of a computer receiving information from a server on the internet is known as
                          [SBI Clerk, 2009]
   (a) pulling   (b) pushing
   (c) downloading   (d) transferring
   (e) None of these

5. Digital Banking can be resorted through
                          [SBI Clerk, 2009]
   (a) Mobile phones   (b) Internet
   (c) Telephones   (d) All of these
   (e) None of these

6. A Web site's main page is called its——
                          [SBI Clerk, 2009, IBPS - PO, 2011]
   (a) Home Page   (b) Browser page
   (c) Search Page   (d) Bookmark
   (e) None of these

7. While sending an e-mail, the—— line describes the contents of the message. **[SBI Clerk, 2009]**
   (a) subject   (b) to
   (c) contents   (d) cc
   (e) None of these

8. Internet access by transmitting digital data over the wires of a local telephone network is provided by   **[IBPS PO, 2011]**
   (a) Leased line
   (b) Digital subscriber line
   (c) Digital signal line
   (d) None of the mentioned

9. The____folder retains copies of messages have started but are not yet ready to send.
                          [IBPS PO, 2011]
   (a) Drafts   (b) Outbox
   (c) Address B   (d) Sent Items
   (e) Inbox

10. You can ______a search by providing more info the search engine can use to select a smaller, more useful set of results.   **[IBPS PO, 2011]**
    (a) refine   (b) expand
    (c) load   (d) query
    (e) slowdown

11. The ______enables you to simultaneously keep multiple Web pages open in one browser window.   **[IBPS PO, 2011]**
    (a) tab box   (b) pop-up helper
    (c) tab row   (d) address bar
    (e) Esc key

12. The process of transferring files from a computer on the Internet to your computer is called
                          [IBPS PO, 2011]
    (a) downloading   (b) uploading
    (c) FTP   (d) JPEG
    (e) downsizing

13. To reload a Web page, press the ________ button.   **[IBPS PO, 2011]**
    (a) Redo   (b) Reload
    (c) Restore   (d) Ctrl
    (e) Refresh

14. Mobile Commerce is best described as
                          [IBPS PO, 2011]
    (a) The use of kiosks in marketing
    (b) Transporting products
    (c) Buying and selling goods/services through wireless handheld devices
    (d) Using notebook PCs in marketing
    (e) None of the above

15. This first step in the transaction processing cycle captures business data through various modes such as optical scanning or at an electronic commerce website. **[IBPS PO, 2011]**
    (a) Document and report generation
    (b) Database maintenance
    (c) Transaction processing start-up
    (d) Data Entry
    (e) None of these

16. The piece of hardware that converts you computer's digital signal to an analog signal that can travel over telephone lines is called a **[IBPS PO, 2011]**
    (a) red wire   (b) blue cord
    (c) tower   (d) modem
    (e) None of these

17. A _________ is the term used when a search engine returns a Web page that matches the search criteria. **[IBPS PO, 2011]**
    (a) blog   (b) hit
    (c) link   (d) view
    (e) success

18. Connection or link to other documents or Web Pages that contain related information is called
    (a) dial-up   **[SBI PO, 2011]**
    (b) electronic commerce
    (c) hyperlink
    (d) e-cash
    (e) domain name

19. Microsoft's Messenger allows users to
    [SBI PO, 2011]
    (a) bypass a browser to surf the Web
    (b) create a blog
    (c) communicate via direct live communication
    (d) identify and eliminate spam
    (e) make graphic presentations

20. In a web site, the 'home' page refers to-
    (a) the best page   **[IBPS Clerk, 2011]**
    (b) the last page
    (c) the first page
    (d) the most recent page
    (e) the oldest page

21. Which of the following is used by the browser to connect to the location of the Internet resources? **[IBPS Clerk, 2011]**
    (a) Linkers   (b) Protocol
    (c) Cable   (d) URL
    (e) None of these

22. Which of the following is not a term pertaining to the Internet? **[IBPS Clerk, 2011]**
    (a) Keyboard   (b) Link
    (c) Browser   (d) Search Engine
    (e) Hyperlink

23. An educational institution would generally have the following in its domain name
    [IBPS Clerk, 2011]
    (a) .org   (b) .edu
    (c) .inst   (d) .com
    (e) .sch

24. The process of trading goods over the Internet is known as **[IBPS Clerk, 2011]**
    (a) e-selling-n-buying (b) e-trading
    (c) e-finance   (d) e-salesmanship
    (e) e-commerce

25. A _________ is a software program used to view Web pages. **[SBI Clerk, 2011]**
    (a) site   (b) host
    (c) link   (d) browser
    (e) None of these

26. _________ allows voice conversations to travel over the Internet. **[SBI Clerk, 2011]**
    (a) Internet telephony (b) Instant messaging
    (c) E-mail   (d) E-commerce
    (e) None of these

27. Which of the following is not true concering user IDs and passwords? **[SBI Clerk, 2011]**
    (a) When you enter your user ID and password the computer knows it is you
    (b) If your computer asks for a user ID and password, you can create your own
    (c) Sometimes you are assigned a user ID and password, for security reasons
    (d) You should share your user ID and password with at least one other person
    (e) None of these

28. ISP exchanges internet traffic between their networks by **[SBI Clerk, 2011]**
    (a) Internet exchange point
    (b) Subscriber end point
    (c) ISP end point
    (d) None of these

29. Unsolicited commercial email is commonly known as **[SBI Clerk, 2011]**
    (a) spam   (b) junk
    (c) hoaxes   (d) hypertext
    (e) None of these

30. A web site address is a unique name that identifies a specific __________ on the web.
    [SBI Clerk, 2011]
    (a) web browser   (b) web site
    (c) PDA   (d) link
    (e) None of these
31. The Internet allows you to   **[SBI Clerk, 2011]**
    (a) send electronic mail
    (b) view web pages
    (c) connect to servers all around the world
    (d) All of these
    (e) None of these
32. Most mail programs automatically complete the following two parts in an e-mail
    (a) From : and Body :   **[SBI Clerk, 2011]**
    (b) From : and Date :
    (c) From : and To :
    (d) From : and Subject :
    (e) None of these
33. An e-mail address typically consists of a user ID followed by the__________ sign and the name of the e-mail server that manages the user's electronic post office box.
    [SBI Clerk, 2011]
    (a) @   (b) #
    (c) &   (d) «
    (e) None of these
34. Which of these is not a means of personal communication on the Internet ?
    [IBPS PO, 2012]
    (a) chat   (b) instant messaging
    (c) instanotes   (d) electronic mail
    (e) None of these
35. Fourth-generation mobile technology provides enhanced capabilities allowing the transfer of both __________ data, including full-motion video, high-speed Internet access, and videoconferencing. **[IBPS PO, 2012]**
    (a) video data and information
    (b) voice and nonvoice
    (c) music and video
    (d) video and audio
    (e) None of these
36. Usually downloaded into folders that hold temporary Internet files, ______ are written to your computer's hard disk by some of the Web sites you visit. **[IBPS PO, 2012]**
    (a) anonymous files   (b) behaviour files
    (c) banner ads   (d) large files
    (e) cookies

37. A program, either talk or music, that is made available in digital format tor automatic download over the Internet is called a __________. **[IBPS PO, 2012]**
    (a) wiki   (b) broadcast
    (c) vodcast   (d) blog
    (e) podcast
38. When a real-time telephone call between people is made over the Internet using computers, it is called __________. **[IBPS PO, 2012]**
    (a) a chat session   (b) an e-mail
    (c) an instant message (d) Internet telephony
    (e) None of these.
39. Your business has contracted with another company to have them host and run an application for your company over the Internet. The company providing this service to your business is called an __________.
    [IBPS PO, 2012]
    (a) Internet service provider
    (b) Internet access provider
    (c) Application service provider
    (d) Application access provider
    (e) Outsource agency
40. A(n) __________ allows you to access your e-mail from anywhere. **[IBPS PO, 2012]**
    (a) Forum
    (b) Webmail interface
    (c) Message Board
    (d) Weblog
    (e) None of these
41. Which of the following would you find on LinkedIn ? **[IBPS PO, 2012]**
    (a) Games   (b) Connections
    (c) Chat   (d) Applications
    (e) None of these
42. Which of the following cannot be part of an email address ? **[IBPS PO, 2012]**
    (a) Period (.)   (b) At sign (@)
    (c) Space ()   (d) Underscore (_)
    (e) None of these
43. Which of the following must be contained in a URL ? **[IBPS PO, 2012]**
    (a) a protocol identifier
    (b) the letters, www.
    (c) the unique registered domain name
    (d) www. and the unique registered domain name
    (e) a protocol identifier, www. and the unique registered domain name

44. Origin of internet can be tracked from
    (a) ARPA net   **[IBPS Clerk, 2012]**
    (b) Radio networks
    (c) Satellite networks
    (d) Indian army networks
    (e) Air Force networks

45. _______ search engine sends request for information to several search engines simultaneously and compiles the results
    [IBPS Clerk, 2012]
    (a) Meta   (b) Individual
    (c) Directory   (d) Subject directory
    (e) None of these

46. To access a website or web content from a web server, the client sends a(n) _______
    [IBPS Clerk, 2012]
    (a) Information   (b) Message
    (c) Request   (d) Response
    (e) Interrupt

47. An http request contains_______ parts
    [IBPS Clerk, 2012]
    (a) 2   (b) 5
    (c) 3   (d) 4
    (e) 1

48. Through _______ an administrator or another user can access someone else's computer remotely **[IBPS Clerk, 2012]**
    (a) Administrator   (b) Web server
    (c) Web application   (d) HTTP
    (e) Telnet

49. What utility to you use to transfer files and exchange messages ? **[SBI Clerk, 2012]**
    (a) Web browsers   (b) WWW
    (c) Email   (d) Hpertext
    (e) search engines

50. In HTML, tags consists of keywords enclosed within **[SSC, CHSL, 2012]**
    (a) flower brackets { }
    (b) angular brackets < >
    (c) parentheses ( )
    (d) square brackets [ ]

51. A (n) _______ appearing on a web page opens another document when clicked.
    [SBI PO, 2013]
    (a) anchor   (b) URL
    (c) hyperlink   (d) reference
    (e) heading

52. An online discussion group that allows direct "live" communication is known as
    (a) webcrawier   **[IBPS Clerk, 2014]**
    (b) chat group
    (c) regional service provider
    (d) hyperlink
    (e) e-mail

53. The _______ enables you to simultaneously keep multiple Web pages open in one browser window. **[IBPS Clerk, 2014]**
    (a) tab box   (b) pop-up helper
    (c) tab row   (d) address bar
    (e) Esc key

54. Computer and communication technologies, such as communication links to the Internet that provide help and understanding to the end user is known as - **[IBPS Clerk, 2014]**
    (a) presentation file
    (b) information technology
    (c) program
    (d) worksheet file
    (e) FTP

55. The _____ folder retains copies of messages that you have started but are not yet ready to send.
    [IBPS Clerk, 2014]
    (a) Drafts   (b) Outbox
    (c) Address Book   (d) Sent Items
    (e) Inbox

56. A Website address is a unique name that identifies a specific _______ on the web.
    [SBI Clerk, 2014]
    (a) Web browser   (b) Web site
    (c) PDA   (d) link
    (e) None of these

57. The _______, also called the Web, contains billions of documents. **[SBI Clerk, 2014]**
    (a) World Wide Web   (b) HTTP
    (c) Web Portal   (d) Domain
    (e) None of these

58. Every device on the Internet has an unique address that identifies it in the same way that a street address identifies the location of a house.
    [SBI Clerk, 2014]
    (a) DH   (b) DA
    (c) IP   (d) IA
    (e) None of these

59. If you are going to a site you use often, instead of having to type in the address every time, you should **[SBI Clerk, 2014]**
    (a) save it as a file   (b) make a copy of it
    (c) bookmark it   (d) delete it
    (e) None of these

60. To navigate a new Web page for which you know the URL in the browser's _________ and press enter   **[SBI Clerk, 2014]**
    (a) Address button   (b) Address baro
    (c) Name button   (d) Domain bar
    (e) None of these

61. A _________ is the term used when a search engine returns a web page that matches the search criteria.   **[SBI Clerk, 2014]**
    (a) blog   (b) link
    (c) view   (d) hit
    (e) None of these

62. Which command on the Ribbon enables the document to be viewed as it would appear on a webpage?   **[IBPS Clerk, 2015]**
    (a) Page Layout   (b) Internet Layout
    (c) Web Layout   (d) All of the above
    (e) None of these

63. What type of software creates a smaller file that is faster to transfer over the Internet?
          [IBPS Clerk, 2015]
    (a) Compression   (b) Fragmentation
    (c) Encapsulation   (d) Unzipped
    (e) None of these

64. Which of the following is used for close a tab on a browser?   **[IBPS Clerk, 2015]**
    (a) Ctrl + Y   (b) Ctrl + A
    (c) Ctrl + W   (d) Ctrl + T
    (e) None of these

65. The _________ enables you to simultaneously keep multiple web pages open in one brower window   **[SBI Clerk, 2015]**
    (a) tab bar   (b) pop-up helper
    (c) tab row   (d) address bar
    (e) None of these

66. The _________ folder remains copies of messages that you have started but are not yet ready to send.   **[SBI Clerk, 2015]**
    (a) drafts   (b) outbox
    (c) address   (d) sent items
    (e) None of these

67. When the pointer is positioned on a _________, it is shaped like a hand.   **[SBI Clerk, 2015]**
    (a) grammar error   (b) formatting error
    (c) screen tip   (d) hyperlink
    (e) spelling error

68. The standard protocol of the internet is_________?
          [SBI Clerk, 2015]
    (a) TCP/IP   (b) Java
    (c) HTML   (d) Flash
    (e) None of these

69. A website address is a unique name that identifies a specific ___ on the web
          [IBPS PO, 2015]
    (a) Web browser   (b) Website
    (c) PDA   (d) Link
    (e) None of these

70. How are the World Wide Web (WWW) and the internet different?   **[SBI PO, 2015]**
    (a) They aren't different; they are two different names for the same thing.
    (b) The internet is text only, the WWW incorporates multimedia.
    (c) The internet is primarilyused by businesses; the WWW can be used by home users.
    (d) The WWW is faster than the more archaic internet.
    (e) None of these

71. What is m-commerce?   **[SSC CGL, 2015]**
    (a) machine commerce
    (b) mobile commerce
    (c) money commerce
    (d) marketing commerce

72. Which among the following is a recently debated principle that Internet service providers and governments regulating the Internet should treat all data on the Internet the same, not discriminating or charging differentially by user, content, website, platform, application, type of attached equipment, or mode of communication?   **[IBPS PO Mains, 2016]**
    (a) Comcast   (b) Net Neutrality
    (c) Oblique-net   (d) Net Fraternity
    (e) Fair Web

73. What can possibly be the drawback of e-mails?
    (a) Emails requires being physically delivered to the user   **[IBPS Clerk Mains, 2016]**
    (b) Emails infects computer.
    (c) Emails are very expensive to transmit
    (d) Emails are slow to load
    (e) people don't check emails regularly

74. Which of the following is a valid email address?
          [IBPS Clerk Mains, 2016]
    (a) name.website@info@edu
    (b) name.website@info.in
    (c) name@website.info.com
    (d) website.name@website.com
    (e) website@info@info.com

75. What is the full form of VoIP?
    [IBPS Clerk Mains, 2016]
    (a) Voice of Internet Power
    (b) Voice over Internet Protocol
    (c) Voice on Internet Protocol
    (d) Very optimized Internet Protocol
    (e) Very official internet Protocol
76. The principal electronic payment systems for electronic commerce is **[IBPS RRB, 2016]**
    (a) Credit card (b) Digital wallet
    (c) Electronic cheque (d) All of the above
    (e) None of these
77. Which of the following is the first graphical web browser? **[IBPS RRB, 2016]**
    (a) MSN (b) Mozilla
    (c) Chrome (d) Mosaic
    (e) Internet explorer
78. An email account includes a storage area, often called _____ **[IBPS RRB, 2016]**
    (a) Attachment (b) Font
    (c) Hyperlink (d) browser
    (e) Mailbox
79. Which of the following is not associated with Browsers? **[IBPS RRB, 2016]**
    (a) Opera (b) Chrome
    (c) Firefox (d) Yahoo
    (e) UC Browser
80. Which of the following is the valid domain name extension? **[IBPS RRB, 2016]**
    (a) .edu (b) .org
    (c) .com (d) .net
    (e) All of these

ANSWER KEY

1.	(d)	15.	(d)	29.	(a)	43.	(d)	57.	(a)	71.	(b)
2	(b)	16.	(d)	30	(b)	44.	(a)	58.	(c)	72.	(b)
3.	(c)	17.	(b)	31.	(d)	45.	(a)	59.	(c)	73.	(e)
4.	(c)	18.	(c)	32.	(b)	46	(c)	60.	(b)	74.	(d)
5.	(d)	19.	(c)	33.	(a)	47.	(c)	61.	(d)	75.	(b)
6.	(a)	20	(c)	34.	(c)	48.	(e)	62.	(c)	76.	(d)
7.	(a)	21	(d)	35.	(a)	49.	(c)	63.	(a)	77.	(d)
8.	(b)	22	(a)	36.	(e)	50.	(b)	64.	(c)	78.	(e)
9.	(a)	23	(b)	37.	(e)	51.	(c)	65.	(a)	79.	(d)
10.	(a)	24.	(e)	38	(d)	52.	(b)	66.	(a)	80.	(e)
11.	(c)	25	(d)	39.	(e)	53.	(c)	67.	(d)		
12.	(a)	26.	(a)	40	(b)	54.	(e)	68.	(a)		
13.	(e)	27	(d)	41.	(b)	55.	(a)	69.	(d)		
14.	(c)	28	(a)	42	(c)	56.	(d)	70.	(b)		

Practice Exercise

1. Which of the following is Web browser?
   - (a) Paint
   - (b) Power Point
   - (c) Fire fox
   - (d) Word
   - (e) All are Web browsers

2. The Internet allows you to __________.
   - (a) send electronic mail
   - (b) view Web pages
   - (c) connect to servers all around the world
   - (d) All of the above
   - (e) None of these

3. Most World Wide Web pages contain commands in the language __________.
   - (a) NIH
   - (b) URL
   - (c) HTML
   - (d) IRC
   - (e) FTP

4. Which is the slowest internet connection service?
   - (a) Digital Subscriber Line
   - (b) TI
   - (c) Cable modem
   - (d) Leased Line
   - (e) Dial-up Service

5. Sending an e-mail is same as
   - (a) writing a letter
   - (b) drawing a picture
   - (c) talking on phone
   - (d) sending a package
   - (e) None of these

6. Which of the following is not true about passwords?
   - (a) A password should be a combination of mixed case alphanumeric characters
   - (b) Password should be maximum 6 characters in length
   - (c) A password that can be memorized easily should be used, so that it need not be noted down
   - (d) A password that can be typed quickly without much effort should be used
   - (e) None of these

7. The secret code that restricts entry to some programs is __________.
   - (a) entry-code
   - (b) passport
   - (c) password
   - (d) access-code
   - (e) None of these

8. What is the storage area for email messages called?
   - (a) A folder
   - (b) A directory
   - (c) A mailbox
   - (d) The hard disk
   - (e) None of these

9. IPv6 addressed have a size of
   - (a) 32 bits
   - (b) 64 bits
   - (c) 128 bits
   - (d) 265 bits
   - (e) None of these

10. The Internet is a system of __________.
    - (a) Software bundles
    - (b) Web page
    - (c) Website
    - (d) Interconnected Networks
    - (e) None of these

11. A __________ shares hardware, software and data among authorized users.
    - (a) network
    - (b) protocol
    - (c) hyperlink
    - (d) transmitter
    - (e) None of these

12. A(n) __________ allows sharing of a broadband Internet connection.
    - (a) hub
    - (b) adapter
    - (c) router
    - (d) switch
    - (e) plug

13. What is Windows Explorer?
    - (a) A drive
    - (b) A personal computer
    - (c) A Web browser
    - (d) A network
    - (e) A file manager

14. __________ is the most popular Internet activity.
    - (a) Art
    - (b) Shopping
    - (c) Searching
    - (d) Entertainment
    - (e) Communication

15. A web site address is a unique name that identifies a specific __________ on the Web.
    - (a) Web browser
    - (b) PDA
    - (c) Website
    - (d) link
    - (e) user

16. Documents on the Web are called __________.
    - (a) Web pages
    - (b) Web sites
    - (c) Web communities
    - (d) Web tags
    - (e) Home pages

17. A Web site containing stories and articles relating to current events, life, money, sports and the weather is considered a(n) __________ Web site.
    - (a) business/marketing
    - (b) portal
    - (c) informational
    - (d) news
    - (e) retailing

18. You can have a live conversation with another connected user via ____________.
    (a) e-mail   (b) instant messaging
    (c) e-commerce   (d) distance learning
    (e) Word package

19. Video-conferencing requires a microphone, speakers, and a ____________ attached to your computer.
    (a) mouse   (b) keyboard
    (c) video camera   (d) scanner
    (e) mobile phone

20. The process of a computer receiving information from a server on the Internet is known as ____________.
    (a) acquisition   (b) pulling
    (c) transferring   (d) pushing
    (e) downloading

21. The communications device that allows the computer to access a network is called a ____________ card.
    (a) modem   (b) video
    (c) sound   (d) network
    (e) dialog

22. With ____________, the computer's modem uses a standard telephone line to connect to the Internet.
    (a) DSL
    (b) dial-up access
    (c) ISDN
    (d) cable television Internet services
    (e) satellite

23. ____________ services are available free at portals on the Web.
    (a) E-mail
    (b) FTP
    (c) Video-conferencing
    (d) Telephone
    (e) All of these

24. An e-mail address typically consists of a user ID followed by the ____________ sign and the name of the e-mail server that manages the user's electronic post office box.
    (a) @   (b) #
    (c) &   (d) *
    (e) None of these

25. A Web ____________ consists of one or more Web pages located on a Web server.
    (a) hub   (b) site
    (c) story   (d) template
    (e) None of these

26. ____________ makes it possible for shoppers to make purchases using their computers.
    (a) E-world   (b) E-commerce
    (c) E-spend   (d) E-business
    (e) None of these

27. A Web site's main page or first page is called its ____________.
    (a) home page   (b) browser page
    (c) search place   (d) bookmark
    (e) None of these

28. Programs such as Internet Explorer that serve as navigable windows into the Web are called
    (a) Hypertext   (b) Networks
    (c) Internet   (d) Web browsers
    (e) None of these

29. ____________ is the act of copying or downloading a program from a network and making multiple copies of it.
    (a) Network piracy   (b) Plagiarism
    (c) Software piracy   (d) Site-license piracy
    (e) None of these

30. Internet works on
    (a) packet switching (b) circuit switching
    (c) network switching (d) both (a) and (b)
    (e) None of these

31. A word in a web page that, when clicked, opens another document.
    (a) anchor   (b) URL
    (c) hyperlink   (d) reference
    (e) None of these

32. A Web site address is a unique name that identifies a specific ____________ on the Web.
    (a) Web browser   (b) PDA
    (c) Web Site   (d) link
    (e) None of these

33. ____________ is a procedure that requires users to enter an identification code and a matching password.
    (a) Paging   (b) Logging on
    (c) Time-sharing   (d) Multitasking
    (e) None of these

34. If you are going to a site you use often, instead of having to type in the address every time, you should
    (a) save it as a file (b) make a copy of it
    (c) bookmark it   (d) delete it
    (e) None of the above

35. To navigate to a new Web page for which you know the URL, type that URL in the browser's ____________ and press Enter
    (a) Address bar   (b) Domain bar
    (c) Address button   (d) Name button
    (e) None of the above

36. When sending an e-mail, the ___________ line describes the contents of the message.
    - (a) subject
    - (b) to
    - (c) contents
    - (d) cc
    - (e) None of these

37. A Web site address is a unique name that identifies a specific ___________ on the Web.
    - (a) Web browser
    - (b) Web site
    - (c) PDA
    - (d) link
    - (e) None of these

38. A ___________ is the term used when a search engine returns a Web page that matches the search criteria.
    - (a) blog
    - (b) hit
    - (c) link
    - (d) view
    - (e) success

39. What is e-commerce?
    - (a) Buying and selling of international goods
    - (b) Buying and selling of products and services over the Internet
    - (c) Buying and selling of products and services not found in stores
    - (d) Buying and selling of products having to do with computers
    - (e) Buying and selling of electronic goods

40. What are the four things required to connect to the Internet?
    - (a) Telephone line, Modem, Computer and an ISP
    - (b) Modem, Computer, PDA and ISP
    - (c) Telephone line, PDA, Modem and Computer
    - (d) Computer, ISP, Modem and Communication software
    - (e) Monitor, Keyboard, Mouse and Modem

41. Which of the following functions is not performed by servers?
    - (a) Email processing
    - (b) Database sharing
    - (c) Processing Websites
    - (d) Storage
    - (e) Word processing

42. The process of transferring files from a computer to the Internet server is called ___________.
    - (a) downloading
    - (b) uploading
    - (c) FTP
    - (d) JPEG
    - (e) downsizing

43. The ___________ controls a client's computer resources.
    - (a) application program
    - (b) instruction set
    - (c) operating system
    - (d) server application
    - (e) compiler

44. To reload a Web page, press the ___________ button.
    - (a) Redo
    - (b) Reload
    - (c) Restore
    - (d) Ctrl
    - (e) Refresh

45. The ___________ enables you to simultaneously keep multiple Web pages open in one browser window.
    - (a) tab box
    - (b) pop-up helper
    - (c) address bar
    - (d) Esc key

46. A popular way to learn about computers without ever going to a classroom is called ___________.
    - (a) i-learning
    - (b) isolated learning
    - (c) e-learning
    - (d) close learning
    - (e) distance learning

47. The ___________ folder retains copies of messages that you have started but are not yet ready to send.
    - (a) Inbox
    - (b) Outbox
    - (c) Drafts
    - (d) Sent Items
    - (e) Address Book

48. A (n) ___________ is not a web browser.
    - (a) FOXPRO
    - (b) Mozilla
    - (c) Netscape navigator
    - (d) Internet explorer
    - (e) None of these

49. One advantage of dial-up Internet access is that
    - (a) it utilises broadband technology
    - (b) it is Indian
    - (c) it uses a router for security
    - (d) modem speeds are very fast
    - (e) it utilises existing telephone service

50. You can use the ___________ bar to type a URL, and display a Web page, or type a keyword to display a list of related Web pages.
    - (a) Menu
    - (b) Title
    - (c) Search
    - (d) Web
    - (e) Address

51. Most mail programs automatically complete the following two parts in an email:
    - (a) From: and Body:
    - (b) From: and Date:
    - (c) From: and To
    - (d) From: and Subject:
    - (e) None of these

52. Which of the following is an advantage of mounting an application on the Web?
    - (a) The possibility of 24-hour access for users
    - (b) Creating a system that can extend globally
    - (c) Standardising the design of the interface
    - (d) All of these
    - (e) None of these

53. Which of the following is called as protocol in the URL ?
    http://www.xyz.com
    (a) .com   (b) www
    (c) xyz   (d) http
    (e) None of these
54. The software that allows users to surf the Internet is called a/an
    (a) Search engine
    (b) Internet Service Provider (ISP)
    (c) Multimedia application
    (d) Browser
    (e) Internet Surfing Provider
55. Online documents containing underlined phrases or icons that a user can click in order to move immediately to related parts of the current document or to other documents with relative information are called
    (a) hypermedia   (b) hypertext
    (c) HTML   (d) URL
    (e) FTP
56. What are the two parts of an e-mail address?
    (a) User name and street address
    (b) Legal name and phone number
    (c) User name and domain name
    (d) Initial and password
    (e) User name and recipient name
57. Why should you delete unknown e-mail attachments?
    (a) It can make you land in jail.
    (b) The person could track you down and hurt you.
    (c) It is a bad manners.
    (d) It might contain a virus that could hurt your computer.
    (e) None of these
58. Which of the following softwares allows the user to move from page to page on the Web by clicking on or selecting a hyperlink or by typing in the address of the destination page?
    (a) Web browser   (b) Web home page
    (c) Web home page   (d) Web service
    (e) None of these
59. A good Web site
    (a) is relevant, reliable, recent and verifiable
    (b) always stays the same
    (c) is well-designed but not necessarily accurate
    (d) contains Terms of Use information
    (e) is attractive in appearance
60. A(n) ___________ Web site offers a variety of Internet services from a single, convenient location.

    (a) protocol   (b) informational
    (c) portal   (d) news
    (e) chat
61. The secret code that gives you access to some programs.
    (a) clue   (b) cue
    (c) password   (d) help
    (e) None of these
62. Which of the following functions is not performed by servers?
    (a) Email processing
    (b) Database sharing
    (c) Processing Websites
    (d) Storage
    (e) Word processing
63. Connectivity is similar to
    (a) Power cord   (b) Internet
    (c) Floppy disk   (d) Data
    (e) None of these
64. Which of the following is not a term pertaining to Email?
    (a) power Point   (b) inbox
    (c) sender   (d) receiver
    (e) None of these
65. What is an E-mail attachment?
    (a) A receipt sent by the recipient
    (b) A separate document from another program sent along with an E-mail message
    (c) A malicious parasite that feeds off of your messages and destroys the contents
    (d) A list of CC: or BCC: recipients
    (e) None of these
66. Which of the following are all considered advantages of e-mail?
    (a) Convenience, speed of delivery, generality and reliability
    (b) Printable, global and expensive
    (c) Global, convenience and Microsoft owned
    (d) Slow delivery, reliable, global and inexpensive
    (e) None of these
67. E-commerce allows companies to ___________.
    (a) issue important business reports
    (b) conduct business over the Internet
    (c) support decision making processes
    (d) keep track of paper-based transactions
    (e) None of these
68. Which of the following is required to create an HTML document?
    (a) browser   (b) internet
    (c) text editor   (d) search engine
    (e) None of these

69. The file that is linked with an e-mail and sent to the receiver of the e-mail is referred to as __________.
    - (a) annexure
    - (b) appendage
    - (c) add-on
    - (d) attachment
    - (e) article

70. Which one of the following is the most important or powerful computer in a internet network?
    - (a) Network station
    - (b) Network client
    - (c) Network Server
    - (d) Desktop
    - (e) None of these

71. The term "host" with respect to the internet, means __________.
    - (a) A computer that is a stand along computer
    - (b) A computer that is connected to the Internet
    - (c) A computer reserved for use by the host
    - (d) A large collection of computers
    - (e) Hyperlink

72. What is the advantage of using basic HTML to create a document?
    - (a) HTML is very easy to use.
    - (b) The document can be displayed by all word processors.
    - (c) The document can be displayed by all programs.
    - (d) The document can be displayed by all browsers.
    - (e) None of these

73. Which of the following will be used if the sender of an e-mail wants to bold, itlalicise etc the text message?
    - (a) Reach Signature
    - (b) Reach Text
    - (c) Reach Format
    - (d) Plain Format
    - (e) Plain text

74. Which of the following terms is not related to Internet?
    - (a) Link
    - (b) Function key
    - (c) Browser
    - (d) Search engine
    - (e) Hyperlink

75. What is included in an e-mail address?
    - (a) Domain name followed by user's name
    - (b) User's name followed by domain name
    - (c) User's name followed by postal address
    - (d) User's name followed by street address
    - (e) None of these

76. Which of the following operations is safe if an e-mail from an unknown sender is received?
    - (a) Open it to know about the sender and answer it.
    - (b) Delete it after opening it.
    - (c) Delete it without opening it.
    - (d) Open it and try to find who the sender is.
    - (e) None of these

77. When browsing the World Wide Web, the browser is a
    - (a) feeder
    - (b) server program
    - (c) application program
    - (d) system program
    - (e) client program

78. Where is the newly received email stored?
    - (a) In your website
    - (b) In Address-box
    - (c) In Inbox
    - (d) In your personal laptop
    - (e) None of these

79. Small programs that act on data received by the user's computer as part of a Web page are called
    - (a) search engine
    - (b) servlets
    - (c) browsers
    - (d) applets
    - (e) feedback

ANSWER KEY

1.	(c)	15.	(d)	29.	(c)	43.	(c)	57.	(d)	71.	(b)
2.	(d)	16.	(a)	30.	(a)	44.	(e)	58.	(a)	72.	(d)
3.	(c)	17.	(c)	31.	(c)	45.	(c)	59.	(a)	73.	(c)
4.	(e)	18.	(b)	32.	(d)	46.	(c)	60.	(c)	74.	(b)
5.	(a)	19.	(c)	33.	(b)	47.	(c)	61.	(c)	75.	(b)
6.	(b)	20.	(e)	34.	(c)	48.	(a)	62.	(e)	76.	(c)
7.	(c)	21.	(a)	35.	(a)	49.	(e)	63.	(b)	77.	(c)
8.	(c)	22.	(b)	36.	(a)	50.	(e)	64.	(a)	78.	(c)
9.	(c)	23.	(a)	37.	(d)	51.	(b)	65.	(b)	79.	(b)
10.	(d)	24.	(a)	38.	(b)	52.	(d)	66.	(a)		
11.	(a)	25.	(d)	39.	(b)	53.	(d)	67.	(b)		
12.	(c)	26.	(b)	40.	(d)	54.	(d)	68.	(c)		
13.	(c)	27.	(a)	41.	(e)	55.	(b)	69.	(d)		
14.	(c)	28.	(a)	42.	(b)	56.	(c)	70.	(c)		

Microsoft Windows

When referring to an operating system, Windows is an operating environment created by Microsoft that provides an interface known a s Graphical User Interface (GUI) for computers/laptops/notebooks etc. Windows eliminates the need for a user to type each command at a command line, like MS-DOS, by using a mouse to navigate through drop-down menus, dialog boxes, buttons, tabs, and icons.

BASICS OF MICROSOFT WINDOWS

Developer(s) Microsoft
Initial release November 19, 1990; almost 24 years ago
Stable release 2010 (14.0.6023.1000 SP1) / June 28, 2011
Development status Active
Written in C++
Operating system Microsoft Windows
Available in Over 35 languages
Type Office suite

GENERATIONS OF MICROSOFT WINDOWS

Upper timeline boxes:

- Microsoft introduced a New version (3.10) or window 3.1 released on April 1992 based on MS-DOS.
- Microsoft introduced a New version NT(3.50)/(3.51) or windows NT 3.50 released on 21 Sept.1994, Next version is windows NT 3.51 released on 30 May 1995.
- Microsoft introduced a New version NT 4.10 or window 98 released on 25 June 1998.
- Microsoft introduced a New version (NT 5.1) or window XP released on 25 Oct.2001.
- Microsoft introduced a New version (NT 6.0) or windows vista, released on 30 January 2007.
- Microsoft introduced a New version (NT 6.2) or window 8, released on 26 October 2012.
- Microsoft introduced a New version (NT 10.0) or window-10, released on 29 July 2015.
- Microsoft announced a New version window 10 (Insider Preview Build 15025) for PC. It will be release on 2017-2018.

Timeline:

1985 to 1990	1992	1993	1994	1996	1998	2000	2001	2005	2007	2009	2012	2013	2015

Lower timeline boxes:

- Microsoft introduced all initial version starting from 1.01 to 3.0 or window 1.01 to window 3.0 released on Nov.1985 to May 1990.
- Microsoft introduced a New version 3.2, 3.11, NT 3.10 or window 3.2 & window NT 3.1 released on Nov.1993.
- Microsoft introduced a New version (4.00) or window 95 released on 24 Aug 1995 & Next version is NT(4.0) or window (NT) (4.07) released on 24 Aug.1996
- Microsoft introduced a a New version NT -(5.00), or window 2000 released on 17 Feb 2000 & Window ME released on 14 Sept.2000.
- Microsoft introduced a a New version (NT 5.2) or windows XP released on 25 April 2005.
- Microsoft introduced a a New version (NT 6.1) or (window 7) released on 22 October 2009.
- Microsoft introduced a a New version (NT 6.3) or window (8.1) released on 17 October 2013.

MICROSOFT WINDOWS VERSIONS

Microsoft Windows Versions for Personal Computers

The following details the history of Microsoft Windows Versions designed for personal computers (PCs).

1. **MS-DOS (Microsoft disk operating system in 1992) :** Originally developed by Microsoft for IBM, MS-DOS was the standard operating system for IBM-compatible personal computers. The initial versions of DOS were very simple and resembled another operating system called CP/M.

2. **Windows NT (New Technology, introduced in 1993)** is a 32-bit operating system that supports preemptive multitasking. There are actually two versions of Windows NT: Windows NT Server, designed to act as a server in networks, and Windows NT Workstation for stand-alone or client workstations.

3. **Windows 95 (August 1995) :** Windows 95 is a GUI(Graphical User Interface) based operating system.

    It supports 32-bit applications, which means that applications written specifically for this operating system should run much faster.

4. **Windows 98 (June 1998) :** It is a graphical operating system by Microsoft. It is the second major release in the Windows 9x line of operating systems. Windows 98 is the successor to Windows 95. Like its predecessor, it is a hybrid 16-bit/32-bit monolithic product with an MS-DOS based boot stage.

5. **Windows ME - Millennium Edition (September 2000) :** The Windows Millennium Edition, called "Windows Me" was an update to the Windows 98 core and included some features of the Windows 2000 operating system. It is designed for single CPU or SMP 32 bit Intel X86 computer.It introduced the Multilingual User Interface(MUI).

6. **Windows XP (eXperience, introduced in October 2001) :** Windows XP is an OS produced by Microsoft for use on personal computers.

    Windows XP comes in two versions, Home and Professional. Microsoft focused on mobility for both editions, including plug and play features for connecting to wireless networks. The operating system also utilizes the 802.11x wireless security standard.

7. **Windows Vista (30 Jan 2007) :** Its is an operating system by Microsoft for use on personal computers, including home and business desktops, laptops, tablet PCs, and media center PCs.

    New features of Windows Vista include an updated graphical user interface and visual style dubbed Aero, a new search component called Windows Search, redesigned networking, audio, print and display sub-systems, and new multimedia tools including Windows DVD Maker.

    Vista aimed to increase the level of communication between machines on a home network, using peer-to-peer technology to simplify sharing files and media between computers and devices.

8. **Windows 7 (October, 2009) :** It is an upgarde to Windows XP. It supports 64 bit processor.Enhancements and new features in Windows 7 include multi-touch support, Internet Explorer 8, improved performance and start-up time, Aero Snap, Aero Shake, support for virtual hard disks, a new and improved Windows Media Center, and improved security.

9. **Windows 8 (October, 2012) :** Windows 8 is a completely redesigned operating system that's been developed from the ground up with touchscreen use in mind as well as near-instant-on capabilities that enable a Windows 8 PC to load and start up in a matter of seconds rather than in minutes. Windows 8 will replace the more traditional Microsoft Windows OS look and feel with a new "Metro" design system interface that first debuted in the Windows Phone 7 mobile operating system. The Metro user interface primarily consists of a "Start screen" made up of "Live Tiles," which are links to applications and features that are dynamic and update in real time. Windows 8 supports both x86 PCs and ARM processors.

10. **Windows 10 (September, 2014) :** It is a personal computer operating system developed and released by Microsoft as part of the Windows NT family of operating systems. It was officially unveiled in September 2014. Its original release in July 2015.

Microsoft described Windows 10 as an "operating system as a service" that would receive ongoing updates to its features and functionality, augmented with the ability for enterprise environments to receive non-critical updates at a slower pace, or use long-term support milestones that will only receive critical updates, such as security patches, over their five-year lifespan of mainstream support.

Microsoft Windows Versions for Servers and Mobile Devices

Apart from Windows Versions designed for use on personal computers (PCs) and laptops, Microsoft has also developed operating systems for services, handheld devices, and mobile phones.

1. **Windows Server (March 2003)** : Windows Server is a series of Microsoft server operating systems. Windows servers are more powerful versions of their desktop operating system counterparts and are designed to more efficiently handle corporate networking, Internet/intranet hosting, databases, enterprise-scale messaging and similar functions. The Windows Server name made its debut with the release of Windows Server 2003 and continues with the current release, Windows Server 2008 R2, which shares its codebase with Windows 7. Windows Server 2008 R2 debuted in October 2009.

2. **Windows Home Server (January 2007)** : Announced in January 2007, Windows Home Server (WHS) is a "consumer server" designed to use with multiple computers connected in the home. Home Server allows you to share files such as digital photos and media files, and also allows you to automatically backup your home networked computers. Through Windows Media Connect, Windows Home Server lets you share any media located on your WHS with compatible devices.

3. **Windows CE (November 2006)** : A version of the Windows operating system designed for small devices such as personal digital assistants (PDAs) (or Handheld PCs in the Microsoft vernacular). The Windows CE graphical user interface (GUI) is very similar to Windows 95 so devices running Windows CE should be easy to operate for anyone familiar with Windows 95.

4. **Windows Mobile (April 2000)** : A mobile operating system for smartphones and mobile devices from Microsoft based on the Windows CE kernel and designed to look and operate similar to desktop versions of Microsoft Windows. Windows Mobile has largely been supplanted by Windows Phone 7, although Microsoft did release, in 2011, Windows Embedded Handheld 6.5, a mobile OS compatible with Windows Mobile 6.5 that's designed for enterprise mobile and handheld computing devices.

5. **Windows Phone (November 2010)** : A mobile operating system for smartphones and mobile devices that serves as the successor to Microsoft's initial mobile OS platform system, Windows Mobile. Windows Phone 7 features a multi-tab Internet Explorer Mobile Web browser that uses a rendering engine based on Internet Explorer 9 as well Microsoft Office Mobile, a version of Microsoft Office that's tailored for mobile devices.

POPULAR MOBILE OPERATING SYSTEMS

1. Android OS (Google Inc.)

It is a Google's open and free software stack that includes an operating system, middleware and also key applications for use on mobile devices, including smart phones. Updates for the open source Android mobile operating system have been developed under "dessert-inspired" code names (Cupcake, Donut, éclair, Gingerbread, Honeycomb, and Ice Cream Sandwich) with each new version arriving in alphabetical order with new enhancements and improvements.

2. iPhone OS / iOS (Apple)

It was originally developed for use on its iPhone devices. Now, the mobile operating system is referred to as iOS and is supported on a number of Apple devices including the iPhone, iPad, iPad 2 and iPod Touch. The iOS mobile operating system is available only on Apple's own manufactured devices as the company does not license the OS for third-party hardware. Apple iOS is derived from Apple's Mac OS X operating system.

3. BlackBerry OS (Research In Motion)

It is a proprietary mobile operating system developed by Research in Motion for use on the company's popular BlackBerry handheld devices. The BlackBerry platform is popular with corporate users as it offers synchronization with Microsoft Exchange, Lotus Domino, Novell GroupWise email and other business software, when used with the BlackBerry Enterprise Server.

4. Bada (Samsung Electronics)

It is a proprietary Samsung mobile OS that was first launched in 2010. The Samsung Wave was the first smart phone to use this mobile OS. Bada provides mobile features such as multipoint-touch, 3D graphics and of course, application downloads and installation

5. MeeGo OS (Nokia and Intel)

A joint open source mobile operating system which is the result of merging two products based on open source technologies: Maemo (Nokia) and Moblin (Intel). MeeGo is a mobile OS designed to work on a number of devices including smart phones, net books, tablets, in-vehicle information systems and various devices using Intel Atom and ARMv7 architectures.

6. Symbian OS (Nokia)

It is a mobile operating system (OS) targeted at mobile phones that offers a high-level of integration with communication and personal information management (PIM) functionality. Symbian OS combines middleware with wireless communications through an integrated mailbox and the integration of Java and PIM functionality (agenda and contacts). Nokia has made the Symbian platform available under an alternative, open and direct model, to work with some OEMs and the small community of platform development collaborators. Nokia does not maintain Symbian as an open source development project.

7. Palm OS (Garnet OS)

It is a proprietary mobile operating system (PDA operating system) that was originally released in 1996 on the Pilot 1000 handheld. Newer versions of the Palm OS have added support for expansion ports, new processors, external memory cards, improved security and support for ARM processors and smart phones. Palm OS 5 was extended to provide support for a broad range of screen resolutions, wireless connections and enhanced multimedia capabilities and is called Garnet OS.

8. Web OS (Palm/HP)

It is a mobile operating system that runs on the Linux kernel. Web OS was initially developed by Palm as the successor to its Palm OS mobile operating system. It is a proprietary Mobile OS which was eventually acquired by HP and now referred to as web OS (lower-case) in HP literature. HP uses web OS in a number of devices including several smart phones and HP Touch Pads.

WINDOWS STRUCTURE

Desktop Applications

1. **Word :** Microsoft Word is a word processor and was previously considered the main program in Office. Its proprietary. DOC format is considered a standard, although Word 2007 can also use a new XML-based, Microsoft Office-optimized format called .DOCX. It is available for the Windows and Mac platforms.

   The first version of MS-Word, released in the autumn of 1983, was for the MS-DOS operating system and had the distinction of introducing the mouse to a large population of computer users. Word 1.0 could be purchased with a bundled mouse, though none was required. Following the precedents of LisaWrite and MacWrite, Word for Macintosh attempted to add closer WYSIWYG (What You See Is What You Get) features into its package. Word for Mac was released in 1985. Word for Mac was the first graphical version of Microsoft Word. Despite its bugs, it became one of the most popular Mac applications.

2. **Excel :** Microsoft Excel is a spreadsheet program that originally competed with the dominant , but eventually outsold it.It is available for the Windows and Mac platforms. Microsoft released the first version of Excel for the Mac in 1985, and the first Windows version in November 1987.

3. **Outlook :** Microsoft Outlook (not to be confused with Outlook Express) is a personal information manager and email communication software. The replacement for Windows Messaging, Microsoft Mail and Schedule+ starting in Office 97, it includes an e-mail client, calendar, task manager and address book. On the Mac, Microsoft offered several versions of Outlook in the late 1990s, but only for use with Microsoft Exchange Server.

4. **PowerPoint :** Microsoft PowerPoint is a popular presentation program for Windows and Mac. It is used to create slideshows and is composed of text, graphics, movies and other objects which can be displayed on-screen and navigated through by the presenter or printed out on transparencies or slides.

Other desktop applications (Windows versions only)

- Microsoft Access — database manager
- Microsoft InfoPath — an application to design rich XMLbased forms
- Microsoft OneNote — note-taking software for use with both tablet and conventional PCs
- Microsoft Publisher — desktop publishing software mostly used for designing brochures, labels, calendars,greeting cards, business cards, newsletters, and postcards.
- Microsoft Office Picture Manager — basic photo management software (similar to Google's Picasa or Adobe's
- Photoshop Elements

WINDOWS DESKTOP

- **Desktop** means the background of your screen on which the various programs run. The computer screen is basically the electronic desk.

    The following terms used to describe the Windows desktop:

1. **Icons :** Icons are those small picture like symbols on the desktop and inside folders that denote various programs, folders and sometimes sub folders also. Icons are small pictures that represent files, folders, programs, and other items.

Dragging - If you move an icon on your desktop with mouse, this is called dragging.

Dropping - After releasing it, it will called dropping.

2. **My Computer :** In Windows, My Computer is the source of all resources in the computer including drives, control panels and data.

3. **The Recycle Bin :** An icon on the Windows desktop that represents a directory where deleted files are temporarily stored. This enables you to retrieve files that you may have accidentally deleted.

4. **My Documents :** My Documents and Documents are Microsoft Windows folders that store computer documents, program settings, and other files associated with programs on your computer.

    For example, when saving a file in Microsoft Word, the default folder is My Documents. Saving all of your personal files into the My Documents folder makes them easier to back up and locate.

    Note: Microsoft has changed "My Documents" to "Documents" in the most recent versions of Windows.

It can open in three ways:

1.   From the Desktop, double-click the My Documents folder icon.

2.   Click the Start button in the lower left corner of the screen. Click Documents on the right side of the menu that pops up.

3.   Open My Computer and then select My Documents.

5.   **My Network Places :** My Network Places is a network browser that displays network connections a computer has to other computers and servers and is what replaces Network Neighborhood found in Windows 95, 98, and NT. In a home network setting, My Network Places can display the other computers, network printers, and other network resources. In an office setting, it can display computers, servers, and network printers in the users local workgroup. With the release of Microsoft Windows Vista and Windows 7, My Network Places has been renamed to Network.

An icon for Network Neighborhood, My Network Places, or Network may be on the Windows Desktop and is also accessible through the Windows Explorer.

6.   **The Windows Task Bar :** It refers to the bar that is used at the bottom of your Windows screen (it can be moved) with the Start Button on the left and the clock on the right.

The following are the main parts of the taskbar.

(a)   **Start Button :** This button resides on the extreme left side of the taskbar. When we click on the start button then the start menu will appear.

(b)   **Quick Launch Icons :** On the right side of the Start Button, there are some little icons. Windows and Internet Explorer, when installed, automatically puts the icons of some of the very helpful things there. For example, with just one click on its icon, Internet Explorer browser can be launch from here. "Show Desktop" icon is a quick way of minimizing all open windows on the desktop at once (with just one click) and revealing the desktop.

(c)   **Open Applications :** The middle and longest portion of the taskbar remains empty until you launch a program . As soon as you open a program in your computer its name appears in this middle part of the taskbar.

(d)   **Tray Icons :** Next on the taskbar are the tray icons. These icons represent programs that are running silently in the background and will jump into action the moment it becomes necessary.

(e)   **Clock:** On the extreme right side of the taskbar resides the computer clock. The clock is actually a part of the tray icons. But the clock will be there even if you run Windows in safe mode.

7.   **The Windows Menu System :** A menu bar is a user interface element that contains selectable commands and options for a specific program. In Windows, menu bars are typically located at the top of open windows.

(a)   **File :** The File menu includes common file options such as New, Open Save, and Print.

(b)   **Edit :** The Edit menu contains commands such as Undo, Select All, Copy, and Paste.

(c)   **View :** The View menu typically includes zoom commands and options to show or hide elements within the window.

(d)   **Help :** The Help Menu for tutorials or helpful informations.

8.   **The Windows Start Menu :** The Microsoft Windows Start Menu is the primary location in Windows to locate installed programs and find any files or folders. By default, the Start menu is located in the bottom left-hand corner of the screen and is accessed by clicking the Start button. Start Menu has following important sections:

(a)   **Left Pane :** The left pane shows recently ran programs or any pinned program shortcuts.

(ii)   **All Programs :** At the bottom of the left pane is the "All Programs" option, which displays all programs that have been installed on the computer.

(iii) Search : The "Search" bar is useful feature allows to type in the name of the program or file looking for and have the results displayed above.

(b) Right Pane : The right pane shows each of the more commonly accessed sections of the computer such as your computer, Control Panel, documents, music, and pictures.

(i) Personal folder : Opens your personal folder, which is named for whoever is currently logged on to Windows.

(ii) Documents : Opens the Documents library, where a user can access and open text files, spreadsheets, presentations, and other kinds of documents.

(iii) Pictures : Opens the Pictures library, where a user access and view digital pictures and graphics files.

(iv) Music : Opens the Music library, where a user can access and play music and other audio files.

(v) Games : Opens the Games folder, where a user can access all of the games on computer.

(vi) Computer : Opens a window where you a user can access disk drives, cameras, printers, scanners, and other hardware connected to computer.

(vii) Control Panel : Opens Control Panel, where you a user customize the appearance and functionality of your computer, install or uninstall programs, set up network connections, and manage user accounts.

(viii) Devices and Printers : Opens a window where you a user can view information about the printer, mouse, and other devices installed on computer.

(ix) Default Programs : Opens a window where you user can choose which program in indows to use for activities such as web browsing.

(x) Help and Support : Opens Windows Help and Support, where a user can browse and search Help topics about using Windows and computer.

(c) Shut down (Turn Off) : The Shut down button allows to Shut down the computer or click the arrow next to the Shut down button to switch user, log off, restart, and sleep the computer.

Folders : A folder is a location that stores multiple files and other folders found on Apple computers, computers running Microsoft Windows, and other GUI operating systems. When in a command line, folders are referred to as directories.

Title bar : Title Bar refers to the bar at the top of an open window that will tell what the folder/window is (the title) and contains the minimize, maximize and close buttons. It can also use the title bar to move a window around.

Cursor : Cursor is the symbol which is used to for action performing. The cursor changes its shape from the default arrow to various shapes according to the purpose it is serving at the time. For instance, it may form an I-beam shape when user selects a text in a document or a double-arrow when use resized a window.

Scroll Bar : Scroll Bar appears when there is some information in the window than can be displayed and the information is more than that. This is usually a vertical scroll bar, but a horizontal scroll bar may display if the width of the window is too narrow.

Address Bar : Address Bar allows you to navigate up and down a series of windows by double-clicking on a folder. The folder with the Back/Fwd Buttons in Windows 7 would allow you to return to the previous folder.

Dialog box : In a graphical user interface operating system, a dialog box or dialogue box is a new window that appears above the rest that lists additional information, errors, or options.

MOUSE CLICKS ON WINDOWS

A mouse has two buttons and most current mouse have a middle button as well. The type of click means the button you push when you click.

- The **left-click** selects items and will be used most often. If no button is specified, this will be the one you use.

- If you **right-click** on an item you will get a context-sensitive menu with a list of the things that you *can* do with the item you clicked on. Like this in the example.

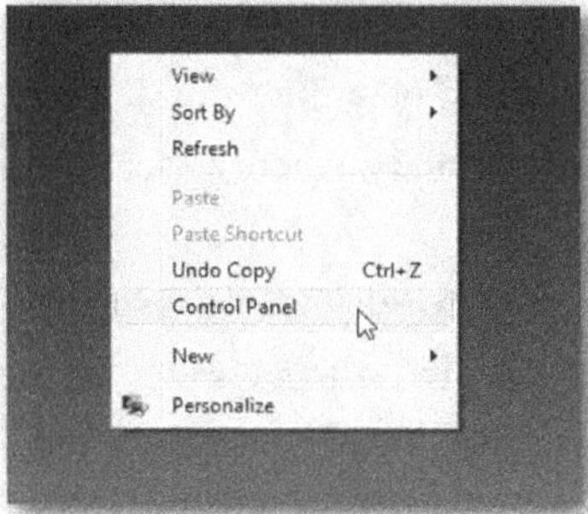

When a user right-click to obtain a menu, it will select the menu with the left button (generally just referred to as selecting or clicking — the left mouse button click is assumed).

Context Sensitive

This refers to the fact that the menu varies when you place it on different items:

- If you right-click an icon on your desktop it will include the option to open it.

- If you right-click on the background (desktop) it will give you options to arrange icons or refresh the desktop.

FILES & FILE EXTENSIONS

A file is an object on a computer that stores data, information, settings, or commands that are used with a computer program. In a graphical user interface (GUI) such as Microsoft Windows, files are shown as unique icons that relate to the program that opens the file.

File extensions are the part of the filename that is *after* the dot in Windows. For example, a text file like **readme. txt** has **txt** as its extension.

Extensions Tell What *Type* of File

The extension tells Windows how to deal with a certain file by identifying the type of file it is. By associating a certain extension with a default program to deal with that sort of file, you can open the program by double-clicking on the filename. The type of file is usually indicated by its icon as well.

Common Extensions

There are hundreds of extensions, many of which are proprietary (e.g. specific to a particular program) and quite a few that are legacy (no longer in active use). Some of the more common ones are:

- **.txt** -text file
- **.doc** -Microsoft Word document
- **.docx-** Microsoft Word open XML document – Word 2007 or later
- **.xls-** Microsoft Excel spreadsheet
- **.xlsx-** Microsoft Excel open XML spreadsheet – Excel 2007 or later
- **.ppt-** Microsoft PowerPoint presentation document

- **.pptx-** Microsoft PowerPoint open presentation document – PowerPoint 2007 or later
- **.html-** Web page (Hypertext Markup Language) file
- **.mp3-**audio (music) file
- **.pdf-** Adobe Portable Document Format file (Adobe Reader)
- **.jpg-** JPEG image file (usually a photo)
- **.bak -** Backup File
- **.tmp -** Temporary File
- **.rar -** WinRAR Compressed Archive
- **.zip -** Zipped File

Dangerous Extensions

Some Windows extensions can indicate programs that can do harm to your computer. You should always be careful with files that have the following extensions, particularly if attached to an email message, because they can be used to install malicious or unwanted programs:

- **.pif** -program information file
- **.exe-** executable (program) file
- **.bat-** batch file – can call other files including program or scripting files
- **.scr -** scripting file – sometimes mistakenly called a screen saver file

Most users should not see any of these sorts of files attached to emails. While any of these could be legitimate files it is more likely that its purpose is to infect your computer with a virus or other malicious program.

Hidden By Default

Windows hides "known" extensions by default (Windows "knows" what the extension is — you may not).

This was probably done to make it look less intimidating, but you should re-enable the display of these extensions (see Folder Options). Many file extensions are not safe to open unless provided by a *trusted* source.

For example, if you see a file attached to an email, you may not know that the attachment is unsafe to open:

- If extensions are hidden, Windows displays **phonelist.txt.scr** as **phonelist.txt**, hiding the actual *.scr* extension) allowing you to assume (mistakenly) that it is a text document and therefore safe to open.
- However, as noted earlier, the *.scr* extension is not safe to open — especially when you are unsure of the source.
- Even if you received the message from a friend, it may not be safe (or could have been attached by a virus on their computer or someone with unauthorized use of their email address).

ACCESSORIES IN WINDOWS

1. **Notepad :** Notepad is a generic text editor included with Microsoft Windows that enables someone to open and read plaintext files. If the file contains special formatting or is not a plaintext file, it will not be able to be read in Microsoft Notepad.

    How to open Windows Notepad

    Click Start→Click Programs and then Accessories→Click the "Notepad" icon.

2. **Wordpad :** Microsoft WordPad is a free rich text editor included with Microsoft Windows 95, 98, ME, NT, 2000, XP, Vista, 7, and future releases of Microsoft Windows. Microsoft Word can create, edit, and save their documents as a plain-text file (.txt), Rich Text Format (.rtf), and Word for Windows 6.0 (.doc) format (Windows 95, Windows 98, Windows ME users only -- XP does not support .doc). In Windows 7, users can now save their document in an OpenDocument (odf) format.

How to open Windows Notepad

Click Start→Click Programs and then Accessories→Click the "WordPad" icon.

3.   **Paint :** Alternatively referred to as MS Paint and Microsoft Paint. Paint is a simple program which allows users to create basic graphic art on a computer. It provides basic functionality for both drawing and painting in both colour or black and white, as well as shaped stencils and cured line tools.

How to open Windows Paint

Click Start→Click Programs and then Accessories→Click the "Paint" icon.

Keyboard Shortcuts for Windows

To	Press
Displays the properties of the selected object.	ALT+Enter
"Close the active item, or quit the active program.	ALT+F4
Switch between open items.	ALT+TAB
Carry out the corresponding command or select the corresponding option in a dialog box.	ALT+Underlined letter
Display the corresponding menu.	ALT+Underlined letter in a menu name
Select a button if the active option is a group of option buttons in a dialog box.	Arrow keys
View the folder one level up in My Computer or Windows Explorer.	BACKSPACE
Open a folder one level up if a folder is selected in the Save As or Open dialog box in a dialog box.	BACKSPACE
Copy selected item.	CTRL while dragging an item
Select all.	CTRL+A
Copy.	CTRL+C
Move the insertion point to the beginning of the next paragraph.	CTRL+DOWN ARROW
Display the Start menu.	CTRL+ESC
Close the active document in programs that allow you to have multiple documents open simultaneously.	CTRL+F4
Move the insertion point to the beginning of the previous word.	CTRL+LEFT ARROW
Move the insertion point to the beginning of the next word.	CTRL+RIGHT ARROW
Highlight a block of text.	CTRL+SHIFT with any of the arrow keys
Move backward through tabs in a dialog box.	CTRL+SHIFT+TAB
Move forward through tabs in a dialog box.	CTRL+TAB
Paste.	CTRL+V
Cut.	CTRL+X
Undo.	CTRL+Z
Delete.	DELETE
Display the bottom of the active window.	END
Carry out the command for the active option or button in a dialog box.	ENTER

To	Press
Cancel the current task.	ESC
Display Help in a dialog box.	F1
Activate the menu bar in the active program.	F10
Rename selected item.	F2
Search for a file or folder.	F3
Display the Address bar list in My Computer or Windows Explorer.	F4
Display the items in the active list in a dialog box.	F4
Refresh the active window.	F5
Cycle through screen elements in a window or on the desktop.	F6
Display the top of the active window.	HOME
Open the next menu to the left, or close a submenu.	LEFT ARROW
Collapse current selection if it's expanded, or select parent folder.	LEFT ARROW
Display the items in the active list in a dialog box.	F4
Refresh the active window.	F5
Cycle through screen elements in a window or on the desktop.	F6
Display the top of the active window.	HOME
Open the next menu to the left, or close a submenu.	LEFT ARROW
Collapse current selection if it's expanded, or select parent folder.	LEFT ARROW
Display the items in the active list in a dialog box.	F4
Refresh the active window.	F5
Cycle through screen elements in a window or on the desktop.	F6
Display the top of the active window.	HOME
Open the next menu to the left, or close a submenu.	LEFT ARROW
Collapse current selection if it's expanded, or select parent folder.	LEFT ARROW
Display the shortcut menu for the selected item.	Menu key
Display all subfolders under the selected folder.	NUM LOCK+ASTERISK on numeric keypad (*)
Collapse the selected folder.	NUM LOCK+MINUS SIGN on numeric keypad (-)
Display the contents of the selected folder.	NUM LOCK+PLUS SIGN on numeric keypad (+)
Open the next menu to the right, or open a submenu.	RIGHT ARROW
Display current selection if it's collapsed, or select first subfolder.	RIGHT ARROW
Display the items in the active list in a dialog box.	F4
Refresh the active window.	F5
Cycle through screen elements in a window or on the desktop.	F6
Display the shortcut menu for the selected item.	Menu key
Collapse the selected folder.	NUM LOCK+MINUS SIGN on numeric keypad (-)

To	Press
Display the contents of the selected folder.	NUM LOCK+PLUS SIGN on numeric keypad (+)
Open the next menu to the right, or open a submenu.	RIGHT ARROW
Display current selection if it's collapsed, or select first subfolder.	RIGHT ARROW
Delete selected item permanently without placing the item in the Recycle Bin.	SHIFT+DELETE
Display the shortcut menu for the selected item.	SHIFT+F10
Move backward through options in a dialog box.	SHIFT+TAB
Select or clear the check box if the active option is a check box in a dialog box.	SPACEBAR
Move forward through options in a dialog box.	TAB
Display or hide the Start menu.	Windows Key
Lock your computer if you are connected to a network domain, or switch users if you are not connected to a network domain.	Windows Key+ L
Show the desktop.	Windows Key+D
Open My Computer.	Windows Key+E
Search for a file or folder.	Windows Key+F
Display Windows Help.	Windows Key+F1
Minimize all windows.	Windows Key+M
Open the Run dialog box.	Windows Key+R
Restores minimized windows.	Windows Key+Shift+M
Opens Utility Manager.	Windows Key+U

Past Exercise

1. The information you put into the computer is called **[SBI Clerk, 2009]**
   - (a) facts
   - (b) data
   - (c) files
   - (d) directory
   - (e) None of these

2. The rectangular area of the screen that displays a program, data and /or information is a **[SBI Clerk, 2009]**
   - (a) title bar
   - (b) button
   - (c) dialog box
   - (d) window
   - (e) None of these

3. Help Menu is available at which button? **[SBI Clerk, 2009]**
   - (a) End
   - (b) Start
   - (c) Turnoff
   - (d) Restart
   - (e) None of these

4. File extensions are used in order to——— **[SBI Clerk, 2009]**
   - (a) name the file
   - (b) ensure the filename is not lost
   - (c) identify the file
   - (d) identify the file type
   - (e) None of the above

5. Files deleted from the hard disk are sent to the— **[SBI Clerk, 2009]**
   - (a) recycle bin
   - (b) floppy disk
   - (c) clipboard
   - (d) motherboard
   - (e) None of these

6. The —— of software contains lists of commands and options. **[SBI Clerk, 2009]**
   - (a) menu bar
   - (b) tool bar
   - (c) title bar
   - (d) formula bar
   - (e) None of these

7. To make the number pad act as directional arrows, you press the —— key. **[SBI Clerk, 2009]**
   - (a) shift
   - (b) arrow lock
   - (c) num lock
   - (d) caps lock
   - (e) None of these

8. Window 7, the latest operating system from Microsoft Corporation has .... Indian languages fonts. **[SSC CGL, 2010]**
   - (a) 14
   - (b) 26
   - (c) 37
   - (d) 49

9. To change selected text to all capital letters, click the change case button, then click **[IBPS PO, 2011]**
   - (a) Uppercase
   - (b) Upper all
   - (c) Capslock
   - (d) Lock Upper
   - (e) Large Size

10. Help menu is available at which button? **[IBPS PO, 2011]**
    - (a) End
    - (b) Start
    - (c) Turnoff
    - (d) Restart
    - (e) Reboot

11. You can keep your personal files/folders in **[IBPS PO, 2011]**
    - (a) My folder
    - (b) My Documents
    - (c) My Files
    - (d) My Text
    - (e) None of these

12. When the pointer is positioned on a ____, it is shaped like a hand. **[IBPS PO, 2011]**
    - (a) Grammar error
    - (b) Formatting error
    - (c) Screen Tip
    - (d) Spelling error
    - (e) Hyperlink

13. To restart the computer the following combination of keys is used **[IBPS Clerk, 2011]**
    - (a) Del + Ctrl
    - (b) Backspace + Ctrl
    - (c) Esc + Ctrl
    - (d) Insert + Esc
    - (e) Ctrl + Alt + Del

14. Which part of the computer helps to store information? **[IBPS Clerk, 2011]**
    - (a) Monitor
    - (b) Keyboard
    - (c) Disk drive
    - (d) Printer
    - (e) Plotter

15. Which key is used to delete one character to the left of the current position of the cursor? **[IBPS Clerk, 2011]**
    - (a) Backspace
    - (b) Delete
    - (c) Insert
    - (d) Esc
    - (e) Ctrl

16. If you change Windows 98 to Windows XP, you are actually performing   **[IBPS Clerk, 2011]**
    (a) upstart   (b) upgrade
    (c) update   (d) patch
    (e) None of these

17. When a chart is placed on this, it is much larger and there is no other data on it
    [IBPS Clerk, 2011]
    (a) Chart sheet   (b) Exclusive sheet
    (c) Primary sheet   (d) Reference sheet
    (e) None of these

18. Which of the following is not true about computer files?   **[SBI Clerk, 2011]**
    (a) They are collections of data saved to a storage medium
    (b) Every file has a filename
    (c) A file extension is established by the user to indicate the file's contain
    (d) All files contain data
    (e) None of these

19. A menu contains a list of   **[SBI Clerk, 2011]**
    (a) commands   (b) data
    (c) objects   (d) reports
    (e) None of these

20. File __________ shrinks the size of a file so it requires less storage space.   **[SBI Clerk, 2011]**
    (a) scanning   (b) synthesizing
    (c) defragmenting   (d) compression
    (e) None of these

21. In addition to the basic typing keys, desktop and notebook computer keyboards include a(n) __________ keypad to efficiently move the screen-based insertion point. **[SBI Clerk, 2011]**
    (a) editing   (b) number
    (c) locked   (d) docked
    (e) None of these

22. What is the name given to those applications that combine text, sound, graphics, motion video, and/ or animation ?   **[IBPS PO, 2012]**
    (a) motionware   (b) anigraphics
    (c) videoscapes   (d) multimedia
    (e) maxomedia

23. Which of the following is the first step in sizing a window ?   **[IBPS PO, 2012]**
    (a) Point to the title bar
    (b) Pull down the View menu to display the toolbar
    (c) Point lo any corner or border
    (d) Pull down the View menu and change to large icons
    (e) None of these

24. What is the significance of a faded (dimmed) command in a pull-down menu ?
    [IBPS PO, 2012]
    (a) The command is not currently accessible
    (b) A dialog box appears if the command is selected
    (c) A Help window appears if the command is selected
    (d) There are no equivalent keystrokes for the particular command
    (e) None of these

25. The Search Companion can __________.
    [IBPS PO, 2012]
    (a) Locate all files containing a specified phrase
    (b) Restrict its search to a specified set of folders
    (c) Locate all files containing a specified phrase and restrict its search to a specified set of folders
    (d) Cannot locate all files containing a specified phrase or restrict its search to a specified set of folders
    (e) (a) & (b)

26. Which file (s) can be executed without mentioning its extension name   **[IBPS Clerk, 2012]**
    (a) .exe   (b) .bat
    (c) .com   (d) .app
    (e) All of these

27. About pasting from the clip board
    [IBPS PO, 2013]
    (a) a part of the clip board contents can be pasted
    (b) whole of the contents of clip board can be pasted

(c) sometimes (a) and sometimes (b)

(d) (a) and (b)

(e) None ol the above

28. To display the contents of a folder in Windows Explorer you should ____________.
[SBI PO, 2013]

(a) click on it   (b) collapse it

(c) name it   (d) give a password

(e) rename it

29. Which of the following refers to the rectangular area for displaying information and running programs ?   **[SBI PO, 2013]**

(a) Desktop   (b) Dialog box

(c) Menu   (d) Window

(e) Icon

30. ____________ is a Window utility program that locates and eliminates unnecessary fragments and rearranges files and unused disk space to optimize operations.   **[SBI PO, 2013]**

(a) Backup   (b) Disk Cleanup

(c) Disk Defragmenter (d) Restore

(e) Disk Restorer

31. ________ are lists of commands that appear on the screen.   **[SBI Clerk, 2014]**

(a) GUIs   (b) Icons

(c) Menus   (d) Windows

(e) None of these

32. To open find window.   **[IBPS Clerk, 2015]**

(a) F1   (b) F2

(c) F3   (d) F5

(e) None of these

33. Which of the following is an operating system?
[SBI Clerk, 2015]

(a) MS Windows   (b) Mac

(c) MS DOS   (d) Windows NT

(e) All of the above

34. Windows 10 is in an example of a ________ ?
[SBI Clerk, 2015]

(a) Application software

(b) Brawser

(c) Operating system

(d) Shareware

(e) None of these

35. Which among the following key combination can be used to close the Current Active Window?
[IBPS PO Mains 2016]

(a) Ctrl+F4   (b) Ctrl+S

(c) Ctrl+G   (d) Alt+S

(e) None of the above

36. Which among the following key can be used as a shortcut to rename a folder in Microsoft Windows 8 and higher versions?
[IBPS Clerk Mains 2016]

(a) F2   (b) F4

(c) F6   (d) F9

(e) F11

ANSWER KEY

1.	(b)	6.	(a)	11.	(b)	16.	(b)	21.	(b)	26.	(e)	31.	(a)	36.	(a)
2.	(d)	7.	(c)	12.	(e)	17.	(a)	22.	(d)	27.	(b)	32.	(d)		
3.	(b)	8.	(d)	13.	(e)	18.	(c)	23.	(c)	28.	(a)	33.	(e)		
4.	(d)	9.	(a)	14.	(c)	19.	(a)	24.	(a)	29.	(d)	34.	(c)		
5.	(a)	10.	(b)	15.	(a)	20.	(d)	25.	(e)	30.	(c)	35.	(a)		

Practice Exercise

1. Window is ___________ and Window 95, Window 98 are ___________.
   (a) Graphical User Interface, Operating System
   (b) Graphics Useful Interface, Executing Systems
   (c) Graph User Interval, Expert Systems
   (d) None of these

2. Text and graphics that have been out of copied are stored in an area called the ___________.
   (a) Pasteboard   (b) Copyboard
   (c) Clipboard   (d) Cuttingboard
   (e) None of these

3. What is the default file extension for all Word documents?
   (a) WRD   (b) TXT
   (c) DOC   (d) FIL
   (e) None of these

4. What are bas, doc, and .htm examples of?
   (a) Databases   (b) Extensions
   (c) Domains   (d) Protocols
   (e) None of these

5. A ___________ is a unique name that you give to a file of information
   (a) device letter   (b) folder
   (c) filename   (d) filename extension
   (e) None of these

6. Computers send and receive data in the form of ___________ signals.
   (a) Analog   (b) Digital
   (c) Modulated   (d) Demodulated
   (e) All of these

7. ___________ are graphical objects used to represent commonly used application.
   (a) GUI   (b) Drivers
   (c) Windows   (d) Application
   (e) Icons

8. Which of the following operating systems is not owned and licensed by a company?
   (a) Unix   (b) Linux
   (c) Windows 2000   (d) Mac
   (e) Windows

9. In any window, the maximize button, the minimize button and the close buttons appear on
   (a) The title bar   (b) Menu bar
   (c) Status bar   (d) Ruler bar
   (e) Tool bar

10. A blinking symbol on the screen that shows where the next character will appear is a/an ___________.
    (a) delete key   (b) arrow key
    (c) cursor   (d) return key
    (e) None of these

11. Date and Time are available on the desktop at ___________.
    (a) Taskbar   (b) My Computer
    (c) Recycle Bin   (d) only 2 and 3
    (e) None of these

12. A ___________ contains buttons and menus that provide quick access to commonly used commands.
    (a) toolbar   (b) menu bar
    (c) window   (d) find
    (e) None of these

13. ___________ Explorer is a tool that lets you more easily navigate the files and folders on your computer.
    (a) Windows   (b) Netscape
    (c) Internet   (d) Microsoft
    (e) Web

14. Which key is used in combination with another key to perform a specific task?
    (a) function   (b) arrow
    (c) space bar   (d) control
    (e) None of these

15. Before the days of Windows, users interfaced with the operating system through a ___________ interface.
    (a) graphical   (b) object oriented
    (c) command utility (d) command line
    (e) Command oriented

16. Different applications and documents of windows desktop are represented by
    (a) Symbols   (b) Labels
    (c) Graph   (d) Icon
    (e) None of these

17. On which button does help menu exist?
    (a) End   (b) Start
    (c) Turn off   (d) Restart
    (e) None of these

18. If you do not want to select any option after opening a menu then click menu title again or press key ___________ to close the menu.
    (a) Shift   (b) Tab
    (c) Escape   (d) FI
    (e) None of these

19. It is easier to change the name of file using
    ____________ process.
    (a) Transforming   (b) Christening
    (c) Renaming   (d) Retagging
    (e) None of these
20. ____________ may be included in other folder
    while making heirarchical structural folder.
    (a) Mainfolder   (b) Tiered folder
    (c) Sub-folder   (d) Object
    (e) None of these
21. To shrink a window to an icon ____________.
    (a) open a group window
    (b) minimise a window
    (c) maximise a window
    (d) restore a window
    (e) None of these
22. A(n) ____________ contains commands that can
    be selected.
    (a) pointer   (b) menu
    (c) icon   (d) button
    (e) None of these
23. If you want to move an icon on your desktop,
    this is called ____________.
    (a) double clicking (b) highlighting
    (c) dragging   (d) pointing
    (e) None of these
24. All the deleted files go to
    (a) Recycle bin   (b) Task bar
    (c) Tool bar   (d) My Computer
    (e) None of these
25. The .... is the entire window that fills
    your computer screen and its contents.
    (a) System Tray
    (b) Taskbar
    (c) Desktop
    (d) Quick Launch Toolbar
    (e) Menu bar
26. A small figure which depicts some application
    on the screen is called
    (a) Menu   (b) Photo
    (c) Modem   (d) Icon
    (e) None of these
27. Which keys enable the input of numbers
    quickly?
    (a) Function keys
    (b) The numeric keypad
    (c) Ctrl, shift and alt
    (d) Arrow keys
    (e) None of these
28. What menu is selected to change font and style?
    (a) Tools   (b) File
    (c) Format   (d) Edit
    (e) None of these

29. ____________ is when the more power-hungry
    components, such as the monitor and the hard
    drive are put in idle.
    (a) Hibernation
    (b) Powerdown
    (c) Standby mode
    (d) The shutdown procedure
    (e) None of these
30. ____________ moves the cursor one space to
    the right or puts spaces in between words.
    (a) Control key   (b) Space bar
    (c) Printer   (d) Mouse
    (e) None of these
31. Use this when you want to make all letters
    capital without having to use the shift key for
    each character.
    (a) shifter   (b) upper case
    (c) caps lock key   (c) icon
    (e) None of these
32. Any letter, number, or symbol found on the
    keyboard that you can type into the computer.
    (a) output   (b) character
    (c) type   (d) print
    (e) None of these
33. A symbol or question on the screen that prompts
    you to take action and tells the computer what
    to do next ____________.
    (a) scanner
    (b) questionnaire
    (c) prompts and dialog box
    (d) information seeker
    (e) None of these
34. Choices are referred to as ____________.
    (a) options   (b) exit
    (c) boot   (d) folder
    (e) None of these
35. Anything written on the screen is called
    ____
    (a) cursor   (b) text
    (c) folder   (d) boot
    (e) None of these
36. Lets you leave a screen or program.
    (a) boot   (b) programs
    (c) exit   (d) text
    (e) None of these
37. A place that a user can create to store files.
    (a) cursor   (b) text
    (c) folder   (d) boot
    (e) None of these
38. Start or restart the computer.
    (a) exit   (b) kick
    (c) boot   (d) kick-start
    (e) None of these

39. The __________ button applies any changes you have made but leaves the Properties window open.
    (a) Apply   (b) cancel
    (c) ok   (d) next
    (e) Delete

40. Commands at the top of a screen such as FILE-EDIT-FONT-TOOLS to operate and change things within programs.
    (a) menu bar   (b) tool bar
    (c) user-friendly   (d) word processor
    (e) None of these

41. To change written work already done.
    (a) file   (b) edit
    (c) cut   (d) close
    (e) None of these

42. A key that will erase information from the computer's memory and characters on the screen.
    (a) edit   (b) delete key
    (c) dummy out   (d) trust key
    (e) None of these

43. To exit the program without leaving the application.
    (a) file   (b) edit
    (c) copy   (d) close
    (e) None of these

44. Screen that comes on when you turn on your computer that shows all the icons.
    (a) desktop   (b) face to face
    (c) viewer   (d) view space
    (e) None of these

45. A button that makes character either upper or lower case and numbers to symbols.
    (a) monitor   (b) shift key
    (c) icon   (d) mouse
    (e) None of these

46. A screen list of options in a program that tells you what is in that program –
    (a) screen   (b) icon
    (c) menu   (d) backup
    (e) None of these

47. Letters, numbers and symbols found on a keyboard are –
    (a) Icon   (b) Screen
    (c) Keys   (d) Menu
    (e) None of these

48. A piece of hardware that is used to enter information into the computer by using keys –
    (a) keyboard   (b) monitor
    (c) hard disk   (d) icon
    (e) None of these

49. Capital letters on a keyboard are referred to as –
    (a) caps lock key   (b) grownups
    (c) big guys   (d) upper case letters
    (e) None of these

50. A symbol on the screen that represents a disk, document or program that you can select –
    (a) keys   (b) caps
    (c) icon   (d) monitor
    (e) None of these

51. Powerful key that lets you exit a program when pushed
    (a) arrow keys   (b) spacebar
    (c) escape key   (d) return key
    (e) None of these

52. The "desktop" of a computer refers to __________.
    (a) the visible screen
    (b) the area around the monitor
    (c) the top of the mouse pad
    (d) the inside of a folder
    (e) None of these

53. To "maximize" a window means __________.
    (a) fill it to capacity
    (b) expand it to fit the desktop
    (c) put only like files inside
    (d) drag it to the Recycle Bin
    (e) None of these

54. The rectangular area of the screen that displays a program, data, and/or information is a __________.
    (a) title bar   (b) button
    (c) dialog box   (d) window
    (e) interaction box

55. Creating a __________ means making a duplicate copy of important files so that when a problem occurs, you can restore those files using the copy.
    (a) mirror   (b) hot file
    (c) printout   (d) hotspot
    (e) backup

56. A file extension is separated from the main file name with a(n) __________, but no spaces.
    (a) question mark   (b) exclamation mark
    (c) underscore   (d) period
    (e) None of these

57. What is MP3?
    (a) A mouse   (b) A printer
    (c) A sound format   (d) A scanner
    (e) None of these

58. A quicker way to launch a program is to click on ……….. in Microsoft window.
    (a) System Tray   (b) Taskbar
    (c) Desktop
    (d) Quick Launch Toolbar
    (e) Menubar

59. In an information system, alphanumeric data normally takes the form of
    (a) Sentences and paragraphs
    (b) Numbers and alphabetical characters
    (c) Graphic shapes and figures
    (d) Human voice and other sounds
    (e) None of these

60. Various applications and documents are represented on the Windows desktop by
    (a) Symbols   (b) Labels
    (c) Graphs   (d) Icons
    (e) None of these

61. A __________ contains buttons and menus that provide quick access to commonly used commands.
    (a) menu bar   (b) toolbar
    (c) window   (d) action bar
    (e) None of these

62. The __________ of software contains lists of commands and options.
    (a) menu bar   (b) title bar
    (c) formula bar   (d) tool bar
    (e) None of these

63. To access a mainframe or supercomputer, users often use a __________.
    (a) terminal   (b) node
    (c) desktop   (d) handheld
    (e) None of these

64. What are bas, doc and htm examples of?
    (a) extensions   (b) domains
    (c) protocols   (d) databases
    (e) None of these

65. Ctrl, shift and alt are called __________ keys.
    (a) adjustment   (b) function
    (c) modifier   (d) alphanumeric
    (e) None of these

66. Which of the following menu types is also called a drop-down menu?
    (a) fly-but   (b) cascading
    (c) pop-up   (d) pull-down
    (e) None of these

67. Which device is used as the standard pointing device in a Graphical User Environment?
    (a) Keyboard   (b) Mouse
    (c) Joystick   (d) Track ball
    (e) None of these

68. Data that is c opied from an application is stored in the __________.
    (a) driver   (b) clipboard
    (c) terminal   (d) prompt
    (e) None of these

69. Codes consisting of bars or lines of varying widths or lengths that are computer-readable are known as __________.
    (a) a bar code   (b) an ASCII code
    (c) a magnetic tape (d) a light pen
    (e) None of these

70. What is the main folder on a storage device called?
    (a) Platform   (b) Interface
    (c) Root Directory   (d) Home Page
    (e) None of the above

71. Which of these keys is not on the number keypad?
    (a) Ctrl   (b) Del
    (c) Enter   (d) Num Lock
    (e) None of the above

72. What menu is selected to cut, copy and paste?
    (a) File   (b) Edit
    (c) Tools   (d) Table
    (e) None of the above

73. A (n) __________ is created by an application.
    (a) executable file (b) software program
    (c) document   (d) operating system
    (e) None of the above

74. The __________ key and the __________ key can be used in combination with other keys to perform shortcuts and special tasks.
    (a) Control, Alt
    (b) Function, toggle
    (c) Delete, Insert
    (d) Caps Lock, Num Lock
    (e) None of the above

75. What is a file?
    (a) A file is a section of main storage used to store data.
    (b) A file is a collection of information that has been given a name and is stored in secondary memory.
    (c) A file is the part of a program that is used to describe what the program should do.
    (d) A file is another name for floppy disk.
    (e) None of the above

76. Applications are often referred to as
    (a) data file
    (b) executable files
    (c) system software
    (d) the operating system
    (e) None of the above

77. Deleted data remains on a disk until
    (a) the data is overwritten
    (b) the recycle bin is emptied
    (c) a file compression utility is used
    (d) the disk is scanned
    (e) None of the above

78. Which is a graphical representation of an application?
    (a) Window 95
    (b) Windows Explorer
    (c) Icon
    (d) Taskbar
    (e) None of the above

79. To restart the computer __________ key is used.
    (a) Del + Ctrl   (b) Backspace + Ctrl
    (c) Ctrl + Alt + Del   (d) Reset

80. Which of the following statements is false concerning file names?
    (a) Files may share the same name or the same extension but not both.
    (b) Every file in the same folder must have a unique name.
    (c) File extension is another name for file type.
    (d) The file extension comes before the dot (.) followed by the file name.
    (d) None of these

81. The __________ is the term used to describe the window that is currently being used.
    (a) Web Window   (b) Display Area
    (c) WordPad window   (d) Active Window
    (e) Monitor

82. The __________ settings are automatic and standard.
    (a) default   (b) CPU
    (c) peripheral   (d) user-friendly
    (e) defaulter

83. Press __________ to move the insertion point to the Address box, or to highlight the URL in the Address box.
    (a) ALT + D   (b) ALT + A
    (c) SHIFT + TAB   (d) TAB + CTRL
    (e) CTRL + S

84. Which process checks to ensure the components of the computer are operating and connected properly?
    (a) Booting   (b) Processing
    (c) Saving   (d) Editing
    (e) Starting

85. __________ is referred to as a path using the proper syntax
    (a) c;/windows/desktop
    (b) c:>c
    (c) c:\windows\desktop\My Documents
    (d) c:winnt/system32
    (e) c:\windows\system32

86. Microsoft's operating system Windows
    (a) is designed for multiple concurrent users.
    (b) has a graphical user interface.
    (c) can perform multitasking.
    (d) All of these
    (e) Both (b) and (c) above

87. The term "user interface" refers to
    (a) what the user sees on the screen and how they can interact with it.
    (b) how the operating system responds to user commands.
    (c) the means by which the user interacts with the peripheral devices on the computer.
    (d) All of these
    (e) None of these

88. The __________ icon represents an e-mail message that has not been read.
    (a) Closed envelope   (b) Red envelope
    (c) Highlighted envelope (d) Flashing letter
    (e) Question Mark

89. To start Internet Explorer, __________ on the Windows taskbar, point to All Programs, and then point to Internet Explorer.
    (a) double click the Internet Explorer button
    (b) click the Start button
    (c) right click My Computer
    (d) all of the above
    (e) reboot the computer

90. What do you see when you click the right mouse button?
    (a) The same effect as the left click
    (b) A special menu
    (c) No effect
    (d) A mouse cannot be right clicked
    (e) Computer goes to sleep mode

91. In Window ME, what does ME stand for?
    (a) Millenium   (b) Micro-Expert
    (c) Macro-Expert   (d) Multi-Expert
    (e) My-Expert

92. Keyboard shortcuts are used to move the
    (a) I-beam   (b) insertion point
    (c) scrollbar   (d) mouse
    (e) None of these

93. When a computer prints a report, this output is called
    (a) Program   (b) Soft copy
    (c) Hard copy   (d) Execution
    (e) None of these

94. A set of choices on the screen is called a(n)
    (a) menu   (b) reverse video
    (c) action plan   (d) editor
    (e) template

95. Which of the following types of menu shows further sub-choices?
    (a) Reverse   (b) Template
    (c) Scrolled   (d) Rapped
    (e) Pulled Down

96. Which menu enables the user to choose toolbars?
    (a) View   (b) Format
    (c) Insert   (d) Edit
    (e) Help
97. By viewing the properties of the local hard disk of a computer, the user can find out
    (a) the amount of space that has been used up and the remaining free space on the disk.
    (b) the name of the user viewing the properties of the disk.
    (c) nothing useful to the user.
    (d) the number of programs available in the computer
    (e) None of these
98. The keyboard shortcut to centralise the selected text in Word is
    (a) Ctrl + Esc   (b) Ctrl + C
    (c) Alt + C
    (d) There is no keyboard shortcut for this operation
    (e) Ctrl + E
99. Windows 95, Windows 98 and Windows NT are known as
    (a) processors   (b) domain names
    (c) modems   (d) operating systems
    (e) None of these
100. To indent the first paragraph of your report, you should use this key ____________.
    (a) space bar   (b) return key
    (c) tab key   (d) shift key
    (e) None of these
101. The ____________ file format is a method of encoding pictures on a computer.
    (a) HTML   (b) JPEG
    (c) FTP   (d) URL
    (e) DOC

ANSWER KEY

No.	Ans	No.	Ans	No.	Ans	No.	Ans	No.	Ans	No.	Ans
1.	(a)	18.	(c)	35.	(b)	52.	(a)	69.	(a)	86.	(d)
2.	(c)	19.	(c)	36.	(c)	53.	(b)	70.	(c)	87.	(a)
3.	(c)	20.	(c)	37.	(c)	54.	(d)	71.	(a)	88.	(a)
4.	(b)	21.	(b)	38.	(c)	55.	(e)	72.	(b)	89.	(b)
5.	(c)	22.	(c)	39.	(a)	56.	(d)	73.	(a)	90.	(b)
6.	(b)	23.	(c)	40.	(a)	57.	(c)	74.	(a)	91.	(a)
7.	(e)	24.	(a)	41.	(b)	58.	(d)	75.	(b)	92.	(c)
8.	(a)	25.	(c)	42.	(b)	59.	(b)	76.	(c)	93.	(c)
9.	(a)	26.	(d)	43.	(d)	60.	(d)	77.	(b)	94.	(a)
10.	(c)	27.	(b)	44.	(a)	61.	(b)	78.	(b)	95.	(e)
11.	(a)	28.	(c)	45.	(b)	62.	(a)	79.	(c)	96.	(a)
12.	(a)	29.	(c)	46.	(c)	63.	(a)	80.	(d)	97.	(a)
13.	(a)	30.	(b)	47.	(c)	64.	(a)	81.	(d)	98.	(e)
14.	(d)	31.	(c)	48.	(a)	65.	(b)	82.	(a)	99.	(d)
15.	(d)	32.	(b)	49.	(a)	66.	(c)	83.	(a)	100.	(c)
16.	(d)	33.	(c)	50.	(c)	67.	(b)	84.	(a)	101.	(b)
17.	(c)	34.	(a)	51.	(c)	68.	(b)	85.	(c)		

Microsoft Office

Chapter

Microsoft Office is an office suite of desktop applications, servers and services for Microsoft Windows and OS X operating systems. It was first announced by Bill Gates of Microsoft on 1 August 1988 at COMDEX in Las Vegas.

BASICS OF MICROSOFT WORD

Microsoft Word is the word processor component of Microsoft Office that allows users the ability to create and save documents. A word document can be a letter, report, or even a web page.

How to Start the MS Word Program

Click Start → All Programs → Microsoft Office → Microsoft Word

File format for document created in word is .docx or.doc

GENERATIONS OF MICROSOFT OFFICE

Above the timeline (left to right):

- Microsoft introduced initial version office 1.0, its contents are word 1.0 Excel 2.0 Power Point 2.0 & office 2.0, both released on Nov. 19, 1990.
- Microsoft introduced a new version office 1.6 released on July 8, 1991. Its contents are window 1.1, Excel 3.0, Power Point 2.0, Mail (2.1).
- Microsoft version 3.0 released on Aug. 30, 1992.
- Microsoft introduced a new version (7.0) or office 95 released on August 24, 1995. It supports window 95, etc.
- Microsoft introduced a new version 8.5 or office 97 powered by word 98 released on June 20, 1997. It supports window 98.
- Microsoft introduced a new version (10.0) or office XP released on May 31, 2001 It supports, window 98, window 2000/XP.
- Microsoft introduced a new version (12.0) or office 2007, released on Jan. 30, 2007. It supports window vista, word 2007, etc.
- Microsoft introduced a new version (15.0) or office 2013 released on Jan. 29, 2013 It supports IA-32, X-64 system, window 7, window server 8.
- Microsoft announced office which supports main stream It will be release on Oct, 2020.

Timeline: 1990 | 1991 | 1992 | 1994 | 1995 | 1996 | 1997 | 1999 | 2001 | 2003 | 2007 | 2010 | 2013 | 2016

Below the timeline (left to right):

- Microsoft introduced a new version office 1.5, released on March 4, 1991. Its contents are Word 1.1, Excel 3.0, Powerpoint 2.0
- Microsoft introduced a new version office 4.0 released on 17 Jan. 1994, office 4.3 on 2 June, 1994 & office NT 4.2 on 3 July, 1994. It supports window NT word 6.0, etc.
- Microsoft introduced a new version (8.0) or office 97, released on Nov. 19, 1996. It supports window 95 and word 97, etc.
- Microsoft introduced a new version (9.0) or office 2000, released on June 7, 1999. It supports windows 95, window 98, word 2000, etc.
- Microsoft introduced a new version (11.0) or office 2003, relesed on Oct. 21, 2003. It supports window XP/ 2000, word 2003, etc.
- Microsoft introduced a new version (14.0) or office 2010, released on June 15, 2010. It supports window XP, vista. It works on both 32-64 bit system.
- Microsoft introduced a new version (16.0), or office 2016, release on 22, Sept. 2015. It support window-10, word 2016, etc.

SOME IMPORTANT MICROSOFT TERMINOLOGY

Microsoft Outlook

Its is a personal information manager from Microsoft, available as a part of the Microsoft Office suite. Although often used mainly as an email application, it also includes a calendar, task manager, contact manager, note taking, journal, and web browsing.

It can be used as a stand-alone application, or can work with Microsoft Exchange Server and Microsoft SharePoint Server for multiple users in an organization, such as shared mailboxes and calendars, Exchange public folders, SharePoint lists, and meeting schedules.

Microsoft OneNote

Microsoft OneNote was included in all Microsoft Office offerings before eventually becoming completely free of charge. OneNote is available as a web application on Office Online, a Windows desktop app, a mobile app for Windows Phone, iOS, Android, and Symbian, and a Metro-style app for Windows 8 or later.

Microsoft OneNote is a freeware note-taking program. It gathers notes (handwritten or typed), drawings, screen clipping-sand audio commentaries. However, OneNote eventually became a core component of Microsoft Office; with the release of Microsoft Office 2013.

Microsoft Office Sway

Microsoft office Sway released by Microsoft in August 2015, Sways is stored on Microsoft's server and are tied to the user's Microsoft account. They can be viewed and edited from any web browser with a web app available in Office Online. They can also be accessed using apps for Windows 10 and iOS. Additional apps are currently in development for Android and Windows 10 Mobile.

Microsoft office, Sway allows users who have a Microsoft account to combine text and media to create a presentable website. Users can pull content locally from the device in use, or from internet sources such as Bing, Facebook, One-Drive, and YouTube.

Microsoft Office 2010

Microsoft Office 2010 (code named Office 14) is a version of the Microsoft Office productivity suite for Microsoft Windows.

It is the successor to Microsoft Office 2007 and the predecessor to Microsoft Office 2013. Office 2010 includes extended file format support, user interface improvements, and a changed user experience.

A 64-bit version of Office 2010 is available, but not for Windows XP or Windows Server 2003. It is the first version of the productivity suite to ship in both 32-bit and 64-bit versions.

Office 2010 marks the debut of Office Web Apps, online versions of Word, Excel, PowerPoint, and OneNote that work in web browsers. Office Starter 2010, a new edition of Office, replaced the low-end home productivity software, Microsoft Works.

Office 2010 is the first version to require product activation for volume licensing editions. Unlike previous versions of the productivity suite, every application in Office 2010 features the ribbon as its user primary user interface. Mainstream support ended on October 13, 2015; extended support ends on October 13, 2020.

PARTS OF WORD WINDOW

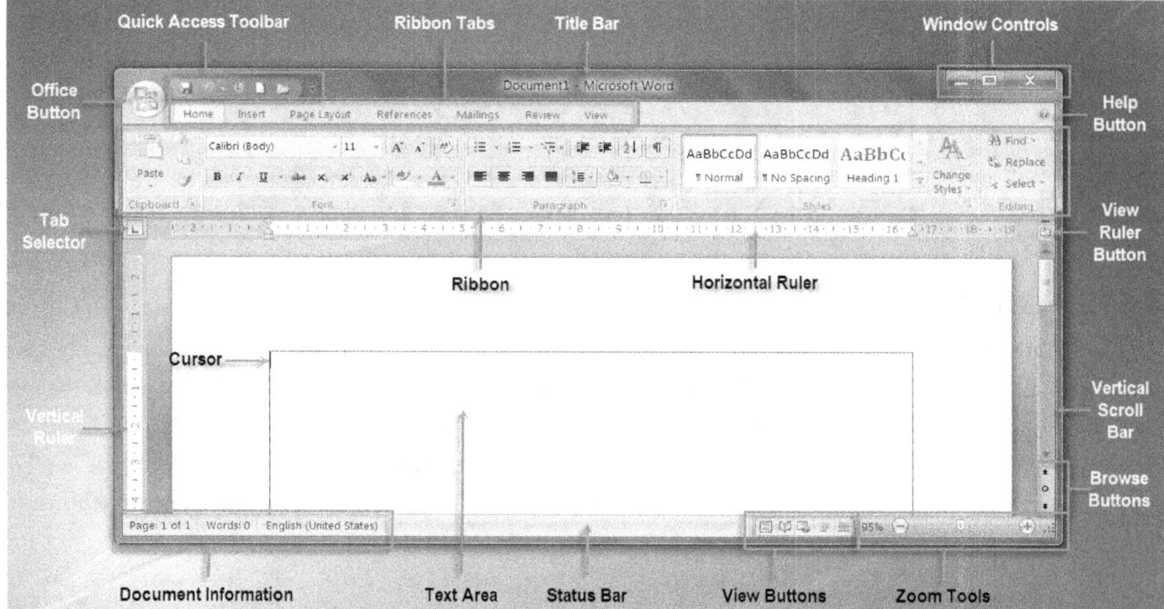

1.   OFFICE BUTTON

It is located in upper left button corner of the office.

The options available in the Office Button menu are :

New	Creates a new document
Open	Opens an existing document form disk
Save	Saves the open document to disk
Save As	Saves the open document to disk under a different name
Print	Prints the open document
Prepare	Prepares the document for distribution, through such tasks as adding a signature on encryption
Send	Sends the document to another user by email or fax
Publish	Makes the document publicly available via a document serve or a public web space
Close	Exits the open document.

2.   RIBBON

The Ribbon is located at the top of the screen and stretches across the window. The Ribbon is organized into 8 different

Tabs; File, Home, Insert, Page Lausert, References, Mailings, Review, and View. Each Tab has several **Groups**, where similar tools and features are found.

(a)   HOME TAB

The Home tab displays a variety of tools and features used to format and move text. The Home tab can change the color, size, font, and alignment of the text. The Home tab can also cut, copy, and paste text.

The Home tab has 5 groups; Clipboard, Font, Paragraph, Styles and Editing.

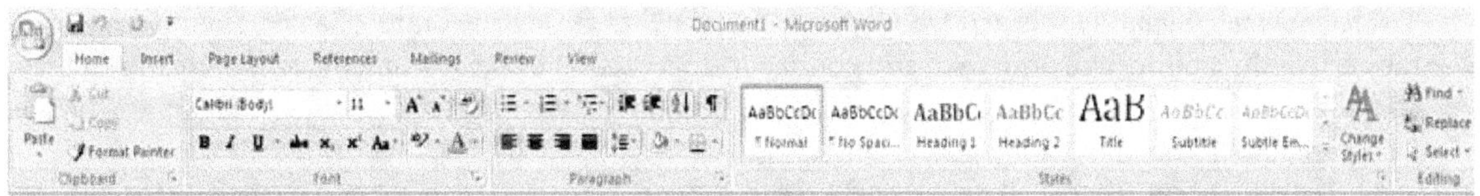

(b) INSERT TAB

The Insert tab displays tools and features used to add an item or special format to the document. The Insert tab can add pictures, symbols, or page numbers to the document. The Insert tab has 7 groups; Pages, Tables, Illustrations, Links, Header & Footer, Text, and Symbols.

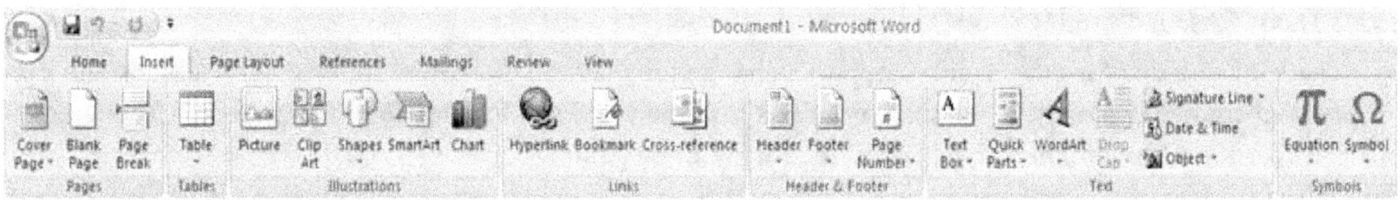

(c) PAGE LAYOUT TAB

The Page Layout tab displays tools and features used to change the way text and images will be positioned in the document. The Page Lausert tab controls the margins and page orientation. The Page Lausert tab has 5 groups; Themes, Page Setup, Page Background, Paragraph, and Arrange.

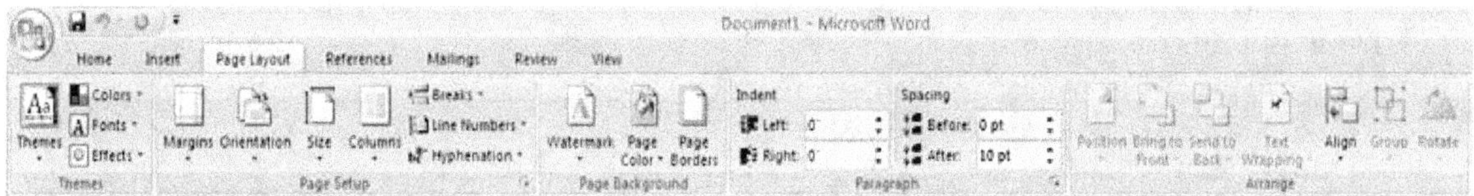

(d) REFERENCE TAB

The References tab displays tools and features used in academic or professional writing. The References tab will assist with using citations, footnotes, and a table of contents. The References tab has 6 groups; Table of Contents, Footnotes, Citations, Captions, Index, and Table of Authorities.

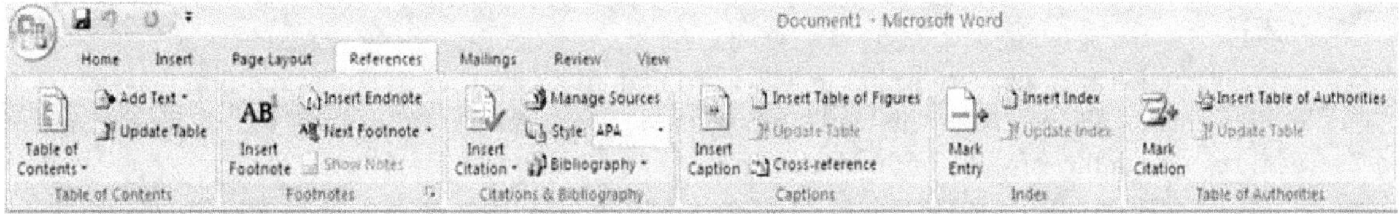

(e) MAILINGS TAB

The Mailings tab displays tools and features used to print envelopes, labels, and send mass communications. The Mailings tab has 5 groups; Create, Start Mail Merge, Write & Insert Fields, Preview Results, and Finish.

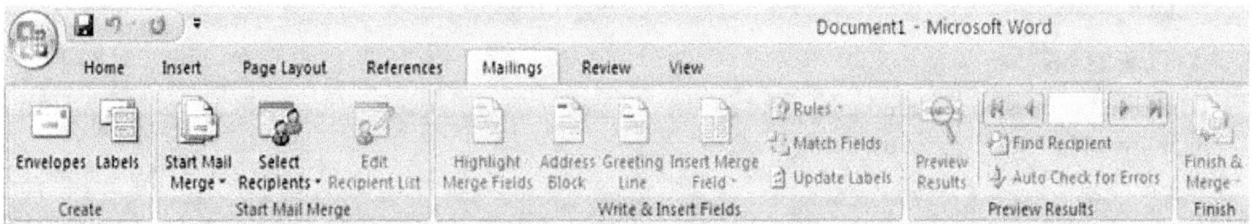

(f) REVIEW TAB

The Review tab displays tools and features used to fix mistakes or write drafts of a document. The Review tab can check spelling and grammar, add comments to a section of the document, or change the language of the document. The Review tab has 7 groups; Proofing, Language, Comments, Tracking, Changes, Compare, and Protect.

(g) VIEW TAB

The View tab displays tools and features to change the way the document looks on the screen. The View tab can change the zoom level, display or position the windows for 2 different documents. The View tab has 5 groups; Document Views, Show, Zoom, Window, and Macros.

3. TAB STOP

A tab stop is a term used to describe the location the cursor stops after the tab key is pressed. Tab stops are used in word processors to enable users to align text by pressing the tab key. In Microsoft Word, the tab selector, also called the tab indicator, is a button to the left of the ruler that supplies the user with a variety of tab marker options.

Types of tab stops–

Below are explanations of each of the five different tab stops.

1. Left - Text is extended to the right of the tab.
2. Center - Text is centered in the middle of the tab.
3. Right - Text is extended to the left of the tab.
4. Decimal - Text before the decimal point extends to the left and text after the decimal point extends to the right.
5. Bar - A vertical bar is shown on the tab.

4. RULER

The ruler is a measurement tool found in MS word that allow the user to align graphics, text, tables, or other elements on a page. When enabled the horizontal ruler appears at the top of the document, and the vertical ruler is on the left-side of the document.

5. STATUS BAR

The status bar, which is a horizontal area at the bottom of the document window in Microsoft Word, provides information about the current state of what user are viewing in the window and any other contextual information.It shows the Page number(Shows the page number) and Number of words in the document itself.

6. TITLE BAR

The title bar is a bar located along the top of a window or a dialog box that displays the name of the window or software program being used.

7. QUICK ACCESS TOOLBAR

Abbreviated as QAT is a toolbar menu that appears in Microsoft Word in the top left corner of the window. The Quick Access Toolbar gives user quick access to commonly used features such as the Save feature. Clicking on the Quick Access Toolbar down arrow gives user the ability to customize the Quick Access Toolbar and add and remove any of the commands shown in the toolbar.

MICROSOFT WORD SHORT CUTS

SHORTCUT	DESCRIPTION
Ctrl + 0	Adds or removes 6 pts of spacing before a paragraph.
Ctrl + A	Select all contents of the page.
Ctrl + B	Bold highlighted selection.
Ctrl + C	Copy selected text.
Ctrl + D	Open the font preferences window.
Ctrl + E	Aligns the line or selected text to the center of the screen.
Ctrl + F	Open find box.
Ctrl + I	Italic highlighted selection.
Ctrl + J	Aligns the selected text or line to justify the screen.
Ctrl + K	Insert link.
Ctrl + L	Aligns the line or selected text to the left of the screen.
Ctrl + M	Indent the paragraph.
Ctrl + P	Open the print window.
Ctrl + R	Aligns the line or selected text to the right of the screen.
Ctrl + S	Save the open document. Just like Shift + F12.
Ctrl + T	Create a hanging indent.
Ctrl + U	Underline the selected text.
Ctrl + V	Paste.
Ctrl + X	Cut selected text.
Ctrl + Y	Redo the last action performed.
Ctrl + Z	Undo last action.
Ctrl + Shift + L	Quickly create a bullet point.
Ctrl + Shift + F	Change the font.
Ctrl + Shift + >	Increase selected font +1pts up to 12pt and then increase font +2pts.
Ctrl +]	Increase selected font +1pts.
Ctrl + Shift + <	Decrease selected font -1pts if 12pt or lower; if above 12, decreases font by +2pt.
Ctrl + [	Decrease selected font -1pts.
Ctrl + <left arrow>	Moves one word to the left.
Ctrl + <right arrow>	Moves one word to the right.
Ctrl + <up arrow>	Moves to the beginning of the line or paragraph.
Ctrl + <down arrow>	Moves to the end of the paragraph.
Ctrl + Del	Deletes word to right of cursor.
Ctrl + Backspace	Deletes word to left of cursor.
Ctrl + End	Moves the cursor to the end of the document.

SHORTCUT	DESCRIPTION
Ctrl + Home	Moves the cursor to the beginning of the document.
Ctrl + Spacebar	Reset highlighted text to the default font.
Alt + Ctrl + F2	Open new document.
Ctrl + F2	Display the print preview.
Ctrl + Shift + F12	Prints the document.
F1	Open Help.
F4	Repeat the last action performed
F5	Open the Find, Replace, and Go To window in Microsoft Word.
F7	Spellcheck and grammar check selected text or document.
F12	Save As.
Shift + F3	Change the text in Microsoft Word from uppercase to lowercase or a capital letter at the beginning of every word.
Shift + F12	Save the open document. Just like Ctrl + S.
Shift + Enter	Create a soft break instead of a new paragraph.
Shift + Insert	Paste.
Shift + Alt + D	Insert the current date.
Shift + Alt + T	Insert the current time.

In addition to the above shortcut keys, users can also use their mouse to perform some common actions. Below some are examples of mouse shortcuts.

MOUSE SHORTCUTS	DESCRIPTION
Click, hold, and drag	Selects text from where user click and hold to the point user drag and let go.
Double-click	If double-clicking a word, selects the complete word.
Double-click	Double-clicking on the left, center, or right of a blank line makes the alignment of the text left, center, or right aligned.
Double-click	Double-clicking anywhere after text on a line will set a tab stop.
Triple-click	Selects the line or paragraph of the text that the mouse triple-clicked on.
Ctrl + Mouse wheel	Zooms in and out of document.

BASICS OF MICROSOFT EXCEL

Microsoft excel is among the most widely used in various business fieds. A lot of fields these days require basic Excel skills. These basic Excel skills are – familiarity with Excel ribbons & UI, ability to enter and format data, calculate totals & summaries through different kinds of formulas, highlighting of data that meets certain conditions, creating simple reports & charts, understanding the importance of keyboard shortcuts & productivity tricks.

How to Start the MS Excel Program

Click Start -> All Programs-> Microsoft Office->Microsoft Excel

File format for the sheets created is .xlsx or .xls

PARTS OF THE EXCEL WINDOW

Besides the usual window components (close box, title bar, scroll bars, etc.), an Excel window has several unique elements identified in the figure below.

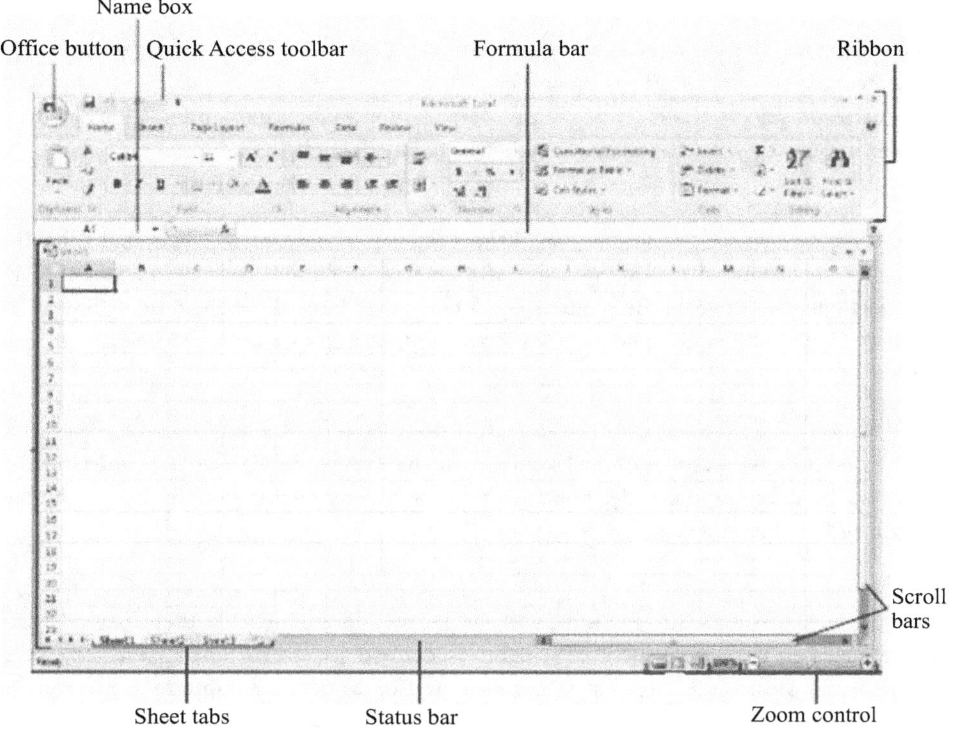

There are some important areas in the screen:

1. **Office logo button**

   It is at the top left corner contains many commands for the document such as New, Open, Save, Save as, Print and Close.

2. **Quick Access Toolbar**

   A small toolbar next to the Office button contains shortcuts for some of the most common commands such as Save, Undo, and Redo buttons.

3. **Ribbon**

   Tabs are part of the horizontal ribbon menu that contains links to various features of the program. Each tab - such as Home, Page Layout, and Formulas - contains a number of related features and options that are activated by clicking on the appropriate icon.

4. **Formula Bar**

   This is where any calculations or formulas user would like to write will appear. This is used to start building formulas.

5. **Spreadsheet Grid**

   This is where all user numbers, data, charts & drawings are present. Each Excel file can contain several sheets. But the spreadsheet grid shows few rows & columns of active spreadsheet. To see more rows or columns user can use the scroll bars to the left or at bottom.

6. **Status bar**

    This tells us what is going on with Excel at any time. User can tell if Excel is busy calculating a formula, creating a pivot report or recording a macro by just looking at the status bar. The status bar also shows quick summaries of selected cells (count, sum, average, minimum or maximum values). User can change this by right clicking on it and choosing which summaries to show.

7. **Sheet Tab**

    In Microsoft Excel, a sheet, sheet tab, or worksheet tab is the current worksheet that is being displayed. Every Excel file is capable of having multiple worksheets, and after opening an Excel file, user will see multiple sheet tabs as shown in the picture. By default, user have three sheet tabs "Sheet1" the default worksheet, "Sheet2", "Sheet3", and an additional tab that allows user to add additional sheets to the Excel file.

8. **Zoom Slider**

    Located in the bottom right corner of the Excel screen, the zoom slider is used to change the magnification of a worksheet by dragging the slider box back and forth or by clicking on the Zoom Out and Zoom In buttons located at either end of the slider.

9. **Name box**

    Microsoft Excel, the Name Box is the box to the left of the formula bar that displays the cell that is currently selected in the spreadsheet. If a name is defined for a cell that is selected, the Name Box displays the name of the cell. User can use the Name Box to define a name for a selected cell as well. The picture shows an example of the Name box in Microsoft Excel.

SOME IMPORTANT TERMS IN EXCEL

ROW NUMBERS : Rows run horizontally in a worksheet and are identified by a number in the row header.

COLUMN LETTER : Columns run vertically on a worksheet and each one is identified by a letter in the column header.

Together a column letter and a row number create a cell reference. Each cell in the worksheet can be identified by this combination of letters and numbers such as A1, F456, or AA34.

Macros - An Excel macro is a set of instructions that can be triggered by a keyboard shortcut, toolbar button or an icon in a spreadsheet.

Macros - are used to eliminate the need to repeat the steps of common tasks over and over.

Tasks such as:

*   adding or removing rows and columns
*   protecting or unprotecting worksheets
*   selecting a range of cells
*   adding the current date to a spreadsheet

In Microsoft Office 2010 version, Office tab is replaced by File tab.

CHARTS

Charts are visual representations of worksheet data. Charts often makes it easier to understand the data in a worksheet because users can easily pick out patterns and trends illustrated in the chart that are otherwise difficult to see.

A chart is a made-up of many parts. Following are the parts of charts:

- **Chart Area :** The chart area in a document or spreadsheet contains the chart, graph, headers and a legend providing information on the various lines or colors in the chart. The chart area is usually is total region surrounded the chart.

- **Plot Area :** This is the area where chart data is plotted. The plot area on a 2-D chart contains the data markers, gridlines, data labels, trendlines, and optional chart items placed in the chart area. The plot area on a 3-D chart contains all the above items plus the walls, floor, axes, axis titles, and tick-mark labels in the chart.

- **Chart title :** The descriptive text aimes at helping user identify the chart.

- **Axis Title :** These are the titles given to three axis i.e. X,Y,Z.

- **Legend :** The Legend helps to identify various plotted data series.

- **Gridlines :** There are horizontal and vertical lines which inserted in the chart to enhance its readability.

- **Data Label :** It provides additional information about a data marker.

DIFFERENT TYPES OF CHARTS SERVE DIFFERENT PURPOSES

- **Column charts :** Data that is arranged in columns or rows on a worksheet can be plotted in a column chart. Column charts are useful for showing data changes over a period of time or for illustrating comparisons among items.

  In column charts, categories are typically organized along the horizontal axis and along the vertical axis.

  Column charts have the following chart subtypes:

  - ○ **Clustered column and clustered column in 3-D :** Clustered column charts compare values across categories. A clustered column chart displays values in 2-D vertical rectangles. A clustered column in 3-D chart displays the data by using a 3-D perspective only.

  - ○ **Stacked column and stacked column in 3-D :** Stacked column charts show the relationship of individual items to the whole, comparing the contribution of each value to a total across categories. A stacked column chart displays values in 2-D vertical stacked rectangles. A 3-D stacked column chart displays the data by using a 3-D perspective only.

  - ○ **3-D column :** 3-D column charts use three axes that user can modify (a horizontal axis, a vertical axis, and a depth axis), and they compare data points along the horizontal and the depth axes.

- **Line charts :** Data that is arranged in columns or rows on a worksheet can be plotted in a line chart. Line charts can display continuous data over time, set against a common scale, and are therefore ideal for showing trends in data at equal intervals. In a line chart, category data is distributed evenly along the horizontal axis, and all value data is distributed evenly along the vertical axis.

  Line charts have the following chart subtypes:

  - ○ **Line and line with markers :** Displayed with markers to indicate individual data values, or without, line charts are useful to show trends over time or ordered categories, especially when there are many data points and the order in which they are presented is important. If there are many categories or the values are approximate, use a line chart without markers.

  - ○ **Stacked line and stacked line with markers :** Displayed with markers to indicate individual data values, or without, stacked line charts can be used to show the trend of the contribution of each value over time or ordered categories, but because it is not easy to see that the lines are stacked, consider using a different line chart type or a stacked area chart instead.

○ **3-D line** : 3-D line charts show each row or column of data as a 3-D ribbon. A 3-D line chart has horizontal, vertical, and depth axes that user can modify.

- **Pie charts** : Data that is arranged in one column or row only on a worksheet can be plotted in a pie chart. Pie charts show the size of items in one data series, proportional to the sum of the items. The data points in a pie chart are displayed as a percentage of the whole pie.

- **Bar charts** : Data that is arranged in columns or rows on a worksheet can be plotted in a bar chart. Bar charts illustrate comparisons among individual items.

- **Area charts** : Data that is arranged in columns or rows on a worksheet can be plotted in an area chart. Area charts emphasize the magnitude of change over time, and can be used to draw attention to the total value across a trend. For example, data that represents profit over time can be plotted in an area chart to emphasize the total profit.

- **XY (scatter) charts** : Data that is arranged in columns and rows on a worksheet can be plotted in an xy (scatter) chart. Scatter charts show the relationships among the numeric values in several data series, or plots two groups of numbers as one series of xy coordinates.

  A scatter chart has two value axes, showing one set of numeric data along the horizontal axis (x-axis) and another along the vertical axis (y-axis). It combines these values into single data points and displays them in irregular intervals, or clusters. Scatter charts are typically used for displaying and comparing numeric values, such as scientific, statistical, and engineering data.

MICROSOFT EXCEL SHORTCUTS

Below is a listing of all the major shortcut keys usable in Microsoft Excel. See the computer shortcut page if user are looking for shortcut keys used in other programs.

SHORTCUT	DESCRIPTION
F2	Edit the selected cell.
F3	After a name has been created, F3 will paste names.
F4	Repeat last action. For example, if user changed the color of text in another cell, pressing F4 will change the text in cell to the same color.
F5	Go to a specific cell. For example, C6.
F7	Spell check selected text or document.
F11	Create chart from selected data.
Ctrl + Shift + ;	Enter the current time.
Ctrl + ;	Enter the current date.
Alt + Shift + F1	Insert New Worksheet.
Alt + Enter	While typing text in a cell, pressing Alt + Enter will move to the next line, allowing for multiple lines of text in one cell.
Shift + F3	Open the Excel formula window.
Shift + F5	Bring up search box.
Ctrl + 1	Open the Format Cells window.
Ctrl + A	Select all contents of the worksheet.
Ctrl + B	Bold highlighted selection.
Ctrl + I	Italic highlighted selection.

Ctrl + K	Insert link.
Ctrl + S	Save the open worksheet.
Ctrl + U	Underline highlighted selection.
Ctrl + P	Bring up the print dialog box to begin the printing process.
Ctrl + Z	Undo last action.
Ctrl + F3	Open Excel Name Manager.
Ctrl + F9	Minimize current window.
Ctrl + F10	Maximize currently selected window.
Ctrl + Page up	Move between work sheets in the same document.
Ctrl + Page down	Move between work sheets in the same document.
Ctrl + Tab	Move between Two or more open Excel files.
Alt + =	Create a formula to sum all of the above cells.
Ctrl + '	Insert the value of the above cell into the cell currently selected.
Ctrl + Arrow key	Move to next section of text.
Ctrl + Space	Select entire column.
Shift + Space	Select entire row.
Ctrl + -	Delete the selected column or row.
Ctrl + Shift + =	Insert a new column or row.
Ctrl + Home	Move to cell A1.

FORMULA BAR

The formula bar is located beneath the toolbar at the top of the Excel worksheet. Use the formula bar to enter and edit worksheet data. The contents of the active cell always appear in the formula bar. When user click the mouse in the formula bar, an X and a check mark appear. User can click the check icon to confirm and completes editing, or the X to abandon editing.

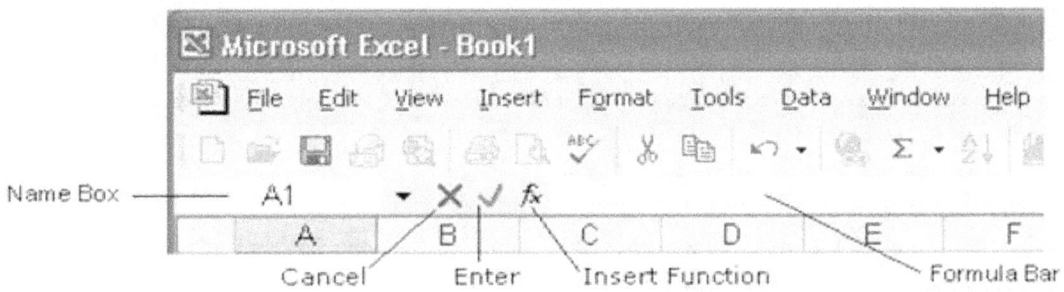

Name box

The Name box displays the reference of the selected cells.

Row and column headings

Letters and numbers identify the rows and columns on an Excel spreadsheet. The intersection of a row and a column is called a cell. Use row and column headings to specify a cell's reference. For example, the cell located where column B and row 7 intersect is called B7.

Active cell

The active cell has a dark border around it to indicate user position in the worksheet. All text and numbers that user type are inserted into the active cell. Click the mouse on a cell to make it active.

Fill handle

The lower right corner of the active cell has a small box called a Fill Handle. User mouse changes to a cross-hair when user are on the Fill Handle. The Fill Handle helps user copy data and create series of information. For example, if user type January in the active cell and then drag the Fill Handle over four cells, Excel automatically inserts February, March, April and May.

Worksheet tabs

An Excel workbook consists of multiple worksheets. Use the worksheet tabs at the bottom of

Alignment

By default, Excel left-aligns labels and right-aligns values in a worksheet. User can change cell alignment using the toolbar or the Format Cells command.

The toolbar has text alignment icons next to the bold and italic icons. User can left-align, right-align, or center text within a cell using these buttons. Select the cell(s) user want to align and click the appropriate alignment button on the toolbar.

The toolbar also has a button that will center a label over a range of cells, for example centering a title over a report. To center data over a range of cells, select the cell user want to center and the columns user want to center it over and click the Center over Cells button (shown at right).

Format Alignment command

User can also change the alignment of data within cells using the Alignment section of the Format Cells dialog. This dialog box also has options to change the orientation of text (i.e. sideways or vertical) and a box to wrap text within a cell.

Changing Numeric Formatting

To change the format of a number, choose the Cells command from the Format menu. In the Format Cells dialog box, Excel displays different tabs for various formatting types. To change numeric formats, click the Number tab. Select the category user want and then the actual format. For example, to display numbers as currency with two decimal places, select the Currency category, enter 2 for the number of decimal places, and select the appropriate currency symbol. Or to display a number as a percentage, choose the Percentage category and select the number of decimals user want to display.

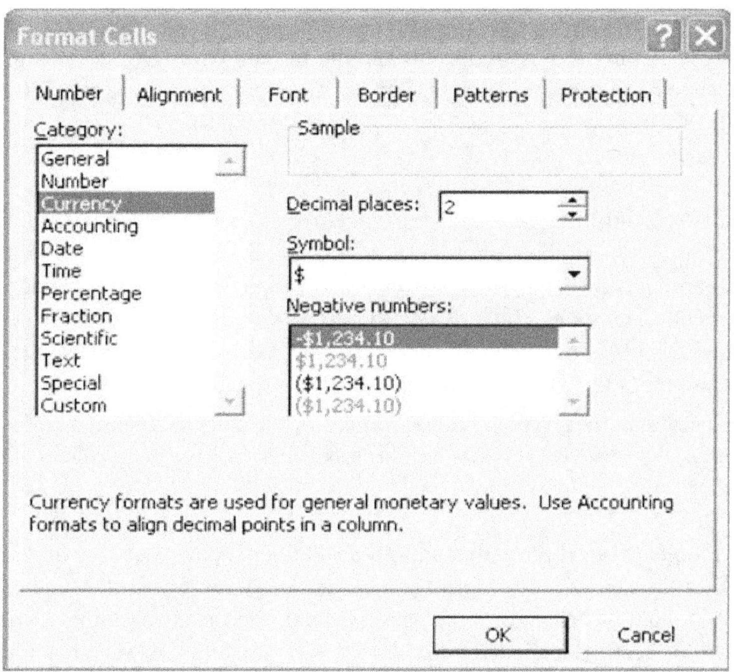

Placing borders around cells

The toolbar has a button for placing borders around cells. User can also use the Border section of the Format Cells dialog box, which provides more options. Select the cells user want a border on and choose the desired format from either the toolbar or the Format Cells dialog box. ▭ ▾ width in this way, a numeric width indicator appears in the upper left part of the formula bar.

FORMULAS AND FUNCTIONS

Formulas and functions that perform calculations are the true power of spreadsheets.

Formulas

To build a formula, first select the cell in which user want the results to appear. In Excel, all formulas start with the = sign. After the = sign, type the cells user want to add or subtract along with the mathematical operation user wish to perform. For example, to add the January sales in the worksheet below, the formula would be =B3+B4+B5. If user want to subtract February Widget Sales from January Widget sales, the formula would be =B3-C3.

	A	B	C	D	E	F	G	H
1								
2		January	February	March	April	May	Totals	%'s
3	Widgets	98	39	40	140	240		
4	Figets	122	18	50	150	250		
5	Digets	56	52	60	160	260		
6								
7	Totals							

Copying Formulas

The easiest way to copy a formula is with the Fill Handle in the lower right corner of the cell. Create user initial formula and then position the mouse on the Fill Handle. When the mouse changes shape to a cross-hair, press and drag over the adjacent cells user want to copy the formula to.

SUM( ) function

The SUM( ) function is probably the most common function in Excel. It adds a range of numbers. To build a SUM( ) function, begin by typing the = sign; all functions begin with the = sign. Next type the word SUM followed by an open parenthesis. User must now tell Excel which cells to sum. Using the mouse, click and drag over the range of cells user wish to add. A dotted outline will appear around the cells and the cell range will be displayed in the formula bar. When user have the correct cells selected, release the mouse button, type a closing parenthesis and press the <Enter> key.

If user do not want to use the mouse, type in the references of the cells user want to sum. For example, to add cells B3 through B5, type =SUM(B3:B5). Excel interprets B3:B5 as the range of cells from B3 to B5.

AutoSum button

In Excel, the standard toolbar has a button that simplifies adding a column or row of numbers. The AutoSum button, which resembles the Greek letter Sigma (shown at right), automatically creates a SUM( ) function. When user click the AutoSum button Excel creates a sum function for the column of numbers directly above or the row of numbers to the left. Excel pastes the SUM( ) function and the range to sum into the formula bar. If the range is not correct, simply select the proper range with user mouse on the worksheet. When user have the correct range entered, press the <Enter> key to complete the function.

Using the Insert Function Button

The Insert Function Button is located by the Formula Bar.

Click the Insert function button in to activate the Insert Function dialog window. *fx*

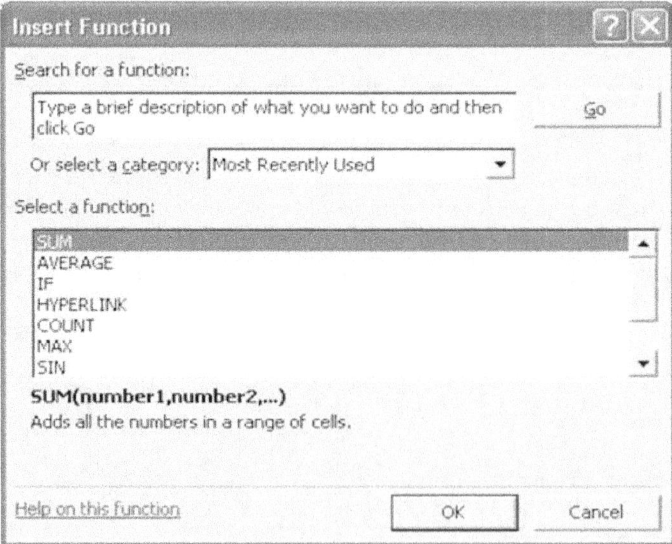

First, choose the Function Category user are interested in from the select a category drop down menu.

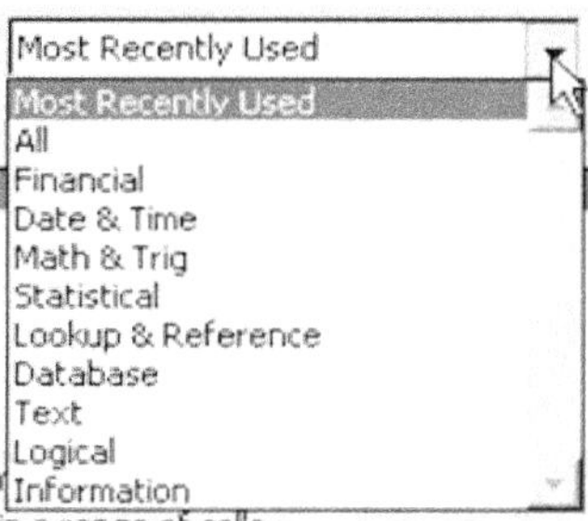

Then select the function user want in that category. When user have selected the proper function click OK.

In the Function Arguements dialog box user specify the cells the function will operate on, which are called its arguments. Select the cells with the mouse and click OK. Notice the creation of the function in the formula bar.

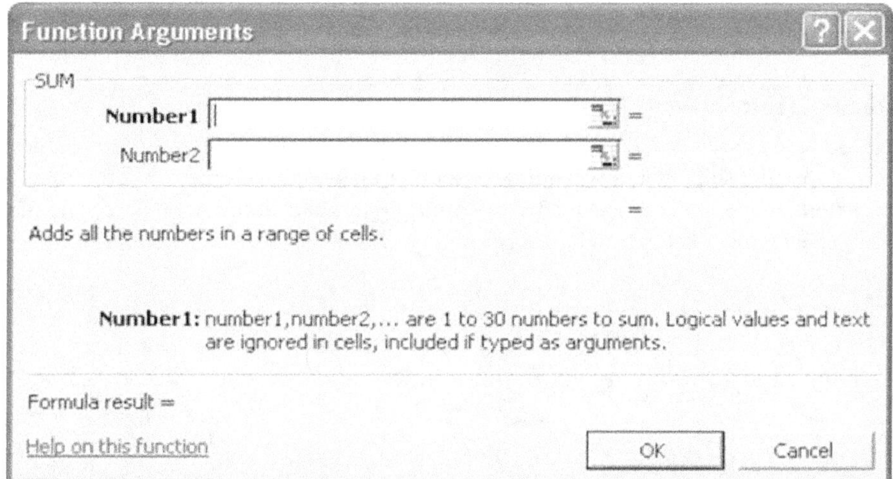

BASICS OF MICROSOFT ACCESS

Microsoft Access is a versatile relational database program that enables user to efficiently store and retrieve data. This will explains how to navigate the Access interface, create simple tables and queries, and relate information from one table to another.

How to start MS Access Program

Click start → All programs → Microsoft office → Microsoft Access.

PARTS COMPONENTS OF THE ACCESS WINDOW

Besides the usual window components (close box, title bar, scroll bars, etc.), an Access window has several unique elements identified in the figure below :

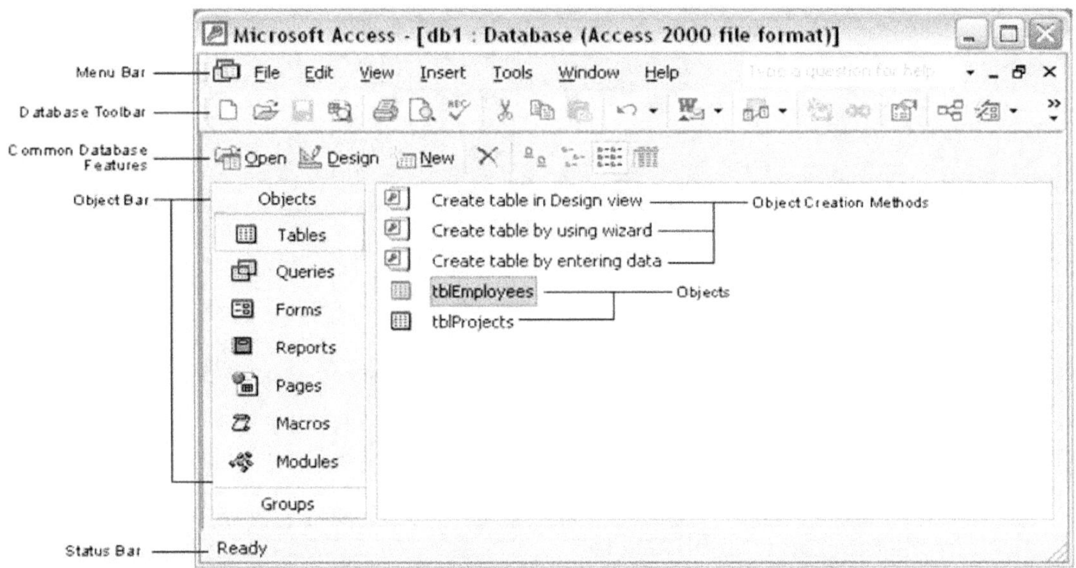

1. The Database Toolbar

The Database toolbar, located beneath the menu bar, has buttons for commonly performed tasks like accessing the Relationships window, adding Objects, Exporting to Office, and other operations. Access let's user customize the toolbar or even display multiple toolbars at the same time. The Standard Access XP toolbar appears undocked in the figure below.

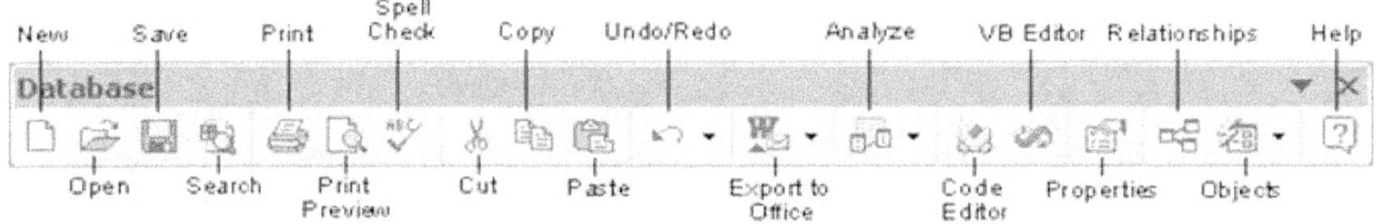

2. The Data sheet Toolbar

The Data sheet toolbar provides common tasks for editing an object in Data sheet view. The Database toolbar will automatically change into the Data sheet toolbar when this view is selected. The Data sheet tool bar exists between different objects, thus, this toolbar largely remains consistent.

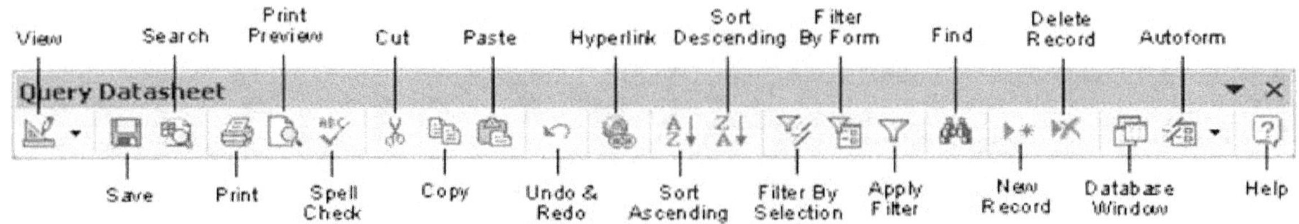

3. The Design Toolbar

The Design toolbar provides common tasks for editing an object in Design view. The Database toolbar will automatically change into the Design toolbar when this view is selected. The Design tool bar exists between different objects, and thus, maintains much of the same functionality.

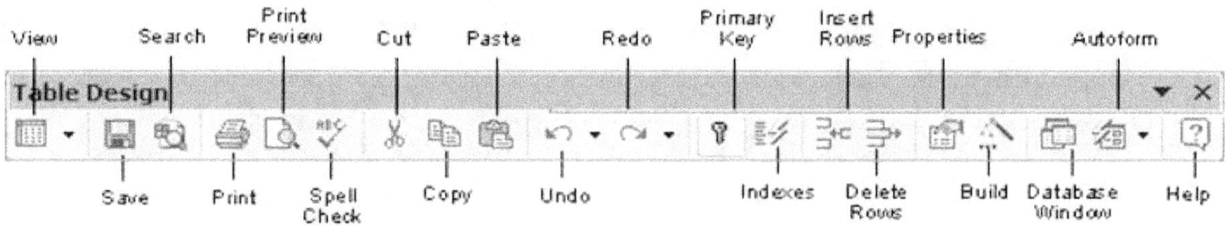

COMMON DATABASE FEATURES

Access provides a quick and convenient method of accessing the most common tasks. This includes switching between views, opening and creating new databases, and a few minor formatting issues

Creating a Database

When user start Access there are no databases open, but the Task Pane is visible and provides quick access to common options such as opening an existing database or creating a new database. To create a database, select Blank Database under the New subgroup.

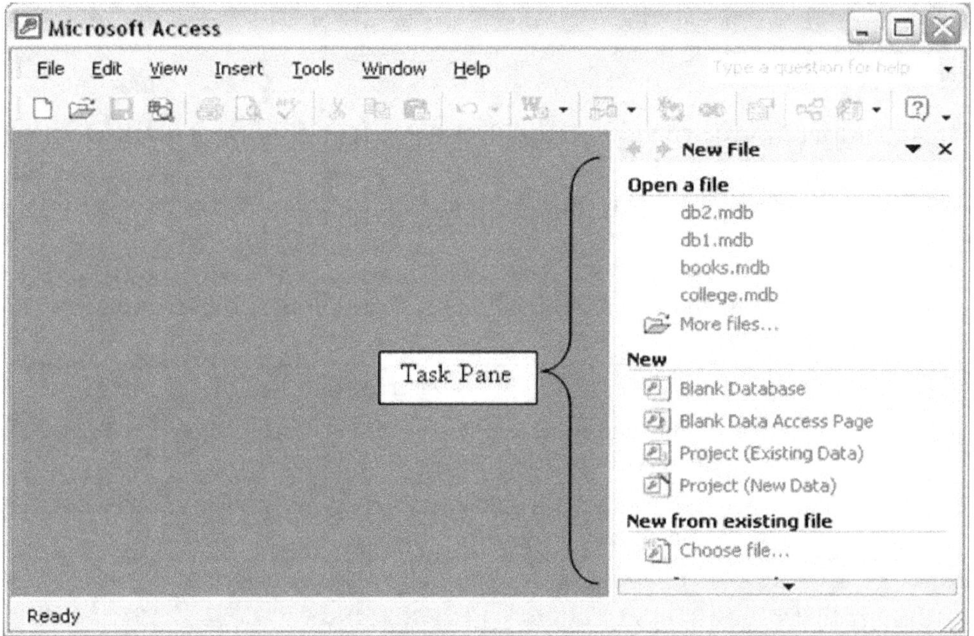

COMPONENTS OF MICROSOFT ACCESS

An Access database consists of seven different components. These are: tables, queries, forms, reports, pages, macros, and modules. Use the buttons in the database window shown below to create and modify these components. Each component listed is called an object.

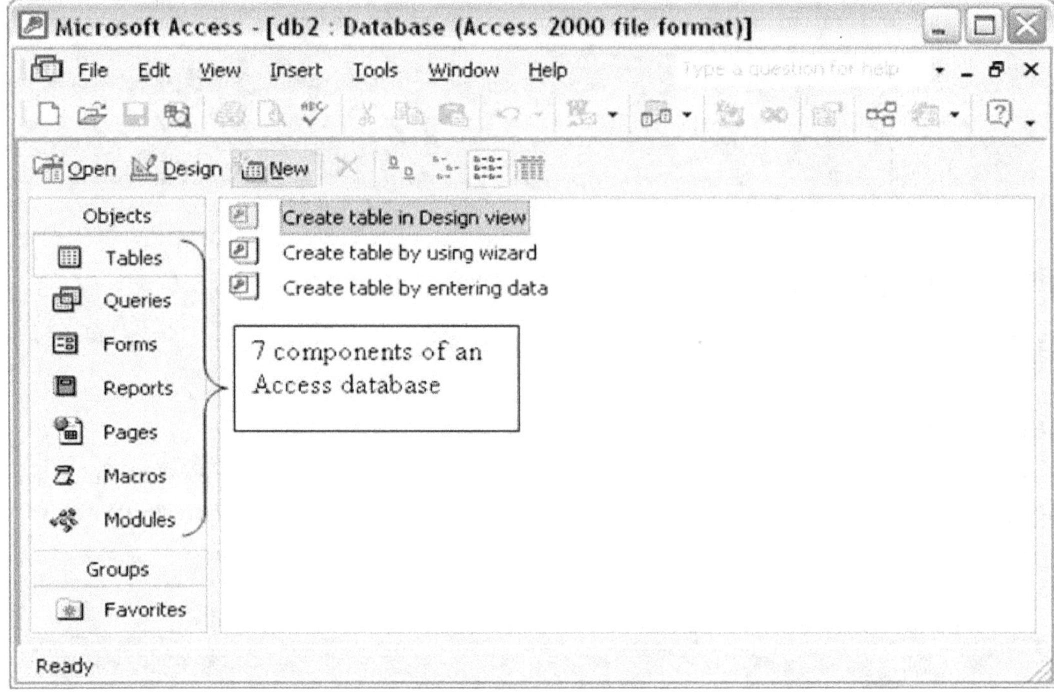

Listed below are the names and descriptions of the different objects user can use in Access. This will focus on the first two objects: tables and queries.

Tables: Tables are where the actual data is defined and entered. Tables consist of records (rows) and fields (columns).

Queries: Queries are basically questions about the data in a database. A query consists of specifications indicating which fields, records, and summaries want to see from a database. Queries allow to extract data based on the criteria user define.

Query Type	Description
Select query	Retrieves data from one or more tables and displays the record set in a datasheet. This is the most common type of query.
Parameter query	Prompts the user to enter values that define the query, such as specified region for sales results or a specified price range for houses.
Cross-tab query	Arranges a recordset to make it more easily visible, using both row headings and column headings.
Action query	Creates a new table or changes an existing table.
SQL query	An advanced query that is created by using an SQL statement.

Forms : Forms are designed to ease the data entry process. For example, To create a data entry form that looks exactly like a paper form.

Reports: When a user want to print records from user database, design a report. Access even has a wizard to help produce mailing labels.

Pages: A data access page is a special type of Web page designed for viewing and working with data from the Internet or an intranet. This data is stored in a Microsoft Access database or a Microsoft SQL Server database.

Macros: A macro is a set of one or more actions that each performs a particular operation, such as opening a form or printing a report. Macros can help user automate common tasks. For example, user can run a macro that prints a report when a user clicks a command button.

Modules: A module is a collection of Visual Basic for Applications declarations and procedures that are stored together as a unit.

Elements of MS-Access

In MS-Access, database holds five major elements for every database operation.

Field Name : It is a label provide for a field that specifies the type of information contained in a particular field.

Field Type/Data Type : It specifies the type of data stored in the field such as textual data and numerical data or combination of both. The default size of data type is 50 in MS-Access.

Data type	Field length or Field size
Text	0-255 characters
Memo	0.65535 characters
Number	1, 2, 4 or 8 bytes
Date/Time	8 bytes
Currency	8 bytes
Auto Number 4 bytes	4 bytes
Yes/No	1 bit (0 or 1)
OLE object	Upto 1 GB
Hyperlink	Each part contains 2048 characters

SOME IMPROTANT TERMS–

Field Length : Field refers length or width to the maximum number of characters that a field can contain.

Primary Key : A field which is used to uniquely identify the records in a table. The primary key cannot contain null value.

Validation Rule : It is a condition that must be met before the data is accepted into the database.

MS-Access View

You can create a table by two most popular ways

Database View : It shows the data in the database and also allows you to enter and edit the data but not allow to change the database.

Design View : It allows you to create or change the table and also set the keys.

Filtering Data : It enables to display only those records in a table that meet a specified filter criterion.

Relationship : It is an association between access table or quarries that use related field. It is a link between tables and enables us to accessed data from both tables simultaneously.

Relationship can be divided in three categories; One-in-One, One-to-Many and Many-to-Many.

Attributes : Attributes can be defined as the characteristics of an entity to identify in uniquely. Such as student's attributes are his Roll-No, Section, Name etc.

MS ACCESS : SHORTCUTS

The following is a list of general shortcuts or hotkeys in Access :

Key Sequence	Description
F1	Display the Microsoft Access Help. This may be context-sensitive help depending on what you are positioned on.
F11	Display the Database window.
F12	Open the Save As dialog box.
CTRL+N	Open a new database.
CTRL+O	Open an existing database.
CTRL+P	Print the current or selected object.
CTRL+S	Save the current database object.
CTRL+W	Close the active window.
ALT+SPACEBAR	Display the Control menu.
ALT+F11	Toggle between the Visual Basic editor and the Access Database window.
SHIFT+F10	Display the shortcut menu (ie: popup menu).

Shortcut Keys For Entering Data In A Datasheet/Form

The following is a list of shortcuts or hot keys for entering data in a Datasheet/Form:

Key Sequence	Description
CTRL+PLUS SIGN (+)	Add a new record.
CTRL+MINUS SIGN (or older)	Delete the current record.
CTRL+SEMICOLON (;)	Insert the current date.
CTRL+COLON (:)	Insert the current time.
CTRL+ALT+SPACEBAR	Insert the default value for the field.
CTRL+ENTER	Insert a new line.
SHIFT+ENTER	Save changes to the current record.
SPACEBAR	Toggle between the values in a check box or radio button.

SHORTCUT KEYS FOR WORKING WITH TEXT/DATA

The following is a list of shortcuts or hot keys for working with text/data in Access:

General

Key Sequence	Description
F7	Check spelling.
CTRL+C	Copy the selection to the Clipboard.
CTRL+V	Paste the contents of the Clipboard to where the insertion point is.
CTRL+X	Cut the selection and copy it to the Clipboard.
CTRL+Z	Undo typing.
CTRL+DELETE	Delete all characters to the right of the insertion point.
CTRL+SEMICOLON (;)	Insert the current date.
CTRL+COLON (:)	Insert the current time.

CTRL+ALT+SPACEBAR	Insert the default value for the field.
ESC	Undo changes in the current field. Press ESC a second time to undo changes to the current record.
SHIFT+F2	Open the Zoom box to enter large amounts of data that can not be properly displayed in a small control.

Finding and Replacing Text

Key Sequence	Description
CTRL+F	Open the **Find** tab on the **Find and Replace** dialog box.
CTRL+H	Open the **Replace** tab on the **Find and Replace** dialog box.
SHIFT+F4	Find the next occurrence of the value entered in the **Find and Replace** dialog box when the dialog box is closed.

Selecting Text in A Field

Key Sequence	Description
SHIFT+RIGHT ARROW	Extends selection one character to the right.
SHIFT+LEFT ARROW	Extends selection one character to the left.
CTRL+SHIFT+RIGHT ARROW	Extends selection one word to the right.
CTRL+SHIFT+LEFT ARROW	Extends selection one word to the left.

Moving The Insertion Point in A Field

Key Sequence	Description
RIGHT ARROW	Move one character to the right.
LEFT ARROW	Move one character to the left.
CTRL+RIGHT ARROW	Move one word to the right.
CTRL+LEFT ARROW	Move one word to the left.
END	Move to the end of the field, in a single-line field.
HOME	Move to the beginning of the field, in a single-line field.
CTRL+END	Move to the end of the field, in a multi-line field.
CTRL+HOME	Move to the beginning of the field, in a multi-line field.

BASICS OF MICROSOFT POWERPOINT

PowerPoint is a program to help create and present presentations. This handout introduces the basic features of Microsoft PowerPoint and covers the basics of creating simple presentations and editing and formatting the PowerPoint slides. PowerPoint 2007 is a presentation software application from Microsoft. With PowerPoint, user can easily create slide shows, presentations, and multimedia applications. Teachers, Trainers and other presenters can use slide shows to illustrate their presentations.

How to start MS-Powerpoint–

Click start → All programs → Microsoft Office → Microsoft Powerpoint

File format for the slides created is .pptx or ppt.

PARTS OF POWER POINT

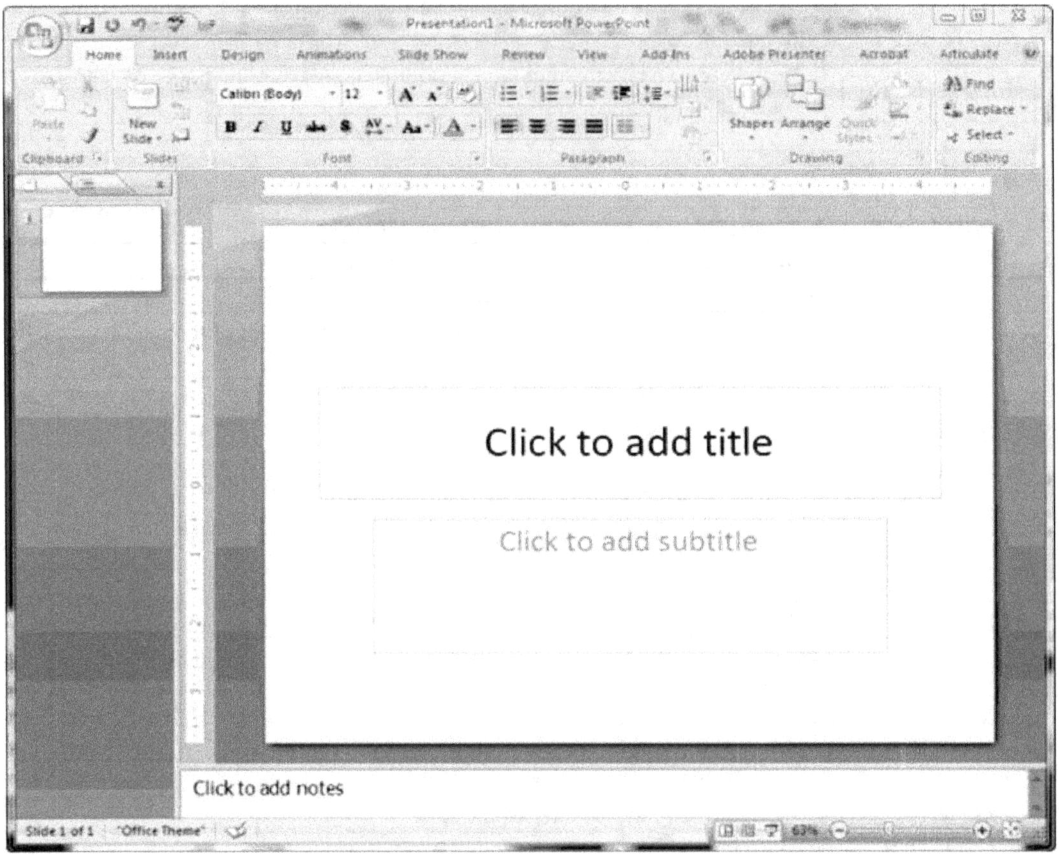

1. The Microsoft Office Button

In the upper-left corner of the PowerPoint 2007 window is the Microsoft Office button. It›s similar to the old File Menu. When user click the button, a menu appears. User can use the menu to create a new file, open an existing file, save a file, print, and perform many other tasks.

2. The Quick Access Toolbar

Next to the Microsoft Office button in the upper left corner is the Quick Access toolbar outlined in red in the image above.

The Quick Access toolbar provides with access to commands that are frequently used. By default, Save, Undo, and Redo appear on the Quick Access toolbar. User use Save to save the file, Undo to rollback an action user have taken, and Redo to reapply an action user have rolled back. User can customize this toolbar by right clicking on it or click the small black down arrow to the right.

3. The Title Bar

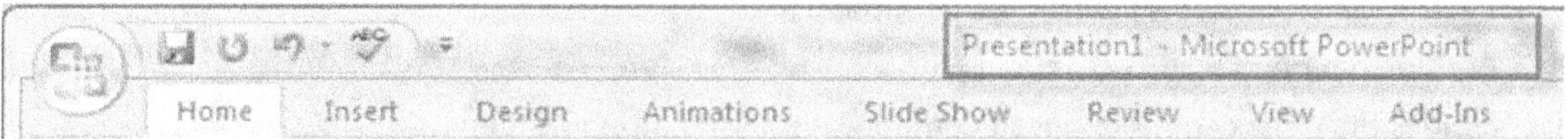

The Title bar is located at the top in the center of the PowerPoint window. The Title bar displays the name of the presentation on which user are currently working. By default, PowerPoint names presentations sequentially, starting with Presentation1. When user save user file, user can change the name of user presentation.

4. The Ribbon

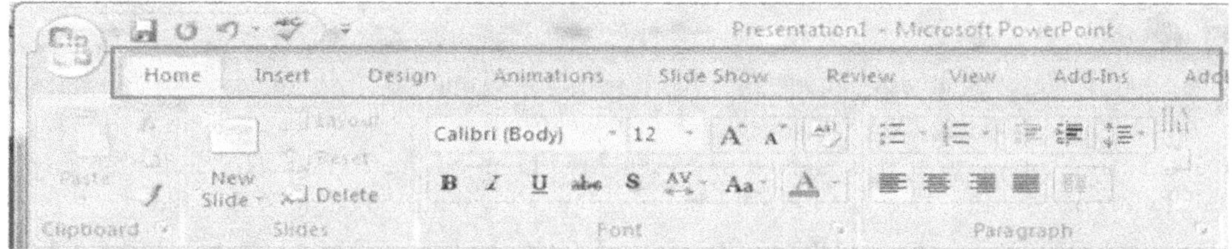

The Ribbon holds all of the commands and features of each of the tabs in the Ribbon. The Tabs are located across the top of the ribbon under the Title Bar. These contextual tabs will appear when user have something highlighted that calls for it. For example, if user have a picture highlighted on its slide, a Picture Tools tab will appear.

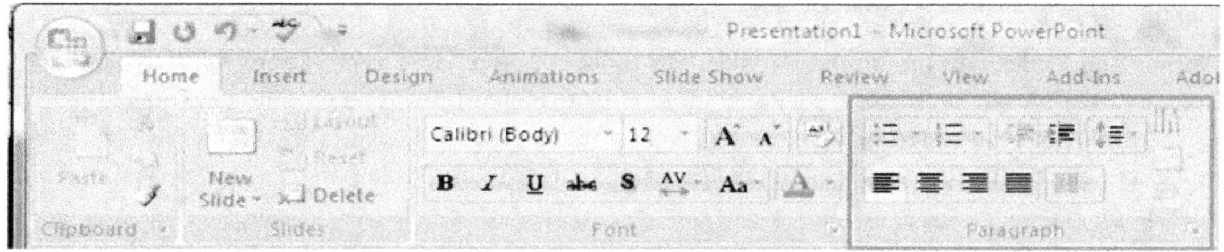

Similar tools are located in Command Groups across the ribbon.

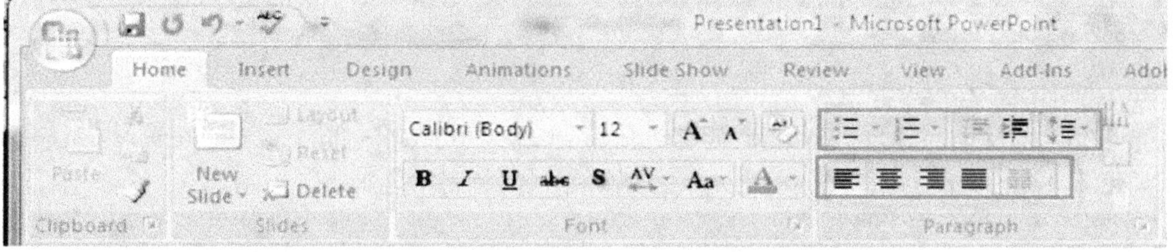

Each Command Group includes Command Buttons to perform various actions on that group of tools.

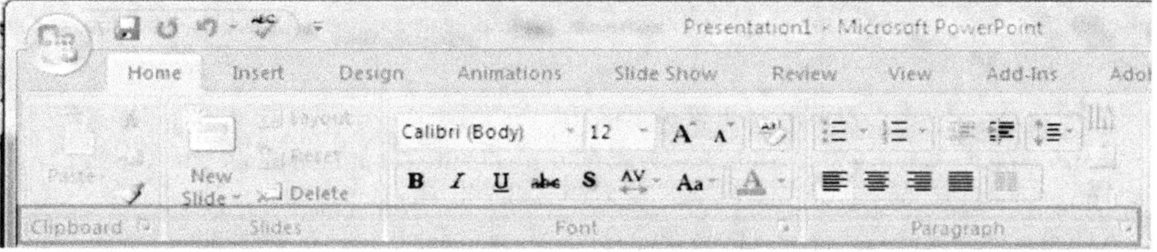

Clipboard : Contains the cut, copy, paste commands. The Format Painter tool is located here as are the Paste Special, Paste as Hyperlink, and Duplicate commands.

Slides : All the commonly used commands for creating new slides

Font : Includes the most commonly used commands for formatting font

Paragraph : Includes all of the paragraph formatting commands, vertical and horizontal alignments, text direction, bullets, numbering, indenting, spacing before and after, columns, etc. It also includes the dialog box for tabs.

Drawing : Allows to add shapes and draw on slides. This is Format Shape Dialog Box. The Status bar generally appears at the bottom of the window.

5.   Status bar

The Status bar displays the number of the slide that is currently displayed, the total number of slides, and the name of the design template in use or the name of the background.

The Outline tab displays the text contained in presentation in an outline format. The Slides tab displays a thumbnail view of all slides. User can click the thumbnail to view the slide in the Slide pane.

The View buttons appear near the bottom of the screen. User can use the View buttons to change between Normal view, Slider Sorter view, and the Slide Show view.

Normal View

Normal view splits the screen into three major sections: the Outline and Slides tabs, the Slide pane, and the Notes area.

The Outline and Slides tabs are on the left side of window. They enable to shift between two different ways of viewing your slides. The Slides tab shows thumbnails of your slides. The Outline tab shows the text on r slides. The Slide pane is located in the center of your window. The Slide pane shows a large view of the slide on which user currently working. The Notes area appears below the Slide pane. User can type notes on the Notes area.

Slide Sorter View

Slide Sorter view shows thumbnails of all slides. In Slide Sorter view, user can easily add, delete, or change their order of your slides.

Slide Show View

Use the Slide Show view when want to view slides, as they will look in final presentation. When in Slide Show view:

Esc - Returns to the view using previously.

Left-clicking - Moves you to the next slide or animation effect. When reach the last slide, automatically return to previous view.

Right-clicking - Opens a pop-up menu. User can use this menu to navigate the slides, add speaker notes, select a pointer, and mark presentation.

Zoom In & Zoom Out

Zoom controls allows you to zoom in and zoom out on the window. Zooming in makes the window larger so focus in on an object. Zooming out makes the window smaller so user can see the entire window.

You can click and drag the vertical and horizontal splitter bars to change the size of your panes.

User use the **Minimize button** to remove a window from view. While a window is minimized, its title appears on the task bar.

Click to the **Maximize button** to cause a window to fill the screen. After maximize a window, clicking the Restore button returns the window to its former smaller size.

Click to the **Close button** to exit the window and close the program.

MS– Power Point Shortcuts

Shortcut Keys	Description
F5	View the Slide Show
Shift + Ctrl + Home	Selects all text form the cursor to the sart of the active text box
Shift + Ctrl + End	Selects all text form the cursor to the end of the active text box
Spacebar or click the mouse	Moves to next slide or next animation
S	Stop the show press S again to restrat the show
Esc	End the side show
Ctrl + A	Select all items on the page or the active text box
Ctrl + B	Applies bold to the select text
Ctrl + D	Duplicates the selected object
Ctrl + F	Opens the find dialog box
Ctrl + G	Opens the grids and guies dialog box
Ctrl + H	Opens the replace dialog box
Ctrl + I	Applies Italics to the selected text
Ctrl + M	Inserts a new slide
Ctrl + N	Opens a new blank presentations
Ctrl + O	Opens the open dialog box
Ctrl + T	Opens the font dialog box
Ctrl + U	Applies underlining to the selected text Paste
Ctrl + V	Paste
Ctrl + W	Closes the presentation
Ctrl + Y	Repeats the last comand entered
Home	Moves cursor to beginning of current line of text
End	Moves cursor to end of current line of text
Ctrl + Home	Moves cursor in beginning of presentations
Ctrl + End	Moves cursor to end of presentation
Shift + Click each side	Selects more than one slide in a presentation
Shift + F1	Help

Past Exercise

1. A hard copy of a document is
   [SBI Clerk, 2009]
   (a) printed on the printer
   (b) stored on a floppy
   (c) stored on a CD
   (d) stored in the hard disk
   (e) None of these

2. The name that the user gives to a document is referred to as **[SBI Clerk, 2009]**
   (a) document-name
   (b) file-name
   (c) name-given
   (d) document-identity
   (e) None of these

3. Microsoft Word is an example of
   [SBI Clerk, 2009]
   (a) an operating system
   (b) a processing device
   (c) application software
   (d) an input device
   (e) None of these

4. If text was highlighted and "Edit" "Copy" was clicked, what would happen ?
   [SBI Clerk, 2009]
   (a) Text would be copied from the document and placed in the clipboard
   (b) Text would be removed from the document and placed in the clipboard
   (c) Text from the clipboard would be placed in the document at the place where the cursor is blinking
   (d) 'b' and 'c'
   (e) None of the above

5. For opening and closing of the file in Excel, you can use which bar ? **[SBI Clerk, 2009]**
   (a) Formatting   (b) Standard
   (c) Title   (d) Formatting or Title
   (e) None of these

6. Data that is copied from an application is stored in the **[SBI Clerk, 2009]**
   (a) Driver   (b) Terminal
   (c) Prompt   (d) Clipboard
   (e) None of these

7. Changing an existing document is called the document. **[SBI Clerk, 2009]**
   (a) creating   (b) deleting
   (c) editing   (d) adjusting
   (e) None of these

8. In a spreadsheet program the —contains related worksheets and documents. **[SBI Clerk, 2009]**
   (a) workbook   (b) column
   (c) cell   (d) formula
   (e) None of these

9. In order to save an existing document with a different name you need to —
   [SBI Clerk, 2009]
   (a) Retype the document and give it a different name
   (b) Use the Save as command
   (c) Copy and paste the original document to a new document and then save
   (d) Use Windows Explorer to copy the document to a different location and then rename it
   (e) None of the above

10. What would you do to highlight a word? You position the cursor next to the word, and then
    ——————— **[SBI Clerk, 2009]**
    (a) Drag mouse while holding button down
    (b) Click mouse once
    (c) Roll mouse around
    (d) Roll and then click mouse
    (e) None of the above

11. Which one of the following software applications would be the most appropriate for performing numerical and statistical calculations?
    (a) Database   **[SBI Clerk, 2009]**
    (b) Document processor
    (c) Graphics package
    (d) Spreadsheet
    (e) None of the above

12. The background of any word document———
    [SBI Clerk, 2009]
    (a) is always white colour
    (b) is the colour you preset under the Options menu
    (c) is always the same for the entire document
    (d) can have any colour you choose
    (e) None of the above

13. What is the default file extension for all word documents? **[SBI Clerk, 2009]**
    (a) TXT   (b) WRD
    (c) FIL   (d) DOC
    (e) None of these

14. Text in a column is generally aligned———— **[SBI Clerk, 2009]**
    (a) justified   (b) right
    (c) center   (d) left
    (e) None of the above

15. In page preview mode———— **[SBI Clerk, 2009]**
    (a) You can see all pages of your document
    (b) You can only see the page you are currently working
    (c) You can only see pages that do not contain graphics
    (d) You can only see the title page of your document
    (e) None of the above

16. A —— is a named set of characters that have the same characteristics. **[SBI Clerk, 2009]**
    (a) type face   (b) type style
    (c) font   (d) pico
    (e) None of these

17. A —— pre-designed document that already had coordinating fonts, a layout and a back ground. **[SBI Clerk, 2009]**
    (a) guide   (b) model
    (c) ruler   (d) template
    (e) None of these

18. Which elements of a Word document can be displayed in colour? **[SBI Clerk, 2009]**
    (a) Only graphics
    (b) Only text
    (c) All elements
    (d) All elements but only if you have a colour printer
    (e) None of these

19. How many different documents can you have open at any one time? **[SBI Clerk, 2009]**
    (a) Not more than three
    (b) Only one
    (c) As many as your computer memory will hold
    (d) No more than your Taskbar can display
    (e) None of these

20. Which of the following can be used to select the entire document? **[IBPS PO, 2011]**
    (a) CTRL+A   (b) ALT+ F5
    (c) SHIFT+A   (d) CTRL+K
    (e) CTRL+H

21. To instruct Word to fit the width of a column to the contents of a table automatically, click the___button and then point to AutoFit Contents. **[IBPS PO, 2011]**
    (a) Fit to Form (b) Format
    (c) Autosize   (d) Contents
    (e) AutoFit

22. The default view in Excel is______view. **[IBPS PO, 2011]**
    (a) Work   (b) Auto
    (c) Normal   (d) Roman
    (e) None of these

23. What displays the contents of the active cell in Excel? **[IBPS PO, 2011]**
    (a) Namebox   (b) Row Headings
    (c) Formulabar   (d) Taskpane
    (e) None of these

24. In Word you can force a page break **[IBPS PO, 2011]**
    (a) by positioning your cursor at the appropriate place and pressing the F1 key
    (b) by positioning your cursor at the appropriate place and pressing Ctrl + Enter
    (c) by using the Insert/Section Break
    (d) by changing the font size of your document
    (e) None of these

25. The basic unit of a worksheet into which you enter data in Excel is called a **[IBPS PO, 2011]**
    (a) tab   (b) cell
    (c) box   (d) range
    (e) None of these

26. In Excel __________allows users to bring together copies of workbooks that other users have worked on independently. **[IBPS PO, 2011]**
    (a) Copying   (b) Merging
    (c) Pasting   (d) Compiling
    (e) None of these

27. A(n)______ is a special visual and aduio effect applied in Powerpoint to text or content. **[IBPS PO, 2011]**
    (a) animation   (b) flash
    (c) wipe   (d) dissolve
    (e) None of these

28. In word, when you indent a paragraph, you **[IBPS Clerk, 2011]**
    (a) push the text in with respect to the margin
    (b) change the margins on the page
    (c) move the text up by one line
    (d) move the text down by one line
    (e) None of these

29. Excel would evaluate the formula, = 20* 10/4 *8 and return the answer   **[IBPS Clerk, 2011]**
    (a) 400   (b) 40
    (c) 6.25   (d) 232
    (e) 600

30. In word, you can use Styles to
    [IBPS Clerk, 2011]
    (a) Make copies of documents
    (b) Save changes to documents
    (c) Delete text in documents
    (d) Format your documents
    (e) None of these

31. In the formula, = B1/B2 + B3, which of the following is the correct precedence?
    [IBPS Clerk, 2011]
    (a) Addition higher precedence than division
    (b) Equal precedence among the two operators: proceed right to left
    (c) Equal precedence among the two operators proceed left to right
    (d) Division higher precedence than addition
    (e) None of these

32. To make a copy of the current document to disk
    [IBPS Clerk, 2011]
    (a) Use the "save" command
    (b) This cannot be done
    (c) Use the "duplicate" command
    (d) Copy the document
    (e) Use the "save as" command

33. This dialog box specifies or modifies the worksheet cell range containing data to be charted   **[IBPS Clerk, 2011]**
    (a) Chart Location   (b) Chart Style
    (c) Chart Options   (d) Chart Source Data
    (e) None of these

34. Using Print Preview is useful when you want to-   **[IBPS Clerk, 2011]**
    (a) Colour the document
    (b) Save the document
    (c) Delete the document
    (d) Copy the document
    (e) View how the document will appear when printed

35. Your position in the text is shown by a
    [IBPS Clerk, 2011]
    (a) Blinker   (b) Cursor
    (c) Causer   (d) Pointer
    (e) None of these

36. To reverse the effect of your last action in word
    (a) Use the cut command   **[IBPS Clerk, 2011]**
    (b) Use the Undo command
    (c) Press the delete key
    (d) Use the Redo command
    (e) None of these

37. A word gets selected by clicking it to select a word, in Word   **[IBPS Clerk, 2011]**
    (a) once   (b) twice
    (c) three times   (d) four times
    (e) None of these

38. In word, you can change Page Margins by
    [IBPS Clerk, 2011]
    (a) Dragging the scroll box on the scroll bars
    (b) Deleting the margin boundaries on the Ruler
    (c) Dragging the margin boundaries on the Ruler
    (d) Clicking the right mouse button on the Ruler
    (e) None of these

39. In word, replace option is available on
    [IBPS Clerk, 2011]
    (a) File Menu   (b) View Menu
    (c) Edit Menu   (d) Format Menu
    (e) None of these

40. In Excel, this is a prerecorded formula that provides a shortcut for complex calculations
    [IBPS Clerk, 2011]
    (a) Value   (b) Data Series
    (c) Function   (d) Field
    (e) None of these

41. This is not a function category in Excel
    [IBPS Clerk, 2011]
    (a) Logical   (b) Data Series
    (c) Financial   (d) Text
    (e) None of these

42. Which of the following is not one of the syntax rules?   **[IBPS Clerk, 2011]**
    (a) The order in which you list the function's arguments
    (b) The precedence of the arguments
    (c) Whether or not the function has arguments
    (d) Properly spelling the function's name
    (e) None of these

43. Editing a document consists of reading through the document you've created, then
    (a) correcting your errors   **[SBI Clerk, 2011]**
    (b) printing it
    (c) saving it
    (d) deleting it
    (e) None of these

44. The name a user assigns to a document is called a(n) **[SBI Clerk, 2011]**
 (a) filename (b) program
 (c) record (d) data
 (e) None of these

45. ___________ allows users to upload files to an online site so they can be viewed and edited from another location. **[IBPS PO, 2012]**
 (a) General-purpose applications
 (b) Microsoft Outlook
 (c) Web-hosted technology
 (d) Office Live
 (e) None of these

46. What feature adjusts the top and bottom margins so that the text is centered vertically on the printed page ? **[IBPS PO, 2012]**
 (a) Vertical justifying
 (b) Vertical adjusting
 (c) Dual centering
 (d) Horizontal centering
 (e) Vertical centering

47. What is the overall term for creating, editing, formatting, storing, retrieving, and printing a text document ? **[IBPS PO, 2012]**
 (a) Word processing
 (b) Spreadsheet design
 (c) Web design
 (d) Database management
 (e) Presentation generation

48. The letter and number of the intersecting column and row is the ___________.
 [IBPS PO, 2012]
 (a) cell location (b) cell position
 (c) cell address (d) cell coordinates
 (e) cell contents

49. In Power Point, the Header and Footer button can be found on the Insert tab in what group ?
 [IBPS PO, 2012]
 (a) Illustrations group (b) Object group
 (c) Text group (d) Tables group
 (e) None of these

50. A typical slide in a slide presentation would not include ___________. **[IBPS PO, 2012]**
 (a) photo images charts, and graphs
 (b) graphs and clip art
 (c) clip art and audio clips
 (d) full-motion video
 (e) content templates

51. The PC productivity tool that manipulates data organized in rows and columns is called a ___________. **[IBPS PO, 2012]**
 (a) spreadsheet
 (b) word processing document
 (c) presentation mechanism
 (d) database record manager
 (e) EDI creator

52. To find the Paste Special option, you use the Clipboard group on the ______ tab of PowerPoint. **[IBPS PO, 2012]**
 (a) Design (b) Slide Show
 (c) Page Layout (d) Insert
 (e) Home

53. What is the easiest way to change the phrase, revenues, profits, gross margin, to read revenues, profits, and gross margin ?
 [IBPS PO, 2012]
 (a) Use the insert mode, position the cursor before the g in gross, then type the word and followed by a space
 (b) Use the insert mode, position the cursor after the g in gross, then type the word and followed by a space
 (c) Use the overtype mode, position the cursor before the g in gross, then type the word and followed by a space
 (d) Use the overtype mode, position the cursor after the g in gross, then type the word and followed by a space
 (e) None of these

54. Which PowerPoint view displays each slide of the presentation as a thumbnail and is useful for rearranging slides ? **[IBPS PO, 2012]**
 (a) Slide Sorter (b) Slide Show
 (c) Slide Master (d) Notes Page
 (e) Slide Design

55. When entering text within a document, the Enter key is normally pressed at the end of every ___________. **[IBPS PO, 2012]**
 (a) Line (b) Sentence
 (c) Paragraph (d) word
 (e) file

56. _______ is used to add or put into your document such as a picture or text. **[IBPS Clerk, 2012]**
 (a) TV (b) Squeeze in
 (c) Push in (d) Insert
 (e) None of these

57. Office Assistant is **[IBPS Clerk, 2012]**
    (a) An application that allows you to take notes and save them in file
    (b) A button on the standard toolbar that executes the Save command
    (c) A collection of Autocorrect options in Word
    (d) An animated character that offers help and suggestions
    (e) None of these

58. Pressing CTRL+9 in Excel **[IBPS Clerk, 2012]**
    (a) Prints 9
    (b) Prints
    (c) Prints 9 followed by spaces
    (d) Inserts 9 cells at the current location
    (e) Hides the current row

59. To change the name of an Excel worksheet **[IBPS Clerk, 2012]**
    (a) Click on the worksheet tab by holing CTRL key and type a new name
    (b) Choose Save, AS option from file menu
    (c) Add a (?) at the end of filename while saving the workbook
    (d) Press CTRL + SHIFT keys and new name
    (e) Double click at the worksheet tab and type a new name

60. A document that explains how to use a software program is called ________ manual **[IBPS Clerk, 2012]**
    (a) User (b) System
    (c) Software (d) Program
    (e) Technical

61. To allow someone else schedule your meetings and appointments, ________ feature of Outlook is used **[IBPS Clerk, 2012]**
    (a) Monthly calendar (b) Event manager
    (c) Appointments (d) Delegate Access
    (e) None of these

62. Macros stored in the global macro sheet can be used **[IBPS PO, 2013]**
    (a) in the current document only
    (b) in any document
    (c) can be used only with other macros of the global macro sheet
    (d) not consistent behaviour
    (e) None of the above

63. Anything that is typed in a worksheet appears
    (a) in the formula bar only **[IBPS PO, 2013]**
    (b) in tho active cell only
    (c) in both active cell and formula bar
    (d) in tho formula bar first and when we press ENTER it appears in active cell
    (e) None of the above

64. Which bar is usually located below the Title Bar that provides categorised options? **[IBPS PO, 2013]**
    (a) Menu Bar (b) Status bar
    (c) Toolbar (d) Scroll Bar
    (e) None of the above

65. How many types of cell references are available in Excel? **[IBPS PO, 2013]**
    (a) 3 (b) 4
    (c) 8 (d) 10
    (e) None of these

66. Table of contents can be prepared by using
    (a) macros **[IBPS PO, 2013]**
    (b) headings as H1, H2, H3 and more in the document
    (c) by table of contents in tools menu
    (d) (b) and (c)
    (e) None of the above

67. Table in Word is a grid of rows and columns, with each cell can have **[IBPS PO, 2013]**
    (a) text or graphics (b) only text
    (c) only graphics (d) both
    (e) None of these

68. Word allows user to import graphics from **[IBPS PO, 2013]**
    (a) the library which comes bundled with Word
    (b) any where in the computer
    (c) various graphics format like gif, bmp, png, etc
    (d) only gif format
    (e) None of the above

69. In Word you can force a page break ______. **[IBPS Clerk, 2014]**
    (a) By positioning your cursor at the appropriate place and pressing the Fl key
    (b) By positioning your cursor at the appropriate place and pressing Ctrl+Enter
    (c) By using the insert /section break
    (d) By changing the font size of your document
    (e) None of these

70. Which of the following can be used to select the entire document? **[IBPS Clerk, 2014]**
    (a) CTRL + A (b) ALT + F5
    (c) SHIFT + A (d) CTRL + K
    (e) CTRL + H

71.. The default view in Excel is ______ view. **[IBPS Clerk, 2014]**
    (a) Work (b) Auto
    (c) Normal (d) Roman
    (e) None of these

72. The basic unit of a worksheet into which you enter data in Excel is called a ______
    [IBPS Clerk, 2014]
    (a) tab   (b) cell
    (c) box   (d) range
    (e) None of these

73. In order to Save an .existing docu-ment with a different name you need to   **[SBI Clerk, 2014]**
    (a) Retype the document and give it a different name
    (b) Use the Save as .. command
    (c) Copy and paste the original document to a new document and then-save
    (d) Use Windows Explorer to copy the document to a different location and-then rename it
    (e) None of these

74. The shortcut key to insert the current date?
    [SBI Clerk, 2014]
    (a) Alt + Shift + D   (b) Alt + Shift + V
    (c) Alt + Shift + C   (d) Alt + Shift + B
    (e) None of these

75. The Zoom control slider located in __________
    [IBPS Clerk, 2015]
    (a) Title Bar   (b) Status Bar
    (c) Formula Bar   (d) Scroll Bar
    (e) None of these

76. The very top of the page in a document is known as__________ **[IBPS Clerk, 2015]**
    (a) Footer   (b) Header
    (c) Tab stop   (d) Navigation
    (e) None of these

77. __________ is used to move a document up and down or left and right on the screen.
    [IBPS Clerk, 2015]
    (a) Title Bar   (b) Status Bar
    (c) Formula Bar   (d) Scroll Bar
    (e) None of these

78. Which of the following tells you the page you are on and the total page count?
    [IBPS Clerk, 2015]
    (a) Title Bar   (b) Status Bar
    (c) Formula Bar   (d) Scroll Bar
    (e) None of these

79. __________is a feature supported by many word processors that enables you to surround a picture or diagram with text.
    [IBPS Clerk, 2015]
    (a) Image Wrap   (b) Text Wrap
    (c) Picture Wrap   (d) All of the above
    (e) None of these

80. Which feature allows you to type words in a paragraph continually without pressing the enter key at the end of each line?
    [IBPS Clerk, 2015]
    (a) Image Wrap   (b) Word Wrap
    (c) Picture Wrap   (d) All of the above
    (e) None of these

81. You can move between two or more Excel files opened by using the   **[IBPS Clerk, 2015]**
    (a) ctrl + tab   (b) ctrl + page up
    (c) ctrl + page down   (d) ctrl + F9
    (e) None of these

82. The default view in Excel is _________ View.
    [SBI PO, 2015]
    (a) Work   (b) Auto
    (c) Normal   (d) Roman
    (e) None of these

83. In word you can force a page break ________
    [SBI PO, 2015]
    (a) by positioning your cursor at the appropriate place and pressing the F1 key
    (b) By positioning your cursor at the appropriate place and pressing Ctrl + Enter
    (c) By using the Insert/section break
    (d) By changing the font size of your documents
    (e) None of these

84. What is used to identify whether a data word has an odd or even number of 1's ?
    [SSC CGL, 2015]
    (a) Sign bit   (b) Zero bit
    (c) Parity bit   (d) Carry bit

85. Which among the following is a cloud computing platform and infrastructure created by Microsoft?   **[IBPS PO Mains, 2016]**
    (a) Simple Storage Service
    (b) Atmos
    (c) Openstack Swift
    (d) OceanStore
    (e) Azure

86. Which is a feature included in Microsoft PowerPoint software that allows the user to see all the slides in a presentation at one time?
    [IBPS PO Mains, 2016]
    (a) Slide Sorter   (b) Slide Master
    (c) Handout Master   (d) Slide Header
    (e) Reading View

87. What is the full form of RTF?
    [IBPS Clerk Mains, 2016]
    (a) Richer Text Formatting
    (b) Rich Text Format
    (c) Right Text Fishing
    (d) Right Text Font
    (e) Rich Text Font
88. Which of the following is the text alignment available in word processing software that adjusts the left margin while keeping the right margin in any way? **[IBPS Clerk Mains, 2016]**
    (a) Justify   (b) Left Justify
    (c) Right Justify   (d) Centre
    (e) Orientation
89. Microsoft Word is a word processor developed by Microsoft. In MS Word Spelling Check is a feature available in which tab?
    [IBPS Clerk Mains, 2016]
    (a) File   (b) Home
    (c) Insert   (d) Review
    (e) References
90. Which of the following is not a FONT EFFECT?
    [IBPS Clerk Mains, 2016]
    (a) Font Color   (b) Super Script
    (c) Engrave   (d) Strike Through
    (e) Bold
91. CTLR + ENTER KEY (Return) is a short cut to insert? **[IBPS Clerk Mains, 2016]**
    (a) Table   (b) Picture
    (c) Clip Art   (d) Page Break
    (e) MP3 files
92. F7 is a short cut key to launch which feature in MS-word? **[IBPS Clerk Mains, 2016]**
    (a) Word Count
    (b) Spelling & Grammar
    (c) Mail Merge
    (d) Translate
    (e) Insert
93. A software that is used to create text based documents is called ________
    (a) DBMS   **[IBPS RRB, 2016]**
    (b) Spreadsheet
    (c) Word Processor
    (d) Presentation Software
    (e) None of these
94. Which is used to change the text in Microsoft Word from uppercase to lowercase or a capital letter at the beginning of every word?
    [IBPS RRB, 2016]
    (a) Shift + F3   (b) Shift + F4
    (c) Shift + F5   (d) Shift + F7
    (e) Shift + F6
95. Which of the following shortcut key is used to insert the current date? **[IBPS RRB, 2016]**
    (a) Shift + Alt + T   (b) Shift + Alt + D
    (c) Ctrl + Alt + T   (d) Ctrl + Alt + D
    (e) Shift + Ctrl + T

ANSWER KEY

No.	Ans	No.	Ans	No.	Ans	No.	Ans	No.	Ans	No.	Ans
1.	(a)	17.	(d)	33.	(d)	49.	(c)	65.	(a)	81.	(a)
2.	(b)	18.	(c)	34.	(e)	50.	(e)	66	(b)	82	(c)
3.	(c)	19.	(c)	35.	(b)	51.	(a)	67.	(a)	83.	(b)
4.	(a)	20.	(a)	36.	(b)	52.	(e)	68.	(c)	84.	(c)
5	(c)	21	(e)	37.	(b)	53.	(a)	69.	(b)	85.	(e)
6.	(d)	22	(c)	38.	(d)	54.	(a)	70.	(a)	86.	(a)
7.	(c)	23	(c)	39.	(c)	55.	(c)	71.	(c)	87.	(b)
8.	(a)	24.	(b)	40.	(c)	56.	(b)	72.	(b)	88.	(b)
9	(b)	25	(b)	41.	(a)	57.	(d)	73.	(b)	89.	(d)
10.	(a)	26	(b)	42	(b)	58.	(e)	74.	(a)	90.	(a)
11.	(d)	27	(a)	43	(a)	59.	(e)	75.	(b)	91.	(d)
12.	(d)	28.	(a)	44	(a)	60.	(a)	76.	(b)	92.	(b)
13.	(d)	29.	(a)	45.	(c)	61.	(d)	77.	(d)	93.	(c)
14.	(d)	30.	(d)	46.	(e)	62.	(b)	78.	(b)	94.	(a)
15.	(a)	31.	(d)	47.	(a)	63.	(c)	79.	(b)	95.	(b)
16.	(c)	32.	(e)	48.	(c)	64.	(a)	80.	(b)		

Practice Exercise

1. The quickest and easiest way in Word, to locate a particular word or phrase in a document is to use the __________ command.
   - (a) Replace
   - (b) Find
   - (c) Lookup
   - (d) Search
   - (e) None of these

2. Editing a document consists of reading through the document you've created, then __________.
   - (a) correcting your errors
   - (b) printing it
   - (c) saving it
   - (d) deleting it
   - (e) None of these

3. Each box in a spreadsheet is called a
   - (a) cell
   - (b) empty space
   - (c) field
   - (d) None of these

4. You cannot link Excel worksheet data to a Word document __________.
   - (a) with the right drag method
   - (b) with the hyperlink
   - (c) with the copy and paste special commands
   - (d) with the copy and paste buttons on the standard commands
   - (e) All of these

5. You Microsoft Word by using __________ button.
   - (a) New
   - (b) Start
   - (c) Program
   - (d) Control Panel
   - (e) None of these

6. Which of the following could you do to remove a paragraph from a report you had written?
   - (a) Delete and edit
   - (b) Highlight and delete
   - (c) Cut and paste
   - (d) Undo typing
   - (e) None of these

7. You click at (Control + B) to make the text __________.
   - (a) Italics
   - (b) Underlined
   - (c) Italics and Underlined
   - (d) Bold
   - (e) None of these

8. In Excel, Charts are created using which option?
   - (a) Chart Wizard
   - (b) Pivot Table
   - (c) Pie Chart
   - (d) Bar Chart
   - (e) None of these

9. For creating a document, you use __________ command at File Menu.
   - (a) Open
   - (b) Close
   - (c) New
   - (d) Save
   - (e) None of these

10. The minimum number of rows and columns in MS Word document is
    - (a) 1 and 1
    - (b) 2 and 1
    - (c) 1 and 2
    - (d) 2 and 2

11. Which of the following commands is used to select the whole document?
    - (a) Ctrl + A
    - (b) Alt + F5
    - (c) Shift + S
    - (d) Can't be done
    - (e) None of these

12. In word processing, an efficient way to move the 3rd paragraph to place it after the 5th paragraph is __________.
    - (a) copy and paste
    - (b) copy, cut and paste
    - (c) cut, copy and paste
    - (d) cut and paste
    - (e) None of these

13. $=SUM(B1:B8)$ is an example of a __________
    - (a) function
    - (b) formula
    - (c) cell address
    - (d) value
    - (e) None of these

14. A __________ is a collection of data that is stored electronically as a series of records in a table.
    - (a) spreadsheet
    - (b) presentation
    - (c) database
    - (d) web page
    - (e) None of these

15. A __________ is a professionally designed "empty" document that can be adapted to the user's needs.
    - (a) file
    - (b) guide
    - (c) template
    - (d) user guide file
    - (e) None of these

16. What is the intersection of a column and a row on a worksheet called?
    - (a) Column
    - (b) Value
    - (c) Address
    - (d) Cell
    - (e) None of these

17. In a spreadsheet, a __________ is a number you will use in a calculation.
    - (a) label
    - (b) cell
    - (c) field
    - (d) value
    - (e) None of these

18. ___________ view shows how the contents on printed page will appear with margin, header and footer.
    (a) Draft
    (b) Full Screen Reading
    (c) Outline
    (d) Page Layout
    (e) None of these
19. We can enter and edit the text efficiently using –
    (a) Spreadsheet
    (b) Typewriter
    (c) Word Processing Program
    (d) Desktop Publishing Program
    (e) None of these
20. The background of any Word document
    (a) is always of white color
    (b) is the colour present under the option menu
    (c) is always the same for the entire document
    (d) can have any colour you choose
    (e) None of these
21. When the margins on both sides are straight and equal, then there is ___________ in document.
    (a) full justification   (b) full alignment
    (c) left justification   (d) right justification
    (e) None of these
22. What happens when you press Ctrl + V Key?
    (a) A Capital V letter is typed into your document at the cursor point
    (b) The selected item is pasted from the clipboard
    (c) The selected item is pasted to the clipboard
    (d) The selected drawing objects are distributed vertically on the page
    (e) None of these
23. Title bar, ribbon, status bar, views and document workspace are factors of ___________ program of Words.
    (a) Windows   (b) Browser
    (c) Explorer   (d) Website
    (e) None of these
24. To ___________ a document means to make changes to its existing content.
    (a) format   (b) save
    (c) edit   (d) print
    (e) None of these
25. The name given to a document by user is called
    (a) Filename   (b) Program
    (c) Data   (d) Record
    (e) None of these
26. A saved document is referred to as ___________.
    (a) File   (b) Word
    (c) Folder   (d) Project
    (e) None of these

27. A hard copy of a document is ___________.
    (a) stored in the hard disk
    (b) stored on a floppy
    (c) stored on a CD
    (d) printed on the printer
    (e) None of these
28. Allows you to print.
    (a) ribbon   (b) monitor
    (c) go now   (d) Control-P
    (e) None of these
29. The different styles of lettering in a word processing program.
    (a) font   (b) calligraphy
    (c) writing   (d) manuscript
    (e) None of these
30. Any ___________ letter, number, or symbol found on the keyboard that you can type into the computer.
    (a) output   (b) character
    (c) type   (d) print
    (e) None of these
31. A program which helps create written documents and lets you go back and make corrections as necessary.
    (a) spreadsheet   (b) personal writer
    (c) word printer   (d) word processor
    (e) None of these
32. To insert a copy of the clipboard contents, whatever was last cut or copied at the insertion point.
    (a) paste   (b) stick in
    (c) fit in   (d) push in
    (e) None of these
33. The command used to remove text or graphics from a document. The information is then stored on a clipboard as you can paste it.
    (a) chop   (b) cut
    (c) clip   (d) cart away
    (e) None of these
34. A command that saves what you working on into the hard drive, or onto a disk.
    (a) view   (b) hold
    (c) save   (d) go
    (e) None of these
35. A command to get a file you working on from the memory where it was stored.
    (a) close   (b) delete
    (c) open   (d) get it
    (e) None of these
36. To move down a page in a document.
    (a) jump   (b) fly
    (c) wriggle   (d) scroll
    (e) None of these

37. What menu is selected to print?
    (a) File   (b) Tools
    (c) Social   (d) Edit
    (e) None of these
38. A(n) __________ contains commands that can be selected.
    (a) pointer   (b) menu
    (c) icon   (d) button
    (e) None of these
39. Saving is the process of __________.
    (a) copying a document from memory to a storage medium
    (b) making changes to a document's existing content.
    (c) changing the appearance, or overall look, of a document
    (d) developing a document by entering text using a keyboard
    (e) None of these
40. To find a saved document in the computer's memory and bring it up on the screen to view __________.
    (a) reverse   (b) return
    (c) retrieve   (d) return
    (e) None of these
41. In word processing, an efficient way to move the 3rd paragraph to place it after the 5th paragraph is __________.
    (a) copy and paste
    (b) copy, cut and paste
    (c) cut, copy and paste
    (d) cut and paste
    (e) None of these
42. By default, on which page the header or the footer is printed?
    (a) on first page   (b) on alternate page
    (c) on every page   (d) none of the above
43. Which key should be pressed to start a new paragraph in MS-Word?
    (a) Down Cursor Key (b) Enter Key
    (c) Shift + Enter   (d) Ctrl + Enter
44. What is the intersection of a column and a row on a worksheet called?
    (a) Column   (b) Value
    (c) Address   (d) Cell
    (e) None of these
45. In a spreadsheet, a __________ is a number you will use in a calculator.
    (a) label   (b) cell
    (c) field   (d) value
    (e) None of these
46. Numbers and formulae entered in a cell are called
    (a) Labels   (b) Numeric entries
    (c) Intersection   (d) Text
    (e) Fillers
47. An essential ingredient for effective multimedia presentations incorporates user participation or __________.
    (a) links   (b) buttons
    (c) interactivity   (d) integration
    (e) speed
48. When writing a document, you can use the __________ feature to find an appropriate word or an alternative word if you find yourself stuck for the right word.
    (a) dictionary   (b) word finder
    (c) encyclopedia   (d) thesaurus
    (e) None of these
49. In Excel, __________ contains one or more worksheets.
    (a) Template   (b) Workbook
    (c) Active cell   (d) Label
    (e) None of these
50. By default, your documents print in __________ mode.
    (a) Landscape   (b) Portrait
    (c) Page Setup   (d) Print View
    (e) None of these
51. Which type of file is created by word processing programs?
    (a) database file   (b) storage file
    (c) worksheet file (d) document file
    (e) graphical file
52. For creating a document, you use __________ command at File Menu.
    (a) Open   (b) Close
    (c) New   (d) Save
    (e) None of the above
53. Documentation of computer program is important so that
    (a) users can learn how to use the program
    (b) other programmers can know how to maintain the program
    (c) the programmer can see why the code is written that way while hunting for sources of error
    (d) All of the above
    (e) None of the above
54. Two different files can have the same name if
    (a) they are in different folders
    (b) they are on different drives
    (c) Never
    (d) the names are capitalised differently
    (e) None of the above
55. When you cut or copy information it gets place in the __________.
    (a) Clipart   (b) Clipboard
    (c) Internet   (d) Motherboard
    (e) None of the above

56. A program that enables you to perform calculations involving rows and columns of numbers is called a ___________.
    (a) spreadsheet program
    (b) word processor
    (c) graphics package
    (d) window
    (e) None of the above

57. What is the term for how words will appear on a page?
    (a) Text formatting
    (b) Character formatting
    (c) Point size
    (d) Typeface
    (e) None of these

58. Microsoft Office is an example of a ___________.
    (a) closed-source software
    (b) open-source software
    (c) horizontal-market software
    (d) vertical-market software
    (e) compiler

59. You can use ___________ to copy selected text, and ___________ to paste it in a document.
    (a) CTRL + C, CTRL + V
    (b) CTRL + C, CTRL + P
    (c) CTRL + S, CTRL + S
    (d) SHIFT + C, ALT + P
    (e) CTRL + D, CTRL + A

60. The operation of combining two cells into a single cell in Excel is referred to as ___________.
    (a) Join Cells
    (b) Merge Cells
    (b) Merge Table
    (d) Join Table
    (e) None of these

61. Data is organized in a work sheet as ___________.
    (a) charts and diagrams
    (b) rows and columns
    (c) tables and boxes
    (d) graphs
    (e) None of these

62. Which bar is usually located below that Title Bar that provides categorized options?
    (a) Menu bar
    (b) Status bar
    (c) Tool bar
    (d) Scroll bar

63. In Excel, when the contents and attributes of a cell or range of cells have to be erased using the menu, the user must ___________.
    (a) Select the cells, choose Edit and select Clear, then All
    (b) Select the cells, and click delete on the keyboard
    (c) Select the cells, choose Tools, and select Clear, then Formats
    (d) Select the cells, choose Tools, and select Formula Audit then Delete
    (e) None of these

64. If an Excel Worksheet is to be linked for use in a Power Point presentation, the following should be clicked ___________.
    (a) Edit, Paste Special
    (b) Edit, Paste
    (c) Edit, Copy
    (d) File, Copy
    (e) None of these

65. In Word, which menu would the user select to print a document?
    (a) Tools
    (b) File
    (c) View
    (d) Window
    (e) None of these

66. In order to choose the font for a sentence in a WORD document ___________.
    (a) select Font in the Format menu
    (b) select Font in the Edit menu
    (c) select Font in the Tools menu
    (d) select Font in the Insert menu

67. In order to delete a sentence from a document you would use ___________.
    (a) highlight and copy
    (b) cut and paste
    (c) copy and paste
    (d) highlight and delete
    (e) select and paste

68. Editing a document that has been created means ___________.
    (a) saving it
    (b) printing it
    (c) scanning it
    (d) correcting it
    (e) None of these

69. In Excel, the contents of the active cell are displayed in the ___________.
    (a) footer bar
    (b) tool bar
    (c) task bar
    (d) menu bar
    (e) formula bar

70. To insert a page break in a WORD document, the following options are used ___________.
    (a) Insert and Copy
    (b) Insert and Enter
    (c) Insert and Delete
    (d) Insert and Page Layout
    (e) Insert and Break

71. Which of the following identifies a cell in Excel.
    (a) formula
    (b) name
    (c) label
    (d) address
    (e) None of these

72. While selecting multiple work sheets in Excel, the following key must also be used when clicking the sheet tab ___________.
    (a) Shift
    (b) Alt
    (c) Ctrl
    (d) Insert
    (e) Esc

73. A word processor would be used best to ______.
    (a) paint a picture
    (b) draw a diagram
    (c) type a story
    (d) work out income and expenses
    (e) None of these
74. The result of a formula in a cell is called
    (a) label   (b) value
    (c) range   (d) displayed value
    (e) None of these
75. Which of the following Excel charts represents only one value for each variable?
    (a) Function   (b) Line
    (c) Pie   (d) Bar
    (e) None of these
76. To see the document before the printout is taken, use
    (a) Insert Table   (b) Paste
    (c) Format Painter   (d) Cut
    (e) Print Preview
77. To move data from one part of the document to another, which of the following is used?
    (a) Cut and Paste   (b) Copy and Paste
    (c) Copy and Delete (d) Copy and Undo
    (e) Cut and Insert
78. Which of the following is the another name for a pre-programming formula in Excel?
    (a) Range   (b) Graph
    (c) Function   (d) Cell
    (e) None of these
79. To save a document for the first time, ____________ option is used.
    (a) Save as   (b) Save
    (c) Save on   (d) Copy
    (e) Paste
80. The user can use ____________ commands to search for and correct words in a document.
    (a) Print and Print Preview
    (b) Header and Footer
    (c) Find and Replace
    (d) Spelling and Grammar
    (e) Copy and Paste
81. Which of the following is the feature that keeps track of the right margin?
    (a) Find and replace (b) Wordwrap
    (c) Right justified   (d) Left justified
    (e) Ragged right
82. To specify margins in Word, the user has to select Page Setup option from the ____________ menu.
    (a) Edit   (b) Table
    (c) Autocorrect   (d) File
    (e) Format
83. What is the package called which helps create, manipulate and analyse data arranged in rows and columns?
    (a) Application package
    (b) Word processing package
    (c) Outlining package
    (d) Outline processors
    (e) Spreadsheet package
84. Which of the following options is used to display information such as title, page number of the document?
    (a) Insert Table
    (b) Auto correct
    (c) Thesaurus
    (d) Spelling and Grammar
    (e) Header and Footer
85. Which of the following justifications align the text on both the sides – left and right – of the margin?
    (a) Right   (b) Justify
    (c) both Sides   (d) Balanced
    (e) None of these

		ANSWER KEY			
1. (b)	16. (d)	31. (d)	46. (b)	61. (b)	76. (e)
2. (a)	17. (d)	32. (a)	47. (c)	62. (a)	77. (a)
3. (a)	18. (d)	33. (b)	48. (d)	63. (b)	78. (c)
4. (d)	19. (d)	34. (c)	49. (b)	64. (e)	79. (a)
5. (c)	20. (d)	35. (c)	50. (b)	65. (b)	80. (c)
6. (b)	21. (a)	36. (d)	51. (d)	66. (a)	81. (c)
7. (d)	22. (b)	37. (a)	52. (c)	67. (d)	82. (d)
8. (a)	23. (a)	38. (c)	53. (d)	68. (d)	83. (e)
9. (c)	24. (c)	39. (a)	54. (a)	69. (e)	84. (e)
10. (a)	25. (a)	40. (c)	55. (b)	70. (e)	85. (b)
11. (a)	26. (a)	41. (d)	56. (a)	71. (b)	
12. (d)	27. (d)	42. (c)	57. (a)	72. (c)	
13. (b)	28. (d)	43. (b)	58. (c)	73. (c)	
14. (c)	29. (a)	44. (d)	59. (a)	74. (d)	
15. (c)	30. (b)	45. (d)	60. (b)	75. (c)	

Computer & Network Security

Computer security (also known as cyber security or IT security) is information security as applied to computing devices such as computers and smart phones, as well as computer networks such as private and public networks, including the whole Internet.

Traditionally, computer facilities have been physically protected for three reasons:

- To prevent theft of or damage to the hardware
- To prevent theft of or damage to the information
- To prevent disruption of service

THE BASIC COMPONENTS OF SECURITY

1. **Confidentiality :** Confidentiality is the concealment of information or resources. The need for keeping information secret arises from the use of computers in sensitive fields such as government and industry. For example, military and civilian institutions in the government often restrict access to information to those who need that information. The first formal work in computer security was motivated by the military's attempt to implement controls to enforce a "need to know" principle. This principle also applies to industrial firms, which keep their proprietary designs secure lest their competitors try to steal the designs. As a further example, all types of institutions keep personnel records secret.

2. **Integrity :** Integrity refers to the trustworthiness of data or resources, and it is usually phrased in terms of preventing improper or unauthorized change. Integrity includes data integrity (the content of the information) and origin integrity (the source of the data, often called authentication). The source of the information may bear on its accuracy and credibility and on the trust that people place in the information. This dichotomy illustrates the principle that the aspect of integrity known as credibility is central to the proper functioning of a system.

3. **Availability :** Availability refers to the ability to use the information or resource desired. Availability is an important aspect of reliability as well as of system design because an unavailable system is at least as bad as no system at all. The aspect of availability that is relevant to security is that someone may deliberately arrange to deny access to data or to a service by making it unavailable.

4. **Access Control System :** Any system designed to prevent and restrict access to users. For example, a primary form of access control is only allowing users who have accounts to login to a system or only allowing the user access to files he or she should be able to see.

TOP SOME SOURCES OF COMPUTER VIRUS ATTACK

The most potent and vulnerable threat of computer users is virus attacks. Virus attacks hampers important work involved with data and documents. It is imperative for every computer user to be aware about the software and programs that can help to protect the personal computers from attacks. One must take every possible measure in order to keep the computer systems free from virus attacks. The top sources of virus attacks are highlighted below:

1. **Downloadable Programs :** Downloadable files are one of the best possible sources of virus. Any type of executable program including games, freeware, screen savers as well as executable files are one of the major sources of computer virus attacks. Executable files having an extension of ".com", ".exe" and "coolgame.exe" contain virus sources too. If in the case a user want to download programs from the internet then it is necessary to scan every program before downloading them.

2. **Illegal Software :** Most people who download cracked and illegal versions of software online are unaware about the reality that they may contain virus sources as well. Such illegal files contain viruses and bugs that are difficult to detect as well as to remove. Hence, it is always a preferable option to download software from the appropriate source.

3. **Email Attachments :** Email attachments are one of the other popular sources of computer virus attacks. Hence, a user must handle email attachments with extreme care, especially if the email comes from an unknown sender. Installation of a good antivirus assumes prime necessity if one desires to eliminate the possibility of virus attacks.

4. **Using Internet :** Using internet is one of the common sources of virus infection. Majority of all computer users are unaware as when viruses attack computer systems. Almost every computer user click/download everything that comes their way and hence unknowingly invites the possibility of virus attacks.

5. **Booting from Unknown CD :** Most computer users believe that one of the most common ways of virus infection is through Data CD. It is a good practice to remove the CD when the computer system is not working. If you do not remove the CD after switching off the computer system then it is every possibility that the computer system may start to boot automatically from the disc.

6. **Using Pendrive/USB Flash drive :** Using pen drive/USB flash drive is another source of virus attacks. It is a good practice to scan the pendrive when it is connected to computer.

7. **Not running the latest updates :** Many of the updates, especially those associated with Microsoft Windows and other operating systems and programs, are security updates. Running a program or operating system that is not up-to-date with the latest updates can be a big security risk and can be a way your computer becomes infected.

TYPES OF ATTACK IN NETWORK SECURITY

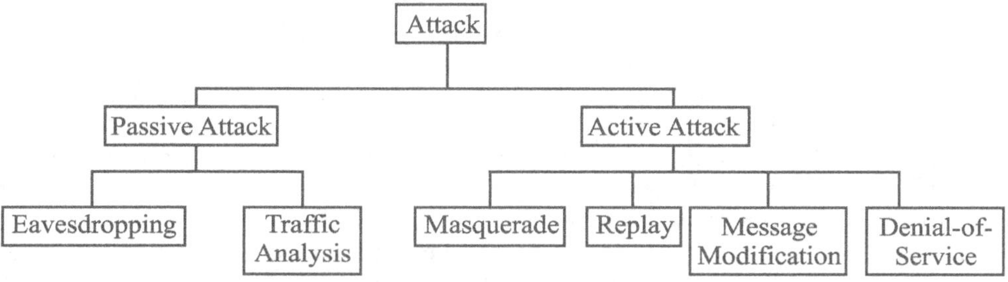

In Network Security, attack is typically divided into two parts.

1. **Passive Attack :** A passive attack monitors unencrypted traffic and looks for clear-text passwords and sensitive information that can be used in other types of attacks. Passive attacks include traffic analysis, monitoring of unprotected communications, decrypting weakly encrypted traffic, and capturing authentication information such as passwords. Passive attacks result in the disclosure of information or data files to an attacker without the consent or knowledge of the user.

2. **Active Attack :** In an active attack, the attacker tries to bypass or break into secured systems. This can be done through stealth, viruses, worms, or Trojan horses. Active attacks include attempts to circumvent or break protection features, to introduce malicious code, and to steal or modify information. These attacks are mounted against a network backbone, exploit information in transit, electronically penetrate an enclave, or attack an authorized remote user during an attempt to connect to an enclave. Active attacks result in the disclosure or dissemination of data files, DoS, or modification of data.

Passive attack further divides into two parts :–

1. **Eaves-dropping:** Eavesdropping is the unauthorized real-time interception of a private communication, such as a phone call, instant message, video conference or fax transmission. The term **eavesdrop** derives from the practice of actually standing under the eaves of a house, listening to conversations inside.

2. **Traffic analysis :** Traffic analysis is a special type of inference attack technique that looks at communication patterns between entities in a system. **"Traffic analysis"** is the process of intercepting and examining messages in order to deduce information from patterns in communication.

Active attack further divides into four parts :

1. **Masquerade attack :** A **masquerade attack** is an **attack** that uses a fake identity, such as a network identity, to gain unauthorized access to personal computer information through legitimate access identification.

2. **Replay attack :** A **replay attack** (also known as playback **attack**) is a form of network **attack** in which a valid data transmission is maliciously or fraudulently repeated or delayed.

3. **Message modification attack :**
   In a **message modification attack**, an intruder alters packet header addresses to direct a message to a different destination or modify that data on a target machine.

4. **Denial-of-service attack :** A **denial-of-service (DoS)** is any type of **attack** where the attackers (hackers) attempt to prevent legitimate users from accessing the **service**. In a **DoS attack**, the attacker usually sends excessive messages asking the network or server to authenticate requests that have invalid return addresses.

TOP ATTACKS IN NETWORK SECURITY

There are some important network security Attacks are:

1. **Distributed Attack :** A distributed attack requires that the adversary introduce code, such as a Trojan horse or back-door program, to a "trusted" component or software that will later be distributed to many other companies and users Distribution attacks focus on the malicious modification of hardware or software at the factory or during distribution. These attacks introduce malicious code such as a back door to a product to gain unauthorized access to information or to a system function at a later date.

2. **Phishing Attack :** In phishing attack the hacker creates a fake web site that looks exactly like a popular site such as the SBI bank or paypal. The phishing part of the attack is that the hacker then sends an e-mail message trying to trick the user into clicking a link that leads to the fake site. When the user attempts to log on with their account information, the hacker records the username and password and then tries that information on the real site.

3. **Hijack attack :** In a hijack attack, a hacker takes over a session between you and another individual and disconnects the other individual from the communication. You still believe that you are talking to the original party and may send private information to the hacker by accident.

4. **Spoof attack :** Spoof attack In a spoof attack, the hacker modifies the source address of the packets he or she is sending so that they appear to be coming from someone else. This may be an attempt to bypass your firewall rules.

5. **Password attack :** An attacker tries to crack the passwords stored in a network account database or a password-protected file. There are three major types of password attacks: a dictionary attack, a brute-force attack, and a hybrid attack. A dictionary attack uses a word list file, which is a list of potential passwords. A brute-force attack is when the attacker tries every possible combination of characters.

MALWARE

Malware, also known as malicious software, is a software that is used to disrupt computer operation, gather sensitive information, or gain access to private computer systems.It can appear in the form of executable code, scripts, active content, and other software. 'Malware' is a general term used to refer to a variety of forms of hostile or intrusive software.The term badware is sometimes used, and applied to both true (malicious) malware and unintentionally harmful software. Some malwares are:

- **Computer Viruses**

  A computer virus or worm is program that replicates itself on its own by by inserting copies of itself into other programs or documents. It can spread by email also. These viruses or worms are malicious programs that aredesigned to infect and gain control over a computer without the owner's knowledge.

- **Viruses and spam**

  Virus-makers and spammers create viruses that infect most of the computers across the globe. These computers become spam-generating machines and cooperate in various manners to send as much spam as possible as efficiently as possible. The infected computers then send massive amounts of spam, unbeknownst to the computer owner.

TYPES OF VIRUS

There are various types of computer viruses, classified in terms of techniques, origin, the types of files affected, damage, OS or Platform attacked, as well as the places they hide. Some of the common types include the following:

- **Resident viruses :** These are permanent viruses dwelling in RAM memory. In this case, they would be in a position to overcome, as well as interrupt, all operations that the system executes. Their effects include corrupting programs and files that are closed, opened, renamed or copied.
- **Overwrite viruses :** These viruses delete information that is in the infected files. In this case, the infected files would be rendered totally or partially useless. Unfortunately, you would only clean the infected file by deleting it completely, therefore losing original content.
- **Direct action viruses :** This virus replicates itself, then acts when executed. Subject to satisfaction of particular conditions, the virus infects files located in the folders or computer directory. It is also in directories specified in the AUTOEXEC.BAT PATH. In most cases, it is located in hard drive's root directory and takes particular action when the computer boots.
- **File infectors :** This virus infects executable files or programs. On running the programs, the virus would be activated, then be able to carry out its damaging effects. Most of the existing viruses are in this category.
- **Boot viruses :** This virus infects the hard disk's or floppy drive's boot sector. This would make the computer unable to boot. These viruses can, however, be avoided by ensuring that the floppy disks and hard drive is well protected. Never start the computer using an unknown disk drive or floppy disk.
- **Directory viruses :** This virus alters the paths indicating a file's location. In this case, when the infected program is executed, you will be running the program unknowingly, since the virus has moved the original program and file to another location. This therefore makes it impossible to locate the moved files.
- **Macro virus :** This virus affects files created using particular programs or applications containing macros. The mini-programs increase their ability to automate some operations, in which case they would be performed as single actions. The user would therefore be saved the trouble of executing them singularly.

ACTION OF A VIRUS

Different computer viruses create different problems in different ways. The most common problems are:

- A virus may destroy all data stored in the hard disk by either formatting it without warning or by destroying some of its sectors.
- A virus may change the boot sector of the hard disk. If the boot sector of a disk is affected, it cannot boot the computer.
- The computer viruses are automatically loaded into the main memory of the computer and remain in the memory. This slows down the data accessing speed of the computer.
- A virus can destroy BIOS of the computer.

COMPUTER WORMS

A computer worm is a standalone malware computer program that replicates itself in order to spread to other computers. Often, it uses a computer network to spread itself, relying on security failures on the target computer to access it. Unlike a computer virus, it does not need to attach itself to an existing program.

TROJAN

Trojans are malicious programs that perform actions that have not been authorized by the user. These actions can include:

- Deleting data
- Blocking data
- Modifying data
- Copying data

Disrupting the performance of computers or computer networks Unlike computer viruses and worms , Trojans are not able to self-replicate.

SPYWARE

Spyware is software that aids in gathering information about a person or organization without their knowledge and that may send such information to another entity without the consumer's consent, or that asserts control over a computer without the consumer's knowledge.

SOME IMPORTANT TERMS RELATED TO SECURITY

Spoofing : It is a situation in which a program successfully masquerades as another by falsifying data and thereby gaining an illegitimate advantage. IP address spoofing or IP spoofing is the creation of Internet Protocol (IP) packets with a source IP address, with the purpose of concealing the identity of the sender or impersonating another computing system.

Hacking : Hacking is the practice of modifying the features of a system, in order to accomplish a goal outside of the creator's original purpose. The person who is consistently engaging in hacking activities, and has accepted hacking as a lifestyle and philosophy of their choice, is called a hacker. Computer hacking is the most popular form of hacking nowadays, especially in the field of computer security, but hacking exists in many other forms, such as phone hacking, etc. and it's not limited to either of them.

Cracking : The original difference between cracking and hacking is that hackers were those who attacked/ penetrated security systems of networks while crackers were those that attacked/penetrated security systems of software. Crackers, cracked software (not networks systems) such that they could be pirated. Crackers are are the profit side of the coin. Their motivation is financial gain and/or to cause damage. Crackers tend to be working for organized crime, services for hire, US, Chinese, Russian goverment employees, competitors commiting corporate espionage etc

Phishing : It is the attempt to acquire sensitive information such as usernames, passwords, and credit card details (and sometimes, indirectly, money) by masquerading as a trustworthy entity in an electronic communication.

Spam : Spam is most often considered to be electronic junk mail or junk newsgroup postings. Some people define spam even more generally as any unsolicited email. However, if a long-lost brother finds your email address and sends you a message, this could hardly be called spam, even though it is unsolicited

Adware : Adware is the common name used to describe software that is given to the user with advertisements embedded in the application. Adware is considered a legitimate alternative offered to consumers who do not wish to pay for software. There are many ad-supported programs, games or utilities that are distributed as adware (or freeware). Today we have a growing number of software developers who offer their goods as "sponsored" freeware (adware) until you pay to register. If you're using legitimate adware, when you stop running the software, the ads should disappear, and you always have the option of disabling the ads by purchasing a registration key.

Rootkits : A rootkit is a type of malicious software that is activated each time your system boots up. Rootkits are difficult to detect because they are activated before your system's Operating System has completely booted up. A rootkit often allows the installation of hidden files, processes, hidden user accounts, and more in the systems OS. Rootkits are able to intercept data from terminals, network connections, and the keyboard.

SOLUTIONS TO COMPUTER SECURITY THREATS

Some safeguards or solutions to protect a computer system from accidental access are described below:

1. Install Anti-Virus Software

Ensure that reputable anti-virus software is installed on all computers. This should include all servers, PCs and laptops. If employees use computers at home for business use or to remotely access the network, these PCs should also have anti-virus software installed.Everyday new computer viruses are being released and it is essential that businesses are protected from these viruses by keeping the anti-virus software up to date. If possible, companies should look at policies whereby computers that do not have the most up to date anti-virus software installed are not allowed to connect to the network.

2. Employ a firewall to protect networks

As computer viruses can spread by means other than email, it is important that unwanted traffic is blocked from entering the network by using a firewall. For users that use computers for business away from the protection of the company's network, such as home PCs or laptops, a personal firewall should be installed to ensure the computer is protected.

Firewall
A method for keeping a network secure. It can be implemented in a single router that filters out unwanted packets, or it may use a combination of technologies in routers and hosts. Firewalls are widely used to give users access to the Internet in a secure fashion as well as to separate a company's public Web server from its internal network. They are also used to keep internal network segments secure. For example, a research or accounting subnet might be vulnerable to snooping from within. Following are the types of techniques used individually or in combination to provide firewall protection.

3. Filter all email traffic

All incoming and outgoing email should be filtered for computer viruses. This filter should ideally be at the perimeter of the network to prevent computer viruses. E-mails with certain file attachments commonly used by computer viruses to spread themselves, such as .EXE, .COM and .SCR files, should also be prevented from entering the network.

4. Scan Internet Downloads

Ensure that all files downloaded from the Internet are scanned for computer viruses before being used. Ideally this scanning should be done from one central point on the network to ensure that all files are properly scanned.

5. Implement a vulnerability management program

Most computer viruses and worms try to exploit bugs and vulnerabilities within the operating system and applications that companies use. New vulnerabilities are introduced into networks every day, be that from installing new software and services, making changes to existing systems or simply from previously undiscovered vulnerabilities coming to light. It is important to regularly review your network and the applications running on it for new vulnerabilities. Any discovered vulnerabilities should be rated and prioritised regarding their criticality and the potential business impact they could have. Once this has been done, a plan on how to manage those vulnerabilities, either by patching, upgrading, or managing the vulnerability using tools such as firewalls or Intrusion Detection Systems should be put into place.

6. Develop an Information Security Policy

The creation and publication of an Information Security Policy is key to ensuring that information security receives the profile it requires in the organisation and is the first critical step in securing the company's systems and data. It is important that senior management support the Information Security Policy and that all users are made aware of their roles and responsibilities under this policy.

7. Password

A password is an unspaced sequence of characters used to determine that a computer user requesting access to a computer system is really that particular user.

Strong password : Term used to describe a password that is an effective password that would be difficult to break. Often a strong password has between six and ten characters (the more the better), numbers, other characters, and both upper and lowercase characters. Below is an example of a strong password.

Weak password : A password that is not an effective password because it's easy to remember. Names, birth dates, phone numbers, and easily guessable words are considered weak passwords. Below is an example of a weak password.

8. Certificate

Many websites use certificates or digital certificates to define their security and identity, so that computers visiting the sites know the sites are legitimate and feature proper security. These certificates must be obtained and from the proper organizations, as well as registered with them. They also expire and must be renewed to remain valid. A web browser may deny access to a website or at least warn the user when a website's certificate has expired and the identity or security of the site cannot be verified.

9. Digital Signature

Alternatively referred to as digitally signed, a digital signature is a mathematical scheme used to verify the authenticity of a digital document or message. They are used when determining authenticity and avoiding tampering are important, such as in financial transactions.

Digital signatures are often used as a means to implement electronic signatures that are encrypted which allows for both authentication and non-repudiation (the signer cannot deny signing a document while claiming his/her private key has not been compromised).

FILE AND FOLDER PERMISSIONS

Most current file systems have methods of assigning permission or access rights to specific users and group of users.

Permission	Meaning for Folders	Meaning for Files
Read	Permits viewing and listing of files and subfolders	Permits viewing or accessing of the file's contents
Write	Permits adding of files and subfolders	Permits writing to a file
Read & Execute	Permits viewing and listing of files and subfolders as well as executing of files; inherited by files and folders	Permits viewing and accessing of the file's contents as well as executing of the file
Modify	Permits reading and writing of files and subfolders; allows deletion of the folder	Permits reading and writing of the file; allows deletion of the file
Full Control	Permits reading, writing, changing, and deleting of files and subfolders	Permits reading, writing, changing and deleting of the file

SECURE SOCKET LAYER

The Secure Sockets Layer (SSL) is a computer networking protocol that manages server authentication, client authentication and encrypted communication between server and client.

TRANSPORT LAYER SECURITY

Transport Layer Security (TLS) is a protocol that ensures privacy between communicating applications and their users on the Internet.

IP SECURITY PROTOCOL

IPsec (Internet Protocol Security) is a framework for a set of protocols for security at the network or packet processing layer of network communication.

IP-sec is said to be especially useful for implementing virtual private networks and for remote user access through dial-up connection to private networks.

IP-security protocol provides two choices of security service:

(i) Authentication Header (AH), which essentially allows authentication of the sender of data.

(ii) Encapsulating Security Payload (ESP), which supports both authentication of the sender and encryption of data as well. Earlier security approaches have inserted security at the Application layer of the communications model.

A big advantage of IP-sec is that security arrangements can be handled without requiring changes to individual user computers. Cisco has been a leader in proposing IP-sec as a standard (or combination of standerds and technologies) and has included support for it in its network routers.

Past Exercise

1. Passwords enable users to– **[SBI Clerk, 2009]**
   (a) get into the system quickly
   (b) make efficient use of time
   (c) retain confidentiality of files
   (d) simplify file structures
   (e) None of these

2. A person who uses his or her expertise to gain access to other people's computers to get information illegally or do damage is a
   [IBPS PO, 2011]
   (a) hacker (b) analyst
   (c) instant messenger (d) programmer
   (e) spammer

3. __________ 'are attempts by individuals to obtain confidential information from you by falsifying their identity. **[IBPS PO, 2011]**
   (a) Phishing trips (b) Computer viruses
   (c) Spyware scams (d) Viruses
   (e) Phishing scams

4. Why is it unethical to share copyrighted files with your friends? **[IBPS PO, 2011]**
   (a) It is not unethical, because it is legal.
   (b) It is unethical because the files are being given for free.
   (c) Sharing copyrighted files without permission breaks copyright laws.
   (d) It is not unethical because the files are being given for free.
   (e) It is not unethical - anyone can access a computer

5. You can protect sensitive data from prying eyes using ________ **[IBPS Clerk, 2012]**
   (a) Encryption (b) Passwords
   (c) File locks (d) File permissions
   (e) None of these

6. If your computer keeps rebooting itself, then it is likely that ________ **[SBI Clerk, 2012]**
   (a) It has a virus
   (b) It does not have enough memory
   (c) There is no printer
   (d) There has been a power surge
   (e) It needs a CD-ROM

7. Why is it unethical to share copyrighted files with your friends? **[IBPS Clerk, 2014]**
   (a) It is not unethical, because it is legal.
   (b) It is unethical because the files are being given for free.
   (c) Sharing copyrighted files without permission breaks copyright laws.
   (d) It is not unethical because the files are being given for free.
   (e) It is not unethical – anyone can access a computer

8. Which of the following is a program that uses a variety of different approaches to identify and eliminate spam ? **[IBPS Clerk, 2014]**
   (a) Directory search
   (b) Anti-spam program
   (c) Web server
   (d) Web storefront creation package
   (e) Virus

9. A person who used his or her expertise to gain access to other people's computers to get information illegally or do damage is a ____.
   [IBPS Clerk, 2014]
   (a) hacker (b) analyst
   (c) instant messenger (d) programmer
   (e) spammer

10. ______ are attempts by individuals to obtain confidential information from you by falsifying their identity. **[IBPS Clerk, 2014]**
    (a) Phishing trips (b) Computer viruses
    (c) Spyware scams (d) Viruses
    (e) Phishing scams

11. Accessing an unsecured Wi-Fi network from your current location without authorization is called __________ **[SBI Clerk, 2014]**
    (a) Hacking
    (b) War Driving
    (c) Wi-Fi Piggybacking
    (d) All of the above
    (e) None of these

12. A collection of hardware and/or software intended to protect a computer or computer network from unauthorized access is called __________ **[SBI Clerk, 2014]**
    - (a) Malware
    - (b) Botnet
    - (c) Worm
    - (d) Motherboard
    - (e) Firewall

13. An unique digital code that can be attached to a file or an e-mail message to verify the identity of the sender and guarantee the file or message has not been changed since it was signed is known as __________ **[SBI Clerk, 2014]**
    - (a) Digital Certificate
    - (b) Hacking
    - (c) Pharming
    - (d) Error! Not a valid embedded object. Dot Con
    - (e) Digital Signature

14. All of the following are examples of real security and privacy risks EXCEPT: **[IBPS Clerk, 2015]**
    - (a) Viruses
    - (b) Hackers
    - (c) Spam
    - (d) Identity theft
    - (e) None of these

15. In IT, the technique of delaying outgoing acknowledgements temporarily is known as
    - (a) AR Acknowledgement **[SSC CGL, 2016]**
    - (b) AR request
    - (c) Piggybacking
    - (d) Piggyframing

16. The scrambling of code is known as:
    [IBPS Clerk Mains, 2016]
    - (a) Encryption
    - (b) Firewalling
    - (c) Scrambling
    - (d) Deception
    - (e) Permuting

17. An act of sending e-mails or creating web pages that are designed to collect an individual's online bank, credit card, or other login information?
    [IBPS Clerk Mains, 2016]
    - (a) Phishing
    - (b) Spam
    - (c) Hacking
    - (d) Cracking
    - (e) Malware

18. Which of the following is the type of software that has self-replicating software that causes damage to files and system?
    [IBPS Clerk Mains, 2016]
    - (a) Viruses
    - (b) Trojan horses
    - (c) Bots
    - (d) Worms
    - (e) Backdoors

19. The conversation of electronic data into another form is called- **[IBPS RRB, 2016]**
    - (a) Biometrics
    - (b) Encryption
    - (c) Compression
    - (d) Encapsulation
    - (e) None of these

20. It is the process in which control information is added to a data packet as it moves through the layers of a communication module is termed as __________ **[IBPS RRB, 2016]**
    - (a) Encapsulation
    - (b) Encryption
    - (c) Decryption
    - (d) Coding
    - (e) None of these

ANSWER KEY

1. (c)	5. (d)	9. (a)	13. (e)	17. (a)
2. (a)	6. (a)	10. (a)	14. (c)	18. (d)
3 (a)	7. (c)	11. (c)	15. (c)	19. (b)
4. (c)	8. (b)	12. (e)	16. (a)	20. (a)

Practice Exercise

1. Firewalls are used to protect against __________
   (a) Unauthorised Attacks
   (b) Virus Attacks
   (c) Data Driven Attacks
   (d) Fire Attacks
   (e) None of these

2. A program designed to destroy data on your computer which can travel to "infect" other computers is called a __________.
   (a) disease   (b) torpedo
   (c) hurricane   (d) virus
   (e) mouse

3. What is the most common way to get a virus in your computer's hard disk?
   (a) By installing games from their CDROMS
   (b) By uploading pictures from mobile phones to the computer
   (c) By opening emails
   (d) By sending emails
   (e) None of these

4. Hackers
   (a) all have the same motive
   (b) is another name for users
   (c) may legally break into computers as long as they do not do any damage
   (d) are people who are allergic to computers
   (e) break into other people's computers

5. A person who uses his or her expertise to gain access to other people's computers to get information illegally or do damage is a __________.
   (a) spammer   (b) hacker
   (c) instant messenger   (d) All of these
   (e) None of these

6. __________ are attempts by individuals to obtain confidential information from you by falsifying their identity.
   (a) Phishing scams
   (b) Computer viruses
   (c) Special function cards
   (d) Scanners
   (e) Keyboards

7. There are several primary categories of procedures. Which of the following is not a primary category of procedures?
   (a) Testing
   (b) Backup and recovery
   (c) Firewall development
   (d) Design
   (e) None of these

8. Physical security is concerned with protecting computer hardware from human tampering and natural disasters and __________ security is concerned with protecting software from unauthorised tampering or damage.
   (a) data   (b) cyber
   (c) Internet   (d) metaphysical
   (e) publicity

9. Unauthorised copying of software to be used for personal gain instead of personal backups is called
   (a) program thievery   (b) data snatching
   (c) software piracy   (d) program looting
   (e) data looting

10. Which of the following are the solutions to network security?
   (i) Encryption   (ii) Authentication
   (iii) Authorization   (iv) Non-repudiation
   (a) i, ii and iii only   (b) ii, iii and iv only
   (c) i, iii and iv only   (d) i, iii only
   (e) All i, ii, iii and iv

11. __________ are often delivered to a PC through an email attachment and are often designed to do harm.
   (a) Viruses   (b) Spam
   (c) Portals   (d) Email messages
   (e) None of these

12. Which one of the following would be considered as a way that a computer virus can enter a computer system?
   (a) Opening an application previously installed on the computer
   (b) Borrowed an illegal copy of software
   (c) Viewing a website without causing any additional transactions
   (d) Running antivirus programs
   (e) None of these

13. A _______ is anything that can cause harm.
    (a) vulnerability   (b) phishing
    (c) threat   (d) spoof
    (e) None of these

14. A _____ is a small program embeded inside of a GIF image.
    (a) web bug
    (b) cookie
    (c) spyware applications
    (d) spam
    (e) None of these above

15. A hacker contacts your phone or E-mails and attempts to acquire your password is called
    (a) spoofing   (b) phishing
    (c) spamming   (d) buging
    (e) Noen of these

16. The phrase _____ describes viruses, worms, trojan horse attack applets and attack scripts.
    (a) malware   (b) spam
    (c) phishing   (d) virus
    (e) None of these

17. Hackers often gain entry to a network be pretending to be at a legitimate computer
    (a) spoofing   (b) forging
    (c) IP spoofing   (d) None of these

18. The main reason to encrypt a file is to
    (a) reduce its size
    (b) secure it for transmission
    (c) prepare it for backup
    (d) include it in the start-up sequence
    (e) None of the above

19. Which one of the following is a cryptographic protocol used to secure http connection ?
    (a) Stream Control Transmission Protocol (SCTP)
    (b) Transport Layer Security (TLS)
    (c) Explicit Congestion Notification (FCN)
    (d) Resource Reservation Protocol (RRP)
    (e) None of the above

20. _____ is a form of virus explicitly designed to hide itself from detection by anti-virus software.
    (a) Stealth   (b) Polymorphic virus
    (c) Parasitic virus   (d) Macro virus
    (e) None of these

21. The first PC virus was developed in
    (a) 1980   (b) 1984
    (c) 1986   (d) 1988
    (e) 1987

22. Abuse messaging systems to send unsolicited is
    (a) phishing   (b) spam
    (c) malware   (d) firewall
    (e) adware

23. _____ are often delivered to PC through an E-mail attachment and are often designed to do harm.
    (a) Viruses   (b) Spam
    (c) Portals   (d) Email messages
    (e) None of these

24. Which one of the following is a key function of firewall?
    (a) Monitoring   (b) Deleting
    (c) Copying   (d) Moving
    (e) None of these

25. The first computer virus is
    (a) creeper   (b) PARAM
    (c) the famous   (d) HARLIE
    (e) Brain

26. A time bomb occurs during a particular
    (a) data or time   (b) logic and data
    (c) only time   (c) All of the above
    (e) None of these

27. First boot sector virus is
    (a) computed   (b) mind
    (c) brian   (d) Elk Cloner
    (e) None of these

28. Which virus spreads in application software?
    (a) Macro virus   (b) Boot virus
    (c) File virus   (d) Anti- virus
    (e) None of the above

29. Some viruses have delayed payload, which is sometimes called a
    (a) time   (b) anti-virus
    (c) bomb   (d) All of these
    (e) None of these

30. An anti-virus is a
    (a) program code
    (b) computer
    (c) company name
    (d) application software
    (e) None of these

31. 'Trend Micro' is a
    (a) virus program
    (b) anti-virus software
    (c) just a program
    (d) All of these
    (e) None of the above

32. It is a self-replicating program that infects computer and spreads by inserting copies of itself into other executable code or documents.
    (a) Keylogger   (b) Worm
    (c) Virus   (d) Cracker
    (e) None of the above

33. Like a virus, it is a self-replicating program. It also propagates through computer network.
    (a) Spyware   (b) Worm Cracker
    (c) Cracker   (d) phishing scam
    (e) None of these

34. Passwords enables user to
    (a) get into the system quickly
    (b) make efficient use of time
    (c) retain confidentiality of files
    (d) simplify file structure
    (e) None of thee above

35. A program designed to destroy data on your compute which can travel to infect other computers, is called is
    (a) disease   (b) tarpedo
    (c) hurricane   (d) virus
    (e) None of these

ANSWER KEY

1.	(a)	7.	(c)	13.	(c)	19.	(b)	25.	(e)	31.	(b)
2.	(d)	8.	(a)	14.	(a)	20.	(a)	26.	(c)	32.	(c)
3.	(c)	9.	(c)	15.	(b)	21.	(c)	27.	(c)	33.	(b)
4.	(e)	10.	(e)	16.	(a)	22.	(b)	28.	(a)	34.	(c)
5.	(b)	11.	(a)	17.	(c)	23.	(a)	29.	(c)	35.	(d)
6.	(a)	12.	(b)	18.	(b)	24.	(a)	30.	(d)		

Abbreviations

Chapter

Computer terminologies and abbreviations are frequently asked in Bank PO/clerk and other exams. Here is an extensive list of short-forms or abbreviations related to computers and information technology:

ACE : Access Control Entry

ADSL : Asymmetric Digital Subscriber Line

ADC : Analog To Digital Converter

AI : Artificial Intelligence

ALGOL : Algorithmic Language

ALU : Arithmetic Logic Unit

ANSI : American National Standards Institute

API : Application Program Interface

ARP : Address Resolution Protocol

ARPANET : Advanced Research Projects Agency Network

ASCII : American Standard Code For Information Interchange

ATM : Asynchronous Transfer Mode

AUI : Attachment Unit Interface

AVI : Audio Video Interleave

BASIC : Beginner`s All Purpose Symbolic Instruction Code

BCD : Binary Coded Decimal

BHTML : Broadcast Hyper Text Markup Language

BIOS : Basic Input Output System

BIU : Bus Interface Unit

BMP : Bitmap

BPS : Bytes Per Seconds

CAD : Computer Aided Design

CADD : Computer Added Drafting And Design

CAI : Computer Aided Instructuion

CAM : Computer Aided Manufacturing

CASE : Computer Aided Software Engineering

CCNA : Cisco Certified Network Associate

CD : Compact Disc

CD RW : Compact Disc ReWritable

CDMA : Code Division Multiple Access

CDROM : Compact Disc Read Only Memory

CGI : Common Gateway Interface

CISC : Complex Instruction Set Computer

CLR : Common Language Runtime

CMOS : Complementary Metal Oxide Semiconductor

COBOL : Common Business Oriented Language

CPI : Clock Cycle Per Instruction

CPU : Central Processing Unit

CRM : Customer Relationship Management

CRT : Cathode Ray Tube

CUI : Character User Interface

DAC : Digital To Analog Converter

DBA : Data Base Administrator

DBMS : Data Base Management System

DCL : Data Control Language

DDL : Data Definition Language

DHCP : Dynamic Host Control Protocol

DHTML : Dynamics Hyper Text Markup Language

DLC : Data Link Control

DLL : Dynamic Link Library

DMA : Direct Memory Access

DML : Data Manipulation Language

DNA : Distributed Internet Architecture

DNS : Domain Name System (Server)

DOM : Document Object Model

DOS : Disk Operating System, Denial Of Service

DRAM : Dynamic Random Access Memory

DSL : Digital Subscriber Line

DSN : Digital Subscriber Network

DTD : Document Type Definition

DVD : Digital Versatile Disc

EAROM : Electrically Alterable Read Only Memory

EBCDIC: Extended Binary Coded Decimal Interchange Code

EDC : Electronic Digital Computer

EDCDIC : Extended Binary Coded Decimal Interchange Code

EEPROM : Electrically Erasable Programmable Read Only Memory

ENIAC : Electronics Numerical Integrator And Calculator

EPROM : Erasable Programmable Read Only Memory

EROM : Erasable Read Only Memory

ERP : Enterprise Resource Planning

EULA : End User License Agreement

FAT : File Allocation Table

FDD : Floppy Disk Drive

FDMA : Frequency Division Multiple Access

FIFO : First In First Out

FORTRAN : Formula Translation

FPS : Frames Per Second

FRAM : Ferro Electric Random Access Memory

FTP : File Transfer Protocol

GB : Giga Bytes

GUI : Graphical User Interface

HDD : Hard Disk Drive

HP : Hewlett Packard

HTML : Hyper Text Markup Language

HTTP : Hyper Text Transfer Protocol

IO : Input Output

IBM : International Business Machines

IC : Integrated Circuit

ICMP : Internet Control Message Protocol

IE : Internet Explorer

IGMP : Internet Group Management Protocol

IP : Internet Protocol

IRC : Internet Relay Chat

IRQ : Interrupt Request

ISDN : Integrated Services Digital Network

ISO : International Standard Organization

ISP : Internet Service Provider

ISR : Interrupt Service Routine

IT : Information Technology

JPEG : Joint Photographic Experts Group

KB : Kilo Bytes

Kb : Kito Bit

KBPS : Kilo Bytes Per Second

L2TP : Layer Two Tunneling Protocol

LAN : Local Area Network

LCD : Liquid Crystal Display

LIFO : Last In First Out

LIPS : Logical Interfaces Per Second

LOC : Lines Of Code

LSI : Large Scale Integration

MAC : Media Access Control

MAN : Metropolitan Area Network

MB : Mega Bytes

MBPS : Mega Bytes Per Second

MCS : Multicast Server

MDI : Multiple Document Interface

MDS : Microcomputer Development System

MFT : Master File Table

MG : Mega Bytes

MICR : MagneticNInk Characters Reader

MIME : Multipurpose Internet Mail Extensions

MIPS : Millions Of Instructions Per Second

MISD : Multiple Instruction Single Data

MODEM : Modulator And Demodulator

MP3 : Motion Pictures Experts Group Layer 3

MPEG : Motion Pictures Experts Group

MS : Microsoft

MSDN : Microsoft Developer Network

MSN : Microsoft Network

MTU : Maximum Transmission Unit

NAS **:** Network Attached Storage

NASSCOM : National Association Of Software & Service Companies

NCP : Network Control Protocol

NDIS : Network Driver Interface Specification

NTFS : New Technology File System

NTP : Network Time Protocol

OCR **:** Optical Character Readers

OLE : Object Linking And Embedding

OMR : Optical Mark Reader

OOP : Object Oriented Programming

OOPS : Object Oriented Programming System

OS : Operating System

OSI : Open System Interconnection

PC **:** Personal Computer

PCI : Peripheral Component Interconnect

PCMCIA : Personal Computer Memory Card International Association

PDA : Personal Digital Assistant

PDF : Portable Document Format

PDL : Page Description Language

PDU : Protocol Data Unit

PIC : Programming Interrupt Control

PLA : Programmable Logic Array

PLC : Programmable Logic Controller

PNG : Portable Network Graphics

PNP : Plug And Play

PPP : Peer To Peer Protocol

PPTP : Point To Point Tunneling Protocol

PROM : Programmable Read Only Memory

QDR **:** Quad Data Rate

QEP : Quoted for performance

QDS : Quality of service

RADSL **:** Rate Adaptive Digital Subscribes Line

RAID : Redundant Array Of Independent Disks

RAM : Random Access Memory

RAMDAC : Random Access Memory Digital To Analog Converter

RAS : Remote Access Network

RD RAM : Rambus Dynamic Random Access Memory

RDBMS : Relational Data Base Management System

RICS : Reduced Instruction Set Computer

RIP : Raster Image Processor

RISC : Reduced Instruction Set Computer

ROM : Read Only Memory

RPC : Remote Procedure Call

RTC : Real Time Clock

RTF : Rich Text Format

RTOS : Real Time Operating System

SACK **:** Selective Acknowledgements

SAP : Service Access Point, Systems Applications Products

SD RAM : Synchronous Dynamic Random Access Memory

SDD : Software Design Description

SDK : Software Development Kit

SDL : Storage Definition Language

SDN : Integrated Service Digital Network

SDRAM : Static Dynamic Random Access Memory

SDSL : Symmetric Digital Subscribes Line

SG RAM : Synchronous Graphics Random Access Memory

SGML : Standard Generalized Markup Language

SIM : Subscriber Identification Module

SIU : Serial Interface Unit

SMS : Short Message Service

SMTP : Simple Mail Transfer Protocol

SNMP : Simple Network Management Protocol

SQA : Statistical Quality Assurance

SQL : Structured Query Language

SRAM : Static Random Access Memory

SRS : Software Requirements Specification

STP : Shielded Twisted Pair

SW : Software

TB : Tera Bytes

TCP : Transmission Control Protocol

TCPIP : Transmission Control Protocol Internet Protocol

TDI : Transport Data Interface

TDMA : Time Division Multiple Access

UDD : User Datagram Protocol

UDP : User Datagram Protocol

UI : User Interface

UML : Unified Modelling Language

UNIX : Uniplexed Information And Computer Systems

URL : Universal Resource Locator

USB : Universal Serial Bus

USRT : Universal Synchronous Receiver Transmitted

UTP : Unshielded Twisted Pair

VAN : Virtual Area Network

VB : Visual Basic

VCD : Video Compact Disc

VGA : Video Graphics Array

VLSI : Very Large Scale Integrated Circuits

VPN : Virtual Private Network

VRAM : Video Random Access Memory

VS : Visual Studio

WAN : Wide Area Network

WAP : Wireless Application Protocol

WINDOWS ME : Windows Millennium Edition

WINDOWS NT : Windows New Technology

WINDOWS XP : Windows Experienced

WORM : Write Once Read Many

WWW : World Wide Web

WYSIWYG : What You See Is What You Get

XHTML : Extensible Hyper Text Markup Language

XML : Extensible Markup Language

XSL : Extensible Style Sheet Language

ZIP : Zone Information Protocol

ZB : Zeta Byte

ZISC : Zone Instruction Set Computer

Past Exercise

1. IT stands for **[SBI Clerk, 2009]**
   - (a) Information Technology
   - (b) Integrated Technology
   - (c) Intelligent Technology
   - (d) Interesting Technology
   - (e) None of these

2. ASCII stands for **[IBPS Clerk, 2011]**
   - (a) American Special Computer for Information Interaction
   - (b) American Standard Computer for Information Interchange
   - (c) American Special Code for Information Interchange
   - (d) American Special Computer for Information Interchange
   - (e) American Standard Code for Information Interchange

3. ____________ is a form of denial of service attack in which a hostile client repeatedly sends SYN packets to every port on the server using fake IP addresses. **[IBPS PO, 2012]**
   - (a) Cyborgaming crime
   - (b) Memory shaving
   - (c) Syn flooding
   - (d) Software piracy
   - (e) None of these

4. What is a URL? **[IBPS PO, 2012]**
   - (a) a computer software program
   - (b) a type of programming object
   - (c) the address of a document or "page" on the World Wide Web
   - (d) an acronym for Unlimited Resources for Learning
   - (e) a piece of hardware

5. What does RAM stand for ? **[SBI Clerk, 2012]**
   - (a) Read Access Memory
   - (b) Read Anywhere Memory
   - (c) Random Anything Memory
   - (d) Random Access Module
   - (e) Random Access Memory

6. VIRUS stands for **[IBPS PO, 2013]**
   - (a) Very Important Record User Searched
   - (b) Verify Interchanged Result Until Source
   - (c) Vital Information Resource Under Siege
   - (d) Very Important Resource Under Search
   - (e) None of the above

7. 'C' in CPU denotes ______________.
   [SBI PO, 2013]
   - (a) Central
   - (b) Common
   - (c) Convenient
   - (d) Computer
   - (e) Circuitry

ANSWER KEY

1.	(a)	2.	(e)	3.	(a)	4.	(c)	5.	(e)	6.	(c)	7.	(a)

Practice Exercise

1. 'WWW' stands for __________.
   - (a) World Word Web
   - (b) World Wide Web
   - (c) World White Web
   - (d) World Work Web
   - (e) None of these

2. What is the full form of USB as used in computer related activities?
   - (a) Universal Security Block
   - (b) Ultra Serial Block
   - (c) United Service Block
   - (d) Universal Serial Bus
   - (e) None of these

3. What does 'C' represent in MICR?
   - (a) Code
   - (b) Column
   - (c) Computer
   - (d) Character
   - (e) None of these

4. ALGOL means –
   - (a) Advance logarithmic language
   - (b) Algorithmic language
   - (c) Algorithmic output language
   - (d) Algorithmic operation language
   - (e) None of these

5. PDA–
   - (a) People's Data Assistant
   - (b) Personal Data Assistant
   - (c) People's Digital Assistant
   - (d) Personal Digital Assistant
   - (e) None of these

6. What is the full form of KB related to computer?
   - (a) Key Block
   - (b) Kernel Boot
   - (c) Kilo Byte
   - (d) Kit Bit
   - (e) None of these

7. CPU stands for __________.
   - (a) CD-run on memory
   - (b) central processing unit
   - (c) call powers up
   - (d) create programs user
   - (e) None of these

8. CD-ROM stands for __________.
   - (a) central processing unit
   - (b) CD-remote open mouse
   - (c) CD-resize or minimize
   - (d) CD-read only memory
   - (e) None of these

9. __________ are often delivered to a PC through an email attachment and are often designed to do harm.
   - (a) Viruses
   - (b) Spam
   - (c) Portals
   - (d) Email messages
   - (e) None of these

10. BIT stands for
    - (a) Megabyte
    - (b) Binary language
    - (c) Binary Information Unit
    - (d) Binary Number
    - (e) Binary Digit

11. ISP –
    - (a) Internet Servant Provider
    - (b) Internet Service Provider
    - (c) Internet Service Protection
    - (d) Internal Server Provider
    - (e) None of these

12. WIMP –
    - (a) Window Icon Menu Pointer
    - (b) Window Icon Mouse Pointer
    - (c) Window Icon Menu Pull down menu
    - (d) Window Icon Menu Pen

13. OCR stands for __________
    - (a) Optical Character Recognition
    - (b) Optical CPU Recognition
    - (c) Optical Character Reader
    - (d) Other Character Restoration
    - (e) None of these

14. What does VGA stand for?
    - (a) Video Graphics Adapter
    - (b) Video Graphics Array
    - (c) Video Game Awards
    - (d) Video Graphics Accelerator
    - (e) Video Girl Ai

15. ERP is an acronym for
    (a)   Enterprise Retirement Planning
    (b)   Enterprise Relationship Planning
    (c)   Enterprise Resource Planning
    (d)   Enterprise Recorder Planning
    (e)   Enterprise Retention Planning
16. What is the full form of CRT?
    (a)   Crystal Ray Tube
    (b)   Cathode Ray Tube
    (c)   Cabin Ray Tube
    (d)   Carbon Ray Tube
    (e)   None of these
17. LAN stands for ___________.
    (a)   Local Access Network
    (b)   Local Area Network
    (c)   Logical Access Network
    (d)   Logical Area Network
    (e)   None of the above

18. RAM stands for ___________.
    (a)   Random Access Memory
    (b)   Ready Application Module
    (c)   Read Access Memory
    (d)   Remote Access Machine
    (e)   None of these
19. What is the full form of LSI?
    (a)   Low Scale Internet
    (b)   Large Scale Internet
    (c)   Low Scale Integration
    (d)   Large Scale integration
    (e)   Local Scale Integration
20. EPROM stands for
    (a)   Erasable Programmable Read-Only Memory
    (b)   Electronic Programmable Read-Only Memory
    (c)   Enterprise Programmable Read-Only Memory
    (d)   Extended Programmable Read-Only Memory
    (e)   Electrical Programmable Read-Only Memory

ANSWER KEY

1.	(b)	5.	(d)	9.	(a)	13.	(c)	17.	(b)
2.	(d)	6.	(c)	10.	(e)	14.	(b)	18.	(a)
3.	(d)	7.	(b)	11.	(b)	15.	(c)	19.	(d)
4.	(b)	8.	(d)	12.	(a)	16.	(b)	20.	(a)

Glossary

A

Access Time : Access time is the time from the start of one access of the storage device to the time when the next access can be started.

Accessory : An Accessory is a device attached to a host computer, but not part of it, and is more or less dependent on the host. It expands the host's capabilities, but does not form part of the core computer architecture.

Examples are computer printers, image scanners, tape drives, microphones, loudspeakers, webcams, and digital cameras.

Active Cell : The cell that continues the value being used or modified in a spreadsheet program, and that is highlighted by the cell pointer. Also known as current cell.

Active Window : The window in Micrddosoft Windows with which the user may interact.

Accumulator : The computer register in which the result of an arithmetic or logic operation is formed (related to arithmetic and logic unit).

Analog Computer : A computer in which numerical data are represented by measurable physical variables, such as electrical.

Antivirus : Computer antivirus refers to a software program that can protect your computer from unwanted viruses and remove any that penetrate your computer's defenses.

Artificial Intelligence : Artificial intelligence (AI) is the intelligence of machines and the branch of computer science that aims to create it. AI textbooks define the field as "the study and design of intelligent agents" where an intelligent agent is a system that perceives its environment and takes actions that maximize its chances of success.

ASCII (American Standard Code for Information Interchange) : ASCII, a code for information exchange between computers made by different companies; a string of 7 binary digits represents each character; used in most microcomputers

Abstraction : The separation of the logical properties of data or function from its implementation in a computer program.

Address : A number, character, or group of characters which identifies a given device or a storage location which may contain a piece of data or a program step.

To refer to a device or storage location by an identifying number, character, or group of characters.

Algorithm : A finite set of well-defined rules for the solution of a problem in a finite number of steps.

Any sequence of operations for performing a specific task.

Alphanumeric : Pertaining to a character set that contains letters, digits, and usually other characters such as punctuation marks.

Analog : Pertaining to data signals in the form of continuously variable wave form physical quantities; e.g., pressure, resistance, rotation, temperature, voltage. Contrast with digital.

Analog device : A device that operates with variables represented by continuously measured quantities such as pressures, resistances, rotations, temperatures, and voltages.

Analog-to-digital converter : Input related devices which translate an input device's sensor analog signals to the corresponding digital signals needed by the computer

Android : It is linux based operating system designed primarily for touch screen mobile devices such as smartphones and tablets computers.

Application software : Software designed to fill specific needs of a user; for example, software for navigation, payroll, or process control. Contrast with support software; system software.

Architecture : The organizational structure of a system or component.

Asynchronous : Occurring without a regular time relationship, i.e., timing independent.

Attribute : The characterstics of an entity is called attributes.

Auxiliary storage : Storage device other than main memory (RAM); e.g., disks and tapes.

Backup : A backup or the process of backing up means making copies of data which may be used to restore the original data after a data loss event.

Bar Code : A bar code (often seen as a single word, barcode) is the small image of lines (bars) and spaces that is affixed to retail store items, identification cards, and postal mail to identify a particular product number, person, or location.

Biometric Device : Biometrics (biometric authentication) consists of methods for uniquely recognizing humans based upon one or more intrinsic physical or behavioral traits.

Bitmap : In computer graphics, a bitmap or pixmap is a type of memory organization or image file format used to store digital images.

Bluetooth : Bluetooth is a proprietary open wireless technology standard for exchanging data over short distances (using short wavelength radio transmissions in the ISM band from 2400-2480 MHz) between fixed and mobile devices, creating personal area networks (PANs) with high levels of security.

Booting : To boot (as a verb; also "to boot up") a computer is to load an operating system into the computer's main memory or random access memory (RAM).

Browse : In database systems, browse means to view data. Many database systems support a special browse mode , in which you can flip through fields and records quickly. Usually, you cannot modify data while you are in browse mode.

Band : Range of frequencies used for transmitting a signal. A band can be identified by the difference between its lower and upper limits, i.e. bandwidth, as well as by its actual lower and upper limits; e.g., a 10 MHz band in the 100 to 110 MHz range.

Bandwidth : The transmission capacity of a computer channel, communications line or bus. It is expressed in cycles per second (Hz), and also is often stated in bits or bytes per second.

Baud : The signalling rate of a line. It's the switching speed, or number of transitions voltage or frequency change made per second.

Bias. A measure of how closely the mean value in a series of replicate measurements approaches the true value.

Binary : The base two number system. Permissible digits are "0" and "1".

Bit. A contraction of the term binary digit. The bit is the basic unit of digital data. It may be in one of two states, logic 1 or logic 0. It may be thought of as a switch which is either on or off. Bits are usually combined into computer words of various sizes, such as the byte.

Bits per second : A measure of the speed of data transfer in a communications system.

Boolean : Boolean algebra is the study of operations carried out on variables that can have only one of two possible values; i.e., 1 (true) and 0 (false).

Bootstrap. A short computer program that is permanently resident or easily loaded into a computer and whose execution brings a larger program, such an operating system or its loader, into memory.

Branch . An instruction which causes program execution to jump to a new point in the program sequence, rather than execute the next instruction.

Buffer : A device or storage area [memory] used to store data temporarily to compensate for differences in rates of data flow, time of occurrence of events, or amounts of data that can be handled by the devices or processes involved in the transfer or use of the data.

Bug : A fault in a program which causes the program to perform in an unintended or unanticipated manner.

Bus : A common pathway along which data and control signals travel between different hardware devices within a computer system.

Byte : A sequence of adjacent bits, usually eight, operated on as a unit.

Blog : It is a discussion or informational site published on the world wide web.

Compressed File : Computer files that have been reduced in size by a compression program. Such programs are available for all computer systems.

Code division Multiple Access (CDMA) : It is a channel access Method used by various radio communication technologies CDMA employs spread spectrum technology and a special coding scheme, where each transmitter is assigned a code to allow multiple users to be multiplied over the same physical channel.

Clock : A device that generates periodic, accurately spaced signals used for such purposes as timing, regulation of the operations of a processor, or generation of interrupts.

Coding : In software engineering, the process of expressing a computer program in a programming language..

Compatibility : The capability of a functional unit to meet the requirements of a specified interface.

Complementary metal-oxide semiconductor : A type of integrated circuit widely used for processors and memories. It is a combination of transistors on a single chip connected to complementary digital circuits.

Complexity : The degree to which a system or component has a design or implementation that is difficult to understand and verify.

Constant : A value that does not change during processing. Contrast with variable.

Cookie. A packet of information that travels between a browser and web server.

Control bus : A bus carrying the signals that regulate system operations.

Crash : The sudden and complete failure of a computer system or component.

Criticality : The degree of impact that a requirement, module, error, fault, failure, or other item has on the development or operation of a system.

Cursor : A movable, visible mark used to indicate a position of interest on a display surface.

CD ROM (Compact Disk- Read Only Memory) : a type of optical disk capable of storing large amounts of data -- up to 1GB, although the most common size is 700 MB (megabytes).

CD-R (Compact Disk-Recordable) : a type of CD disk that enables you to write onto it in multiple sessions.

Central Processing Unit (CPU) : The CPU is the computer's control center. Think of it as the brain that does all the thinking (computation); thus it is called the Central Processing Unit. The actual CPU is about 4 cm square, yet it is the most critical part of the computer. Having a fast CPU (speed measured in MegaHertz or Gigahertz) greatly aids in the overall speed of your computer.

CMOS : Acronym for "Complimentary Metal Oxide Semiconductor". A CMOS computer ciruit consumes very little power and is used in computers to keep track of the system setup information, data, time, type of disk and hard drives, etc, that a computer has installed.

Data : Representations of facts. The raw material of information. (Plural of datu m.)

Database : The integrated data resource for a computer-based information system.

DDR : This is a new type of RAM called Double Data Rate RAM. It is used in some of video cards such as the Nvidia GeForce cards.

Digital : Term used to describe any information that has been translated into a corresponding series of 1s and 0s; any information text, sound, image, color etc. may be digitized.

Digital Computer : A reference to any system based on discrete data, such as the binary nature of computers.

Digital Video/ Versatile Disk (DVD) : The successor technology to the CD-ROM, that can store up to 10 gigabytes or more.

Data bus : A bus used to communicate data internally and externally to and from a processing unit or a storage device.

Default : Pertaining to an attribute, value, or option that is assumed when none is explicitly specified.

Default value : A standard setting or state to be taken by the program if no alternate setting or state is initiated by the system or the user. A value assigned automatically if one is not given by the user.

Demodulation : Converting signals from a wave form analog to pulse form digital. Contrast with modulation.

Design : The process of defining the architecture, components, interfaces, and other characteristics of a system or component.

Developer : A person, or group, that designs and/or builds and/or documents and/or configures the hardware and/or software of computerized systems.

Digital-to-analog converter : Output related devices which translate a computer's digital outputs to the corresponding analog signals needed by an output device such as an actuator.

Direct memory access : Specialized circuitry or a dedicated microprocessor that transfers data from memory to memory without using the CPU.

Disk : Circular rotating magnetic storage hardware. Disks can be hard, flexible, removable and different sizes.

Disk drive : Hardware used to read from or write to a disk or diskette.

Documentation : The aids provided for the understanding of the structure and intended uses of an information system or its components, such as flowcharts, textual material, and user manuals.

Driver : A program that links a peripheral device or internal function to the operating system, and providing for activation of all device functions.

Downloading : Retrieving a file or group of files from the Internet so that they can be stored on a local hard drive. By accessing a page, you have, in fact, downloaded all the information on the page so that it can be viewed and interpreted by your web browser.

Desktop: The screen in Windows upon which icons, windows, a background, and so on are displayed.

Desk Top Publishing (DTP): Software that allows users to produce near-typeset-quality copy for newsletters, advertisements, and many other printing needs, all from the confines of a microcomputer.

Dial up: A dial-up Internet account allows you to use a computer with a modem and appropriate software to connect to the Internet through an Internet Service Provider (ISP). The software "dials" the ISP's access numbers and you can then send e-mail, browse the World Wide Web or engage in other Internet activities.

Disk Operating System (DOS): A disk operating system manages disks and other system resources. It is a subset of OSes, sort of an archaic term for the same. MS-DOS is the most popular program currently calling itself a DOS. CP/M was the most popular prior to MS-DOS.

Domain Names: A name given to a host computer on the Internet; E-mail domain names are good examples of domain names (for example in bijendra@kbscontent.com, the domain name is 'kbscontent.com').

E

Ethernet :A transport method (protocol) used to connect computers to a LAN (Local Area Network) and exchange data.

Embedded computer : A device which has its own computing power dedicated to specific functions, usually consisting of a microprocessor and firmware.

Error : A discrepancy between a computed, observed, or measured value or condition and the true, specified, or theoretically correct value or condition.

Exception : An event that causes suspension of normal program operation.

End user. Any individual who uses the information generated by a computer based system.

Electronic Mail: When a message is sent, the message is sent first to the SMTP server, which acts as an "outbox" for users. The message is then relayed to the appropriate mail server, which can be found listed after the @ symbol in the recipient's E-mail address. The message then waits on that server until the recipient accesses the message.

F

File : (1) A collection of related records. (2) A named area on a disk-storage device that contains a program or digitized information (text, image, sound, and so on). (3) A component of an overall program or application.

Font : In a simplistic sense, a font can be thought of as the physical description of a character set. While the character set will define what sets of bits map to what letters, numbers, and other symbols, the font will define what each letter, number, and other symbol looks like.

Format : (1) Noun : The logical or physical arrangement of the tracks and sectors on a floppy diskette or a hard disk. To be usable, a disk must be formatted so that the tracks and sectors are laid out in a manner compatible with the operating system in use.

(2) Verb : To prepare a disk or diskette, dividing it into sectors so that it is ready to receive data.

Fax. It stands for faccismile machine. It is used to transmit a copy of a document electronically.

Failure : The inability of a system or component to perform its required functions within specified performance requirements.

Fault : An incorrect step, process, or data definition in a computer program which causes the program to perform in an unintended or unanticipated manner.

Fiber optics : Communications systems that use optical fibers for transmission.

Firmware : The combination of a hardware device; e.g., an IC; and computer instructions and data that reside as read only software on that device. Such software cannot be modified by the computer during processing.

Flag : A variable that is set to a prescribed state, often «true» or «false», based on the results of a process or the occurrence of a specified condition.

G

Gopher : A program that searches for file names and resources on the Internet and presents hierarchical menus to the user. As users select options, they are moved to different Gopher servers on the Internet. Where links have been established, Usenet news and other information can be read directly from Gopher. There are more than 7,000 Gopher servers on the Internet.

Gigahertz : One gigahertz is equivalent to 1000 megahertz, or 1,000,000,000 hertz.

H

Hacker : An individual with vast experience with security protocols who attempts to illegally access secure servers in an attempt to download private information, damage systems, or act in some other way to "free information".

Hard Copy : A readable printed copy of computer output.

Hard Disk : Hard disk (internal) is a permanent file and data storage device housed in a computer case.

Home Page : The Web page which is the starting point for accessing information at a site or in a particular area.

Host : A computer, attached to a network which provides services to another computer beyond simply storing and forwarding information.

Handshake : An interlocked sequence of signals between connected components in which each component waits for the acknowledgement of its previous signal before proceeding with its action, such as data transfer.

Hazard : A condition that is prerequisite to a mishap.

Hertz : A unit of frequency equal to one cycle per second.

Hexadecimal : The base 16 number system. Digits are 0, 1, 2, 3, 4, 5, 6, 7, 8, 9, A, B, C, D, E, & F. This is a convenient form in which to examine binary data because it collects 4 binary digits per hexadecimal digit; e.g., decimal 15 is 1111 in binary and F in hexadecimal.

Hardware: Collective term for any computer-related object that can be touched physically.

Hyper Text Markup Language: This is the code by which web pages are created so they can be graphically organized in various ways. The web browser downloads the text of the HTML file, and then decodes the text into what you can see here. Many books and online manuals are available to anyone wishing to learn this code.

Acronyms for «Hyper Text Mark-up Llanguage» which is used to format information so that it can be structured and made accessible to the World Wide Web.

HTTP: Acronym for «Hypertext Transfer Protocol» The protocol that forms the basis of World Wide Web technology. HTTP is the set of rules governing the software that transports hyperlinked files along the Internet.

I

Information Technology (IT) : including ICT (Information and Communication Technology) is the application of appropriate (enabling) technologes to information processing.

Input/output (I/O) : A generic reference to input and/or output to a computer.

IP : Acronym for "Internet Protocol". The standard protocol used by systems communicating across the Internet.

Inkjet Printer : A non-impact printer in which the print head contains independently controlled injection chambers that squirt ink droplets on the paper to form letters and images.

Integrated Services Digital Network (ISDN) : A digital telecommunications standard for data delivery over twisted-pair lines with transmission speeds up to 128 Kbps (two 64 Kbps line pairs).

InterFace : (1) A specific hardware or software connection. (2) Making two devices capable of communication. Used most often to refer to the design of hardware and software that allows connection of network components and transfer of information.

Internet : Internet is the largest wide area network in the world which links millions of computers. Through internet information can be shared, business can be conducted and research can be done.

IP Address (Internet Protocol Address) : A unique numerical Internet address identifying any piece of equipment hooked up to the Internet.

Intranet : An Internet-like network whose scope is restricted to the networks within a particular organization.

Installation. The phase in the system life cycle that includes assembly and testing of the hardware and software of a computerized system. Installation includes installing a new computer system, new software or hardware, or otherwise modifying the current system.

Instruction : A program statement that causes a computer to perform a particular operation or set of operations.

Instruction set : The complete set of instructions recognized by a given computer or provided by a given programming language.

Instruction cycle

Interrupt : The suspension of a process to handle an event external to the process.

Java : Java is a programming language and has a "sandboxed" code interpreter which permits programs to be downloaded to PC's from the Web, but isolates these applications from access to other applications running on the PC.

JPEG (Joint Photographic Experts Group) : A bit-mapped file format that compresses image size.

Jukebox : A storage device for multiple sets of CD-ROMs, tape cartridges, or disk modules enabling ready access to vast amounts of online data.

Job. A user-defined unit of work that is to be accomplished by a computer. For example, the compilation, loading, and execution of a computer program.

Kernel : It is a fundamental part pf program, such as an operating system, that resides in a memory at all times.

Keyboard : is one of computer components which used to input data to a computer. It is called an input device.

Laptop : Laptop is a small and lightweight computer in which all the main parts are fitted into single unit. It is designed to be carried around. Particularly, it is ideal for travellers, journalists, commentators and professionals who want to work both at the office and home.

LCD : Acronym for "Liquid Crystal Display". It is the technology used for displays in notebooks and monitors for computers.

Linux : An open source spinoff of the UNIX operating system that runs on a number of hardware platforms and is made available for free over the Internet.

Log on & Log off : Each server that is accessed must have some way to ensure security of their sensitive information. Thus, servers restrict access by forcing users to "log on" with either personal access codes or anonymously. Anonymous access usually requires the individual's e-mail address, and the user's IP address is also logged. Once the desired information has been obtained, the user can "log off", disconnecting access to the server.

Large scale integration : A classification of ICs [chips] based on their size as expressed by the number of circuits or logic gates they contain. An LSI IC contains 3,000 to 100,000 transistors.

Latency : The time interval between the instant at which a CPU's instruction control unit initiates a call for data and the instant at which the actual transfer of the data starts.

Local Area Network (LAN) : Many multiple-computer homes have found ways to link their computers through a central device called a «hub». This way, each computer can share information directly, without the need to transfer data via a portable storage device, like a floppy disk. A properly set up LAN can also permit the connected computers to access the Internet through a single Internet account.

Monitor : The high-resolution TV-like device that displays your computer's output. Today's monitors have much better quality displays than any TV is capable of producing.

Motherboard : is the core of a computer system. It is the circuit board where all other parts connect. It communicates and controls the overall system. No motherboard means no computer system.

MP3 : this stands for "MPEG I Audio Layer- 3" and is a digital. compressed music file (their file names always end with an mp3 extension). MP3 files are often downloaded or exchanged between people online.

MPEG : Acronym for "Motion Picture Experts Group" A video file compression system which is used on the web.

Multimedia application : Computer applications that involve the integration of text, sound, graphics, motion video, and animation.

Multitasking : The concurrent execution of more than one program at a time.

Macro : In software engineering, a predefined sequence of computer instructions that is inserted into a program, usually during assembly or compilation, at each place that its corresponding macroinstruction appears in the program.

Mainframe : Term used to describe a large computer.

Mean time between failures[MTBF] : A measure of the reliability of a computer system, equal to average operating time of equipment between failures, as calculated on a statistical basis from the known failure rates of various components of the system.

Medium scale integration : A classification of ICs [chips] based on their size as expressed by the number of circuits or logic gates they contain. An MSI IC contains 100 to 3,000 transistors.

Megabit : Approximately one million bits. Precisely 1024 K bits, 220 bits, or 1,048,576 bits.

Megabyte : Approximately one million bytes. Precisely 1024 K Bytes, 220 bytes, or 1,048,576 bytes.

Megahertz : A unit of frequency equal to one million cycles per second.

Memory : Any device or recording medium into which binary data can be stored and held, and from which the entire original data can be retrieved. The two types of memory are main; e.g., ROM, RAM, and auxiliary; e.g., tape, disk. See: storage device.

Metal-oxide semiconductor : One of two major categories of chip design [the other is bipolar]. It derives its name from its use of metal, oxide and semiconductor layers. There are several varieties of MOS technologies including PMOS, NMOS, CMOS.

Microcomputer : A term used to describe a small computer.

Minicomputer : A term used to describe a medium sized computer.

Mnemonic : A symbol chosen to assist human memory and understanding.

Modem : A functional unit that modulates and demodulates signals. One of the functions of a modem is to enable digital data to be transmitted over analog transmission facilities. The term is a contraction of modulator-demodulator.

Modulation : Converting signals from a binary-digit pattern [pulse form] to a continuous wave form [analog]. Contrast with demodulation.

Multiplexer : A device which takes information from any of several sources and places it on a single line or sends it to a single destination.

Machine Language: Machine language consists of the raw numbers that can be directly understood by a particular processor. Each processor›s machine language will be different from other processors› machine language. Although called «machine language», it is not usually what people think of when talking about computer languages. Machine language dressed up with mnemonics to make it a bit more human-readable is called assembly language.

Microprocessor: A computer on a single chip. The central processing component of a microcomputer.

Mouse: A small, handheld device attached to a computer; includes one or more buttons that allow the user to select graphics or text onscreen.

Network Interface Card (NIC) : It is a computer hardware component that connects a computer to a computer Network. It provides a physical access to a networking medium.

Network : A system [transmission channels and supporting hardware and software] that connects several remotely located computers via telecommunications.

Nibble : Half a byte, or four bits.

Node : A junction or connection point in a network, e.g. a terminal or a computer.

Null : A value whose definition is to be supplied within the context of a specific operating system. This value is a representation of the set of no numbers or no value for the operating system in use.

Offline : Pertaining to data that is not accessible by, or hardware devices that are not connected to, a networked computer system.

Online (a) Noun : Pertaining to data and/or hardware devices accessible to and under the control of a networked computer system.

(b) Adverb : Connected. You are online if you are working on your computer while it is connected to another computer. Your printer is online if it is connected to your computer and ready to accept data.

Object code. A code expressed in machine language [«1»s and «0»s] which is normally an output of a given translation process that is ready to be executed by a computer.

Object program. A computer program that is the output of an assembler or compiler.

Octal. The base 8 number system. Digits are 0, 1, 2, 3, 4, 5, 6, & 7.

Optimization. Modifying a program to improve performance; e.g., to make it run faster or to make it use fewer resources.

Operating System or Platform : Operating systems create an environment in which a user and hardware interact to each other. These terms refer to the software that your computer uses to operate (otherwise known as your OS) and not to a manufacturer or company. Windows 2000, Windows XP, and OSX (Mac) are common platforms.

P

Password : Password is a series of characters used to protect resources in a computer from unauthorized access. It is one of the ways to secure computer information from unauthorized users.

Peripheral : A physical device (such as a printer, scanner, or disk subsystem) that is externally attached to a workstation or to the network.

Plugin : A helper application that works within a browser. It adds more functionality to a browser; commonly associated with the Netscape Navigator browser software.

Personal Computer : A small computer designed for use by an individual, a microcomputer.

Processor : The logical component of a computer system that interprets and executes program instructions.

Program:(1) Noun : Computer instructions structured and ordered in a manner that, when executed, causes a computer to perform a particular function.

(2) Verb : The act of producing computer software to perform some application.

Programming : The act of writing a computer program.

Programming language : A language programmers use to communicate instructions to a computer.

Parallel : Pertaining to the simultaneity of two or more processes.

Parity : An error detection method in data transmissions that consists of selectively adding a 1-bit to bit patterns (word, byte, character, message) to cause the bit patterns to have either an odd number of 1-bits [odd parity] or an even number of 1-bits (even parity).

Parity bit : A binary digit appended to a group of binary digits to make the sum of all the digits, including the appended binary digit, either odd or even, as predetermined.

Pixel : In computer graphics, the smallest element of a display surface that can be assigned independent characteristics.

Packet Switching : It refers to method of digital networking communication that combined all transmitted data regardless of content, type or structure into suitable sized blocks, known as packets. Each packet has header information about the scurce, destination, packet numbering etc.

Printed circuit board : A flat board that holds chips and other electronic components. The board is "printed" with electrically conductive pathways between the components.

Prototyping : Using software tools to accelerate the software development process by facilitating the identification of required functionality during analysis and design phases.

Pseudocode : A combination of programming language and natural language used to express a software design.

Q

Qwerty : It one of the standard computer keyboard, with the character Q,W,E,R,T and Y on the top row of letters.

Quality assurance : The planned systematic activities necessary to ensure that a component, module, or system conforms to established technical requirements.

Quality control : The operational techniques and procedures used to achieve quality requirements.

Query : A request for information from a database.

R

Recursion : The process of defining or generating a process or data structure in terms of itself.

Register : A small, high speed memory circuit within a microprocessor that holds addresses and values of internal operations; e.g., registers keep track of the address of the instruction being executed and the data being processed. Each microprocessor has a specific number of registers depending upon its design.

Reliability. The ability of a system or component to perform its required functions under stated conditions for a specified period of time.

Risk. A measure of the probability and severity of undesired effects. Often taken as the simple product of probability and consequence.

Robustness. The degree to which a software system or component can function correctly in the presence of invalid inputs or stressful environmental conditions.

RAM: Acronym is Random Access Memory. Random Access memory, the computers short term memory is used whenever an action is performed by a program. It is also called the active memory. RAM is what the computer uses to run all applications. RAM is usually specified in Megabytes or MB. (The other kind of memory dealers refer to is storage memory or hard drive size. it usually is specified in Gigabytes or GB).

ROM: Acronym is Read Only Memory, in which information is saved once and can never be altered For example. CD-ROM drives read information saved on compact disks (CD). A CD-ROM drive can read that information, but cannot make changes to it. For that you need a CD- RW drive. Some ROM is built into your computer to help it get started when you turn it on.

Routine. A subprogram that is called by other programs and subprograms. Note: This term is defined differently in various programming languages.

Routing. The process of choosing the best path throughout the LAN.

RS-232-C. An Electronic Industries Association (EIA) standard for connecting electronic equipment. Data is transmitted and received in serial format.

S

Scanner : A scanner is a piece of hardware that will examine a picture and produce a computer file that represents what it sees. A digital camera is a related device. Each has its own limitations.

Search Engine : A tool used which matches key words you enter with titles and description on the Internet. It then displays the matches allowing you to easily locate a subject. Similar to a card catalog, but not as efficient. Common search engines are Webcrawler, Yahoo, Alta Vista, Infoseek, Google and Lycos.

Server : (1) A computer or its software that "serves" other computers by administering network files and network operations. Three types of Internet servers are Web servers, e-mail servers, and Gopher servers. **(2)** A high speed computer in a network that is shared by multiple users. It holds the programs and data that are shared by all users.

Surfing : The random, aimless exploration of web pages achieved through following links that look interesting within a document

Software : Software is the set of instructions developed by programming language which tells a computer what to do.

System software : controls the overall operation of a computer. Some of the activities include managing system memory, controlling system resources, executing computer hardware functions and interfacing a user with computer hardware and applications.

Sensor : A peripheral input device which senses some variable in the system environment, such as temperature, and converts it to an electrical signal which can be further converted to a digital signal for processing by the computer.

Serial : (1) Pertaining to the sequential processing of the individual parts of a whole, such as the bits of a character or the characters of a word, using the same facilities for successive parts. (2) Term describing the transmission of data one bit at a time.

Small scale integration : A classification of ICs [chips] based on their size as expressed by the number of circuits or logic gates they contain. An SSI IC contains up to 100 transistors.

Software engineering : The application of a systematic, disciplined, quantifiable approach to the development, operation, and maintenance of software; i.e., the application of engineering to software.

Source code : Computer instructions and data definitions expressed in a form suitable for input to an assembler, compiler or other translator.

Source program : A computer program that must be compiled, assembled, or otherwise translated in order to be executed by a computer. Contrast with object program. See: source code.

Specification : A document that specifies, in a complete, precise, verifiable manner, the requirements, design, behavior,or other characteristics of a system or component, and often, the procedures for determining whether these provisions have been satisfied.

Storage device : A unit into which data or programs can be placed, retained and retrieved.

SSL/Secure Socket Layer : The leading security protocol on the Internet. When an SSL session is started, the browser sends its public key to the server so that the server can securely send a secret key to the browser.

Structured programming : Any software development technique that includes structured design and results in the development of structured programs.

Subroutine : A routine that returns control to the program or subprogram that called it. Note: This term is defined differently in various programming languages.

Synchronous : Occurring at regular, timed intervals, i.e. timing dependent.

Syntax : The structural or grammatical rules that define how symbols in a language are to be combined to form words, phrases, expressions, and other allowable constructs.

Swapping : Storing program on a disk and then transferring these programs into main storage as and when they are needed.

Synchronisation : This method ensures that the receiving end can recognise characters in order, in which the transmitting end sends them in a serial data transmission.

Terabyte : Approximately one trillion bytes; precisely 240 or 1,099,511,627,776 bytes. See: kilobyte, megabyte, gigabyte.

Terminal : A device, usually equipped with a CRT display and keyboard, used to send and receive information to and from a computer via a communication channel.

Test : An activity in which a system or component is executed under specified conditions, the results are observed or recorded and an evaluation is made of some aspect of the system or component.

Test case : Documentation specifying inputs, predicted results, and a set of execution conditions for a test item.

Testing : The process of operating a system or component under specified conditions, observing or recording the results, and making an evaluation of some aspect of the system or component.

Touch screen : A touch sensitive display screen that uses a clear panel over or on the screen surface. The panel is a matrix of cells, an input device, that transmits pressure information to the software.

Traceability : The degree to which a relationship can be established between two or more products of the development process, especially products having a predecessor-successor or master-subordinate relationship to one another; e.g., the degree to which the requirements and design of a given software component match.

Trojan horse : A method of attacking a computer system, typically by providing a useful program which contains code intended to compromise a computer system by secretly providing for unauthorized access, the unauthorized collection of privileged system or user data, the unauthorized reading or altering of files, the performance of unintended and unexpected functions, or the malicious destruction of software and hardware.

Truth table : (1) (ISO) An operation table for a logic operation. (2) A table that describes a logic function by listing all possible combinations of input values, and indicating, for each combination, the output value.

Twisted pair : A pair of thin-diameter insulated wires commonly used in telephone wiring. The wires are twisted around each other to minimize interference from other twisted pairs in the cable. Twisted pairs have less bandwidth than coaxial cable or optical fiber. Abbreviated UTP for Unshielded Twisted Pair.

Unix : UNIX is a family of OSes, each being made by a different company or organization but all offering a very similar look and feel.

Upload : The process of transferring information from one computer to another, generally from a client to a server. For example, you upload a file from your computer to a server or the internet.

USB : Acronym for "Universal Serial Bus". This is a style of port connection that is used by many peripheral devices such as Palm Pilots, phones, scanners, printers etc. This type of connection is much faster than more traditional kinds of connections such as serial and parallel ports.

URL: Acronym for "Universal Resource Locator" The specific path to a World Wide Web file, including filename and extension.

UPS : "Uninterruptible Power Supply". An uninterruptible power supply (UPS) is a device that allows your computer to keep running for at least a short time when the primary power source is lost.

Unit : (1) A separately testable element specified in the design of a computer software element. (2) A logically separable part of a computer program. Syn: component, module.

Usability : The ease with which a user can learn to operate, prepare inputs for, and interpret outputs of a system or component.

User : Any person, organization, or functional unit that uses the services of an information processing system.

Virus : A virus is a program that will seek to duplicate itself in memory and on disks, but in a subtle way that will not immediately be noticed. A computer on the same network as an infected computer or that uses an infected disk (even a floppy) or that downloads and runs an infected program can itself become infected.

Version : An initial release or a complete re-release of a software item or software element.

Version number : A unique identifier used to identify software items and the related software documentation which are subject to configuration control.

Very large scale integration : A classification of ICs [chips] based on their size as expressed by the number of circuits or logic gates they contain. A VLSI IC contains 100,000 to 1,000,000 transistors.

Virus : A program which secretly alters other programs to include a copy of itself, and executes when the host program is executed. The execution of a virus program compromises a computer system by performing unwanted or unintended functions which may be destructive.

Volume : (ANSI) A portion of data, together with its data carrier, that can be handled conveniently as a unit; e.g., a reel of magnetic tape, a disk pack, a floppy disk.

Web Page : A single screen (document) on a Web site.

Webcasting : "Webcasting" is a term that describes the ability to use the Web to deliver delayed versions of sound or video broadcasts.

World Wide Web or WWW : This is the part of the Internet that you acces. The World Wide Web is so named because each page in the WWW has links to other pages, which have links to other pages, and so on, creating what could visually be seen as a web-like network of links.

Workstation : Any terminal or personal computer.

Worm : An independent program which can travel from computer to computer across network connections replicating itself in each computer. They do not change other programs, but compromise a computer system through their impact on system performance.

WAN: Acronym for «Wide Area Network». A larger computer network that is geographically dispersed, such as one that stretches across a university campus.

Website: The location of published hypertext content. Physically, a Website can occupy an entire Web server or a part of a server; or it can be spread out among different servers as long as its sections are all linked directly, to the same home page.

WLAN: Acronym for «Wireless Local Area Network». In a wireless local area network (WLAN), an access point is a station that transmits and receives data, sometimes refered to as a transceiver.

XHTML:

XHTML is Stands for "Extensible Hypertext Markup Language." "Extensible" starts with an "X".

XHTML is a spinoff of the hypertext markup language (HTML) used for creating Web pages. It is based on the HTML 4.0 syntax, but has been modified to follow the guidelines of XML, the Extensible Markup Language. Therefore, XHTML 1.0 is sometimes referred to as HTML 5.0.

XML:

Stands for "Extensible Markup Language." (Yes, technically it should be EML). XML is used to define documents with a standard format that can be read by any XML-compatible application. The language can be used with HTML pages, but XML itself is not a markup language. Instead, it is a "meta-language" that can be used to create markup languages for specific applications. For example, it can describe items that may be accessed when a Web page loads. Basically, XML allows you to create a database of information without having an actual database. While it is commonly used in Web applications, many other programs can use XML documents as well.

XSLT:

Stands for "Extensible Style Sheet Language Transformation." While XML is supposed to be a standardized language, not all XML documents use the same type of formatting. Therefore, the documents sometimes need to be "transformed," or modified so that another script or program will be able to read them. XSLT make this transition possible.

Y2K:

Y2K Stands for "Year 2000". However, this term is more often used to refer to the "Millennium Bug." This bug is a little creature that lives inside older computers. When the year 2000 rolls around, the little bug will self-destruct; blowing up the computer it was residing in. because computers using only last two digits of year, like; four digit year '1999' conveated into two digit i.e. '99', so millions of ruppes have been spent to handle this practically non existent problem.

YOBIBYTE:

A yobi-byte is a unit of data storage that equals 2 to the 80th power, or 1,208,925,819,614,629,174,706,176 bytes.

Zoom : The enlarging and reducing the image displayed on a computer process of proportionately monitor.

Zombie : A computer that has been hijacked by a cracker without the owner's knowledge and used to perform malicious tasks on the internet.

ZIP : A ZIP file (ZIP) is a "zipped" or compressed file.

Zone file : A zone file is stored on a name server and provides information about one or more domain names each zone file contains a list of DNS records with mappings between domain names and IP Address.

Technologies and Terms used in Internet Banking

Chapter 14

Online banking was long considered to be a tremendous new technology breaking offering that would not only enhance the banks' capabilities in terms of services offered on the go but also as a possible change in various types of operational and strategic business models.

Now almost all the banks across the globe are there to offer online banking with different capabilities in their respective fields. With ever-increasing competition, banks have devised new ways to maintain their revenue streams. The core of the idea, however, still remains to offer more value, convenience and satisfaction to the customer.

INTERNET BANKING TECHNOLOGIES

ATM (Automated teller machine)

ATM is known as an automated banking machine cash machine, cashpoint, or cashline machine that is an electronic telecommunications device which enables the customers of a financial institution to perform financial transactions without the need for a human cashier, clerk or bank teller.

On most modern ATMs, the customer is identified by inserting the ATM card with a magnetic stripe or a plastic smart card with a chip that has a unique card number and some security information such as an expiration date or CVVC (CVV). Authentication is provided by the customer entering a personal identification number (PIN).

Using an ATM, customers can access their bank deposit or credit accounts in order to make a variety of transactions such as cash withdrawals, check balances, or credit mobile phones. If the currency being withdrawn from the ATM is different from that in which the bank account is denominated the money will be converted at an official exchange rate. Thus, ATMs often provide the best possible exchange rates for foreign travellers, and are widely used for this purpose.

Mobile banking

It is a service provided by a bank that allows its customers to conduct financial transactions remotely using a mobile device such as a mobile phone or tablet. It uses software, usually called an app, provided by the bank. Mobile banking is usually available on a 24-hour basis. Some bank has restrictions on which accounts may be accessed through mobile banking, as well as a limit on the amount that can be transacted. Transactions through mobile banking may include obtaining account balances and lists of latest transactions, electronic bill payments, and funds transfers between a customer's or another's accounts. Some apps also enable copies of statements to be downloaded and sometimes printed at the customer's premises; and some banks charge a fee for mailing hardcopies of bank statements.

Model of mobile banking

According to the model mobile banking can be said to consist of three inter-related concepts:

- Mobile financial information services
- Mobile accounting
- Mobile brokerage

Most services in the categories designated accounting and brokerage are transaction-based. The non-transaction-based services of an informational nature are however essential for conducting transactions - for instance, balance inquiries might be needed before committing a money remittance. The mobile accounting and brokerage services are therefore offered invariably in combination with information services. Information services, on the other hand, may be offered as an independent module.

Advantage of mobile banking

Mobile banking reduces the cost of handling transactions by reducing the need for customers to visit a bank branch for non-cash withdrawal and deposit transactions.

Mobile banking does not handle transactions involving cash, and a customer needs to visit an ATM or bank branch for cash withdrawals or deposits.

Many apps now have a remote deposit option; using the device's camera to digitally transmit cheques to their financial institution.

Future functionalities in mobile banking

There are many types of future functionalities in Mobile Banking such as:

- Communication enrichment: - Video Interaction with agents, advisors.
- Pervasive Transactions capabilities: - Comprehensive "Mobile wallet"
- Customer Education: - "Test drive" for demos of banking services
- Connect with new customer segment: - Connect with Gen Y – Gen Z using games and social network ambushed to surrogate bank's offerings
- Content monetization: - Micro level revenue themes such as music, e-book download
- Vertical positioning: - Positioning offerings over mobile banking specific industries
- Horizontal positioning: - Positioning offerings over mobile banking across all the industries
- Personalization of corporate banking services: - Personalization experience for multiple roles and hierarchies in corporate banking as against the vanilla based segment based enhancements in the current context.
- Build Brand: - Built the bank's brand while enhancing the "Mobile real estate".

Website Security

With the advent of Online transactions, there has come a need that has forced banks to concentrate more on website security initiatives. Providing a safe, secure and robust website with well defined fraud resolution processes is one such initiative to handle frauds that happen online. User identification, data encryption (below 128 bit), audits and alarms, card verification codes (CVV/ CVV2/CID), online security portal, virtual keyboard and dedicated fraud management team are some of the standard security measures implemented by banks.

In order to monitor and prevent Internet banking fraud and other security breach attempts the following technologies and procedures are a "must have" for all the banks in addition to the standard features: extended validation SSL certificates working in conjunction with anti-phishing and malware protection on browsers, utilization of multiple factor password authentication, enforcing re-authentication while accessing sensitive tools, hiding accounts, Verified by Visa/Secure Code, digital signature, digital certificates, secure tokens, session log out, Back and Refresh activity, hot listing and blocking of fraudulent accounts, use scramble pads against key-logging viruses.

Further to the primarily front-end authentication controls listed above, the following security measures are really cutting-edge and competitive differentiators for any bank. These security measures will provide holistic end-to-end security for consumers as well as corporate clients:

- **Date/Time and IP/ISP Restriction :** Customers can select the days and specify time interval, the IP address and the Internet Service Provider (ISP) from which they connect to personal internet banking.

- **Geolocation :** Geolocation services provide detailed information about a consumer's worldwide location, line speed, domain, etc while performing online transactions.

- **Biometrics :** Biometrics are used to verify a person's identity by a unique physical attributes (e.g. fingerprint, iris recognition, palm print) that distinguishes the individual from any other person.

- **Securing the perimeter :** Denying access to the environment in which the Internet service operates by unauthorized external parties is a key target for ensuring the overall security of the system. Some of the measures in place to achieve this include Multi-Tier Infrastructure segregated into separate security trust domains and industry standard Intrusion Detection System (IDS), monitored 24/7 by a centralized security-monitoring group.

- **Customer Application Control Features :** Some functional features to enable the customer to more easily control the use of the system, activity log tools (audit trail) and advance authorization structure.

- Security and fraud monitoring and incident response, including new vulnerability notification and response, security incident response program, contingency and recovery and rule-based and anomalous behavior. Fraud monitoring should be done on customer Internet sessions, profile information, and transaction details to obtain a risk score.

TERMS RELATED TO INTERNET BANKING

ACH/AUTOMATED CLEARING HOUSE : An "ACH" is a transfer between accounts. When a user of an Internet banking system requests to move $50 from a checking to a savings account, the transfer ends up in an ACH file. This ACH file contains the instructions for the bank's core software on various transactions to perform.

ACCOUNT ANALYSIS : Method by which a bank will wave certain "hard charges" to their customers account depending on their average balance.

CASH MANAGEMENT : Software that allows retail Internet banking, plus features designed for corporate banking, such as payroll, wire transfers, tax payments and more.

EBPP/ELECTRONIC BILL PAYMENT & PRESENTMENT : Allows the customer to view bills (such as cable TV or utilities) via their browser and allows the option of payment. There are four stages to EBPP:

(1)   enrollment of customer

(2)   presentment of bill

(3)   customer's approval of payment

(4)   payment of bill

EFT/ELECTRONIC FUNDS TRANSFER : The transfer of money from one account to another by computer.

EFTPS : The payment of taxes over the Internet.

EDI : Electronic data interchange (EDI) is the exchange of documents in a structured form between computers via telephone lines.

FASTPAY OR QUICKPAY : A local electronic transfer from one account to another. Payments are routed internally from the sender's account to the receiver's account without leaving the bank.

FED FILE : This is the file that contains ACH's, which are moving money from an end user's Account inside the bank (or credit union) to an account at another bank or credit union.

FEDI : Financial Electronic Data Interchange (FEDI) involves the computer to computer transmission of both payment instructions and remittance details using international message standards. An example would be trade payments - e.g. a retailer sending a payment to a supplier in payment of multiple invoices.

INTERNET BANKING : The technology, tools and processes that give you access to your bank accounts and banking transactions from your personal computer. Typically this includes checking account balances, obtaining a list of transactions affecting an account, and perhaps transferring funds from one online account into another.

MEMO POST : A file that gets posted to your account when you perform a transaction that has not officially cleared. This is the feature that adds and subtracts funds from your account throughout the day, even though technically the money hasn't left your account, because your bank operates in the batch mode. Real Time financial institutions do not need Memo Post.

NSF : "Not Sufficient Funds" in your account to cover the specific amount of a transaction.

Page Counter : Normally found at the bottom of a webpage, a page counter actually counts the number of times people have viewed the webpage.

SET : (Secure Electronic Transaction) A standard protocol from MasterCard and Visa for securing online credit card payments via the Internet. It is a three-way transaction: the user, merchant and bank must use the SET protocols. Credit card data and a digital certificate (for authentication) are stored in a plug-in to the user's Web browser.

TIN : "Taxpayer Identification Number" assigned to you by the internal revenue service.

TRANSACTIONAL WEBSITE : A website that allows transactions, such as Internet Banking allows you to pay bills or transfer funds, or an e-commerce site that allows you to make purchases.

Latest Development in IT Related to Banking

With the globalization trends world over it is difficult for any nation big or small, developed or developing, to remain isolated from what is happening around. For a country like India, which is one of the most promising emerging markets, such isolation is nearly impossible. More particularly in the area of Information technology, where India has definitely an edge over its competitors, remaining away or uniformity of the world trends is untenable. Financial sector in general and banking industry in particular is the largest spender and beneficiary from information technology. This endeavours to relate the international trends in it with the Indian banking industry. The last lot includes possibly all foreign banks and newly established Private sector banks, which have fully computerized all the operations. With these variations in the level of information technology in Indian banks, it is useful to take account of the trends in Information technology internationally as also to see the comparative position with Indian banks. The present article starts with the banks perception when they get into IT up gradation. All the trends in IT sector are then discussed to see their relevance to the status of Indian banks.

INDIAN GOVERNMENT INITIATIVES

The government and the regulator have undertaken several measures to strengthen the Indian banking sector.

1. In July 2016, the government allocated Rs 22,915 crore (US$ 3.41 billion) as capital infusion in 13 public sector banks, which is expected to improve their liquidity and lending operations, and shore up economic growth in the country.

2. To reduce the burden of loan repayment on farmers, a provision of Rs 15,000 crore (US$ 2.2 billion) has been made in the Union Budget 2016-17 towards interest subvention.

3. Under Pradhan Mantri Jan Dhan Yojna (PMJDY), 250.5 million accounts! Have been opened and 192.2 million RuPay debit cards have been issued as of October 12, 2016. These new accounts have mustered deposits worth almost Rs 44,480 crore (US$ 6.67 billion).

4. To provide relief to the state electricity distribution companies, Government of India has proposed to their lenders that 75 per cent of their loans be converted to state government bonds in two phases by March 2017

5. The Reserve Bank of India (RBI) has released the Vision 2018 document, aimed at encouraging greater use of electronic payments by all sections of society by bringing down paper-based transactions, increasing the usage of digital channels, and boosting the customer base for mobile banking.

6. The Reserve Bank of India (RBI) has issued guidelines for priority sector lending certificates (PSLCs), according to which banks can issue four different kinds of PSLCs—those for the shortfall in agriculture lending, lending to small and marginal farmers, lending to micro enterprises and for overall lending targets – to meet their priority sector lending targets.

7. The Reserve Bank of India (RBI) has allowed additional reserves to be part of tier-1 or core capital of banks, such as revaluation reserves linked to property holdings, foreign currency translation reserves and deferred tax assets, which is expected to shore up the capital of state-run banks and privately owned banks by up to Rs 35,000 crore (US$ 5.14 billion) and Rs 5,000 crore (US$ 734 million) respectively.

8. The Reserve Bank of India (RBI) plans to soon come out with guidelines, such as common risk-based know-your-customer (KYC) norms, to reinforce protection for consumers, especially since a large number of Indians have now been financially included post the government's massive drive to open a bank account for each household.

9. The Government of India is looking to set up a special fund, as a part of National Investment and Infrastructure Fund (NIIF), to deal with stressed assets of banks.

10. Government of India aims to extend insurance, pension and credit facilities to those excluded from these benefits under the PradhanMantri Jan DhanYojana (PMJDY).

11. To facilitate an easy access to finance by Micro and Small Enterprises (MSEs), the Government/RBI has launched Credit Guarantee Fund Scheme to provide guarantee cover for collateral free credit facilities extended to MSEs upto Rs 1 Crore (US$ 0.15 million).

12. Scheduled commercial banks can grant non-fund based facilities including partial credit enhancement (PEC), to those customers, who do not avail any fund based facility from any bank in India.

DEVELOPMENT BY INDIAN GOVERNMENT IN IT FIELD

Government Working on New National E-Mail Service

- The DeitY (Department of Electronics and Information Technology) is working on creating a user friendly Indian email service on the lines of popular email service providers like Gmail and Yahoo.

- New National E-Mail Servicevice will first be made available to the Central government, then the State government, and then to the citizens for communicating with the government.

- Importance is placed on this project to ensure national security by ascertaining that the communication systems and data transfers are effective and not hackable. The service is also expected to be fast because of enhanced bandwith and servers that will be located in India.

- This project is a part of PM Modi's "Digital India" programme.

Dot Bharat domain lauched by Govt

Union Government launched a new domain Dot Bharat in Devanagari script . Originally the domain will cover 8 languages like Hindi, Bodo, Dogri, Konkani, Maithili, Marathi, Nepali and Sindhi.

These 8 languages are from the list of 22 languages that has been contained in the Schedule-8 of the Constitution of India.

Objective

To connect individuals with social media and deliver content in regional languages, particularly to those who are not acquainted with English.

To deliver information to persons in their own regional languages which will help in advancement of e-governance.

The domain was developed by the joint efforts of National Internet Exchange of India and CDAC (Centre for Development of Advanced Computing). Dot Bharat (.भारत) would substitute the normally used top domains like .com, .in, .net, etc.

'Digital Cloud' for every Indian

PM Narendra Modi's next giant drive to free up service delivery from the hold of the lower bureaucracy will be in the form of a 'digital cloud' for every Indian.

Now, Certificates issued by the Govt.: Education, residential, medical records, birth certificates, etc. will be saved in separate 'digital lockers' and a communication protocol will be established for Govt Departments to access them without actually having to see the hard copy.

The idea is very clear, it is not desired that copies of certificates issued by the government itself to be carried everywhere by people to government offices for several services, e.g. if a student is applying for a government college and has studied in a government-aided school, his birth certificate, identity details and educational certificates, school-leaving details, et al should be available to Govt. institutes where he is applying. Likewise his medical records, etc.

Ministry of Railways Launches New Improved e-Ticketing System

Now booking rail tickets through the IRCTC website will be faster and smoother than before with the new e-ticketing system developed by Centre for Railway Information Systems (CRIS). IRCTC has developed and introduced following e-systems:-

(1) New e-Ticketing system : This would enable booking of 7200 tickets per minute against 2000 tickets through the current system. The new system will enable passengers to easily get information relating to arrivals and departure timings of trains and other information on their mobile phones as CRIS has launched mobile app and desktop app for Windows 8 platform. The app is available free of cost for window 8 phones and the railways is expected launch for android very soon.

(2) Spot Your Train : The 'spot your train' which provides information such as current position, expected time of arrival and departure at a particular station is the most striking feature of this app. Other key features are 'train schedule', 'train between stations', 'information on cancelled, rescheduled and diverted trains' and 'live station'.

(3) 'Live Station' query : Passengers would get the list of trains expected to arrive at or depart from any station in next 2 or 4 hours through 'Live Station' query.

(4) Go-India smart card : Railways also started an array of IT-enabled initiatives for rail users including Go-India smart card. The card would cut down the transaction time at booking counters as there will not be cash dealing during issuance of tickets.

(5) Online Systems e-Demand and e-Diversion : The railways has also introduced online system like e-Demand and e-Diversion for freight service for online booking of wagons and making payment without going to counters.

Reserve Bank issue draft guidelines for 'anytime anywhere' Bharat Bill Payment System

To introduce an 'anytime anywhere payment system', the Reserve Bank of India (RBI) issued draft guidelines for the implementation of Bharat Bill Payment System (BBPS). The draft mentions the requirements and the basic framework of operating the BBPS, and stipulates the eligibility criteria, standards for settlement model and customer grievance redressal, roles and responsibilities and scope for entities seeking to be part of BBPS. RBI's plan to implement an 'anytime anywhere' centralized payment system is based on a report submitted by the GIRO (Government Internal Revenue Order) Advisory Group. GIRO Advisory Group (GAG) was constituted by the RBI in October 2014, under the chairmanship of Prof. Umesh Bellur, Indian Institute of Technology, Bombay to implement a national GIRO-based Indian Bill Payment System. The panel had recommended a mechanism for centralized bills payment system in India, mainly by laying out 2 organizations:

1. Bharat Bill Payment Services (BBPS)
2. Bharat Bill Payment Operating Units (BBPOUs)

India set to build supercomputer grid

Determined to raise India's ranking in the world of high-performance computers, the government is set to clear a ₹. 4,500-crore ($730 million) mission to build supercomputers nearly 40 times quicker than our fastest one. The mission intends to set up 73 supercomputing facilities on a buy-and-build approach at academic and research institutions across the country and network them into a grid. Three of them — the first ones to be set up over the first three years — would be India's first supercomputers capable of peta-scale computing and would join a global league of just 37 such machines.

The seven-year plan has been divided into two phases — the first three years for construction of the machines and the next four for the applications that will use this grid. The supercomputers will occupy a space of over 20,000 square feet, or the size of 10 three-bedroom apartments.

At present, India has two supercomputing machines in the world's top 100, and nine in the top 500.

Its fastest supercomputer at the Pune-based Indian Institute of Tropical Meteorology is ranked 52.

A little less than half of all supercomputers in the top 500 — 233 — are in the US. But the world's fastest, Tianhe-2 (MilkyWay-2), belongs to China's National University of Defense Technology. A late entrant, China has 75 other supercomputers on the list — nearly as many as Japan (30), France (27) and Germany (23) put together.

IMPORTANT BANKING SCHEMES & APPs

3D PRINTING IN BANKING

3D printing will disrupt the traditional economics of global industry, which means it will disrupt banking. How far it goes depends on how successful 3D printing is - and how quickly - but to finish off, here's a final thought.

3D printing means faster product development, lower costs in the prototyping phase, an increase in the amount of products that can be developed and also more niche products.

The price of 3D printable materials will rise, making the raw commodities prices change. Oil will become less important as a fuel and more valuable where it's used in plastics. Recycled materials and recycling processes will become more valuable (they are a source of 3D print materials) which will upset mining and ore prices, may be even staples like steel, silver and gold.

How will 3D printers help improve banking KYC?

3D printers are widely known to offer the potential to be a game changer in the physical supply chain across many sectors and industries. However, the opportunity in Financial Services seems less likely, particularly in any form of real, practical application. Do you agree, or not with my statement here? Well, either way, I suggest you read on to find out more.

Unified Payments Interface (UPI)

"Unified Payment Interface" (UPI) enables all bank account holders to send and receive money from their smart-phones without the need to enter bank account information or net banking user-id/ password.

It is a system that powers multiple bank accounts (of participating banks), several banking services features like fund transfer (P2P), and merchant payments in a single mobile application.

UPI was launched by National Payments Corporation of India with Reserve Bank of India's (RBI) vision of migrating towards a 'less-cash' and more digital society. UPI has built on the Immediate Payment Service (IMPS) platform.

UPI platform can be used for:

* UPI can be used to send and receive money from individuals or to pay directly to merchants
* Immediate money transfer through mobile device round the clock 24*7 and 365 days.
* Single mobile application for accessing different bank accounts
* Single Click to Factor Authentication.
* Virtual address of the customer for Pull & Push provides for incremental security with the customer not required to enter the details such as Card no, Account number; IFSC etc.
* Bill Sharing with friends.

- Scheduling PUSH and PULL Payments for various purposes.
- Utility Bill Payments, Over the Counter Payments, Barcode (Scan and Pay) based payments.
- Donations, Collections, Disbursements Scalable.
- Raising Complaint from Mobile App directly.

How UPI app works

Any Android smart-phone user who has an account with a UPI-partnered bank can download a UPI app such as iMobile (for ICICI Bank customer) and Pockets (for ICICI/ non-ICICI Bank customers) and create their own Virtual Payment Address (VPA) such as xyz@pockets or xyz@icici to start using UPI.

Bhim APP

BHIM is a digital paymants soluation app based on Unified Payments Interface (UPI) from the National Payments Corporation of India (NPCI). If you have signed up for UPI based payments on your respective bank accounts, which is also linked to your mobile number, then you will be able to use the BHIM app to conduct digital transection.

Payment bank

Payments banks are a new model of banks conceptualized by the Reserve Bank of India (RBI). These banks can accept a restricted deposit which is currently limited to INR 1 lakh per customer and may be increased further. These banks cannot issue loans and credit cards. Both current account and savings accounts can be operated by such banks. Payments banks can issue services like ATM cards, debit cards, online banking and mobile banking. Airtel has launched India's first live payments bank. Paytm is the second such service to be launched in the country. India Post Payments Bank is the third entity to receive payments bank permit after Bharti Airtel and Paytm.

Airtel money

Airtel has started a new m-commerce platform called Airtel Money in collaboration with Infosys and Smart Trust (now Giesecke & Devrient). The platform was launched on 5 April 2012, at Infosys' headquarters in Bangalore. Using Airtel Money, users can transfer money, pay bills and perform other financial transactions directly on the mobile phone. It has an all-India presence, certain charges are levied per Airtel Money transaction.

Branch on Wheel – ICICI Bank in Odisha

India's ICICI adds 'Branch on Wheels' Sept. 9, 2013. ICICI Bank Ltd. has launched its "Branch on Wheels" as part of a financial inclusion plan that aims to provide banking services to unbanked villages in India. The initiative is the first of its kind to be implemented by one of the country's private sector banks.

Digital Banking "POCKET" – ICICI

India's largest private sector lender, ICICI Bank, has launched an e-wallet called 'Pockets', which can do everything payments banks can do. Pockets' is a mobile application, which can be used to send money, pay utility bills, book movie tickets, send gifts and share expenses. One can use this service even if one doesn't have an ICICI Bank account. With this app, one can also open a zero-balance account.

Chillr–HDFC Bank

Chillr is launching first for HDFC Bank and is available exclusively for customers of HDFC Bank. As an HDFC Bank customer, you can also transfer money to your contacts having other bank accounts. Chillr is a revolutionary new app that lets you send money immediately to anyone in your phone book, 24 hours a day, 7 days a week.

We-Bank

It is a Chinese first online banking system. Chinese Internet giant Tencent Holdings Ltd made first online banking affiliate We-Bank is close to raising fresh funds from investors including U.S. private-equity firm Warburg Pincus in a deal that values the year-old venture at more than $5 billion, people familiar with the matter said.

We-Bank, which is 30%, owned by Tencent, is raising more than $450 million in the round led by Warburg Pincus as well as Singapore's state-owned investment firm Temasek Holdings Pte. Ltd., the people said.

The online bank's first fundraising round since its operations began a year ago puts a roughly $5.5 billion price tag on the company including the fresh funds, the people said.

Kay-Pay

Kotak Mahindra has launched world's first Face-book based instant funds transfer platform: Kay-Pay. The beauty of this online based Social banking platform is its simplicity: now anyone can transfer funds between their Face-book friends without using internet.

SBI eforex

State Bank of India said it has launched SBI eforex -SBI launched an initiative to provide doorstep services and expedite home loans application process -State Bank of India jointly launched a cyber crime awareness campaign.

E-KYC – SBI

State Bank Group has developed the e-KYC application which will read the customer's

Aadhaar Number and Fingerprints for e-KYC verification. This will be sent to UIDAI and on successful verification from UIDAI, this application will display, print and issue an e-KYC certificate which can be used by the BC to open an account subject to satisfying other account opening requirements.

All VLEs are advised to make best use of it for customer account opening keeping in view the Prime Minister Dhan Jan Yojana. VLEs should open maximum number of accounts given the ease involved in account opening.

SBI has started the implementation of e-KYC for account opening.

I-Mobile app for windows phone – ICICI:

I-Mobile is ICICI Bank's official mobile banking application. I-Mobile, the most comprehensive and secure Mobile Banking application, getting payments done through Unified Payment Interface (UPI), offers over 100 banking services on your windows mobile.

India's first" transparent credit card "in association with American Express – ICICI:

ICICI Bank on 12 dec 2014 launched India's first credit card with a unique transparent design and a distinctive look. The credit card named ICICI Bank coral American express credit card. The card is a part of gemstone collection of ICICI Bank in association with American express.

M-Pesa

It is a mobile phone-based money transfer, financing and micro-financing service, launched in 2007 by Vodafone for Safari-com and Vodacom, the largest mobile network operators in Kenya and Tanzania

 M-Pesa customers can deposit and withdraw money from a network of agents that includes airtime resellers and retail outlets acting as banking agents. The service enables its users to:

*   deposit and withdraw money
*   transfer money to other users
*   pay bills

- purchase airtime
- Transfer money between the services and, in some markets like Kenya, a bank account.
- That offers expanded banking services like interest-bearing accounts, loans, and insurance

M-Wallet

It is a very young concept in India that has taken on consumer psyche rapidly. Everyone is loving mobile wallets and embracing them with open arms. Today, mobile wallet is one of the successful business ideas for start-ups. The evidence lies in the fact that it has surpassed credit cards in terms of the number of users in just a fraction of time.

TAB BANKING FACILITY

SBI has launched the **facility** of **TAB banking** for customers opening of Savings Bank accounts and another for Housing Loan applicants. SBI will offer its valued customers the facility of opening accounts at their door step through **Tab**.

Tap and pay – ICICI

ICICI Bank has launched Proximity Payment Solution, a simple **Tap and Pay** experience using NFC (Near Field Communication) enabled tag. The solution has several benefits:

1. Replaces Cash/Card/Vouchers with just a Tap N Pay tag
2. Saves time and effort
3. Sends instantaneous SMS payment confirmation to customer with the transaction amount and balance

Go cashless and card-less with mobile payment technology Ultra-cash:

Merchant payments in India are still considered a cash-driven space. However, one can start reverse counting to see the world going cashless and card-less with the next generation of mobile payments. What if you discover that you forgot to carry your wallet after reaching a retail store? The Ultra cash app aims to help users in such a situation to shop seamlessly.

Three types of cashless transaction options via prepaid payment instruments for you:

With limited cash in hand and an indefinite crunch in sight, most people are rushing to cashless transactions. "Digital transactions bring in better transparency, scalability and accountability.

The RBI classifies every mode of cashless fund transfer or transaction using cards or mobile phones as 'prepaid payment instrument'.

These can be issued as smart cards, magnetic stripe cards, Net accounts, Net wallets, mobile accounts, mobile wallets or paper vouchers. These are classified into three types:

Closed: Issued by an entity for purchasing goods and services only from it, these don't allow cash withdrawal or redemption. Ola Money is one such closed wallet.

Semi-closed: These are used to buy goods and services, including financial services, from merchant that have a specific contract with the issuer. These too don't allow cash withdrawal or redemption and include wallets offered by service providers like Paytm and State Bank Buddy.

Open: These can be used to buy goods and services, including fund transfers at merchant locations, and also permit cash withdrawals at ATMs. All Visa and Master-Card cards fall into this category.

CASHLESS MODES

Mobile wallet: This is basically a virtual wallet available on your mobile phone. You can store cash on the mobile to make online or offline payments. Various service providers offer these wallets via mobile apps, which you need to download on the phone. You can transfer the money into these wallets online using credit/debit card or Net banking. This means that every time you pay a bill or buy online via the wallet, you won't have to furnish your card details. You can use these to pay fees, bills and make online purchases.

Net banking: This does not involve any wallet and is simply a method of online transfer of funds from your bank account to another bank account, credit card, or a third party. You can do it through a computer or mobile phone. Log in to your bank account on the Net and transfer money via national electronic funds transfer (NEFT), real-time gross settlement (RTGS) or immediate payment service (IMPS), all of which come at a nominal cost ranging from Rs (5 to 55).

Plastic money: This includes credit, debit and prepaid cards. The latter can be issued by banks or non-banks and can be physical or virtual. These can be bought and recharged online via Net banking and can be used to make online or point-of-sale purchases, even given as gift cards.

Plastic Bank: it has a mission statement to create and lead a movement for 'Social Plastic' towards worldwide demand for the use of Social Plastic in everyday products. The higher the worldwide demand becomes, the higher the reward will be for harvesting Social Plastic. This is achieved through 'Plastic Banks' established strategically in impoverished areas with an existing abundance of plastic waste. The Plastic Bank will offer people both education and the opportunity to trade re-usable plastics for credits that can be used for the printing of 3D products, re-purposed necessities and/or micro-finance loans.

LATEST DEVELOPMENT IN IT FIELD:

Electronic Digital Paper

Electronic paper utilizes new display technology called gyricon this gyricon sheet is thin layer of transparent plastic sheet. It developed at Xerox Palo Alto Research Center (PARC), electronic paper is new kind of display somewhere between paper and conventional computer screen like paper, it is thin, lightweight, and flexible like computer display, it is dynamic & rewritable wide range of potential applications, including:

- Electronic paper newspapers offering breaking news, incoming sports scores, and up to the minute stock quotes, even as paper is being read
- Electronic paper magazines that continually update with breaking information and make use of animated images or movie pictures
- Electronic paper textbooks, which could be updated as technology changes

Plastic Displays

Researchers have recently made break throughs in developing displays out of poly-ethylene tere phthalate (PET) it is a thin, flexible, rugged plastic that you can bend, roll up, fold, or form into practically any shape.

Applications could include notebook and desktop displays, hand-held appliances, it also, wearable displays sew into clothing, and paper thin electronic books and newspapers

Power Paper

Computers and other electronic devices becoming thinner and thinner, laptop computer could be as thin as a sheet of paper power supplies must slim down as well power paper, an Israel-based company, has developed paper-thin battery technology.

Power electronic devices, games, greeting cards, smart cards, luggage tags, medical devices Imagine smart tickets to sporting events to avoid counterfeiting and give directions to seat could be very useful in computerized clothing and wearable computers

Power Paper cell will be one-half millimeter thick, and will generate 1.5 volts.

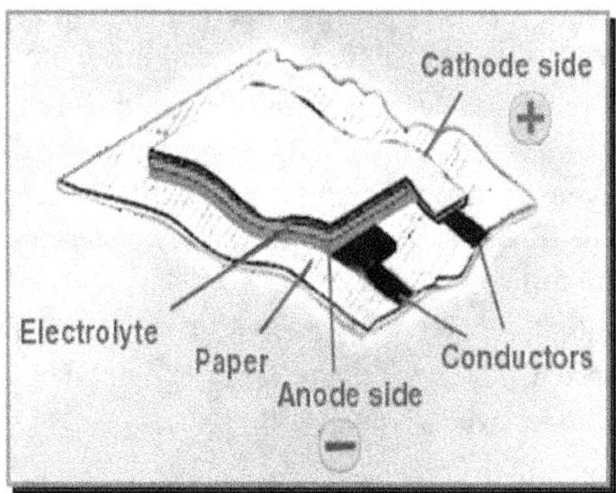

Printable Computers

In printable computer researchers developing ink-based, plastic processor & printable computer components not designed to replace silicon (about 100 times slower) plastic offers some benefits over silicon & silicon is rigid, while plastic chips are flexible & it will lead to simple computers to give intelligence to everyday objects could be integrated into clothes, food labels, simple appliances, toys

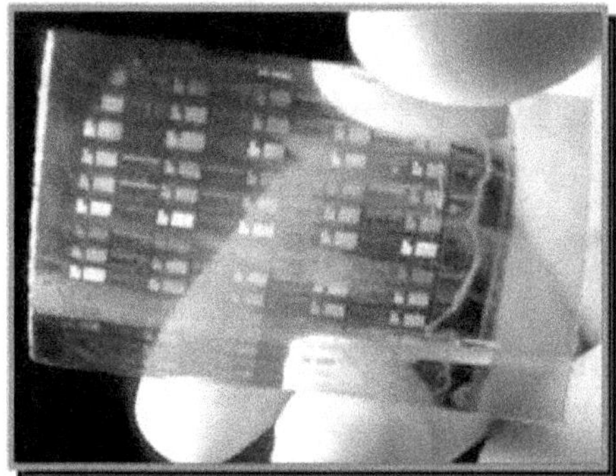

Wearable Computers

Applications like hearing aids with sound enhancement software & "Glasses" with multi-informational display about what is being seen, where you are Wrist computers, PDAs, cell phones. Next step is computerized clothing Including computers in standard clothing items like shoes, pants, shirts, jackets, belts even underwear Some of these devices already making their way into consumer market.

Working to integrate computers and related devices directly into clothing, so that they are virtually invisible interaction via sensors, all fabric keypads, speakers, voice recognition receivers, thin light-emitting diode (LED) monitors, flat screen (plastic) displays, holographic projectors another step in making computers and devices portable without having to carry and manipulate plethora of gadgets.

Other development in IT field

Vehicles – cars, bicycles, lawn mowers, snow blowers, chain saws, etc.

Appliances – Home security, heating/air conditioning, refrigerator, oven, dishwasher, lighting system, entertainment systems, washer, dryer, garage door opener, "watering" systems etc.